ALPINE TRAGEDY

BY CHARLES GOS

Solitude Montagnarde

L'Epopée Alpestre

Alpinisme Anecdotique

Voyageurs Illustres en Suisse

Notre-Dame des Neiges (*fiction*)

La Nuit des Drus (*fiction*)

La Croix du Cervin (*fiction*)

etc.

In Preparation
Histoire du Cervin

Alpine Tragedy

by CHARLES GOS

TRANSLATED FROM THE FRENCH

BY MALCOLM BARNES

LONDON

GEORGE ALLEN AND UNWIN LTD

FIRST PUBLISHED IN ENGLISH IN 1948

First published in 1940
under the title *Tragédies Alpestres*, by Editions de France
in Paris and subsequently by Librairie Payot
Lausanne

PRINTED IN GREAT BRITAIN
in 12-point Baskerville type
BY UNWIN BROTHERS LIMITED
LONDON AND WOKING

ACKNOWLEDGEMENTS

THE engravings which appear throughout this book are by Edward Whymper. That on the title page and those on pages 17, 23, 34, 42, 50, 115, 217 and 246 are reproduced from the 1936 edition of *Scrambles Amongst the Alps* with the permission of John Murray. Those on pages 4, 77, 87, 151 and 203 are reproduced from *Swiss Pictures in Pen and Pencil* with the permission of the Lutterworth Press.

The photographs were reproduced from originals by the following photographers: *Emile Gos*, Lausanne, 1, 11, 12, 13, 17, 18, 35; *Photoglob*, Zurich, 2; *Gugliermina*, Borgosesia, 3, 24; *Vittorio Sella*, Biella, 4, 7, 8, 9, 10, 14, 19, 20, 25, 28, 30, 32; *E. Gyger*, Adelboden, 6, 16, 21, 29; *Ugo de Amicis*, Turin, 26; *Guido Rey*, Turin, 27; *Max Willmann*, Chamonix, 34.

CONTENTS

ACKNOWLEDGEMENTS

INTRODUCTION   *page* 1

1. *The Hamel Affair*   5

2. *Disaster at the Col du Géant*   12

3. *The Garibaldi of the Guides*   18

4. *The Matterhorn Catastrophe*   24

5. *The Disappearance of Captain Arkwright*   35

6. *The Accident on the Schreckhorn*   43

7. *The First Feminine Tragedy*   51

8. *The Tragic Bivouac*   58

9. *The Glacier by Moonlight*   78

10. *The Treachery of a Cornice*   88

11. *The Glory and Terror of the Matterhorn*   99
   I. A Boast that Ended Badly
   II. A Solitary Agony

12. *The Blast of an Avalanche*   116

13. *Mysterious Disasters*   125
   I. The Deaths at the Aiguille Blanche
   II. The Deaths on the Wetterhorn
   III. The Deaths on the Dent Blanche

14. *The Brightness that will Never Fade*   152

15. *Night on the Matterhorn*   165

16. *Tragedy on the Jungfrau*   176

17. *Three Who Vanished*   204

18. *Carrel the Great*   218

CONTENTS

page

19. *When Luck Runs Out*   229

20. *The Annihilation of an English Family*   247

21. *The Collapse of a Bas-Relief*   256

22. *The Maddened Waves of Snow*   270

GLOSSARY   279

DRAMATIS PERSONAE   281

ILLUSTRATIONS

Half-tone plates to be found after page 282:

1. *The Tomb of Michel Croz in the Old Cemetery at Zermatt*
2. *Mont Blanc, from La Flégère*
3. *The Col Du Géant, from the Italian Side*
4. *The North Face of the Matterhorn, from the Zinal Rothorn*
5. *Edward Whymper, (a) in 1865 and (b) in 1908*
6. *The East Face of the Schreckhorn*
7. *The Upper Slopes of Mont Blanc, from the Air*
8. *The Italian Side of Mont Blanc, from the North-West Buttress of the Aiguille du Géant*
9. *The East and South-East Faces of Mont Blanc, from L'Herbetet*
10. *The Eastern Summit of the Lyskamm, South-East Face*
11. *The North Face of the Lyskamm, from the Gornergrat*
12. *The Matterhorn, showing the East and North Faces*
13. *The Italian Face of the Matterhorn, from Breuil*
14. *The Macugnaga Face of Monte Rose, seen from the Italian Approach to the Monte Moro Pass*
15. *The Aiguille Blanche de Péteret*
16. *The Wetterhorn*
17. *The West Face of the Dent Blanche, from the Air*
18. *The Matterhorn (Zermatt Aspect), from the Air*
19. *The Meije, from the Pyramide Duhamel*
20. *The Meije, from the Neighbourhood of the Refuge Chatelleret*
21. *The Summit of the Jungfrau, from the Rottalhorn*
22. *The Jungfrau, from the South-East*
23. *The Victims of the Jungfrau Tragedy*

ILLUSTRATIONS

24. *The South-West Sector of Mont Blanc, from the Aiguille de L'Aigle*

25. *The Italian Face of the Matterhorn, from the Chateau des Dames*

26. *Guido Rey beside Carrel's Cross at Rionde*

27. *Landscape at Breuil*

28. *The Aiguille Du Géant, from the Aiguille Marbrée*

29. *The Petite Dent de Veisivi, from Arolla*

30. *The North and East Faces of the Dent Blanche, from the Aiguille de la Tsa*

31. *Bergli*

32. *The Eiger and the Monch, from the Mettenberg*

33. *Burgener and his Employers a few minutes before their Death*

34. *Alexander Burgener*

35. *The Author, Charles Gos*

The thirteen tail-pieces by
EDWARD WHYMPER

SKETCH MAPS

	page
The Mont Blanc Massif	57
Monte Rosa and Lyskamm	98
La Meije	164
The Matterhorn and Surrounding Glaciers	175
The Dent Blanche and Zermatt	269
The Jungfrau Region	278

INTRODUCTION

ROM the hundreds of fatal accidents that occurred in the
High Alps between the birth of alpinism (the conquest of
Mont Blanc at the end of the eighteenth century) and the
beginning of the twentieth century, I have chosen those which
seem to me to be the most characteristic. Various considerations
have dictated my choice: first, the status of the victims (famous
guides or climbers); then, the scene of the tragedy (this or that
famous mountain); lastly—a consideration which was often
associated with the other two or was, on the other hand, sufficient
in itself—the mysterious conditions or the particularly tragic
circumstances of the drama. Therefore my intention is not,
as can be seen, to set forth any sort of alpine necrology—one
might almost say martyrology—a funereal list which grows from
year to year, and which can be found more or less complete in
the alpine journals.

It is intentional that I have concluded my investigations with
the opening of the twentieth century; but if I overstep my limits
by recalling the death of Alexander Burgener in 1910, it is because
I had the privilege of knowing this grand mountaineer and of
profiting by his friendship. The violent death of the conqueror of
the Grépon and the Dru has its evident place in this sad chronicle.
But it should be understood that all mountain tragedies, whoever
the victims may be, without distinction of status or place or
circumstance, have a touching human quality; and the most
cruel death among the heights will always derive from the scene
a little of its grandeur and poetry.

We are badly informed concerning the earliest alpine tragedies.
Information is missing, and detail is faulty. One is obliged step
by step to reconstruct the plan of the tragedy, to fit together its
many elements, and to pass from the inductive method to the
deductive. But as the years pass so the documentation becomes

more abundant. Then it is enough to go back to the sources and to distinguish the more precise among them.

Since 1900, but above all since 1919, accidents have multiplied at a frightful rate. The great peaks which once seemed reserved for the élite are becoming, little by little, something like a public stadium. Then the inevitable results: the High Alps, a lovely gift to some, become for others a pretext for displaying the shallowest of vanities. Thus besmirched, the noble ideal of yesterday loses its virtue, and the accidents themselves—without wishing in any way to state a paradox—change character. They are no longer—certain of them—anything but horrifying episodes in an athletic and acrobatic spectacle, the inevitable dénouement of the contemptible sentiments which animate certain climbing parties. Recent tragedies, notably on the Matterhorn, on the arête de Péteret, on Mont Blanc and elsewhere, are its noisy and melancholy demonstration. Ruskin's famous likening of the peaks to a "soaped pole" makes us smile to-day. But disregarding the symbol, the "soaped pole" has become an acute reality; it is so real that more than one modern alpine record makes us think of a record of insanity. To which must be added the departure for high places of inexperienced alpinists and innumerable improvised skiers; hence these hecatombs whose victims constantly increase in numbers. I can still hear Guido Rey confide to me, in a voice veiled with melancholy and vibrant with concealed indignation: "We ought to surround certain mountains with barbed wire and only allow real alpinists to climb them." Which is all very well in theory, but alas! . . . That was in September 1934, at Breuil, after terrible mishaps on the Matterhorn, and just before those on the north faces of the Grandes Jorasses and the Eiger.

I have, finally, limited my work to the Alps. There are still other mountains and everywhere the dead. But the Caucasus are quite a long way off, and the Rockies too, and the Himalayas still farther. And it was not my object to undertake a statistical work.

In bringing this preamble to a close, I would like to underline two aspects of these mountain tragedies: the work of the rescue parties, and the affection of the climber for his guide; features which bring light to many a picture otherwise so dark. The heroic work of the rescue parties is appreciated too little. These frequently obscure men who, completely scornful of danger, obey only their consciences in attempting to rescue parties in distress, unknown to themselves display incomparable spiritual qualities. How many of them have died, victims of their inflexible sense of duty!

Lastly, there is the quality of the feelings which unite the traveller and his guide. For months each year, often throughout a lifetime, a man from the towns entrusts himself entirely to a man of the mountains, or perhaps to two. Together they will face the worst obstacles, together they confront unfettered brute forces, undergo the worst privations and come close to death a thousand times. And when the rope is untied, their separation is only superficial. Inner riches develop which, despite the differences of their social spheres, are never exhausted.

Every climber, whatever his nationality, has an infinite gratitude for his guide and is sensible of his courage, his hardiness and his devotion. But it is the British climber, above all, who throughout the history of the Alps provides moving and magnificent examples of this attachment. More than any other he has understood the quality of these rough characters, has divined their charm and fathomed their feelings. Each time that one of these favourite guides falls prey to anxiety or victim to sickness, he intervenes at once: he will help his friend of the mountains, will busy himself with his affairs, and when death steps in it is he who takes care of his family. It is enough to read the pages dedicated to the guides in English alpine literature to be convinced of this admirable fellowship. Even death cannot break the ties. At Chamonix, St. Niklaus, Courmayeur, Zermatt, La Grave, Valtournanche, Grindelwald—almost all the village cemeteries of the Alps are decorated with modest monuments dedicated by climbers to their dead guides. Those stones, on which the greatest names of the conquerors of the peaks are inscribed, give utterance to one of the most beautiful aspects of alpinism: between men of wholly different social categories there is this permanence of simple, loyal, and poetic friendship.

The mountains are not homicidal. Paul Hervieu, when proclaiming some fifty years ago the formula that made his fortune— *l'Alpe Homicide*—the title of a collection of alpine stories—gave expression to a flagrant misconception. The mountains are no more homicidal than any other part of nature. Have we ever heard of the desert or the sea described as homicidal? Yet men die equally on mountains, in the deserts, and on the sea. Why, then, regard the glacier, the sand or the waves as homicidal only because they are the places where a life is brought to a close?

And after all, if relentless fate should seize a man upon the summits and free him of his life so close to that perfection which he loves and which fascinates him, is it then so great an evil?

Lastly, I should like to express my thanks to Mr. H. E. G. Tyndale, editor of the *Alpine Journal*, who has allowed me to make free use of material from that remarkable publication.

Сн. G.

La Fouly, val Ferret (Valais).

CHAPTER ONE

THE HAMEL AFFAIR[1]

The death of the guides Auguste Tairraz, Pierre Balmat and Pierre
Carrier (Mont Blanc, August 1820)

THE first great alpine catastrophe had for its scene the snowy solitudes of Mont Blanc. It was 1820. Conquered in 1786, Mont Blanc until then had claimed no victim, while in the space of thirty-four years only eight parties had reached its summit, a frozen islet in the ocean of the sky. Dr. Hamel, a Russian, aulic councillor to Alexander the First, will have the melancholy honour of opening this series of celebrated alpine tragedies, but though three of his men died there, the doctor himself survived.

On the 17th August, 1820, Dr. Hamel arrived at Chamonix from Geneva. Two young men on holiday in that town, Joseph Durnford and Gilbert Henderson, students from Oxford, were with him, lured by the attraction of climbing Mont Blanc. With him also was an optician from Geneva, named Selligue, the inventor of a barometer that was to be tried out during the climb. That same evening two mountaineers of repute, Joseph-Marie Couttet (later to be Ruskin's alpine mentor) and Mathieu Balmat, were entrusted with the organisation of the party. In all, twelve strong young men of Chamonix, as many guides as porters, were engaged, the porters being laden with baskets of provisions, with camping equipment, physical instruments, and a cooking-pot that served as a cage for a carrier pigeon.

The little troop left Chamonix on the 18th, on a perfect morning, all blue and delicate light. They were in the best of spirits. But

[1] Notes are to be found at the end of each chapter.

5

in the mountains or on the sea, how long such joy will last is never known; with the least oscillation of the atmosphere anything may happen. And that evening, at the Grands Mulets, the bivouac was scarcely set up when the weather suddenly changed. A horde of black clouds obliterated the snows. A terrifying tempest broke out. The rain fell in torrents. The night was nothing but a cataract of giant waters lit by flashes of lightning, during which the glaciers trembled under the shock of the thunder. Its hoarse roar echoed with crushing fury against the rampart of the neighbouring Aiguille du Midi. Chilled, sodden to the bone, cowering among the rocks or in the tents, the climbers held fast.

Dawn brought back peace and the sun. Above the white arêtes the clouds dispersed in the blue sky, stretching themselves into tatters, and hope was reborn. The men stretched themselves and laughed, looked at one another, questioned each other, relit their pipes. The men of Chamonix, scenting only a temporary improvement in the weather, wanted to take advantage of it by descending, but Hamel, on the contrary, wanted to go on. Dispute broke out. The doctor was angry (it is said that he even treated his guides as cowards).[2] Finally, it was the sky that settled the dispute. Under the renewed threat of an approaching squall, it was agreed to wait another day, then the question would be considered again.

Two men were despatched to Chamonix to reassure their families and to bring back provisions. Another storm broke, punctuated by dense showers of rain and squalls of sleet. On the heights it snowed; it snowed everywhere. Unseen avalanches broke loose in the obscurity with the uproar of the sea pounding at a breakwater. The guides could not conceal their anxiety.

At midnight, however, a star lit up like a tiny flower, then whole clusters of stars. Soon they opened up in every part of the darkness and glistened above the glaciers. And as the sun gently placed the petal of a rose upon the summit snows, the party was under way. Three men were left behind: the optician, who had had enough and was going down again to the valley, with two Chamoniards to guide him.

In three hours, over soft snow, the eleven men (three travellers and eight guides) reached the Grand Plateau (about 13,000 feet). This vast, gently inclined plain of snow lies in a semicircle at the frozen feet of the Dôme de Goûter (14,205 feet), of Mont Blanc

6

(15,771 feet) and, to the east, of Mont Maudit (14,664 feet). Furrowed by crevasses with turquoise shadows, this gulf of snow can be an enchantment despite the menace of the glaciers, tentacle-like and of bluish structure, which overlook it. A wondrous light plays there; an air, icy and pure, circulates throughout its infinite serenity. The lower edge of the plateau, like a white wing outstretched, masks the valley. The earth no longer exists. In dazzling light the traveller rises towards a sky of the deepest blue.

At half-past ten the eleven men, in Indian file but unroped, crossed slantwise the dangerous slopes of the "Ancien Passage" through which Balmat and Saussure had ventured. The heavy layer of snow that had fallen in the night, slightly frozen, favoured progress. On they went, to the right the mountain, to the left the void. The slope fell away to the ice precipices of the Maudit. A yawning crevasse, known as the Grande Crevasse, divided it throughout its length.

A group of six guides led the train, their baskets throwing strange shadows; in the rear came the tourists and two guides. The green veils which they had tied to their hats hid their faces. Their long alpenstocks grated on the snow. Hamel, breathless and light-headed, counted his steps, his eyes on his feet. The pigeon could be heard cooing at the head of the column.

Then, silently, swift as a panther, the avalanche leapt. The earth moved under the feet of the climbers, then ran like lava. The snow on the higher slopes slid in its turn and poured down upon the party which was already off its feet. Cries of terror were raised, and cries for help; bodies were whirled around like wrecks in the fury of this Niagara of snow. The enormous mass set upon the company, roaring like a cataract, and engulfed it in the depths of the Grande Crevasse, which it partly filled; then, towards the lower end, it slackened its pace before rebounding against the walls of the Rochers Rouges.[3] And then a calm, a miraculous calm, reconquered the mountains. Two minutes of silence passed under the blue sky and crossed these peaceful solitudes in open flight.

Then the surface of the snow moved at several places and broke open. Here a head emerged, there an arm, human forms swathed in white; Hamel first, then Henderson, then Durnford; lower down, David Couttet and Folliguet; higher up, Mathieu Balmat. And these torsos that shook themselves, these arms that rose in suppliant and despairing gestures, these bodies truncated by the glacier, seemed like the tragic and living presentation of the damned in frozen Cocytus, projected from Dante's *Divine Comedy*.

"The others?—Where are the others?—Over there—Where?— Down there, in the crevasse!"

A little lower down, in fact, the gigantic crevasse opened its huge jaws. The avalanche spanned it like a lowered drawbridge suspended on crystal pillars. Muffled voices arose from its depths. These were the voices of Julien Devouassoud and Joseph-Marie Couttet, already half asphyxiated and purple in the face. An axe was thrown to them and, one helping the other, they freed themselves, cut steps in the ice and, pulling on the sticks that were held out to them, they at last rejoined their comrades. Devouassoud owed his life solely to the Genevese optician's barometer; for this instrument, fixed to a stout board, had anchored the porter between two ledges of ice while the avalanche poured around him.

The survivors counted themselves; three were missing— Auguste Tairraz, Pierre Balmat and Pierre Carrier. Despair gave the survivors courage. Hamel, Durnford, Balmat and Couttet (Joseph-Marie) dared to leap into the gulf on to the mattress of snow and to dig into it. Above their heads curved the menacing lip of the crevasse. About them was a gloomy whiteness, half-dark, between the blue, glassy walls, and below them were invisible depths filled with mysterious sounds. At any moment the arch of snow they were probing might give way. But what of that? Three men were buried there, injured perhaps and in pain. They must be snatched from death.

Trying for an answer to their anxious calls, one of the rescuers, playing the part of listener, held between his teeth the end of a stick that had been driven into the snow. The other group had meanwhile explored the snow that had fallen on the slope. An hour passed, terrible, heavy with anxiety, overwhelming, and filled with unforeseeable dangers. The sun blazed in the zenith on these frozen expanses, scorching them, preparing a murderous offensive of further avalanches. At last there was nothing to do but accept the evidence: the three brave mountaineers were irretrievably lost.

The party reassembled and, turning its back upon the coveted summit, began silently to descend. Hamel was the last to leave the sinister spot. And the same evening the eight survivors re-entered Chamonix. The passing-bell tolled heavily.[4]

*　　*　　*

This catastrophe has a pathetic epilogue. Ten years after the accident Joseph-Marie Couttet, who was leading Mr. Wilbraham's party to Mont Blanc, halted not far from the crevasse. Contemplating it with a melancholy eye, he said: "They are down there!"

To which the tourist added sententiously: "They are there till the day of judgement!"

But Couttet and his traveller were mistaken; "they" were not there. In fact, forty years after the disaster the Glacier des Bossons threw out some tragic wreckage at its extremity: fragments of clothing, human remains perfectly preserved, all the materials for an alpine expedition. Fragments of skull still retained tufts of hair, some fair, others dark. A hand, at the end of an arm, but with no body, still tightly gripped a fragment of stick; a jawbone, shining with teeth; a foot severed below the calf; flanks, scraps of limbs, even a frozen pigeon in its pot.

Dr. Million stated in his report that all the flesh was equally white and fresh. It was possible quickly to recognise these human debris as the remains of the unfortunate guides swallowed up in 1820, and, carried down by the imperceptible current of the glacier (it is well known that glaciers, being of a plastic nature, move continuously), had just been cast up like drowned mariners on a distant shore.[5]

Two survivors of the disaster were summoned as witnesses: Joseph-Marie Couttet and Julien Devouassoud. The former was seventy-two years of age; the latter was over eighty. Devouassoud, having become weak in his mind, leaned vacantly over the sinister display. But Couttet could definitely identify each object. Moreover, among the severed arms he pointed to one that had belonged to his best friend, the guide Pierre Balmat. Very moved, he clasped this livid hand, saying (according to the police report): "I had never dared to believe that, before leaving this world, it would be granted me to grasp once more the hand of one of these fine comrades, the hand of my good friend Balmat!"

Such was the *Affaire Hamel*, the first of the great alpine tragedies.

* * *

Four months before this melancholy discovery, it is related that the famous guide, Auguste Balmat, particularly well thought of by the élite of the English alpinists, was in London. The illustrious climber and physicist, Tyndall, met his friend at the British Museum. An old man, who bore himself very well, accosted them before one of the showcases, saying: "You come from Chamonix, Mr. Balmat?"

"Yes, monsieur."

"Have they yet discovered the bodies of my three guides? I am Dr. Hamel!"

"Alas! No, monsieur."

"Oh, well! You will find them sooner or later."

"That is Mr. Tyndall's opinion too. Sooner or later the glacier will surrender its unhappy victims."

"Certainly, certainly! I well believe it. It will be a very good thing for Chamonix. It will provide you with a very interesting museum to attract the tourists."

A little later, as we have seen, Dr. Hamel's lugubrious prophecy was realised.

For the scene of "The Hamel Affair," see Plates 2 and 7.

[1] It is by the bizarre name *"l'Affaire Hamel"* that this accident is known in alpine historiography.

[2] The following is an extract from the letters of Miss Edgeworth (from Chamonix, 1820):

"*September 6th.*—Mrs. Marcet has just told us that at a breakfast given by M. Prévost and M. Arago and many scientific and literary people, a few days after the accident, parties ran high on this as on all affairs. Some said it was M. Hamel's fault; some said it was all the guides' own fault. One said he wished one of the English gentlemen who was of the party was present, for then they should know the truth. At this moment the servant announced a stranger; 'Monsieur Rumford' the name sounded like as the man pronounced it, and they thought it was Count Rumford come to life. M. Prévost went out and returned with Mr. Dornford, one of the Englishmen who had been of Dr. Hamel's party, who came, he said, to beg permission to state the plain facts, as he knew they had been told to Dr. Hamel's disadvantage. He, Dr. Hamel, Mr. Henderson, and M. Lelleque, a French naturalist, set out; the guides had not dissuaded them from going up Mount Blanc—only advised them to wait until a threatening cloud had passed. When it was gone they all set out in high spirits, the guides cutting holes in the snow for their feet. This, it is supposed, loosened the snow newly fallen, and a quantity poured down over their heads. Mr. Dornford pushed on before the guides; he shook off the snow as it fell, and felt no apprehension. On the contrary, he laughed as he pawed it away, and was making his way on when he heard a cry from his companions, and looking back he saw some of them struggling in the snow. He helped to extricate them, saw a point moving in the snow, went to it, and pulled out Marie Coutay, one of the guides. He was quite purple, but recovered in the air. Looking round, two guides were missing; looked for them in vain, but saw a deep ravine covered with fresh snow, into which they must have fallen."—(*Alpine Journal*, Vol. XVII, 1895.)

[3] "We suddenly heard a dull rumbling like a hidden torrent, and at the same instant, from the top of the slope as far as the place where our steps had ploughed a furrow ten to twelve inches deep, the snow moved. I saw the four or five guides in front of me at once overturned, with their feet in the air; only one seemed to remain standing,

charges on a lead, tied to the same rope. It was this detestable system that both humiliated and amused the English alpinist, Alfred Wills, a President of the Alpine Club, who was also held on a lead by his guides. He wittily compared himself with a dancing bear,[3] and it was some of these dancing bears who, on the 15th of August, 1860, arrived at the Col du Géant (11,053 feet) in the Mont Blanc massif, on the Italian frontier.

The party totalled six men, three travellers, all English— J. M. Rochester, F. Vavasseur and B. Fuller, and three guides from Chamonix. They had left the Tacul bivouac at dawn. By way of the séracs, an astonishing labyrinth of crevasses, buttresses, bastions, slender arches and massive pillars of ice, menacing ruins wreathed in frost, the climbers emerged from the cold shadow into the light of the Bédière plateaux, an area to-day beloved by skiers. Above them stretched the pallid line of the col. It was the end of a beautiful day, of alternating haze and azure skies.

At the col they were immobilised by a dense mist, but this soon dispersed. Nothing could be more soporific than the monotony of these vast snowy plateaux. There was no shelter on the crest from the sweeping winds, for already the remains of Saussure's bivouac were only a small heap of stones in the midst of others.

They ate a little, looking abstractedly at the view, which between two flights of cloud displayed prodigious effects. Down in the peaceful depths lay the pastures of Courmayeur. Against the sky, directly to the right, rose the cyclopean architecture of the south-eastern face of Mont Blanc: from the Brenva glacier to the summit enormous cascades of ice unrolled their livid folds. The savage profile of the Aiguilles de Péteret, the Noire and the Blanche, looked in their broken outline like the temperature chart of a feverish patient. The whole horizon was filled with the airy immensity of the alps of Piedmont: an ocean wave, supple and harmonious, but terribly immobile.

* * *

It is time to go. The Mont-Fréty refuge, where they will pass the night, is still a long way off: over there, on that moraine already in shadow, a grey silhouette beside the humps of rock. The guides measure the intervals in the rope and pass the running knots around the waists of the travellers. Docile and confident, they allow themselves to be tied. They are weary and in a hurry to reach the hut. What a fine rest they will have this evening on the fresh straw, under the blankets! But those who slowly begin the descent are already marked out for death. Those about to die salute the peaks for the last time. In a moment of time the mountain will be their tomb.

The route they should take is to the right: a rock arête reached by a slope of snow. It is the usual way: perhaps a little longer, but much safer than the steep glacier itself, which widens between its frame of rocks.

The leading guide is about to take to the slope. His hesitating feet test the snow, patting it lightly. It gives, sinking, then resists, his feet supporting themselves in the depressions they make. The snow is a little soft on its hardened bed, but with care all will be well. The man in the lead turns round:

"Yes, monsieur," he says, "it's all right, you can come on."

Stones fall past them and spin in parabolas over the ice. And soon the entire party has taken to the slope, vertically, the rope taut between each man. The slope is not so very steep. They have only to keep their eyes open and go boldly.

Exhausted, one of the Englishmen slips. He falls seated, but the rope holds him. He gets up and starts afresh. These repeated false steps set the party laughing. Yet, while it is true that the dangers are not very great, in the mountains the worst is un-foreseeable. At this moment the chief guide, to use a pilot's terms, ought to swing the helm to the right and bring the ship to the rocks. There it would be safer—all the more so with these exhausted "messieurs," who might fall at any step. But the party continues its descent staircase-wise, very slowly, very ponderously, straying even a little to the left.

Now it is interesting to note this curious, even terrifying fact: the three travellers are roped together, a tight knot encircling each of them. This is customary and indispensable, *but the guides themselves are not attached to the rope*, and to a twentieth-century climber this is not only abnormal, but contrary to all the elementary rules of alpine technique and to the principles of alpine morality and honour. But these men, tried mountaineers and men of spirit, believe they are acting rightly. At the head of the column is a guide: he holds the rope in one hand and his ferruled staff in the other. Two travellers follow him, then the second guide, Frédéric Tairraz, one hand on the line. The third

14

and on the other:

> A LA MEMOIRE DE
> FREDERIC TAIRRAZ
> GUIDE DE CHAMOUNIX
> PERI AVEC DES ANGLAIS
> AU COL DU GEANT
> LE 15 AOUT 1860[7]

For the scene of the disaster on the Col du Géant, see Plate 3.

[1] Cf. Charles Gos: *L'Hôtel des Neuchâtelois*, Payot, Lausanne.
[2] J. D. Forbes, *Travels Through the Alps of Savoy*, Edinburgh, 1843.
[3] Sir Alfred Wills, *The Eagle's Nest*, London, 1860.
[4] See Chapter 3.
[5] Cf. John Tyndall: *Hours of Exercise in the Alps*, London, 1871.
[6] In Whymper's intimate diary the following passage can be found: "21st August, 1860. . . . [at Kandersteg] our landlord told me of a fatal accident to three English gentlemen which occurred on Wednesday last on the Col du Géant. It appears that they started with four guides just after great quantities of fresh snow had fallen: their guides remonstrated but to no purpose. They had passed the col in safety and descending to Courmayeur when they came to a precipice which they had to skirt. They went along it tied together when the middle gentleman went through the crust of snow over the precipice. He pulled the two others down after him and two of the guides, the remaining two must have inevitably followed as they were within an inch of the precipice had they not cut the ropes when, of course, the unfortunate men having no support fell to the bottom. There are many details in connection with this melancholy accident which I have yet to hear, but of this I feel assured, that the most experienced Alpine men will do well to leave such mountains as the Weisshorn and the Jungfrau alone this year, and other parts and places where the snow is calculated to deceive and hide real existing dangers, as although it is probable that, even in this case, if the man next to the one who broke through had been walking with greater care and watchfulness, an accident would not have occurred; yet there are so great varieties of dangers in connection with new snow that making such expeditions at like times savours very much of foolhardiness."
(In a footnote Mr. Smythe draws attention to the fact that the details of the accident as told to Whymper and recorded by him are far from exact.)
(Cf. F. S. Smythe: *Edward Whymper*. Hodder & Stoughton, London, 1940.)
[7] (Trans.) "To the memory of Frédéric Tairraz, Guide, of Chamonix, who perished with some Englishmen on the Col de Géant on the 15th August, 1860."

CHAPTER THREE

THE GARIBALDI OF THE GUIDES

The death of the guide Johann-Josef Bennen and of the climber
Boissonet at the Haut de Cry (February 1864)

COMPARED with Mont Blanc, the scene of the first alpine disaster, the Haut de Cry (9,742 feet) in the Valais, a summit of the Préalpes[1] of no importance, scarcely exists. But what of that? Death in the mountains passes from one summit to another, just as in war it passes from front to front. And from the frozen heights of Chamonix and Courmayeur death now aims at this obscure peak in the Rhône valley, where a great guide is about to die.

Johann-Josef Bennen is at the height of his power. He is forty-five years of age. He comes from Lax, a village in the Haut-Valais, where at his chalet live his old mother and three sisters. He is, moreover, engaged to be married. He is very quick, and the British climbers have noticed it: Tyndall, Tuckett and others besides. Daring and prudent at the same time, and of a sensitive nature, he has achieved a great renown and has classed himself with the famous guides of the Oberland. He has some fine victories in his record: the Aletschhorn, the Weisshorn, Mont Blanc by way of the Aiguille du Goûter and les Bosses, to say nothing of two memorable attacks on the still inviolate Matterhorn, when he attempted to forestall Whymper and Carrel. He was the first who dared to guide some travellers upon it, and of the first fifteen attempts up till 1862 his was the one that reached the highest point.

Tyndall named him "the Garibaldi of the Guides," On the first

18

ascent of the Weisshorn (14,804 feet) in 1860, he contemplated momentarily the dizzy arête which thrusts its blade into the sky like an inverted ploughshare, and said, turning towards Tyndall: "A terrible long way off, that summit . . . but we shall have it."

His words galvanised his companion. "His voice, as he spoke," Tyndall observes, "rung like steel in my heart." These are the qualities of a leader; this strength of belief which frees the spirit is, in high places, the most admirable virtue. Nietzsche would have loved such ease on the edge of the abyss. Unknown to himself, Bennen, a poor alpine peasant, brilliantly illustrated the doctrine of the will to power a long time before Nietzsche created his Zarathushtra. But Bennen's impetuous flight is about to dash itself to pieces in full trajectory.

The winter mountains had their adepts fifty years before the appearance of skis: some out of ignorance, like Kennedy in his attempt on the Matterhorn in January 1862, and others seduced by the charms of the alpine landscape under its deep covering of snow, with its skies of so pure a blue above the fogs of the plains. Mr. Gosset and Mr. Boissonet, both of them English, love the winter mountains, and the Haut de Cry, a secondary summit which even in summer has attracted none but a few hunters from the valley, has lured them. Why, it is impossible to tell. But eventually they succumb to their caprice and set forth.[2]

It is the 28th February, 1864, and Bennen, to acquire a few extra francs (for he is shortly to be married) has agreed to accompany them. Three local guides, Nance, Rebot and Bevard, who are probably chamois-hunters, complete the party. Leaving Sion at two in the morning the climbers, passing through Ardon, rise rapidly on the south-east side of the mountain. They quickly reach the edge of the snow, and it is at once very thick. The men sink to their thighs. None of them has snowshoes. As for skis, except for Honoré de Balzac and the Scandinavian countries, nobody in Europe knows of them.

Progress is so exhausting that the guides take five-minute turns in leading. If this state of affairs continues, they will have to give up. Such hard labour is breaking. But in the nick of time the snow hardens. Not for long, however, and the party is again entangled. This adventure amuses Bennen. He laughs heartily, covered in snow to the stomach. This is certainly a change for him from the brass-hard summer ice.

Above the forest the Haut de Cry raises its sharp, limestone arêtes, streaked with white ledges, like an inclined M. At the edge of the wood the party halts to recover its breath. In the distance, rising above a bluish wave of summits, the peak of the Matterhorn raises its black shield aloft. The men are looking at it, and Mr. Gosset asks:

"Do you think it will be reached one day?"

Bennen tosses his head: "Yes, perhaps. The last time I was there with Mr. Tyndall was in '62. We had climbed very high, as far as the crevasse, and then we had to go down again. But I can assure you that the people of Zermatt would have seen our flag that day."[3]

The frozen snow of a secondary crest brings the party rapidly to the base of the summit peak. This is no more than a wide combe. Here they make their last halt. Bennen, like an old wolf, examines the mountain. He seems to be smelling out the way, and his face is screwed up. Suddenly he is anxious. But since this slope is so easy, since there is no glacier with treacherous crevasses to cross, nor rock walls, what is it that worries him? While they wait they uncoil the rope. The Haut-Valaisian is assailed by imponderables; dimly he senses a menace.

"Are there no avalanches in this quarter?" he asks his comrades who live at the foot of the massif.

Unanimously their answer is "No." This corner is quite peaceful. The guides jest in patois and prepare the rope. But Bennen is only partly reassured. The nearness of the summit gives zest to the party, and soon, in Indian file, it is engaged upon the slope, cutting across it horizontally. At first all goes well. The surface bears. Bennen has exaggerated. His doubts disappear.

Then suddenly Bevard and Nance, in the lead, sink to the waist. His anxiety renewed, Bennen secures the rope and waits. But the others continue. They look like bathers entering the water, cleaving the snow with their bodies, opening a trench instead of a furrow. Bennen has not moved. This moving earth tells him nothing. He watches in silence, his whole being apprehensive, his mind and muscles filled with the imminent and developing tragedy.

Turning towards his travellers, he repeats his fears. The answer comes back to him from the head of the party. Over there the snow is hard again. So, let us go on, and all will be well! Then they draw near to the rocks.

The snow in the high mountains must be treated gently. It can suddenly acquire the fury of a lioness, particularly if one should find oneself at grips with it where it would be better not to have been, a fact which climbers á l'eau de rose or worldly skiers irrationally ignore.

So the rest of the party sets off once more and enters the trench in its turn, keeping their elbows to their sides to avoid contact with its walls.

Suddenly, under a divinely blue sky, there is a sound as if a tree has fallen, splitting the glowing silence: an enormous and powerful tree, a massive oak, as high as a poplar, tumbling in one piece. But a tree at these heights? The last firs were more than 3,000 feet below. Then it is the snow!

With a dry crack, deep and hard, a sound horizontal and decisive, the combe of snow has split from side to side only a yard above the men. A crevasse—a fissure, rather—as wide as a thumb, now traverses the slope with the rectilineal and elegant neatness of a surveyor's projection. There is a silence for some seconds, a terrifying silence, filled with strange shudders. Then the voice of Bennen is heard, pronouncing the inexorable words: "We are all lost."

He speaks slowly, in a low voice, a little solemnly. They are his last words. With a man of his character no equivocation is possible.

A new pause suspends both earth and spirit. And the six men await the chaos, transfixed. No one speaks. One of the travellers, Mr. Gosset, attempts to fix his alpenstock in the snow, and it disappears as if into a vase. Then Bennen turns slowly to face the valley, extending his arms like a cross. And as if the avalanche has only awaited this signal, the entire mountain, convulsed, begins to move. Its movement is swift. Joined to one another by the rope, the bodies disappear in the eddies, rise again to the surface, thrashing, and vanish once more. The waves of snow crouch, swell, spring forward, follow one another like waves of the sea. Here, where the rope, striking a rock, leaps and breaks, the bodies drift apart. The head of the avalanche spreads like the tail of a white peacock and rolls on with the uproar of a tempest, while the main mass, less noisy, slides down with the soft and silken sound of water against the hull of a ship.

The enormous mass runs aground on a shelf. But before it is

definitely immobilised, heavy palpitations convulse it, due to the formidable pressure of the snows behind on those in front, and to the settling at the centre of the telescoping, overlapping, coagulating mass.

The avalanche has hardly halted before it freezes hard. The unfortunate victims, gripped in this vice, are about to die—one might say, to die living—flattened by the pressure and sculptured by the frost. Mr. Gosset, half asphyxiated, is buried upright, with his arms raised, unable to move a muscle, a toe or a knee. He is a living statue, except for his hands which project beyond the surface. He is petrified by the darkness and the silence. But he can still think and feel, though there is no room for his chest to expand. Only his ten fingers, he says, could still move.

By a supreme instinctive act this expiring life concentrates itself in these two hands. Their movements are not those of supplication. They are content simply to move, to affirm that they are not yet dead. A survivor, Rebot, sees these fingers in frantic agitation above the snow, like the legs of a huge insect. He throws himself upon them, drags at them, digs around them. The hands are prolonged into arms. A head appears, livid; the eyelids flutter under the frost. A neck, shoulders and chest follow. Mr. Gosset draws in a great breath. His eyes open, and in that instant, though buried firmly to the chest, he sees quite close to him a foot. He points it out to Rebot, and Rebot and Gosset between them pull at it. But they can do nothing: the foot resists them like a beam firmly fixed in its socket.

Twenty minutes later, Nance and Bevard, pale as ghosts, appear. They have been able to release themselves, one helping the other, the blind helping the paralytic. And the three men dig with their axes around Mr. Gosset, who is at last exhumed from his verticle tomb. The four men are worn out. They sit down, a tragic conventicle, around the foot and contemplate it silently.

They wait . . . for what? They do not know. Nothing, probably. This is Mr. Boissonet's foot: they have recognised it. As for Bennen, nothing can be found of him. A fragment of rope rests on the snow like a snake. The four men lift it up; it sinks into the avalanche perpendicularly. They pull at it, they struggle. In vain. Nothing can be done about it; the rope is anchored. At its extremity, several yards down, is the body of Bennen. And this body, this Bennen, even in death remains true to himself, according to his own words on the Matterhorn arête: *Fest wie eine Mauer.*

Several days later the rescue party released the bodies. Bennen's watch had disappeared. The following summer a shepherd discovered it among the stones. He rewound it; it started again.

Bennen is buried at Ernen, near Lax, in the Valley of Conches, between Brigue and Gletsch. His mother became mad with grief. A simple monument perpetuates the memory of this great guide:

DEM GELIEBTEN J. J. BENNEN

FÜHRER IN LAX

GEBOHREN 1819,

GESTORBEN 1864

VON J. TYNDALL

F. V. HAWKINS

UND F. F. TUCKETT

EINGEWEIHT

Job xvi. 22.[4]

[1] Dr. Hch. Dübi, in his *Guide* (*Hochgebirgsführer durch die Berner Alpen*, Berne, 1907), links this massif to the Bernese Alps.

[2] Cf. *Alpine Journal*, Vol. I. 1863–64.

[3] An allusion to the attempt made with Tyndall and the guides Anton Walters (from the Bernese Oberland), Jean-Antoine and César Carrel (of Valtournanche), these last two serving as porters, on the 27th and 28th July, 1862 (the 15th attempt). Bennen himself always believed in victory. It was he who, before Carrel, reached the highest point on the Italian arête and made in passing the first ascent of the southern Shoulder of the Matterhorn, known as the Pic Tyndall (14,008 feet).

[4] (*Trans.*) "To the very dear J. J. Bennen, Guide, of Lax, born in 1819, died in 1864, this monument was raised by J. Tyndall, F. V. Hawkins and F. F. Tuckett."

With time the inscription was slowly effaced, and in 1902 Tyndall, faithful to his guide, renewed it as follows: "*Bergführer Johann Joseph Bennen, aus Lax, Geboren 11 Nov. 1819; Verunglückt 28 Feb. 1864, am Haut de Cry. Errichtet von John Tyndall, F. Vaughan Hawkins und F. F. Tuckett. Erneuert von John Tyndall, 1902.*" (*Trans.*: "Johann Joseph Bennen, guide, of Lax, born on the 11th Nov., 1819; died accidentally on the 28th Feb., 1864, on the Haut de Cry. This monument was raised by John Tyndall, F. Vaughan Hawkins and F. F. Tuckett. Restored by John Tyndall, 1902.")

CHAPTER FOUR

THE MATTERHORN CATASTROPHE

The death of the Rev. Charles Hudson, of Lord Francis Douglas, of R. D.
Hadow, and of the guide Michel Croz (July 1865)

No mountain in the Alps, no mountain in the world, has had a vogue equal to that of the Matterhorn, which raises its prodigious pyramid 14,780 feet into the summit skies of the Valais.

Until the end of the eighteenth century the Matterhorn played no known role. That, however, was the lot of all the summits. Man, for religious reasons (deriving from ancient mythology and from the beliefs of the Middle Ages), feared the mountains. His attention since before the Christian era had been concentrated on the passes. These would see the increasing passage for century after century of all humanity, of kings and vagrants, emperors and troubadours, popes and pilgrims, rich men and knife-grinders, to say nothing of the movements of innumerable armies. But man's perspective was limited to the pass, and everything above its level was lost in nebulosity. Nevertheless, with the awakening of intellect and of the sensibilities—the development of science and the taste for travel, and so forth—man began slowly to raise his eyes. It was then that the peaks ceased to be anonymous and by acquiring personality achieved a civil status.

In 1732 Albert de Haller wrote his famous poem *Die Alpen*, subsequently translated, then expanded into a novel by Jean-Jacques Rousseau, *La Nouvelle Héloïse*, and later imitated by a whole bleating literature.

At this moment—the end of the eighteenth century—a man

looked at the Matterhorn for the first time, contemplated it curiously and found it beautiful. This man's name was already inscribed in the annals of alpine history and science: Horace-Bénédict de Saussure, the Genevese scholar. Already in 1787 the conqueror of Mont Blanc, Saussure was the first to discover the poety of the high mountains in general and the aesthetics of the Matterhorn in particular.[1] For in the astonishing history of this mountain it is no exaggeration to say that its beauty lent a bewitching glory to its conquest.

From Saussure to Ruskin all the intellectuals and all the artists who followed one another to Zermatt were literally hypnotised by the fantastic allure of this fascinating titan. Theirs was a harmony of distracted lyricism, from which the French Romantics were unhappily missing; Théophile Gautier excepted, they ignored the very existence of the Matterhorn. Musset dedicated a poem to the Jungfrau, Hugo some resounding pages to the Aiguilles of Chamonix, Lamartine loved Mont Blanc, but nobody in French literature had seen the Matterhorn or been heard to speak of it: alone, George Sand named it once, as if by accident. But the crowds which swarmed to its feet bowed before it in ecstacy. Even its shadow inspired fear, as if, projected upon the valley and almost too heavy to rise, it drew with it the maleficence of its precipices.

As early as 1857 one man dared an assault on this terrible but wonderful peak. Jean-Antoine Carrel, a simple peasant of the Valtournanche (the Italian valley to the south of the Matterhorn), is the spirit of this first timid attempt, and he remains one of the leaders of this redoubtable adventure in the years of ardent struggle which are about to begin, to appear nine years later as the conqueror of the Italian summit.[2]

But the British alpinists are alert. Indeed, all the daring skirmishers of the peaks are attracted to the Matterhorn. They draw close to it, examine it, take the measure of it, as a player examines the field before the match. Three attempts have already been made upon the Swiss and Italian faces when, in 1860, he who will be the hero of this odyssey, the young Englishman, Edward Whymper, enters the scene. He is only twenty years old and a beginner in the Alps. A draughtsman, he has been sent to Switzerland to illustrate a book. And these mountains whose profiles he should be recording have captured him instead. He is fascinated; he sees the Matterhorn and desires it. He is going to be attached to this formidable mountain, not with a lover's passion, but with a kind of desperate tenacity. One can hardly tell if it is the Matterhorn that is the prey or Whymper himself.

An extraordinary climber, of tenacious nature, energetic, cool, even glacial, nevertheless, in his great love for the savage Matterhorn Whymper produced some exquisite flights of poetry.

But he is not alone in his desire to possess it, and he quickly takes account of the fact. Carrel is there, and Carrel too intends to be the conqueror of the Matterhorn, the mountain that belongs to his native valley. And so it happens that in the six years that follow a fierce and tenacious struggle is played out between the two rivals, both splendid combatants, both determined to win. Attempt succeeds attempt, pushed very high into the inviolate ramparts. Sometimes they are allies, sometimes enemies. Tempests baffle their audacity; avalanches of stones fall upon them; snow blocks their paths. It matters little. Whymper falls in a couloir of ice and just escapes death, but he has scarcely recovered from his wounds before he returns to the mountain. And Carrel is always there.

The years slip by and the Matterhorn still remains unconquered. Of the thirty men whose rivalries have contended and united in turn only two remain face to face. The others have abandoned so severe an assault. They vanish from the scene and do not reappear, while in the monumental décor of these rocks, in the silence of their solitudes, alone, Carrel and Whymper pass and repass, conducting the passionate tournament with such fierceness that one can sense the tumult of their minds and their exasperated wills. And the Matterhorn itself, protagonist in the drama whose action is about to begin, at the touch of so much exalted living seems truly to stir and to assume the sombre power of certain mythological heroes.

But the dénouement draws near. Whymper, weary of the checks sustained on the Italian side, looks for another way. On the 9th July, 1865, he is at le Breuil, abandoned by Carrel, "I was," he says, "in the position of a general without an army," when on the 11th there unexpectedly appears a young Englishman, Lord Francis Douglas, likewise an enthusiast for the high mountains, and a new pretender to the title of conqueror of the Matterhorn. Douglas and Whymper are kindred spirits; they agree to join forces. On the 12th they leave together for Zermatt.

On arriving there in the evening, Whymper is surprised to meet Michel Croz of Chamonix, his favourite guide and his companion in many great conquests, one of the best guides of his time. Croz has arrived the day before with two Englishmen, the Rev. Charles Hudson and Mr. R. D. Hadow, with the intention of attempting the ascent of the Matterhorn. With the Rev. Charles Hudson he has just made the first ascent of the Aiguille Verte by the arête du Moine.

The two Englishmen agree to surrender their guide on the express condition that they will take part in the expedition planned by Whymper and Douglas: a determined assault on the Matterhorn from the Zermatt side. Whymper accepts, being very happy to have secured the valiant Croz. He further engages the guide Peter Taugwalder *père*, of Zermatt, with Taugwalder *fils* as porter. And the party, organised in this fortuitous manner, leaves Zermatt for the Matterhorn on the morning of the 13th. "If," says Whymper, "any one of the links of this fatal chain of circumstances had been omitted, what a different story I should have to tell."

On the 14th July, 1865, at 1.40 in the afternoon, "the world was at our feet," writes the celebrated alpinist, "and the Matterhorn was conquered." To the very real surprise of the climbers the ascent, although difficult and dangerous, presented nothing in its arduous defences comparable with those on the Italian side.[3] A single passage, a short wall of blackish rock, set in the snow and the ice, and overhanging a bottomless abyss, broke the climbers' speed with its treachery. It is there, moreover, that the tragedy will take place on the descent.

What does Whymper do on arriving at the summit? His first thought is to discover if Carrel has preceded him. He examines the snow anxiously, but it is immaculate. Carrel has left no footprints. Whymper is the victor.

But this victor is not without nobility. Leaning over the precipice of the Italian face, he scans the walls that he knows so well, knowing that at this very moment Jean-Antoine Carrel and his companions are making the supreme effort (the eighteenth and last attempt). And when at last he perceives his unhappy rivals and knows himself to have been seen by them, he has this generous thought: "I would that the leader of that party [Carrel] could have stood with us at that moment, for our victorious

27

shouts conveyed to him the disappointment of an ambition of a lifetime. He was *the* man of all those who attempted the ascent of the Matterhorn who most deserved to be the first upon its summit. He was the first to doubt its inaccessibility, and he was the only man who persisted in believing that its ascent would be accomplished."[4] Then, thoughtful, Whymper passes a solemn hour on the summit rocks, "one crowded hour of glorious life," says he, enthralled by the dazzling view which meets his astonished gaze on all sides.

Then Whymper and his comrades prepare to descend. There they all are, trampling about, buckling up their knapsacks, chattering amongst themselves, adjusting their gaiters, fastening their boots, uncoiling the ropes and measuring the intervals along them. A whole band of men happy in their victory. But a little nervous all the same on account of the accursed descent in prospect; a little strained at contemplating that snowy rampart with which they will presently be struggling. All that enormous and mysterious wall to descend before reaching the morning's bivouac and more hospitable regions! Oh! to know at last the feeling of liberation, to savour the relief of having finished with the inexorable ice-encrusted rocks! To have nothing before one but grassy slopes and the paths between the arollas! Ah! to stretch oneself out beside the peaceful Schwarzee!

Everything is ready. They are all roped, but the ropes have been chosen a little haphazardly. Here is the Alpine Club rope, there the heavy manilla. Between the elder Taugwalder and Lord Francis Douglas is the thinnest of the three. But Douglas is well aware of this. He has certainly seen it, but it worries neither him nor Taugwalder, nor does it worry the others. So the descent begins.

Michel Croz leaves first, tied to Hadow, the latter not very sure of himself. The Rev. Charles Hudson follows, a confident, lively fellow; next the little Lord Douglas, light and slender, still very young. He turns to Taugwalder, his guide and old comrade, and with a smile points to their earlier conquest, where they had almost perished together, the Obergabelhorn, over there on the other side of the Zmutt valley, gleaming in the bluish air. And old Taugwalder grunts: *"Herr Gott! Ja, ja, Herr Douglas!"*

Whymper finishes a drawing and packs up. The younger Taugwalder waits for him silently, a little uneasy. Uneasy?

Why? The day is so pure, the mountain so beautiful, and life is so beautiful too! The rope between Whymper and the younger Taugwalder is soon joined to the others, Whymper thus being placed between father and son. And it is a procession of seven men, all tied together, which descends.[5] One hour later death will cut the party down.

In his letter to *The Times* (8th August, 1865), still famous, Whymper tells the story as follows (the climbers finding themselves at the top of the short wall where they had encountered dangerous difficulties on the way up):

"Poor Croz had laid aside his axe, and in order to give Mr. Hadow greater security was absolutely taking hold of his legs and putting his feet, one by one, into their proper positions.[6] From the movements of their shoulders it is my belief that Croz, having done as I have said, was in the act of turning round to go down a step or two himself; at this moment Mr. Hadow slipped, fell on him and knocked him over. I heard one startled exclamation from Croz, then saw him and Mr. Hadow flying downwards; in another moment Hudson was dragged from his steps and Lord Francis Douglas immediately after him. All this was the work of a moment, but immediately we heard Croz's exclamation, Taugwalder and myself planted ourselves as firmly as the rocks would permit; *the rope was tight between us, and the shock came on us both as on one man.* We held; but the rope broke midway between Taugwalder and Lord F. Douglas. For two or three seconds we saw our unfortunate companions sliding downwards on their backs, and spreading out their hands endeavouring to save themselves; they then disappeared one by one, and fell from precipice to precipice on to the Matterhorn glacier below, a distance of nearly 4,000 feet in height. From the moment the rope broke it was impossible to help them.

"For the space of half an hour we remained on the spot without moving a single step. The two men, paralysed by terror, cried like infants, and trembled in such a manner as to threaten us with the fate of the others. Immediately we had descended to a safe place, I asked for the rope that had broken, and to my surprise —indeed, to my horror—found that it was the weakest of the three ropes. . . .

"For more than two hours afterwards I thought every moment that the next would be my last; for the Taugwalders, utterly

unnerved were not only incapable of giving any assistance, but
were in such a state that a slip might have been expected from
one or the other at any moment. . . . There is no occasion to say
more of the descent. I looked frequently, but in vain, for traces
of my unfortunate companions, and we were in consequence
surprised by the night when still at a height of 13,000 feet. We
arrived at Zermatt at 10.30 on Saturday morning."

* * *

On the 16th July, a party comprising Edward Whymper,
several friends and guides, arrived on the Matterhorn glacier.[7]
At the foot of the immense precipice of the north face, in the
middle of a terrace dazzling with snow, the bodies were recovered.
But there were only three : the fourth, that of Lord Francis Douglas,
had vanished. It was never discovered. The abyss has kept its
secret.[8]

A week after the accident, the Valaisian government took
proceedings at an inquest to clear up the story of the wretched
rope. Whymper was questioned, then his guides. Their answers
throw no light on the question.[9] Was the rope cut? In spite of the
energetic denials of Whymper himself, in spite of the pre-emptory
and negative arguments of numerous climbers, there are still
people to-day who, in order to explain the tragedy, say: "Ah!
yes. The story of the cut rope!"

So let us repeat here firmly and plainly, for what our testimony
is worth : No, the rope was not cut; the elder Taugwalder, a
brave guide and an honest man, did not cut the rope. No guide,
in order to save his own life, severs the rope that ties him to his
traveller; he dies with him. In all the long history of the Alps,
in all its tragedies (and there are hundreds of them), no single
case is found contrary to this testimony.

* * *

In July 1906, Edward Whymper, whom I knew well from
having met him several times either at Zermatt or in the studio
of my father, the painter Albert Gos, at Geneva, was staying at
St. Nicolas. It happened that I was there at the same time, and
Whymper one evening invited me to dinner. On the day before,
I had with my young brother climbed the Matterhorn for the
first time, and for us it was obviously a great day. The illustrious

alpinist—author of so many fine pages about the High Alps, their grandeur, their terrible risks, their poetry—listened benevolently to a banal recital which told him absolutely nothing, though it was pleasant to him, perhaps, to catch in this youthful enthusiasm an evocation of great and distant memories which left him musing. And then, carried away by these memories, Whymper told me in his turn, in clear and moving words, the story of the catastrophe which at twenty-five years of age had permanently darkened his life and changed his destiny. I can still see him, seated, mimicking the unfortunate Hadow whose extended legs had struck Michel Croz in the back and thrown him down.

On the following day Whymper presented me with a photographic reproduction of a portrait of Croz, showing his strong and loyal features. Beneath it the conqueror of the Matterhorn had written these words:

Michel Croz, du Tour, Vallee de Chamonix, one of the best mountaineers I have ever known. He was killed miserably, par betise, sur la première ascension de Mont-Cervin. Juillet 14e 1865. Au revoir, cher Michel.

St. Nicolas, juillet 26e 1906.   *Edward Whymper.*

*   *   *

The museum at Zermatt, besides a few crystals and articles of local folklore, contains a rather unusual collection. In effect all the neighbouring mountains are represented and catalogued there, not by their rocks or outlines, but by the relics of alpine expeditions which have come to grief on them. It is a macabre exhibition serving only to excite either the curiosity or the pity of the visitors. For my own part, I remember little of all these relics but those of the catastrophe of the first ascent of the Matterhorn. One day the famous case was opened for me. In it was a boot belonging to the young, vanished Lord Douglas, side by side with one of Hadow's boots—tragic footwear these last, if one may say so, since it was their defects which seem to have precipitated the tragedy. I slowly and piously turned over the leaves of Hudson's prayer-book, printed at the Oxford University Press in 1835; this little old book was carried to the top and then made that terrible fall of close on 4,000 feet. Croz's hat is there too; I turned and turned it in my fingers, careful not to damage it; and I examined for a long time the pieces of the famous ropes, among them the one that broke. On the body of Michel Croz, as it lay stretched out upon the bloodstained snow, was found a rosary, and this too is among the exhibits in the case. The beads still hold together; only the cross is missing, and there is nothing more moving than the presence of this frail relic.

Every time that I recall the fabulous story of the conquest of the Matterhorn, itself as lovely as an heroic poem, I think of these lines from the *Chanson de Roland:*

> Très noblement se bat le preux Roland . . .
> Le preux Roland est de si fier courage . . .
> Anges du Ciel descendent près de lui . . .
> Et tous les trois portent son âme au Ciel.

Thus died Michel Croz, one of the finest knights in the history of the conquest of the Alps.

Among the blue irises and the little crosses in the cemetery of Zermatt can be seen the graves of the victors of the Matterhorn.[10] On Croz's stone there is this epitaph, composed by Whymper himself:

A LA MEMOIRE
DE
MICHEL-AUGUSTE CROZ
NE AU TOUR VALLEE DE
CHAMOUNIX. EN TEMOIGNAGE
DE REGRETS DE LA
PERTE D'UN HOMME BRAVE
ET DEVOUE AIME DE SES
COMPAGNONS ESTIME DES
VOYAGEURS. IL PERIT NON
LOIN D'ICI EN HOMME DE
VOEUR ET GUIDE FIDELE[11]

Through the beautiful nights of summer, above the reflecting snows and the slumbering glaciers, when the silence itself is silent, when the mountains dream and the night-hours sigh, the stars gleam upon their graves.[12]

THE MATTERHORN CATASTROPHE

For the scene of the Matterhorn catastrophe, see Plate 4. See also Plate 12 for the salient features of the northern (Zermatt) aspect of the mountain. For a portrait of Whymper in 1865, and for a photograph of Croz's grave at Zermatt, see Plates 1, and 5.

[1] Cf. de Saussure: *Voyage dans les Alpes*, Vol. IV. Edition de Neuchatel, 1796.

[2] Regarding the death of Carrel, see Chapter 18, *Carrel the Great*.

[3] It is curious to note that Whymper eventually climbed the Matterhorn by a route which he had never attempted before, and which he had regarded as inaccessible or at least infinitely more dangerous and difficult than the Italian arête. It was on this north-north-east arête, known as the Zermatt arête, that the Parker brothers' attempt had taken place in 1860 and 1861, and Kennedy's in 1862.

[4] Three days afterwards (17th July), Jean-Antoine Carrel, accompanying Jean-Baptiste Bich, accomplished the second ascent, and the first from the Italian side. Their two comrades, the Abbé Aimé Gorret and Jean-Augustin Meynet, sacrificed themselves in order to assure the result, and awaited the others at the foot of the terminal tower, at the extremity of the "gallery."

[5] Capt. J. P. Farrar, former President of the Alpine Club, has severely criticised the composition of the party on its descent, "the want of coherence in the 'fortuitously' formed party." "Had the parties been separate, then it can hardly be doubted that the order of descent of Hudson's party would have been as follows:

1. Hudson, leading down.
2. Hadow.
3. Croz, last man.

The order of the second party would in all probability have been:

1. Whymper, leading down.
2. Young Taugwalder.
3. Douglas.
4. Old Taugwalder, last man.

Had this order been adopted we should, in all probability, have not had to chronicle any accident.

For the whole party on one rope the most prudent order, in my opinion, would have been:

1. Hudson, leading down, since he had led on the way up to the shoulder and was used to going without guides.
2. Douglas.
3. Young Taugwalder.
4. Hadow.
5. Croz, who would here be not too far away to give Hudson any advice if required, while at the same time he would be in the best position to ensure the safety of the less experienced of his Messieurs.
6. Whymper.
7. Old Taugwalder, last man."

(Alpine Journal, Vol. XXXII, 1918.)

[6] On the 7th July, 1865, the Rev. Charles Hudson, R. D. Hadow, T. S. Kennedy and the Rev. J. McCormick, with the guides Michel Croz and Peter Perren, made the ascent of Mont Blanc by the Chamonix side (through the Ancien Passage, between the walls of the Rochers Rouges) in record time (less than $4\frac{1}{2}$ hours from the Grands Mulets to the summit, and in 5 hours, less a halt of 20 minutes, from the summit to Chamonix.) In T. S. Kennedy's brief account of this expedition a reflection may be noticed which appears to be of no importance, but which, when we consider the awkward behaviour of Hadow on the Matterhorn, and his hesitation, above all on the descent, seems as if it might explain with irrefutable certainty, taken in conjunction with his defective footwear, the origin of the Matterhorn disaster. Hadow had then to his credit only a single ascent, the peaceful Buet (an easy mountain of 10,164 feet, north-west of Chamonix)! While descending Mont Blanc, says Kennedy, "The snow was very soft, and Hadow, although of wonderful pluck and strength, had not yet acquired sufficient practice to make him quite secure upon his feet. So I left Perren to bring up the rear and afford Hadow support . . ." (Cf. *Alpine Journal*, Vol. III, 1867.)

[7] This rescue party comprised Edward Whymper, the Rev. J. McCormick, the Rev. J. Robertson, and J. Phillpotts, with the guides Josef-Marie and Alexander Lochmatter, Franz Andermatten, and two Chamonix mountaineers, Frédéric Payot and Jean Tairraz.

[8] The mysterious disappearance of Lord Francis Douglas has given rise to several hypotheses, of which the most reputable is that the body, submerged by the glacier, had remained wedged in a fault in the rock foundation. Personally, I do not believe it. Two arguments seem to me to be fundamentally opposed to this conjecture: (1) When he recovered the bodies on the 16th July, Whymper did not mention any crevasses into which the young Englishman could have disappeared; (2) three articles of Lord Douglas's equipment were found near the victims (who were horribly shattered)—a pair of gloves, a belt and a boot. This fact seems to me incompatible with the crevasse hypothesis. I am, moreover, inclined to believe that the body of the young climber was literally torn to pieces, reduced to nothing by a rock wall which the other three victims only touched lightly or sprang over. Some other mountain accidents give eloquent testimony to this belief.

Lord Francis's sister (their father was Archibald William, Marquis of Queensberry) went several times to Zermatt and ascended to the Matterhorn glacier, passing close to its edge to see if by chance her poor brother's body, thrown up by the glacier flow, had come to light.

[9] The report of this interrogation may be found in the *Alpine Journal*, Vol. XXXIII, or as an appendix to the 6th Edition of Whymper's *Scrambles Among the Alps*, Murray, 1936.

[10] Their epitaphs:
1. "Douglas Robert, eldest son of Patrick Douglas and Emma Hadow, who perished in descending the Matterhorn, July 14, 1865, aged 19 years. 'Even so, Father, for so it seemed good in Thy sight.' St. Matthew xi. 26."
2. "Charles Hudson, Vicar of Skillington, Lincolnshire, killed in descending the Matterhorn, July 14, 1865, aged 36 years. 'Be ye therefore also ready.' St. Luke xii. 40."

[11] (*Trans.*) "To the memory of Michel-Auguste Croz, born at Tour, in the valley of Chamonix. As a mark of regret at the loss of a brave and devoted man, loved by his companions and esteemed by travellers. He perished, not far from here, a brave man and a faithful guide."

[12] As for Edward Whymper, he died a natural death at Chamonix in 1911. He is buried down there at the foot of the great conquests of his youth. On his tombstone these words are inscribed: "Edward Whymper, author-explorer-mountaineer, born in London 27th April, 1840, died in Chamonix 16th September, 1911."

Many works have been published about the Matterhorn and its history, but I restrict myself to naming these: Edward Whymper: *Scrambles Amongst the Alps*, Murray, 6th Edition 1936, and *A Guide to Zermatt*, Murray. Guido Rey: *The Matterhorn*, Blackwell, Oxford, 1947.

LORD FRANCIS DOUGLAS

CHAPTER FIVE

THE DISAPPEARANCE OF
CAPTAIN ARKWRIGHT

*The death of Captain Arkwright, of the guide Michel Simond, and of the
porters François and Joseph Tournier (Mont Blanc, Chamonix side, October
1866)*

CAPTAIN Henry Arkwright, soldier of Her Britannic Majesty, and aide-de-camp to the Lord Lieutenant of Ireland, is at the Grands Mulets refuge on the 12th October, 1866.[1] With him is an enchanting lady, young and very fair. Her presence lights up the sorry hut with a touch of romance.

But this is not by any means an amorous occasion. This lady is neither a weeping wife nor a mistress, determined not to leave till the last moment the man who is about to leave for the high and dangerous places. No; this is simply Miss Arkwright, the captain's younger sister, and for these two young people the mountain is an unexplored spectacle. From the beginning they have loved it for its exalting grandeur. And if the captain himself has resolved to climb Mont Blanc before rejoining his post at the headquarters of the Lord Lieutenant, his sister has wanted at least to complete the first stage to the Grands Mulets.

This excursion is both beautiful and picturesque. We penetrate at once to the wild heart of a confusion of glaciers. The air has the savour of snow. The light which irradiates this mass of ice is so pure that it lights up the sky. Especially in autumn. A light pure and limpid, without vapour, with translucent shadows.

The month is October. It is already terribly late to climb Mont Blanc. The days are so short, and the twilight at morning

35

and night is deathly cold. There must be no loitering by the way; every hesitation can complicate the situation.

This will probably be the last ascent of the year. Sylvain Couttet, the tenant of the Grands Mulets refuge, is about to close down, for the season is finished. Only three parties during the last few days have come up, and Chamonix itself can only count upon rare visitors, of which this English family is one. Mrs. Arkwright and her elder daughter have remained at the hotel; the two youngest have left for the glaciers, escorted by guides and porters. It has been agreed that as soon as night has fallen those at the Grands Mulets will fire a Bengal Light and that Chamonix will respond with a cannon-shot.

In front of the hut Captain Arkwright and his sister are sitting muffled up in blankets. The black night engulfs everything. Around them is something like the livid palor of the polar landscape. The lights of the valley founder in the sooty flood. Suddenly a red flame embraces the Grands Mulets. The neighbouring snows purple. A palpitating phantasmagoria emerges briefly from the shadows and then returns. The firework goes out, and a dull detonation rises from afar off, making its way laboriously through the immensity of the night. It is Chamonix saluting in its turn. Mrs. Arkwright and her daughter should be in the square where the mortar is fired.

The captain takes his pipe from his mouth, and turning towards his young sister smiles.

"Did you hear it?" he asks.

"Yes, of course," she replies. "Isn't it strange to think that Mother and Phoebe are down there?"

*   *   *

Two parties, in a moonless night, follow one another silently over the glacier. The luminous specks of the lanterns waver. In front is the roped party of Captain Arkwright and his three men —the guide Michel Simond, and the porters François and Joseph Tournier. Behind is that of Sylvain Couttet and a friend, Nicolas Winhart, a German chef-de-cuisine at Chamonix. The snow bears well. The pace is fast. Very gently dawn breaks. A frozen white wave overhangs everything, emerging slowly from the darkness. A rosy edging trembles on the arêtes. Day is born.

The two parties have traversed the Grand Plateau. They

rejoin. Seated on the snow they take breakfast and hold council on what route to follow—the Ancien Passage or the Corridor? The Ancien Passage, the Balmat-Saussure route, is over there, opposite, to the right. It stretches out its wide rising cornice, its steps of crevassed snow, between the tumultuous ice escarpments that support the summit of Mont Blanc and the upper ramparts of the Rochers Rouges. The Corridor, parallel to the Ancien Passage but exactly beneath it, is separated from it by a double rock belt. Discovered in 1827, it is longer but less dangerous than the other. The two routes rejoin on the far side of the Rochers Rouges, at the foot of the dome of Mont Blanc. And in order to gain two hours, Sylvain Couttet and Michel Simond decide, after much discussion, to take the Ancien Passage. To shorten the climb by two hours; then to die. A strange calculation. Ah! if they had but known!

The column reforms. The Couttet party goes in front. In a few minutes the men arrive at the estuary where the Grand Plateau dies out and the slopes of the Ancien Passage rise up. A flank advance on snow now very hard. If this continues they will have to cut steps. Directly above them, at about three hundred feet, stands a jagged group of séracs, some leaning, some upright, of glistening enormity, their walls polished like glass, the whole forming a massive architecture, terribly unstable and menacing. Very fine to look at from a long way off, this exhibition of Murano glass. But let us leave in haste this shadowy gulf where imminent danger lurks. Those exposed névés down there, despite the crevasses that yawn in the sun like crocodiles, have a very pleasing look. Yet life there is held by less than a thread.

Couttet cuts several steps. He precedes the other party by a mere five or six yards. He remarks that it is a little higher up that in 1820 an avalanche developed under the feet of the Hamel party. . . . A fearful sound of cracking answers to his words. But it is not the snow that gives beneath him, but an avalanche of ice severed from the heights above. A large segment of a hanging glacier has detached itself in a single piece and descends upon the party. Couttet utters a cry:

"To the right! To the right! Lie down!"

Simultaneously and instinctively he throws himself forward so violently that he upsets his companion, the chef-de-cuisine, and drags him along. Behind them a panting voice is raised:

"No! No! This way."

Already the squall is upon them.

"Lie down!" Couttet cries again.

He throws himself to his knees, anchors himself with his steel-shod stick, lowers his head, which is turned towards the cyclone, one arm protecting his forehead. There is a terrifying prelude; a shower of powder snow envelops them, and then the hurricane follows with the roar of an express: tons of ice, of icicles, jets of snow under pressure, a chaotic mass of matter which, striking a lurking crest of rock, rebounds and forms above the two recumbent men a fearful vault, dark and muffling.

The minutes pass. The bombardment slackens and scatters. A few delayed missiles pass by singly, awkwardly, slipping by with soft sounds. For ten minutes an opaque cloud, a fog of powdered ice and snow, fills the air and hovers over the site of the disaster. Little by little it lightens and clears and, pursued by the wind, drifts off towards the west.

It is then that Sylvain Couttet stirs and raises his head. Six feet above him the chef-de-cuisine, shrinking beside his alpenstock, is safe and sound. The rope between them is intact. Lower down, a little to the left, in the midst of gently inclined slopes, the avalanche spreads itself like an open fan over more than three hundred yards: an accumulation of scattered blocks, a confused pile of snow and ice of indescribable structures, a cataclysmic heap. Over these debris delicately play all the chromatic scales of blue and green. From this pacified chaos a wonderful sensation of silence rises. A yellow butterfly flutters across the diaphanous wilderness.

Couttet unropes. He hurries towards the place where his comrades were. But he encounters a high barier of debris, a cathedral overthrown, resplendent even in its ruins. The two men enter the place of death. They hoist themselves up, slide down, stride about, tumble over, take soundings. But their anxious cries fall flat, vainly.

But a black spot attracts their attention. A knapsack. And then, not far from the knapsack, a body. A corpse, frightfully mutilated, sprinkled with snow but hardly buried. It is François Tournier, the porter, his skull crushed, his face partly torn away, his right leg broken in two places. A fragment of rope still hangs from his body, cut clean a yard on either side.

38

At the end of two hours, able to do no more, Couttet and Winhart abandon their search. There is no more to do, no more to hope. Captain Arkwright and his men are definitely erased from the roll of the living. Into his sombre kingdom Hades welcomes them. The one body is dragged beyond the avalanche and piously stretched upon the inviolate snow. And mournfully, with broken hearts, the two survivors descend to the Grands Mulets.

* * *

Miss Arkwright's guide and porters are seated in the sun in front of the hut. They smoke their pipes, their hats over their eyes, and talk among themselves in patois. They know nothing, doubt nothing, have no presentiments. But what of the noise of the avalanche? But there are ten—even twenty—avalanches a day in this concourse of glaciers where the rock of the Grands Mulets stands out like a semaphore—a semaphore in miniature, although at over ten thousand feet, dominated on all sides by snowy crests five thousand feet higher.

Briefly Couttet acquaints the Chamoniards with the facts. Then, changing his tone: "Why do I find you here?" he asks. "Hasn't his sister gone down yet?"

"No. She's waiting for him."

"Ah! *Mon Dieu!*"

"She had to be told," Couttet relates, "and the others had no wish to be entrusted with the message. For my own part, I did not dare. At last I take courage. I enter the hut. She is seated there, at the far end, the window open, a sketchbook on her knees, painting a water-colour of the Dôme du Goûter. Seeing her there, so peaceful, I am so distraught by what I have to say to her that I remain at the door, all my features distorted, unable to say a word. She turns. 'Well, Sylvain?'

"My throat is very tight. I raise my arms like this.

"She cries: 'My brother!'

" 'Be brave, mademoiselle!'

"Then she became as white as snow, rose, went to the window, knelt there with her hands together and prayed while looking at the mountain. Afterwards she came straight towards me and said:

" 'You can tell me everything now, Sylvain. I am ready.'
And when I had finished, she said: 'We will go and search for
him to-morrow.' "

* * *

The rescue parties from Chamonix searched the avalanche for
ten days. A second victim was exhumed, the porter Joseph Tournier. His body was riveted to the snow by his blood, clothed in
roseate ice, vitrified. It had to be released with hammer blows.
Lower down the body of the guide Michel Simond at last appeared.
Above the rescuers grouped around this icy tomb, the immensity
of the hanging glaciers, hollowed out like a quarry, provided a
constant menace. One hollow, very blue, more blue than the
wall itself, formed an elegantly pointed arch at the foot of the
rampart. This turquoise of so pure a quality was where the
avalanche had broken loose.

On the tenth day it was necessary to abandon the recovery of
the Captain's body. An intense cold reigned at these heights
(about 13,000 feet). The sky became overcast. Squall followed
squall, forerunners of the hurricane. The rescue parties fled
before the tempest that boiled already on the arêtes.

On the 31st October it was possible to resume the task. A
stranger, slight and elegant, had joined the parties. He looked
with a sort of melancholy stupor upon the place where his elder
brother had vanished. It was Lieutenant Arkwright, an officer
of the Guards, who had arrived the day before from England.
A second avalanche had fallen and had entirely covered the
debris, submerging them. The excavations were filled, levelled.
Apart from this nothing had changed in all this gigantic mountain,
save that it was whiter where the new snow had fallen, and that
up there, among the séracs, the turquoise arch was slightly larger.

There was nothing now to do but descend. The abandoned
spoils were about to begin their long glacier journey.

* * *

Thirty-one years later (1897) the body of Captain Arkwright,
one-time soldier of Her Britannic Majesty, and aide-de-camp to
the Lord Lieutenant of Ireland, reappeared. A fissure in the
tongue of the Glacier des Bossons, there where the verdure
already surrounds it, tightly enclosed the dead man. The head,

an arm and a leg were missing, torn away by the crashing together of a crevasse. A fragment of rope still encircled these remains. His sister, a little fair Englishwoman, came from London for the funeral. She was accompanied by her brother, the young lieutenant of 1866. He had become a Colonel.[3]

*   *   *

In the English cemetery at Chamonix no epitaph recalls this drama. But in the English Church one may read on a plaque:

IN MEMORY OF HENRY ARKWRIGHT, BORN DEC. 16, 1837, FOURTH SON OF JOHN ARKWRIGHT OF HAMPTON COURT, HEREFORDSHIRE, CAPT. IN H.M. 34TH REGT. OF FOOT AND AIDE-DE-CAMP TO THE LORD LIEUTENANT OF IRELAND. HE WAS LOST IN AN AVALANCE WHILE ASCENDING MONT-BLANC, OCTOBER 13, 1866.—"HE SHALL GIVE HIS ANGELS CHARGE OVER THEE, THEY SHALL BEAR THEE UP IN THEIR HANDS."

For the scene of the Arkwright tragedy, see Plates 2 and 7.

[1] Cf. *Alpine Journal*, Vol. II, 1865–66.
[2] It was on the 22nd August, 1897. On the left bank of the glacier were found, together with the remains of the body, the following objects: a handkerchief with the captain's name embroidered in full; an alpenstock, the wood having rotted around the metal; a gold pencil, the lead being intact; a gold chain, neat and clean, as if it had just left the jeweller.
[3] The mutilated corpse was buried on the 31st August, 1897, at the English cemetery in Chamonix. The ceremony was imposing: all the population of Chamonix, led by the guides, escorted the bier. The service was conducted by Colonel Arkwright. The grave of the captain is close to that of Prof. R. L. Nettleship, tutor of Balliol College, Oxford, who died on the Dôme du Goûter in 1892.
The editor of a small Chamonix paper had photographed the remains. A short while after the burial this paper published the following notice:
"We have promised our readers a picture of the principal remains discovered at the Glacier des Bossons. When we were about to put the engraving to press we were informed that Colonel Arkwright formally opposed its publication. We could not but defer to this injunction, but we will make use of the strict right we possess to send to our friends, individually, proofs of this engraving which, moreover, shows absolutely nothing unseemly."
Two months later (October) Edward Whymper found the upper part of Captain Arkwright's trousers while walking along the Glacier des Bossons. In one of the pockets there were two handkerchiefs marked with the captain's name, and a woollen scarf; these effects were perfectly preserved, like new, and only the trousers had deteriorated. (Cf. *Alpine Journal*, Vol. XVIII, 1896–97.)
In the *Echo des Alpes*, in 1899, appeared the following:
"On the 25th May, 1899, the guide Désailloud, of Chamonix, was conducting three tourists to the Glacier des Bossons, and when they arrived at about thirty yards above the chalet des Bossons he discovered in a crevasse a human foot enclosed in a sock; the foot appeared to have been detached from the leg at the height of the shoe.

"A little further off the same guide found a rusted axe with a broken handle, a large knife with several blades, a part of a skull, and finally a gold watch very little deteriorated.

"These objects have been identified as having belonged to Captain Arkwright, who died on Mont Blanc in 1866, and whose almost intact remains were recovered in 1897. It is estimated that, from the place where the accident occurred to the place where they were recovered, these articles and bones had covered about twelve kilometres (7½ miles). The remains have been interred at the cemetery in Chamonix; the watch and knife have been sent to the deceased's family."

MICHEL-AUGUSTE CROZ
(see Chap. 4.)

CHAPTER SIX

THE ACCIDENT ON THE
SCHRECKHORN

The death of the Rev. J. M. Elliott (July 1869)

ON the 26th July, 1868, Théophile Gautier met the young
Rev. J. M. Elliott at Zermatt. Gautier was then discovering
the Matterhorn for himself, which Elliott had just climbed,
and to Elliott he dedicated pages which burned with admiration.

Elliott was the first, after Whymper's tragic victory in 1865,
to dare to attack this terrible mountain from the Swiss side,
where the catastrophe had occurred. Leaning upon his hotel
balcony, finding some amusement in watching the parade of
the tourists waiting for the hour of dinner, the poet observed a
stir of curiosity in the crowd. "Cleaving the groups," he says,[1]
"appeared a procession, preceded by a tall young man, robust
but elegant, in jacket and waistcoat and breeches of brown
velour, gaitered to the knees, his felt hat pulled down to his eyebrows, manly and determined in his features, having the air of
a perfect gentleman despite the rusticity of his dress. He was a
member of the Alpine Club who had just happily accomplished
the ascent of the Matterhorn. The light of his campfire had been
seen in the night from the Riffel Inn, like a red spangle on the
flank of the mountain. Behind him walked the guides, with coils
of rope encircling their bodies like bandoliers, with axes for
cutting steps in the ice, with their spiked staffs and all the
apparatus necessary for an assault upon so savage a peak. On
all their brown and resolute faces shone the satisfaction of a

43

difficulty vanquished, and the reflection of their triumpth mingled with the burn of the snow.

"The guides[2] entered the hotel, and the Englishman remained for a moment on the threshold, leaning his shoulder against the door-post, in an indolent attitude and with a perfectly detached air, as if he were just leaving his club in Pall Mall. He was practising, perhaps without thinking of it, that precept of dandyism formulated by Brummel and revived from Horace: *nil admirari*."

Thus, thanks to the Rev. J. M. Elliott, alpinism takes its place in French literature through Théophile Gautier, and is annexed by romanticism. This is the first time since Rabelais that a great French writer speaks in intelligent terms about mountain-climbing. Henceforth Elliott belongs somewhat to literary history. So let us find out something about him.

Looking at him, Gautier first thinks of Brummel and Horace. This is a mere figment of the poetic imagination. Elliott was simply a young Anglican clergyman. Aged twenty-seven years, he was a product of Cambridge. Doubtlessly he had worked hard there and played cricket while studying theology. And now he was the incumbent of a Brighton parish.

Founded in 1857 in London, the famous Alpine Club brought together the élite of English climbers. British alpinism was then at its apogee, and the most formidable peaks fell one after another. The "British flag" floated not only over the ocean waves, but over those of the mountains too, immobile and gigantic. "Rule Britannia, Britannia rules the waves"—"of the Alps" one might almost add.

Julius Marshall Elliott began to love the mountains while very young, and following tradition he first trained in the hills of his own country. Then he came to the Alps. From his first steps he showed himself to be a great climber. And when he climbed the Matterhorn and unknown to himself took his place in French literature, he had accounted for an imposing number of summits. One might almost say that Théophile Gautier met him *in extremis*. And as if, by divination, he had presentiment of the approaching catastrophe, the author of *Mademoiselle de Maupin* turned his thought to the terrible risks of the high mountains.

"Looking at this fine young man, rich without a doubt and

accustomed to all comforts and refinements, who had just risked his life so carelessly in a useless and perilous enterprise, we muse upon the unconquerable passion of some men for dangerous ascents. No example reforms them. This young member of the Alpine Club[3] had certainly seen, in passing, the graves of his three compatriots in the cemetery of Zermatt.[4] But the peak, like the abyss, has its fascination: it calls and it attracts. It is an attraction of the same kind which draws the chamois hunter; he knows that one day his feet will slip, that he will fall into the gulf, into the torrent, into the cleft of a glacier, unless he is swallowed up by an avalanche or crushed by a falling mass of rock. He scales the walls to the very summit, he leaps the deep crevasses, he treads the narrow cornices, he crosses the snowbridges as if he has wings; he has a frenzy for high places, and his daring seems not to know the laws of gravity. These without doubt are keen delights that make the peaceful pleasures of the plain appear insipid; once they have been tasted, he cannot do without them, but must return until he finds there his own destruction."

"He must return until he finds there his own destruction." A sad prophecy! It is as if from the deep past could be heard an echo of the voice of the sybil. But Elliott has climbed Mont Blanc, which has had a monopoly of the great tragedies, and he has safely returned; he has climbed the Matterhorn, which since 1865 has shared the sinister reputation of the bloodstained snows of Chamonix, and from it too he has safely returned. He has returned safely from many other peaks, and still further peaks await this young clergyman from Brighton. But the prescribed hour approaches. Elliott will be the man to extend the horrors of alpine tragedy to the Bernese Alps from Mont Blanc and the Valais.[5]

*   *   *

There is great animation in front of the Hôtel Adler at Grindel-wald on Monday, 26th July, 1869. A party of climbers is making its preparations for departure to high places. Its two principals are the Reverends J. M. Elliott and P. W. Phipps. This evening they will bivouac at the Kastenstein. Blankets and cooking-pots curiously surmount their packs. Elliott travels with two moun-taineers from Zermatt, the celebrated guide Franz Biener and the porter Joseph Lauber. It is in Biener's footsteps that Elliott has been fashioned and, besides the Matterhorn ascent, they have roamed together on the 4,000 metre summits for four summers. Biener is proud of his pupil, whose reputation for courage and daring is well known.

The Rev. P. W. Phipps has but one man, Peter Baumann, a well-known Oberlander, to serve both as guide and porter. But Phipps is without pretentions. Nevertheless, the ensuing dawn is so fine that he changes his plans—the charming snows of Strahlegg—in order to follow Elliott to the Schreckhorn.

The Schreckhorn (13,386 feet) is a notable mountain. Its name ("Terror Peak") like Mont-Maudit ("the Accursed Mountain") evokes the same sombre romanticism. These names sum up the psychology of a vanished people, which, from antiquity until the eighteenth century, grew up in fear of the heights. With time the spirit of man has changed, but the formidable names remain, which no longer mean anything except as vestiges of an out-dated feeling. The Schreckhorn, conquered in 1861, is still a splendid mountain—more or less the Aiguille Verte of the Oberland. Its high solitary pyramid can be seen from Berne to the left of the enormous bas-relief, dark against a pale screen of snow. With a cloud resting on its summit one might describe it as a cyclopean glacier-table.

The parties advance rapidly along the Schreckfirn. Above the ramparts of rock, sprinkled with snow and engraved with couloirs still in shadow, explodes all the beauty of space. Sheets of light, combed by the crenellations of the arêtes, quiver against the gilded blue of the sky. There is a murmurous silence as if the chasms themselves are speaking.

Now the climbers are busy on the face of the Schreckhorn. They rise by the rocky edge of a couloir. The mountain is in an ideal condition, the dry rock not too cold, the snow firm so that the nails can bite, and no ice. And if you add to these the magnificent strength of will that quickens these climbers' spirits, what more could be desired? But the combination of material and moral elements is not enough. There is a further necessary element: technique, a prosaic sounding word in these exalted conditions, yet it asserts its rights. The man who throws himself into the water, without knowing how to swim, sinks; and the man who undertakes a hazardous climb, ignorant of certain elementary conditions, falls—not always, of course, but it is better not to rely on luck.

46

The ramparts rise straight up. Branches of snow, prolifically sprouting like ivy, crawl against the rock and break the climbers' impetus. Baumann passes the rope around his traveller's waist. But Biener hesitates. He holds the coil in his hands, and knowing that Elliott is not one of those who consider the rope indispensable in the high places, he asks, perplexed:

"Mr. Elliott, shall we . . . "

"No, my dear Biener," Elliott replies. "You're not serious! What's the good of it! There's no danger here."

Lauber refixes the rope to his pack and the party moves on, each of them independent of the other, unroped. Elliott is renowned for his speed. The gap between the two parties increases rapidly, and soon, hidden by a steep slope, the men in the lead are out of sight.[6]

When the Baumann–Phipps party reaches the gap in the final arête (the Saddle, 13,047 feet), the Elliott party is already half-way to the summit. They are following a snowy crest and are nearing a breastwork of rock which divides it. Lauber, in front, draws his axe, cuts several steps, lays hold of the rock, hoists himself up, stands in a niche, turns round and, having no rope to make fast, awaits his companions. Baumann raises a shout of joy and Lauber answers him.

What a marvellous day! The glaciers crackle. Very close, the Finsteraarhorn raises its needlelike summit, and its mighty, ice-armoured steps flash like mirrors. Steps for Titans to climb the sky! Along the horizon all the Alps from Mont Blanc to the Bernina raise their rugged alabaster waves. Over towards Berne it is like a flower-bed of indistinct greenery.

This glance around the horizon has lasted a few seconds. Elliott places his feet in the niches cut by Lauber. He reaches the last step, supports himself with his axe, and leaps to the rock. But . . . Good God! . . . he is suddenly on his back and has lost his axe. Lauber leans over, gesticulates, shouts. Biener can be seen to throw himself forward and with one arm to lay hold of the body as it passes. And there we see a tragic group on a steep slope of snow, almost of ice, on the very edge of the abyss.

Clinging to his ice-axe with his right hand, Biener, flattened against the slope, with his left hand holds Elliott back by the middle of one arm. Elliott is on his back and quite unable to right himself; his heels strike desperately at the ice without finding the least point of support. Ten feet above them Lauber can do nothing to help. It is impossible for him to intervene in time to untie the rope and throw it to his comrades; for to do this he would have to take off his knapsack, untie and uncoil the rope and then to throw it—quick to say but much slower to perform, and he is probably not in a position in which he can make these movements.

Biener seems to lean over more and more, spread-eagled between his axe to the right and Elliott's body to the left. Already his balance is terribly precarious. Millimetre by millimetre, imperceptibly, inexorably, his shoulders shift, lean over. At one and the same time he resists and slowly yields. Now his body seems to have reached the extreme limit of stability beyond which there can be but one thing certain—disaster. You cannot play with impunity with the laws of gravity. Then, suddenly, Elliott is seen, still on his back, shooting at high speed down the icy slopes of the northeastern face. The body passes a reef of broken stone like a meteor; then, taking to the snow again, plunges very swiftly into the sheaves of light that expand from the Lauteraar Glacier 1,300 feet below.

Biener has now regained a normal posture. He is motionless and at an acute angle to the slope. Panting, he looks at his large peasant hand, that loyal hand which, for five, ten, fifteen, perhaps twenty seconds has held back a life, young and ardent, but heavy, heavy as a whole world ready to collapse—that tanned and parchment-like hand, that large hand which has been forced to open, now empty and useless.

The two men from Zermatt descend towards the Phipps party. Everything must be done to save Elliott. But what? Together they look silently into the gulf. To attempt to descend the precipice would be sheer madness, but Baumann, at the end of ropes which have been knotted together to make about two hundred feet, attempts it. His reconnaissance is futile. Not far away he sees some traces of the fall, a slight furrow where a little powdery snow trickles down, softly hissing. He shouts and shouts, leaning out as far as he can. "Herr Elliott! Herr Elliott!" he shouts again and again. But his cries are lost in the immensity of the mountain.

* * *

48

The same evening the men reached Grindelwald. Two rescue parties were organised and they left at once, one by the upper Grindelwald Glacier and the Lauteraarsattel, the other by the opposite face of the mountain, by the Lower Glacier. Fifteen hours later the first party had returned with the body. Elliott had fallen in a straight line to the Lauteraar Glacier. A furrow, a vertical track, as straight as an arrow, divided the dazzling snow.[7]

The burial took place at Grindelwald. Over the grave the village pastor opened a prayer-book, read a few lines and made his comments. It was Elliott's own prayer-book. It had been found in one of his pockets. Various phrases in it had been underlined, witnessing to the nobility of the young clergyman's sentiments and to his mystic love of the mountains.[8]

* * *

Théophile Gautier concluded the reflections prompted by his encounter with Elliott at the foot of the Matterhorn with these words: "Although reason may reject it, man's struggle with the mountain is poetic and noble. The multitude, which has an instinct for great things, surrounds these daring men with respect. They signify the will challenging the blind obstacle, and they plant the flag of human intelligence upon the inaccessible."

For the scene of the Elliott tragedy see Plate 6.

[1] Gautier: *Vacances du Lundi*, Paris, 1869.

[2] Two well-known guides accompanied Mr. Elliott: Josef-Marie Lochmatter (who died on the Dent Blanche in 1882—see Chapter 13, Part III), father of the celebrated Franz Lochmatter (who died on the Weisshorn in 1933), and Peter Knubel (father of the no less celebrated Josef Knubel—still living—both of St. Niklaus).

[3] Gautier was mistaken. Elliott was only a candidate for membership of the Alpine Club. He was accepted in the month of November, 1868. (Regarding Théophile Gautier's sojourn in Zermatt, see C.-E. Engels, *Th. Gautier, le Cervin et l'Alpiniste*, Journal de Genève, 1936; and Charles Gos, *Voyageurs Illustres en Suisse*, Berne, 1937.)

[4] Those who died on the Matterhorn on the 14th July, 1865, on the occasion of the first ascent of the mountain. See Chapter 4.

[5] Cf. *Alpine Journal*, Vol. IV, 1868–69.

[6] Apart from the Matterhorn, Elliott had made almost all his ascents with Franz Biener. Elliott was endowed with a violent and dictatorial character, which explains his clear refusal to use the rope and his guide's immediate submission, since he knew his employer's temperament perfectly well. On the Matterhorn (26th July, 1868) Elliott had shown his character well. In the story of this climb which he left behind, he abused his guides to such a degree that Whymper himself took up their defence in eloquent terms. Elliott even brought the abilities of the two men into question. (*Alpine Journal*, Vol. XXVIII, 1914, and Charles Gos, "La Deuxième Ascension du Cervin par le Versant de Zermatt," *Gazette de Lausanne*, 1st October, 1942.)

[7] The name *Elliottplatte* has been given to the place where the unfortunate English climber slipped, and the name *Elliottwand* to the precipice where he perished.

The first ascent by the face down which Elliott fell had been made on 4th August, 1864, by the Swiss climber E. de Fellenberg, with the guides P. Michel, P. Inäbnit and P. Egger.

[8] It was in 1866 that the Elliott–Biener partnership began. Captain Farrar describes Elliott as: "one of the most entertaining and active English mountaineers of his day." The guide Franz Biener, nicknamed "Weisshorn," was one of the best guides of the epoch, and Elliott, "who, as we know, was not quite an easy employer," nevertheless wrote in his guide's *führerbuch*:

"His first-rate qualities as a guide, his activity, willingness, carefulness, endurance, and instinctive power of solving difficulties on ice or rock, together with his simple and perfectly natural character . . . makes his society in a Swiss tour a very considerable addition to one's happiness."

Two or three pages later Elliott writes:

"Franz Weisshorn Biener has been with me this year for nearly four weeks. In that time he has guided me up the Galenstock, over the Strahleck pass, up the Wetterhorn, over the Mönch Joch and Mönch, up the Finsteraarhorn, over the Alphubel Joch and Alphubel, up the Dom and up the Weisshorn. With the exception of the Weisshorn each was his first ascent; yet nothing could have surpassed his quickness of eye and correctness of judgement often proved under trying circumstances in mist and rain and snow. Of his strength and willingness to carry I have spoken in a previous year, but I have never put it to such proof as now. In all but the last two expeditions he was my sole guide and porter, and led the way up the Mönch most perseveringly after gaining the Mönch Joch under the very heavy disadvantages of fresh and deep snow, and not-withstanding the discouragement of Grindelwald guides who assured him that it was "impossible." The ascent to the summit of the Dom but for him would have been impracticable, for the other guide of our party, though counted first-rate, entirely collapsed under the difficulties of the way. But most of all I like to mention his genuine-ness, his extreme simplicity, his perfect straightforwardness and candour, his trustworthi-ness, and his kindliness of heart. His care of me and his consideration for me when very tired shew qualities that would fit him for the charge of ladies, were they not combined with better qualities which make him a first-rate guide and friend." —Julius M. Elliott, P.C. of St. Mary's, Brighton, 1868. (*Alpine Journal*, Vol. XXXI, 1917.)

THE REV. CHARLES HUDSON
(*see Chap. 4.*)

CHAPTER SEVEN

THE FIRST FEMININE TRAGEDY

The death of Mrs. G. B. Marke and of the porter Olivier Gay
(Mont Blanc, Chamonix side, August 1870)

A TRAGEDY of swift and terrifying simplicity. On a glacier of Mont Blanc, at an altitude of 14,000 feet, an unexpected hole opens in the snow beneath the very feet of the climbers. A trap is drawn, two victims are swallowed up and are never seen again. For the first time a woman's name is inscribed on the lugubrious roll of the mountain dead. And Mont Blanc is once again the scene.

Splendid in its dazzling effulgence of light, with its snowy plateaux, its undulations, its white terraces, spacious glistening avenues leading to the infinite, Mont Blanc, which seems from below to be so good-natured, attracts like a lover. The mere sight of it gives birth to desire. How can one be so close to it and yet renounce it, the highest peak in the Alps and yet so easy to reach? Many are the tragedies on Mont Blanc which have had their origin in this psychological complex: that the victims did not know how to renounce it. To leave, moreover, for these high oceans of snow without experience and training is rather like a novice rower taking a frail skiff upon the high seas.

That is how this party finds itself on the way to the Grands Mulets on the 1st August, 1870.[1] Mr. G. B. Marke is familiar with the mountains, though he is not a climber of repute. He has come from Switzerland with his two Valaisian guides, Franz Burgener and Peter Zurbriggen, from the valley of Saas.[2] But what of Mrs. Marke, his young wife, and Miss Wilkinson, their friend? There is a very clear impression that it is during this first stage that the idea of accompanying Mr. Marke to the summit is born in the minds of the young Englishwomen.

The guides assure them, when questioned, that the climb is not difficult, in fact much less difficult than the climbs in the Swiss Alps.

"But isn't there any danger?" they ask.

"None," the guides reply.

"But what about the crevasses?"

"Crevasses! *Parbleu!* You can see them and avoid them. Certainly, it's a long journey. Tiring, too, because of the height. But if the weather is fine it can be climbed quite easily."

Nevertheless, two guides for three tourists, of whom two are completely inexperienced women, are not enough. But that will sort itself out at the Grands Mulets, where there is certain to be company.

Unfortunately, at the Grands Mulets there is nobody but the servant, Olivier Gay, a young Swiss from Trient on the other side of the Col de Balme. Gay has been for three years in the service of Sylvain Couttet, the well-known guide and tenant of the hut. Couttet has just gone down to Chamonix, but Gay himself agrees to accompany the English party the next day. He is familiar with the mountain. It should be possible to return before midday, with a quick gain of one or two louis.

"But where," he asks, "is the rope for me and the ladies?"

The guides have only one and there are none at the hut. Then they see, hanging on the wall, an old rope now only used for carrying wood. But that's of no consequence; on Mont Blanc there is no use for a rope except to drag the exhausted tourists along. As for crevasses, you just go round them. That at least is the generally accepted view, apparently shared by the Marke party.

* * *

Marke and his two Swiss guides are in front, Gay and the two Englishwomen are behind, and the two parties rise slowly on the slopes of the Grand Plateau. The two young women are painfully affected by its monotony and the refracted glare from the snow. They stop repeatedly to recover their breath and to quieten the pounding of their hard-tried hearts. Olivier Gay, courteous and obliging, understands and excuses their shortcomings.

"You will see," he says, "it will be better higher up in the keener air. Here the air is so still and it makes you sleepy."

The Ancien Passage, the grave of Dr. Hamel's guides and of Captain Arkwright's party, is passed to the right in order to take the Corridor, a glacier belt below it, at the foot of the Rochers Rouges. At the far end of it lies the saddle between the Maudit and Mont Blanc, and to reach the summit from that point only the last slopes, the Mur de la Côte and the Calotte, remain to be climbed. The two parties at last reach the foot of the Mur de la Côte, at about 14,000 feet, and there they halt. They sit down on the snow. Knapsacks are opened. Provisions are unpacked. But only the guides eat. The weather is fine, but it is dismally cold. The squally wind can be heard sweeping the hoary slopes of the Calotte. A dust of snow hovers in the air.

But the guides are already on their feet, ready to proceed. Mrs. Marke and Miss Wilkinson, prostrated, do not look like starting. Torpor overwhelms them. Their heads feel as if caught in a vice. The early symptoms of mountain-sickness are worse even than those of sea-sickness; for on the sea the ship takes you away, but on the mountain salvation can only come from within, and if your nerve is broken and your reserves of energy are wasted, the situation can be serious, even very serious. Burgener grumbles:

"Are we going on, or are we not?"

The men decide to proceed, but not the women. Only Mr. Marke and his guides will attempt to reach the summit, while Gay and the women will await their return.

The three men ascend the slope and vanish. For a while the blade of an axe can be heard cutting at the ice to excavate some steps. Fragments fall hissing down. The wind blows violently all the time. It bears down in huge waves, surges back, foams invisibly, whistles, whispers, wheels about. The two women are benumbed. The splendid scenery before their eyes—the opal flanks of Mont Maudit and the tawny rock spear of the Aiguille du Midi, piercing the wondrous blue of the sky—does not interest them at all. They fall into complete indifference, a kind of anaesthesia. When a climber reaches this state it is a bad sign. Gay himself, of course, feels perfectly well and his morale is unaffected. These two poor women fill him with pity. He would like to do something for them, to shelter them from the cold, to

53

bring back a smile to their pretty faces, so touching and childlike in their disarray. He tries to comfort them with words, but they make no difference. His words of encouragement strive vainly against a desperate, silent resignation, forming an hermetically sealed barrier between him and them.

However, Mrs. Marke rises, her frail shoulders trembling. She is pale. She speaks a few short words. She is hardly able to move her jaws. She points to a spot at the foot of a snowy declivity a little lower down, where perhaps they might find shelter from the increasingly icy gusts of wind. This little gesture with her finger traces the inexorable line of her expiring fate. Olivier Gay puts the knapsack over his shoulder, picks up the rope which has not been untied, and, supporting Mrs. Marke with a strong hand, they move off. Miss Wilkinson follows at a distance of some six or eight yards, tied to the same rope.

Then follows the bewildering and terrible tragedy. No *mis en scène*; no roaring avalanche; no hanging glacier to break away; no noise; no commotion. In fact, nothing. In fact, it is almost as if nothing has happened at all—except that a snowbridge has given way beneath the weight of two people and in silence, discreetly, Mrs. Marke and Olivier Gay have disappeared. Only Miss Wilkinson remains on her knees in the snow, and the terrifying silence is abruptly broken by her cries, her hysterical shrieks of terror.

Only ten minutes have passed since the parties separated. The higher party is clambering up the steep icy slopes of the Mur de la Côte when they hear the shrill cries, muted by the wind. The men stop and listen, and anguish grips them. They turn about, carefully treading in their own tracks. They reach the Corridor once more and perceive Miss Wilkinson, still on her knees, her hands to the ground, screaming like one demented on the edge of a hole scarcely a yard across. A scrap of rope still hangs from the young woman's waist.

A concealed crevasse is there. On the way up the hard crust had held, but it had given way on the descent under the combined weight of two persons. Miss Wilkinson had been thrown down and dragged towards the chasm. She, too, was about to disappear when the decayed rope broke, and she remained face to face with this gaping hole.

Mr. Marke's despair can be imagined, and the commotion of

the guides. They carefully approach the menacing brink and lean over the dark pit. They shout, they call, they implore the victims to reply, they beg for a sign. There is silence. A rope is let down, but it does not touch bottom. There is nothing to do but leave the fatal place. But Mr. Marke cannot thus abandon his young and adored wife.

"No! no! How can you? She's there . . . quite close . . . perhaps unconscious on a heap of snow. Any moment she may come to herself and call me, beg us to come to her help. And we shouldn't be there. She'll be able to see the blue sky through the gap. She'll guess we are going away, getting smaller, vanishing in this white infinity. She'll think I'm abandoning her. No, Burgener, we can't. Look, Gay might call us too and shout for help. He lost his axe when he fell. He has nothing but his hands and teeth to cling with to those smooth walls. They'll never get out of this trap without us. No, no! Burgener, I beg you, no! Don't go. We can't leave them—can we, Zurbriggen? Don't leave them. No! no! . . . Oh God!"

*　　*　　*

Climbing hurriedly from Chamonix, twelve men arrived at three o'clock the following morning at the Grands Mulets. After a brief halt they moved on again for the Grand Plateau and the Corridor. Franz Burgener was their leader. Unfortunately, the fine weather was breaking up as they approached the foot of the Corridor. Lost in the thick mists, blinded by the dense snow which began to fall in the head wind, the rescuers strayed for three hours at the risk of vanishing too. Then they had to go back. Two days of tempest kept them at the Grands Mulets. On the third day the thick mists dispersed. Reascending the Corridor, the guides soon located the stick planted by Burgener beside the hole, like the outline of a cross upon a grave.

A wooden beam was laid across the crevasse. A guide was slowly lowered attached to three ropes. At a depth of nearly one hundred feet the walls of the crevasse narrowed to a funnel, there was nothing more than a pipe too narrow to squeeze through. But the victims, falling vertically to the axis of the cleft, had passed this point, forced through by the impetus of their fall and flattened. Traces of blood still marked a scarlet trail on the porous ice.

For six hours four men took turns at the end of a rope to

enlarge the funnel with their axes. Sylvain Couttet, one of the survivors of the Arkwright disaster, stayed down there for four hours alone. A wan light filtered through the airhole far above. Then at last it was possible to go a few feet further, and lower down still could be seen a mass of snow. Beyond that complete darkness reigned. A lantern, lowered on a string, showed that the chasm enlarged. Strange sounds, rumblings, furtive creakings, gave a mysterious life to these terrifying subterranean labyrinths. Couttet probed the snow with a pole; it revealed nothing.

The afternoon drew to a close and the weather clouded over. The evidence had to be faced: neither that day nor the next would the bodies be reached, nor was there any reason to suppose they would ever be reached. The cleft could not be enlarged in less than two days. And then? Only uncertainty.

At five o'clock in the evening a thunderstorm broke loose, one of those high alpine thunderstorms which seem to be born on the spot—by spontaneous generation so to speak—sly, swift and brutal. It is hard to say how they develop. A small cloud explodes and suddenly becomes immense and terrible. There was only time for the parties to be reorganised on their ropes, and the retreat—rather, the flight—began. At the Grand Plateau they ran into heavy falls of snow. The thunder loosed its bombardment in rapid fire, a farandole of roars amidst the continuous blaze of lightning, the murky ceiling afire with hallucinating lights. Snow in the sky, snow on the earth, and white sheeted shadows where the mountaineers—those courageous rescuers so often ignored by the crowd—plunged along. Their axes crackled. They had to get rid of them to escape the murderous discharges. They threw them ahead as far as possible, retrieving them between the flashes, then throwing them away once more—a tragic game of hide-and-seek with the storm. This time the storm lost the game, for soon the floorboards of the refuge resounded under their feet. They emerged from the hurricane as white as ghosts.

*   *   *

The bodies of Mrs. Marke and the porter, Olivier Gay, have never been recovered. Thrust by the glacier current into a hollow in the rock foundation, they rest there perhaps for eternity—and eternally young.

For the scene of the Marke tragedy, see Plates 2 and 7.

[1] Cf. *Alpine Journal*, Vol. V, 1870–72.

[2] The old visitors' book at the Monte Rosa Hotel in Zermatt contains the following entry:

"I ascended the Matterhorn on September 3 with Nicolas Knubel and Pierre Zurbriggen (Saas) as guides. Left Zermatt on September 2 at 9 a.m. and reached the chalet at 4.50 p.m. Started next morning at 4.30 a.m. and after an exceedingly difficult and dangerous climb reached the summit at 7.15 a.m. Rested at the summit for five minutes and then descended with great difficulty to the chalet, which we reached at 12.45 p.m. We rested there an hour and reached Zermatt at 5.50; then ascended immediately to the Riffel, which I reached at 1.35. The expedition is an exceedingly difficult one, requiring at least two guides for each traveller. The weather was magnificent."— (Signed) G. B. Marke. (*Alpine Journal*, Vol. XXXI, 1917.)

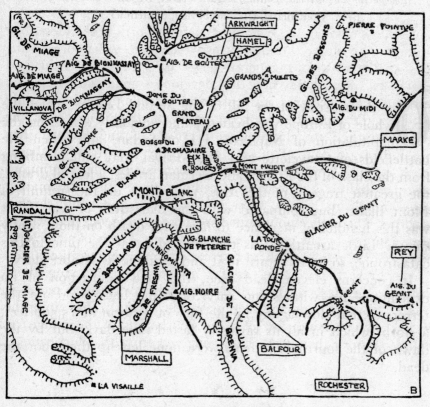

THE MONT BLANC MASSIF

CHAPTER EIGHT

THE TRAGIC BIVOUAC

The death of Dr. J. G. Bean, the Rev. G. McCorkindale, Mr. J. Randall; of the
guides Jean Balmat, Edouard Simond, and Joseph Breton; and of the porters
Alphonse Balmat, Fernand Tairraz, Auguste Couttet, Auguste Cachat and Johann
Graf (Mont Blanc, Chamonix side, September 1870)

O N the morrow of the fall of the Second Empire, when the whole of Europe was heatedly and anxiously discussing the capitulation of Napoleon III at Sedan, and when the battlefields of Gravelotte and Saint-Privat were still trembling from the clash of the French and German armies, a fearful drama, the greatest tragedy of the Alps, took place on the summit of Mont Blanc. But compared with the maelstrom of war, what was this handful of men face to face with death on those windy snows? Little attention was therefore given at the time to this catastrophe, so let us return to it and examine its sombre story.

It concerns eleven dead men, the total destruction of an expedition. No witness, no survivor came back to relate the terrors of that slow agony in the fury of a storm at 15,500 feet, a storm which in all its savagery lasted nine days. But by the dawn of the fourth day there were none left up there but the dead.

* * *

26th August, 1870: the smoking-room of an hotel at Chamonix. After dinner, two English climbers, J. M. Marshall and J. Stogdon, a member of the Alpine Club, were drinking coffee and smoking their pipes. That same day they had ascended

Mont Blanc with two Swiss guides, Moritz Andermatten of Visp and the elder Peter Taugwalder of Zermatt, one of Whymper's guides on the first ascent of the Matterhorn, a witness and survivor of the tragedy. It was between him and Lord Francis Douglas that the rope had broken.

The two alpinists were deeply burned by the glaciers. Surprised by a cyclone at the summit of Mont Blanc, lost in the thick mists and the snow, they had only just escaped death. So now they were happily savouring their peaceful comforts, while between puffs at their pipes they recalled their impressions.

The hotel porter entered. He handed Stogden a visiting card, on which was written intriguingly: "*John Randall, Quincy, Mass., U.S.A., asks permission to introduce himself and to talk with the gentlemen about Mont Blanc.*"

But Marshall preferred not to sit up. He had had enough, and when Mr. Randall entered he excused himself and retired. Stogdon invited the stranger to sit down, and the two men chatted together. The American, a man in his fifties, asked to be excused for his rather inconsiderate approach, but as soon as he had known that the two climbers had just descended from Mont Blanc, he had but one wish—to ask them about their climb and to hear their impressions.

"But why," Stogdon asked, amused, "should Mont Blanc interest you so much?"

Then, with a candour that was almost confidential, Randall revealed the feelings that he had repressed for many years, which only an alpinist could understand. Unquestionably he adored the mountains. This was the first time he had seen the Alps, but he knew their magnificent history thoroughly: all the peaks, all the glaciers, all the passes, all the famous climbers, the dates of the great first ascents—he knew them all, had read all about them in Saussure, Forbes, Wills, the *Alpine Journal*, and in the tales of Stephen, Tyndall and Whymper. They had filled him with enthusiasm. "To see, not necessarily to climb, Mont Blanc had been the dream of his life."[1] At the first opportunity he had crossed the ocean and arrived at Chamonix. Mont Blanc was hardly glimpsed before he was fascinated. It surpassed in splendour all that he had imagined.

Touched by such confidence and simplicity, and perhaps a little flattered too by the admiration of which he was the object,

Stogdon responded by recalling the meetings of the Alpine Club, where was to be found the élite of British alpinism. He ended by relating his own alpine adventures, especially that of the day just ended, with the storm sweeping the summit of Mont Blanc and they, Stogdon and Marshall and their guides, lost in that infuriated immensity, owing their salvation to the unexpected luck of discovering their own tracks in the ice of the Grande Bosse.

To this Randall listened, transported with joy. Such a revelation of high mountain adventure acted on him violently. An irresistible force stirred his spirit and carried him away. Like the man who, having encountered Love in its ultimate form and, free henceforth, is dead to all other desires because he is one with his destiny and is lost in it, so Mr. Randall is going to know those divine joys he had never dared to hope for, and to die cruelly in the realisation of his dream.

"The consequence," Stogdon philosophically concludes, "was that I didn't get to bed till two."

Shortly after this curious interview, Stogdon left Chamonix to return to his own country. He was to hear no more from his enthusiastic friend of an evening, except to learn from the newspapers of the catastrophe in which he perished. As for Randall, more and more enamoured of Mont Blanc, and hypnotised by its glaciers, he was living as one possessed. To climb the mountain became an obsession. Uncertain weather did not lessen his desire. But the east wind blew without respite—"the wind of the Aiguille Dru,"[2] as it is called in Chamonix. On the silver arêtes, engraved upon a white sky, the winds strove with one another in stirring up the plumes of snow. In such conditions it was untimely to prepare for the heights, but, so that he might not be taken unawares by a sudden return of good weather and lose precious hours, Randall organised his expedition. He won over to his project two acquaintances from the hotel, one of them a compatriot, Dr. J. G. Bean, of Baltimore (Maryland), and the Rev. George McCorkindale, of Gourock, who were no better trained for mountaineering than he was himself. At the guides' bureau Fate chose the following mountaineers to go with them: as guides, Jean Balmat,[3] Edouard Simond and Joseph Breton, and as porters, Alphonse Balmat, Auguste Couttet, Auguste Cachat and Fernand Tairraz.

On the 4th September the wind dropped. In the ashen twilight Mont Blanc glowed with coral light. Then the first constellations came out. To-morrow it would be possible to start.

*　　　*　　　*

5*th. September* The long caravan left Chamonix in the morning and added yet another to its number in passing the Pierre Pointue, the young Johann Graf, of Kandersteg, in the Bernese Oberland, a servant at the chalet. But the weather, though radiant in the morning, was already changing, and Randall, having examined the sky, which was clouding over, and having consulted his guides, entered the inn with melancholy and wrote these words in the visitors' book: "Bad weather. My pet scheme is gone up, and I go down." A touching confidence whose moderation reveals the depth of the passion which tormented his spirit. One might speak of it as a triumphant love, taking delight in scarcely concealing its wonderful secret, as if all humanity was interested in its "pet scheme" and shared the ardour of a heart which closed up on itself with jealousy.

Mr. Randall was thus about to abandon his climb when the sun reappeared and flooded the terrace. The massed clouds lightened and fled in confusion. The snows of Mont Blanc re-assumed their place, inlaid upon a sky of lake blue: it was certainly an invitation to proceed. After all, why should they not go at least as far as the Grands Mulets? On that they were unanimous: they would sleep that night at the refuge, and they would discuss later what to do after that. So the "pet scheme" was reborn, more exciting than ever. An hour later, trembling with happiness, Mr. Randall, on whom the rope had just been tied for the first time, trod with emotion the snows of Mont Blanc.

6*th September*. In the candlelit resting-place the guides breakfasted, prepared the haversacks and ropes. Randall himself was the first to be ready. He rose, anxious to depart. From the top of the steps he anxiously examined the immense pale solitudes before him. Then the whole caravan, probably divided between four ropes, slowly began its march in the uncertain dawn. The snows still mingled with the stars. This was the poetic preamble of a terrible tragedy of which, from Chamonix, they were able through a telescope to catch certain scenes, abruptly cut short and dislocated from one another by the furious flight of the clouds.

61

The weather broke up very quickly. The long column was crossing the Grand Plateau when suddenly a rounded cloud, coming from nowhere, exactly capped the summit of Mont Blanc.

"A bad sign," said Chamonix at the telescope. "The wind is rising. They will have to stop and come down again."

But the column continues on its way. At the Corridor sunlight still plays intermittently on the snow. Dishevelled clouds cross the bluish abyss of a sky already veiled by thin vaporous layers. A peevish wind blows in gusts. Dark clouds, forerunners of the tempest, pour from behind the peaks.

"Are they coming down?" ask those around the telescope.

"I can't tell yet. . . . They are at the end of the Corridor. . . . they have stopped . . . they seem to be consulting."

A voice, that of an old guide, mutters: "It would be better if they were to pack up, and quickly too."

Other voices break in, questioning: "What are they doing? . . . Can you still see them? . . . Are they coming down?"

The man at the telescope does not answer. He is standing beside the levelled tube like a gunner beside his battery. He watches those up on the mountain, and the faces of all the others are turned there too, where, foundering in an accumulation of cloud, Mont Blanc is about to be engulfed.

But beyond that screen of cloud which slides between the valley and the high glacier regions are wide spaces swept by gusts of wind which keep the menacing storms at bay. Under a ceiling hollowed out of the clouds the parties continue to advance along a kind of brightened glade, soon, however, to be abruptly ravaged. After cutting a flight of steps in the ice of the Mur de la Côte, they then find themselves at the foot of the last slopes of the Calotte, the frozen cupola at the top of which Mont Blanc comes to an end.

They stop to recover their breath, and the guides put their heads together again.

"Shall we go on, or shall we stop here? This storm may, after all, pass and break elsewhere. Haven't we seen that sort of thing happen many times before? Why, it happened only the other day. *Tiens!* It was like that with the two Englishmen, Mr. Stogdon and Mr. Marshall, and I had a talk about it with Taugwalder. It was just like it is to-day, and the same evening they slept at Chamonix."

This reminiscence strengthens their shaken confidence. Randall, shivering in his woollens, catches the sense of the argument and approves with a secret smile. But when the four parties approach the summit, like a minute procession clinging to a frozen roof, bending to a wind that now blows without respite and with crushing violence, the disordered sky is suddenly joined to the mountain with the finality of a closing lid. The horizon is brought at once to the closest dimensions—to the snow at their feet, to the phantom-like silhouette in front, to the swinging rope, to the perpetual slope, the perpetual snow, the perpetual grey monotony of earth and sky. The wind rushes upon them with the force of a battering-ram, blowing from all sides at once, as if the unfathomable depths encircling the summit exhale impassioned breaths which struggle violently with one another and interlock in a dark hurricane.

The climbers know they have reached the summit only because there is no more to climb. It is two-thirty in the afternoon. They cannot wait a second. There is time only to arrive and to turn back, quickly and in silence, before their tracks are effaced. The tracks?—that chain of little marks which, like Ariadne's clue, stretches out upon the snow, runs down the Calotte, makes a turn at the foot of the Mur de la Côte, passes down the Corridor, twists in and out of the crevasses of the Grand Plateau, descends with the exactness of a telephone wire to the Grands Mulets, traverses the Junction and in all safety reaches the moraine at last near the Pierre à l'Echelle, there joining the footpath to Chamonix. And so, theoretically, Chamonix—the village, the chalet, the family, all the good life down there—is at the end of this imaginary line. To follow it is salvation: to lift it up from the earth, to seize it in both hands, to cling to it as to a handrail and run down in giant strides, to flee from this inexorable wind and cold.

In one minute the cruel situation becomes tragic. With bent backs, enveloped in a cloud of snow blown up from the surface of the mountain, fine as the desert sand, the men lower themselves slowly. One party is blown to its knees by a squall; they rise again with the ponderous movements of deep-sea divers. For a moment they are forced to cling to the earth with feet and hands and axes, or be swept away like straws and cast over the edge. The frost-swollen ropes, now as thick as cables, trail on the ground under their feet.

Suddenly there is a halt at the head of the column. The second party collides with the three men of the first. The third and fourth parties almost stumble into the rest.

"What's the matter now? . . . Move on. Move on, for the love of God! . . . Get a move on. We can't take root here . . . die like dogs."

But the wind seals their mouths and closes their ears. The cold cements their jaws and the words are never spoken. It is almost impossible to speak at all. The guides huddle together. The syllables form between half-clenched teeth.

"Now, what's the matter?" they ask.

The leader does not answer; he simply points to the snow, white, immaculate, unmarked. The tracks have vanished.

At this moment a rent appears in the cloud. In an instant the short horizon leaps to miles. There, beyond the white crests and the sullied glaciers, can be seen the green of the valley and the village of Chamonix. It is as beautiful as a mirage, this distant vision of peaceful humanity, like the vision of a distant shore to shipwrecked sailors in a wild sea.

* * *

Meanwhile, the telescope at Chamonix is always levelled. The villagers have rightly thought that the column has abandoned its rash project because of the mist. During the brief clearing the glaciers are hastily scanned, but nothing is seen. "Undoubtedly," they say, "they are waiting at the Grands Mulets for the storm to end." Hope recovers. Mechanically the telescope rises again towards the summit, dips, becomes stationary, searches. Then the observer cries: "I can see them!"

"You can see them? . . . What? . . . Where?"

"High up, near the summit!"

"Where did you say? . . . Near the summit? . . . *Mon Dieu!*"

Everyone wants to look, and an agonising silence weighs heavily around the telescope. It is three o'clock. The eleven men, grouped in the middle of the Calotte at the point known as the Petits Mulets, seem to be looking for a way down. Waves of snow, sprays of frost torn from the glaciers, sweep over them. Then, their way located, the group breaks up. Hesitating, one party moves off. A second follows it, then the two last at close intervals. From the man at the telescope comes a stifled exclamation. With one eye to the glass he describes what he sees:

"They move forward—they stop—they start again—they stop once more—they throw themselves down on the snow—they are on all fours—they are not moving any more—oh! what a wind! —they are still on their knees—they are putting their heads together again—my God! the wind will carry them all off." He is silent for a while; then he says: "The mists are rising. I can't see any more."

Several minutes pass silently, heavy with the confusion of their spirits. The watcher stays at his post, his eye always to the lens, searching the cloud. Then suddenly he begins to speak again.

"I can see them again—they are descending—one, two, three, six, nine, eleven—they are all there, on their feet—ah! what fine fellows they are—stick to it!—*nom de Dieu!*"

The clouds close up. They wait. But the clouds remain clinging to the mountain, wheeling about. They wait for a long time. They wait until the evening. They wait until even the most powerful telescope would be useless against the encroaching darkness. Then the crowd that had come for news disperses slowly, abandoning the sightless telescope, alone in the centre of the deserted square. Someone weeps. It is the wife of Jean Balmat.

The following morning they gather once more. But the storm continues on the heights. They wait until evening. They wait until the next morning. Then till the morning after that. But the storm is endless. The days pass. They wait for eight days, and for eight days Mont Blanc is invisible.

*   *   *

As the clouds close up again between the valley and the parties blockaded at the Petits Mulets, the men move off again with courage, cheered by the sight of the valley, as if that lovely vision itself has the power to save them. In a glance they have been able to discover their position, to fix their landmarks. Below them the slopes of the Calotte run down towards the Mur de la Côte; and the Corridor, where the storm will be less furious, is hidden by the Rochers Rouges. Lower down, the Grand Plateau and the Petit Plateau spread their easy snows to that haven of refuge, the black reef of the Grands Mulets.

In short, only the Mur de la Côte must not be missed. In a

65

direct line it is from six to seven hundred yards distant from the Petits Mulets, and about six hundred feet lower down; so the descent does not require much effort. At the Mur de la Côte they will find their own steps in the ice, and at the foot of the Mur, to the left, the Corridor begins. After that it will be impossible to make a mistake, thanks to the wall of the Rochers Rouges. Once at the Grand Plateau the trick is played, and they will be able to reach the Grands Mulets with their hands in their pockets.

The men stir themselves. They have hardly reformed their line than a squall, more violent than the rest, fells them like toy soldiers. They rise and move off again. But not for long. A dense cloud, a column of darkness, rises from the depths and, swift as a wild tide, climbs and climbs, reaches the level of the climbers, sweeps over them and, still rising, covers the summit of the mountain, suddenly submerging all. (It was at this moment that the final curtain falls between Chamonix and the climbers.) And so, in this desert of ice, at almost 15,500 feet, the tragedy begins. We will try to reconstruct it.

With the coming of this complete obscurity, snow begins to fall: a dense, compact snow carried on a disordered wind. Blinded and suffocated, as if sunk in fantastic regions where the unchained elements join in furious combat, the men immediately lose their way. The landmarks vanish. There is no longer anything on which to fix their eyes. The first party gropingly advances, then stops. It starts again, obliquely, to the right. The second party overtakes it. They become stationary again. The guides shout into each other's ears. In their gestures they contradict themselves. One points to the right, the other to the left. The third and fourth parties, hove-to, a little to the rear, take no part in the debate, as if indifference already consumes their strength. They will follow the others.

The wind meanwhile redoubles its blows and seems to lift the mountain up, letting it fall back heavily. The snow descends in masses, as if a cloudy scaffolding has given away. The sky no longer exists. There is nothing in this fearful emptiness but the panting dialogue of the elements and these men who are about to die.

Now they are grouped together again, silent white ghosts born of the tempest and its prisoners. And as it is impossible to advance, and even more impossible to retreat, they will have to stay where they are, to bivouac and to wait. To wait for what? Death! Death?—surely, you say, eleven men full of strength and courage can wait for something better than death—wait at any rate for the storm to end, and to-morrow to cross again the bridge over the Arve? Why not?

Guides and porters have dumped their haversacks. Their frozen ropes are as hard as iron and difficult to untie. Because of their ignorance of the language, the travellers have little to do with the shelter which the guides improvise. With axes and feet and hands the mountaineers dig into the snow. A kind of burrow soon appears, whose entrance, facing away from the wind, forms a vaguely protecting penthouse. After two or three hours of intense work, the men crawl into the burrow one after the other, the travellers at the back, the Chamoniards to the front. And there they all are, piled one on top of the other, crammed in haphazardly, their necks hard against the ceiling, their legs twisted up, their arms closely pressed to their sides.

Evening falls. Nothing changes in the sinister twilight; the wind continues to blow in heavy gusts, by fits and starts, and its uproar is like the noise of a torrent. It snows and snows. The dense mists glide past tirelessly. In their hole, barricaded against the cold, the eleven men slowly thaw. Their ice-encrusted faces, their frosted lashes and beards and hair, begin to melt. Little by little the phantoms take on a human appearance. Conversation breaks out. It is brief. A knapsack is opened and a bottle of wine extracted; it is nothing but a block of red ice, which nobody has any wish to eat. Nobody, in fact, is either hungry or thirsty. Pipes are lit. The flames of the matches curiously illuminate these masks of fatigue lined up under the roof of snow, with the brims of their hats pulled down over their ears by kerchiefs knotted under their chins. In this tragic company, where una-vowed distress already finds its way into the depths of the sub-conscious mind, in this storm-battered bivouac where eleven men strive against an adverse fate, snores are heard. One by one these unfortunate beings fall asleep.

* * *

An hour had hardly passed when they were already awake, believing that day was about to break. It was not yet eight in the evening. Their bruised flesh pained them. Their stiffened limbs adhered to the icy floor. It was impossible to move them. In reaction, their defenceless bodies no longer resisted the invading cold.[4] A sick man complained, his groans alternating with the snores of an obstinate sleeper. Sighs arose with a rising modulation. Their teeth chattered with the cold.

Outside the tempest was ceaseless. In the vehement darkness a tumult of wind stirred up the snow. The maddened heavens ran with the uproar of a wild sea against the thin parapet which isolated the men from the world. One gust made a sudden break in the shelter. It blew upon the pale faces, lashed them with sleet, covering those in front with snow, and even to the back of the burrow sprinkled the benumbed heap with flakes. None moved. Their spirits, like their bodies, slid into a state of mournful prostration in the inexorable night.

*   *   *

The great hope among the guides was to see the hurricane yield with the new dawn to a fine day. It was a vain hope. When dawn paled (*Wednesday, 7th September*) the snow was still falling. It began slowly to pile up under the penthouse like an inundation. The night wind passed with the same cruel passion into the wind of the day. Its immense waves followed one another without respite. In the darkness its blows had shaken the summit of the mountain, and in the dawn equally heavy blows replied. In the intervals long cries could be heard like the notes of a strange organ, heralding renewed squalls. A crueller coldness froze the first uncertain hours. In their crumpled clothes, stiffened by the frost, the men submitted sadly to a new torment. The guides consulted among themselves. It was impossible to dream of starting out. Everywhere the blizzard swept with unrelenting fury.

"Later, we will see. Perhaps in the afternoon . . . then there will just be time to reach the Grand Mulets before dark. But there will be fresh snow to deal with."

They explain all this to the tourists, who dumbly accept it without understanding very much. Silence reigns in the shelter, but for the groans of the sick man. Their teeth continue to chatter almost as if replying to one another. One of the young porters, unnerved, has not the strength to conceal his fears. "*Mon Dieu! Mon Dieu!*" he repeats, like a litany.

But no one hears him. Each is isolated from the others in his own thoughts, each escapes towards his secret horizons, each sees a picture of what is most dear to him. In this unmoving human mass, eleven souls drift imperceptibly to obscure depths. Randall thinks of Quincy: "How far away it is, on the other side of the ocean!" The Scottish clergyman can see again his peaceful Gourock presbytery: "This wind, these clouds," he thinks, ". . . all the heroes of Ossian have never seen anything like this!" The visions of the Chamoniards are not far off, five or six miles at the most. And for all of them, without visible sign, begins a *tête-à-tête* with death.

Dr. Bean, coming straight back from Baltimore, where he has seen his charming home again, is abruptly plunged into this cruel reality. He is courageous enough to move his arms, by which he had been hoarding the slender remnants of the warmth of his body, and from a pocket he takes a notebook and he writes:

"Tuesday, 6th September.—I have made the ascent of Mont Blanc with ten persons—eight guides, Mr. McCorkindale and Mr. Randall. We arrived on the summit at half-past two o'clock. Immediately after leaving it, I was enveloped in clouds of snow. We passed the night in a grotto excavated out of the snow, affording very uncomfortable shelter, and I was ill all night."[5]

He puts the notebook back in his pocket, tries vainly to button the jacket again, but has to give it up because of the insuperable difficulties. He squeezes his elbows to his sides again. Then, shivering, he waits. He waits, like the others, the martyrdom of the day now beginning.

*   *   *

On the other side of the clouds at Pierre Pointue, Sylvain Couttet,[6] tenant of the chalet, persuaded that the climbers have reached the Grands Mulets (*Tuesday, 6th September, evening*) and are passing the night there, is sleeping peacefully. The eleven men will come down to him, without a doubt, first thing in the morning. On Wednesday, the 7th, towards eight-thirty, when up there at the heart of the hurricane Dr. Bean has just recorded the pathetic note we have quoted, Sylvain Couttet, surprised that no one has arrived, takes his telescope and climbs a neighbouring slope to examine the Grands Mulets route.

The weather is grey, sullen, but sufficiently broken in the valley and its environs to see quite a long way. On the Aiguilles and on Mont Blanc, on the contrary, the clouds come down as far as the Grands Mulets. All the glaciers are covered with fresh snow, but there are no tracks visible to indicate the arrival or departure of the climbers.

Couttet regains his chalet anxiously and in haste. He has laid his plans quickly. His telescope may have misled him. He equips himself and leaves at once for the Grands Mulets with a servant. At the same time he dispatches a workman to Chamonix with a note addressed to the mayor and the chief guide. This message explains his fears of an accident and his departure for the Grands Mulets: "If I find no one, I will place a sign on the snow to the right of the chalet. In that case, organise a rescue party for immediate departure."[7]

In two hours of fast walking Sylvain reaches the refuge: it is deserted. He lays out the sign on the snow and runs down into Chamonix. There he meets the rescue party of fourteen guides which is just starting out, and joins them in their climb up again. During this time the clouds have been drifting down. On the road to the Pierre Pointue the wind and the rain rage furiously. The heavy mist reaches to the moraines; at Pierre à l'Echelle it is snowing. A premature twilight falls. It is impossible to go on. The fourteen guides return to Pierre Pointue and there take up their quarters.

* * *

At the top of the mountain the day, which had never begun, was ending. The opaque and swirling gloom, the snow, the cold, the tumult of the wind and its long howls, still found the eleven men crouching in their shelter. They were plunged in the same immobility as the day before. Closely packed one on top of the other, and sunk in silence and resignation, they trembled with the cold. Their faces were lined with distress. They had no distraction but to listen to the same eternal uproar outside, to the groans of the sick man, and to the castanet-like chattering of their own teeth. They were waiting, always waiting.

And when the white obscurity was about to turn black, Dr. Bean, at the far end of the burrow, once more made the movements which permitted him to reach his notebook. As he had not been able to button up his jacket in the morning, he succeeded without much effort. His fingers were numb; he turned over the pages awkwardly, and wrote painfully, conscientiously, the thoughts that had come to him during the day:

"7th September—evening. We have been on Mont Blanc for two days in a terrible snowstorm; we have lost our way and are in a hole scooped out of the snow at a height of 15,000 feet. I have no more hope of descending. Perhaps this book may be found and in that case it will be sent to you. We have no food; my feet are already frozen and I am exhausted . . . (here the writing becomes awkward and shaky) *. . . I have hardly the strength to write a few words. I die in faith in Jesus Christ, with affectionate thoughts of my family; my remembrances to all. I trust we may meet in Heaven. My effects are in part at the Hôtel Mont Blanc and partly with me in two portmanteaux. Send them to the Hôtel Schweizerhof at Geneva, pay my bills at the hotel, and heaven will reward your kindness.—Jos. G. Bean."*

As he intended to complete his pathetic monologue *in extremis*, and as he knew his powers were failing, Dr. Bean did not put his book away; he felt that he would never be able to make those movements again. His hand gripped the morocco binding. And for the second time night descended in the roar of the hurricane and the long wait.

*   *   *

On the following day, *Thursday the 8th*, Mont Blanc still lies under a mass of clouds. They are perpetually agitated; they sink, roll about, break up, reform ceaselessly. The sky is very low over the valley.

On high, at the tragic bivouac, where the force of the hurricane has not abated, dawn spreads its sad light; cloud follows cloud, squall follows squall, and columns of snow follow one another endlessly—an unbroken chain of days and nights, majestic in the obstinacy of its monotonous cataclysm. The frost continues to weave its impalpable texture. Having slowly coated each body and numbed its tissues, it now works deeply, slowing the flow of the blood and congealing the veins, progressively anaesthetizing the nervous centres. They have hardly noticed the fact that their limbs are frozen. The sick man is quiet at last, but no one pays attention to the fact. And when we look at these castaways in the wan light of the morning, these unhappy faces with their sprouting beards, these ever tightly huddled bodies, welded together by the frost, is it quite certain they are all alive?

Look, for instance, at Auguste Cachat, the porter, with fixed eyes and rigid eyelids; or at Fernand Tairraz and his pinched nostrils. They are congealed between two still living comrades. Perhaps they are only asleep. But this suspicious slumber may well be that of eternity which at last opens its peaceful doors. One of the guides pulls himself together. His dark presentiments release a surge of energy, of revolt. This may be Jean Balmat. The instinct of struggle with the mountains, that domination of the elements and that self-mastery of which his grandfather, Jacques Balmat, one of the conquerors of Mont Blanc, was so admirable an expression, suddenly revives. He has had enough of this abominable waiting in a hole where they are doomed to perish one after the other.

"We had better try a sortie. In a straight line the Mur de la Côte is just down below. In a quarter of an hour we could be there."

Jean Balmat has had his say. Edouard Simond and Joseph Breton, the guides, have listened to him gravely. They argue. They reckon their chances. Alphonse Balmat, the porter, agrees. Maybe their comrades from Chamonix have climbed up to see what is happening, and they might meet them at the Corridor. Johann Graf, the youngster from the Oberland, the servant at Pierre Pointue, knows his master well and says with conviction, "Sylvain will certainly be with them."

The plan of escape is explained to the travellers. Randall approves and thinks: "Good gracious! What a story to tell at Quincy! Never in any book has such a story been told before!" So Randall is one of the party. But not Dr. Bean, nor the Scottish clergyman; they are very weary, prostrated, and prefer to stay where they are and wait. As for the others they say nothing; better not to ask.

A guide moves towards the opening. His stiffened limbs refuse to function; they have to be forced. A stooping silhouette, unable to straighten itself, blocks the entrance. But the hurricane charges the obstacle with tenfold rage and blows it down. The man re-enters the burrow backwards, partly asphyxiated, whitened, as if a white cloak has fallen over his shoulders from the heavens. All are silent.

Perhaps it would be best not to leave just yet. The Chamoniards argue the matter afresh, their courage shaken. Randall, watchful without understanding, holds himself ready to go. As for Dr. Bean, who knows that his last hour is approaching, he makes one desperate effort to open his notebook and hold his pencil. He succeeds by degrees, with the obstinacy of a drunken man. And laboriously, like a small boy, he writes in very large, almost illegible letters: "*Morning—intense cold. Much snow which falls uninterruptedly. Guides restless.*"

That is all. His thoughts become confused and his hand stiffens. He relapses into apathy, that torpor which, once the painful phase is past, becomes a peaceful deliverance.

* * *

At Pierre Pointue rain mingles with the snow. It is impossible to make a start, and the fourteen guides sadly descend again to Chamonix. The tempest lasts for another six days, which brings to nine the number of days during which Mont Blanc and its eleven victims have been isolated from the world.

On Thursday, the 15th September, in the morning, eleven days after the departure of Randall's caravan from Chamonix, the sky is blue and the sun shines gaily. In the brilliant light Mont Blanc spreads its snowy folds above the greenish depths. It reappears after ten days of snowstorm, adorned with divine whiteness and as fascinating as on that day when the unhappy Randall had been seduced by its loveliness.

Sylvain Couttet and M. Mouchet, justice of the peace, decide to go up to la Flégère in order to examine the mountain for what can be discovered—no longer tracks, but bodies, since all hope has been abandoned a long time since. At Praz des Violaz they focus their glasses, and they can see five black spots in the middle of the Calotte, to the left of the Petits Mulets, spread over the snow. Broken stones? Impossible at that point; they have never been seen there before. A little perplexed, and to assure himself that he has not been deceived, Sylvain Couttet returns to Chamonix, where he arms himself with a telescope and climbs the slope of the Brévent with a few guides. Near Plan-Praz a new scrutiny is made. The guides take turns at the eyepiece; their opinion is unanimous. Those five black spots are bodies.

73

The same evening the indefatigable Couttet organised a new rescue party of twenty-three guides. And so, on the 16th, by way of the Pierre Pointue, the small company reached the Grands Mulets, where they slept. On the 17th, following exactly the route of the vanished party, the rescuers arrived, by way of the Grand Plateau and the Corridor, at the Mur de la Côte and ascended it. A little higher they came upon the first body, that of the Rev. McCorkindale. A little above it lay the bodies of the porters Auguste Couttet and Fernand Tairraz, and separated from these by about a hundred yards of the slope, fifty of them of ice, Dr. Bean and a third porter, Auguste Cachat. The American was stretched out, "his head leaning on one hand, his elbow resting on a knapsack"; near him Cachat was seated in a natural position. The two men looked as if they were chatting peacefully and admiring the view. Coils of rope, sticks, ice-axes, knapsacks ("one of which still contained bread, cheese and a little meat") were scattered around them. "The limbs of the first three," writes Couttet in his report, "extended in all directions, although the heads pointed upwards and the bodies had no injuries. Their clothes were more or less in tatters, as if they had slid."

Of the other six men there was no trace. A little further to the right, however, someone had tried to make a descent, as revealed by the end of an axe-shaft embedded in the ice.[8] The five bodies, completely frozen, were between the top of the Mur de la Côte and the Petits Mulets, but quite outside the proper line of descent; that is, much too far to the right as one leaves the summit of the mountain.

The bodies were put into large canvas sacks, but they could not be carried farther on that day than the Grand Plateau. The following day (the 18th) three were taken as far as the Jonction and two close to Pierre Pointue. Only on the third day (the 19th) did the funereal convoy arrive at Chamonix.[9]

On the 20th, 21st and 22nd the rescue party, which had returned to the Calotte, continued its work. Soundings were made, trenches were dug in all directions, but always centring on the line of descent from the place where Dr. Bean was found (very probably the site of the bivouac)[10] down to the broken axe-shaft, embedded in the hard snow. Several articles were brought to light: straps, gloves, blouses, etc. These scattered remains were spread all along the slope which, on the Italian face, joined a large crevasse, the first of the icy precipice of the Brenva, above Courmayeur.

But of the fugitives from the bivouac nothing was found: the four Chamoniards—Jean Balmat, Edouard Simond, Joseph Breton, the guides, and Alphonse Balmat, the porter; all had disappeared, and with them the little Overlander, Johann Graf, servant at the Pierre Pointue, and also the poor, but touching Mr. John Randall, of Quincy, who, "in order to see Mont Blanc, the great thing of his life," died, carried away by his dream and swept from human sight.

*　　*　　*

What has happened since the moment when the guides decided to abandon the bivouac on the morning of Thursday the 8th? By his sudden access of energy the initiator of the sortie has revived the flagging spirits of his comrades. Around him these human remnants have refound their pride, have become men once more. Their wills have freed their spirits from the fetters that torment them like trapped beasts. Sudden courage has invaded minds already filled with the shadow of death. In this confusion of equally terrible circumstances and conditions, to act as these men do, to co-ordinate their thoughts and to carry out the simple movements of preparing to depart, is a form of heroism.

It is easy to imagine the voice of Jean Balmat saying, "Are you all ready?"

They are all ready. Crouching, the men tie themselves to one another for better or for worse, for it is impossible to dream of roping up outside. Randall, a pale smile on his defeated features, grasps the failing hands of Dr. Bean and the Rev. McCorkindale;[11] he tells them how the guides hope to dispatch a rescue party without delay. Then, on all fours, one after the other, the men leave the hole and enter the hurricane, galvanised by the hope of approaching victory. Now they are standing up, stumbling in the snow. They make several steps forward, holding their distances, bending to the slope, dwarfing themselves in the storm, and descend for a few yards. And suddenly, losing their feet, they vanish, caught by the icy slope and the mist. Nothing more is known of them.[12]

THE TRAGIC BIVOUAC

For the scene of the tragedy in which Mr. Randall and ten others died, see Plates 2, 7, 8 *and* 9.

[1] This phrase is taken from Stogdon's "The Late Accident on Mont Blanc." (*Alpine Journal*, Vol. V.)

[2] Quoted by Stogdon.

[3] Grandson of Jacques Balmat, one of the conquerors of Mont Blanc and de Saussure's guide.

[4] It is very nearly certain that the entrance to the grotto had not been closed by a wall of snow after the fashion of an igloo. Otherwise the unfortunate party would have been able to wait, without suffering too much from the cold, as other parties have done, even in winter, when surprised in the same way by storms.

[5] Dr. Bean's notes are the only clues which permit us to reconstruct the tragedy.

[6] A worthy guide and a great-hearted man; he proved it many times, notably on the occasion of the Arkwright and Marke accidents. (See Chapters 5 and 7.)

[7] From Couttet's own report.

[8] This broken axe is an enigma. Hypotheses accumulate in vain. It is difficult to understand, not less so since the Glacier des Bossons several years ago threw up a piece of an axe with the initials "J. G. B." engraved on the steel head. This was a remnant of Dr. Bean's axe, a part of which Sylvain Couttet had discovered planted in the ice. This fragment had taken about fifty years to reach the valley.

[9] All the quotations from Sylvain Couttet's report are taken from Durier's *Le Mont-Blanc*.

[10] It can be taken for certain that this really was the site of the camp. Its destruction can be explained by the constancy and strength of the tempest. By beating down upon and tearing away the roof of snow, the wind at last broke in and therafter achieved the rapid devastation and levelling of the bivouac. According to Sylvain Couttet's report, it may be assumed that a gust more violent than the rest had thrown the Rev. G. McCorkindale and the porters Auguste Couttet and Fernand Tairraz, *still living*, down the slope; "their limbs extended in all directions" does not correspond, in fact, with bodies already petrified by the frost. As for Dr. Bean and Auguste Cachat, they must have died of the cold in the bivouac in the natural positions in which they were found, in the midst of the articles deposited there when the camp was made. On the other hand, it might be objected that the mass of snow which fell during the eleven days should have buried everything, and that the above conclusions are therefore illogical. Theoretically yes; but in reality no. It must not be forgotten that at great altitudes the force of the wind is such that the snow, swept without respite, cannot accumulate except in certain favourable places, as this particular tempest well proved.

Finally, some Alpine historians thought they could throw some doubt on the courage and ability of the guides and, from the fact that the caravan had neither map nor compass, accuse them of improvidence. It is easy to make such accusations, but I believe that in this case they are absolutely unjustified. By definition a guide is certainly not a super-man, and it is possible that in certain circumstances a guide may be found unfit for his job. Such cases are extremely rare. As for the absence of a map or a compass, even if the caravan had had one, or every member of it had had two, the disaster would still have occurred. To assert the contrary is completely to ignore the violence of the wind which unfettered elements can loose at heights of 4,000 metres (aprox. 13,000 feet) and over.

[11] The Rev. G. McCorkindale and Mr. J. G. Bean were buried side by side in the English cemetery at Chamonix (situated opposite the station). Their stones still exist, and on them may be read the following epitaphs:

(1) "*Ubi crux ibi patria*. In memoriam Rev. George McCorkindale, Minister of Gourock, Scotland; perished on Mont Blanc, 7th September, 1870, aged 40 years. A man greatly beloved."

(2) "James G. Bean of Balt., Md. U.S. of America, perished near the summit of Mount Blanc about the 7th September, 1870, aged 54. On his person was found a diary and among the last words which he pencilled to his wife were these: 'I die in good faith in Jesus Christ and hope we will meet in Heaven.'"

in the form of half-open pincers, the Glacier du Brouillard and the Glacier de Fresnay, separated by the rocky chain of the Inno-minata (12,192 feet). Its exploration had been going on for ten years. Four attempts had miscarried, although pressed quite high.[1] Marshall's attempt, which ended tragically in 1874, is thus the fifth.

James Aubrey Garth Marshall came from Leeds. Like many young Englishmen of his day he was attracted to the Alps, and he made his début there in 1872 by a very creditable conquest, the first ascent of the Aiguille des Leschaux (12,366 feet) in the Mont Blanc massif, accompanied by T. S. Kennedy and the guides Johann Fischer and Julien Grange. So the summer of 1874 was his third alpine season. Nevertheless, he had been through a good school; famous guides had fashioned him—Johann Fischer, his old friend from Zaun, near Meiringen, and Ulrich Almer from Grindelwald, bearing a legendary name. Ulrich was the son of the celebrated Christian Almer, one of the glories of alpine history.[2]

At the end of August the Marshall party arrives at Courmayeur. They have just completed a brilliant series of climbs in the Swiss mountains, including the first north-south traverse of the Aletsch-horn (13,721 feet) by unexplored routes on both the ascent and the descent; also the traverse of the Rothorn in ten hours from Zinal to Zermatt. From Zermatt they have reached Courmayeur by the high level route, that is, by the cols and glaciers.

On the 25th August the climbers spend the night at the chalets of Pré de Bar, a solitary alp on the Italian side of the Petit-Col-Ferret; and on the 26th they accomplish the first ascent of the Aiguille de Triolet (12,697 feet). The same evening they sleep at Courmayeur. Johann Fischer feels rather at home in this Italian village; he meets his friends there, and the local guides receive him joyfully. He has often stayed there with his English "monsieur," T. S. Kennedy, one of the finest climbers of the time, with whom, in company with the famous Jean-Antoine Carrel of Valtournanche (one of the heroes of the conquest of the Matterhorn),[3] he had made the first ascent of Mont Blanc by the Glacier du Mont-Blanc (Miage basin) in 1872.

Fischer has been at Courmayeur only a few weeks ago.[4] He and his comrade, Jaun, also an Oberlander, had undertaken to climb Mont Blanc by the Brouillard face with T. S. Kennedy and T. Middlemore. The attempt had miscarried because of bad weather; they had, nevertheless, climbed high enough for Fischer, lured by the adventure, to be tempted to repeat it.[5] And we can be certain that when, in his turn, Marshall, following Birbeck, Utterson-Kelso, Durazzo, and Kennedy–Middlemore, arrives at Courmayeur and raises his eyes towards the gigantic ramparts of the Brouillard, it is Johann Fischer who murmurs the bewitching words in his ear.[6] On the 30th August, at ten in the morning, the party leaves the Hôtel Royal at Courmayeur.

In their three rest-days since their "first" on the Triolet, the men have had time to recover their strength. Heavily laden, they reascend the Val Veni. The angelus from the chapel of Notre-Dame de Berrier greets them in passing. The bells of a multitude of cattle and the murmur of the River Doire mingle their harmonies. Over the rhododendron thickets can be seen the greenish walls skirting the glaciers on the edge of the valley. Then the track loses itself in the alpine pasture of Fresnay. Above the chalets open the mountain spaces: a cascade, a grassy terrace where pink saxifrage grows side by side with the grey-velour edelweiss and perfumed artemesia, some shepherdless sheep which have grown almost wild in their solitude. Soon the party is engaged in the desert-like region of the old moraines.

In order to turn the rocky foot of the arête of the Aiguille de l'Innominata, they make a left turn on the Glacier du Brouillard and, after about an hour, rejoin its bank. There, at about 10,500 feet, a favourable spot invites a bivouac. The loads are deposited on a slab-covered place. A rivulet murmurs among the stones. In a trice a wall raised under the shelter of a rock forms an agreeable resting-place. The fire crackles under the pot. Pipes are lit. And while the soup simmers the men, their hands in their pockets, comfortable in their discovery of such a bivouac, walk a little way from the edge of the glacier to survey the next day's itinerary.

Johann Fischer has an idea at the back of his mind. The last time that he came this way, a few weeks ago, on his attempt with Kennedy, he had noticed a herd of chamois on the Innominata arête. So, to avoid the ascent of the Glacier du Brouillard—steep, terribly crevassed, and exposed to avalanches—he has told himself that it would be simple to discover the route used by these beasts and to reach the crest as low down as possible. It could then be followed throughout its length in the direction of Mont Blanc.

stretched out on the smooth surface betrays the presence of a crevasse. Wave-like icy prominences gleam, rounded like domes. The murmur of water rises monotonously in the milky solitude. The slanting shadow of a sérac falls like the arm of a sundial over a glacier torrent, and the water, a luminous whirling spindle, runs swiftly and eternally changing under the barrier of shadow.

At this moment Fischer halts, turns round to Almer and asks the time. Almer takes his great silver watch from his pocket, consults it without striking a match, and replies that it is almost midnight.

Almost midnight! Fischer's destiny is completed. Five minutes separate them from the bivouac down there on the moraine, near those large rocks. The snow is firm; the glacier is easy to move on, like a calmed sea after the furious and menacing surge higher up, with its high waves, hard and green, and its motionless whirlpools.

The tragedy develops suddenly. A snowbridge opens under Fischer's feet; he falls vertically, dragging Marshall with him into the chasm. And Almer, who in this light has had no time to parry the blow, surprised on the uneven ice floor, is snatched up by the rope, dragged furiously along, and disappears in his turn. Meanwhile the full moon rises slowly in the great clear spaces, bathing the sleeping mountains with its icy serenity.

*   *   *

When Almer recovers consciousness a total darkness surrounds him. They have fallen one on top of the other, in a heap. He does not call them. He knows. Their silence is already that of eternity. With difficulty he turns around, and in this terrifying blackness peers about the icy tomb of which he is a living prisoner. He feels himself; his bruised muscles work painfully, and to move his limbs is agony. His wounds are slight; he suffers only from an overall bruising. He sits down beside the dead and reflects. But in his musings he sees before him, on the crevasse wall, a pale light that penetrates the darkness—the trembling starlight that slips through the hole above.

The moon has set. The approaching dawn proclaims itself with a greyish light. The tomb lights up little by little. Almer rises; he examines the tragic roof. By climbing the wall of ice he can escape. A sad hope is reborn. He unties the bloodstained rope which still links him to his motionless comrades, recovers an axe and begins his difficult task. He ascends slowly, cutting notches for his torn hands and steps for his feet, makes a move upward, rising as if on a ladder, until at last his head touches the ceiling. The light coming through the hole surprises him. His hands pass through it; he grips the edge of the ice, pulls himself up by it, establishes himself on his elbows. Then his chest emerges from the chasm, and at last he is standing upright. And the rising run, flushing the summit of Mont Blanc, falls too upon the solitary human silhouette, stumbling over the glacier. The bivouac is scarcely a hundred yards away.[10]

*   *   *

Despite his exhaustion and bruises, Ulrich Almer has the courage to make the descent to Courmayeur. The sheep on the Alp de Fresnay watch the strange pedestrian pass. The chalets are closed; nobody is there to help him. He continues his long errand. He reaches Courmayeur enfeebled, and leaves again the same afternoon, by mule, for the Brouillard glacier, following the rescue party which is under the orders of the guide Emile Rey. At Fresnay he gets down and continues with the others.

At seven in the evening Emile Rey, who has been let down into the crevasse, brings up the bodies.[11] The crevasse is twenty-eight feet wide and thirty-two deep. James Aubrey Garth Marshall has a fractured skull and his death must have been instantaneous. As for poor Fischer, his wounds are such that he could not have survived his traveller by more than a few minutes.[12]

The cemetery at Courmayeur received their remains. On their common stone are these words:

JAMES AUBREY GARTH MARSHALL
BORN AT HEADINGLEY NEAR LEEDS IN ENGLAND
ON THE ELEVENTH OF JUNE 1841
JOHANN FISCHER
BORN AT ZAUN NEAR MEIRINGEN IN SWITZERLAND
ON THE TWELFTH OF JANUARY 1834
AT MIDNIGHT ON AUGUST 31, 1874 FELL TOGETHER
INTO A CREVASSE IN THE BROUILLARD GLACIER AND
THEIR BODIES NOW LIE ON EITHER
SIDE OF THIS CROSS

*   *   *

On the day following the burial a solitary horseman slowly ascended the Grand Col Ferret; his forehead was swathed in bandages and his arm was in a sling. It was Ulrich Almer who, without his rope, his axe, his traveller, or his old comrade Johann, was returning to Martigny, and to Grindelwald, his native village.[13]

For the scene of the Garth Marshall tragedy, see plate 9.

[1] These four attempts were as follows: John Birbeck, Jr., 1864; the Marquis Durazzo, 1870 and 1872; Capt. E. V. Utterson-Kelso and the Rev. A. G. Girdlestone, with guides from Courmayeur, 1873; T. S. Kennedy and T. Middlemore, with the guides Johann Fischer and Johann Jaun and two porters from Courmayeur, 1874. Eccles made the sixth attempt in 1875, a year after the Marshall tragedy. (See also note 7 to this chapter.)

[2] Ulrich Almer was born at Grindelwald on the 8th May, 1849. At the time of the accident on the Glacier du Brouillard he already had to his credit the first ascent of the Gross Nesthorn (1865), the second ascent of the western summit of the Grandes Jorasses (1867), the first ascents of the Meije (Pic Central) and the Ailefroide (1870), the first ascent of the Weisshorn by the northern face (1871), and of the Aiguille de Blaitière (northern summit) and the Col des Hirondelles (1873). After 1874 he was second guide to the famous climber W. A. B. Coolidge, his father being the leader of that memorable party. He was, furthermore, one of the pioneers of winter climbing in the Bernese Oberland. One cannot record the career of Ulrich Almer, as remarkable as he was modest, without recalling the following brave incident: on the 14th August, 1880, on the Obergabelhorn, a cornice collapsed, dragging Almer's party with it into the abyss (H. W. Majendie and R. L. Harrison and the guide Josef Brantschen). Almer, without losing his head, leapt backwards, fixed his ice-axe in the snow, held it there with all his strength, and thus saved his three comrades who were suspended above a precipice roughly 2,000 feet deep. (Cf. *Les Alpes*, No. 7, 1936.)

[3] See note 6 (*c*) to Chapter 17; also Chapter 18.

[4] During July.

[5] See note 8 to this chapter.

[6] Dr. Emil Zsigmondy, the famous Austrian climber who died on the southern face of the Meije in 1885 (see Chapter 14), describes Garth Marshall as the "celebrated climber." Among other exploits Garth Marshall took part in the first attempt to climb the Aiguille du Dru (1873) with T. S. Kennedy and the guides who accompanied him to the Brouillard. (Cf. Clinton Dent, *Above the Snow Line*, 1885.)

[7] The first ascent of Mont Blanc by the itinerary chosen on this wall by Johann Fischer was not achieved until 1919 (August 10th), by E. G. Oliver and S. L. Courtauld, with the guides Adolph and Henry Rey (sons of the celebrated Emile Rey) of Courmayeur, and Adolf Aufdenblatten, of Zermatt. The first descent was made by E. Thomas and R. L. M. Underhill, with the guides Josef Knubel and Franz Biener in 1928. (Cf. *Alpine Journal*, Vol. XXXIII, 1921, and *Guide Kurz*, It. 779.)

The ascent of Mont Blanc by the Brouillard and Fresnay glaciers and the arête de Péteret was made by the English climber James Eccles, with the guides Michel-Clément Payot and Alphonse Payot of Chamonix (30th–31st July, 1877). During a reconnaissance of the Brouillard side in 1875, the same climber, with Michel-Clément Payot and two porters, spent the night at Garth Marshall's bivouac, the walls of which still remained intact. (Cf. *Alpine Journal*, Vol. VIII, 1878.)

[8] Dr. Andreas Fischer, himself a guide, one of Johann Fischer's sons, says in his book, *Hochgebirgswanderungen in den Alpen und im Kaukasus*, that the attempt was pressed very high, directly up the face of Mont-Blanc de Courmayeur. Ulrich Almer confided to him that "this very hard climb left on him an indelible impression, and that it had been difficult and dangerous." (*Op. cit.* Chap. "Im Mont-Blanc Revier," p. 112.) Kennedy, Stephen, Moore, Melchior Anderegg, Johann Jaun, Christian Almer, his son Ulrich himself, and others amongst the best, advised against this expedition.

On the other hand, in January 1920 Dr. Claude Wilson (later President of the Alpine Club) talked to Ulrich Almer at Grindelwald about this attempt. Almer confirmed the fact that the party had followed the arête between the Fresnay and Brouillard glaciers as far as the point where the glaciers join (then the Col de Fresnay), and higher, the ridge of the buttress in the wall, but rather to the left. However, the fresh snow on the rocks had forced the party to turn back; "the rocks were *schneebedeckt*" and it was impossible to continue. (Quoted by Capt. J. P. Farrar: "The traverse of the Aiguille Blanche de Péteret and of Mont-Blanc de Courmayeur.—A memorial to a great guide, Daniel Maquignaz." *Alpine Journal*, Vol. XXXIII, 1921.)

This information, given to Dr. Wilson by Ulrich Almer, completely corresponds to the beginning of the present itinerary of Mont Blanc by the Brouillard face, known as the "arête de l'Innominata."

Finally, T. Graham Brown quotes these words of Almer's: "It was impossible to go any farther, we found not time enough to look for another place to go farther. ("The early attempts on Mont-Blanc de Courmayeur from the Innominata basin," *Alpine Journal*, Vols. LII and LIII, 1940 and 1941).

[9] Now Col Eccles. The party had accomplished in passing, both in the ascent and the descent, the "firsts" on the Col de Fresnay (11,808 feet), the Pic Eccles (13,218 feet) and the Col Eccles (13,120 feet) attributed subsequently and erroneously to other climbers.

[10] Interesting evidence from Sir Leslie Stephen:

'J'espère que notre ami Loppé sera bientôt en Angleterre. Je l'ai vu à Courmayeur au mois Septembre et nous sommes montés ensemble au glacier du Brouillard pour voir la crevasse où le pauvre Fischer a péri avec M. Marshall. C'était un bien triste accident! Encore cinq minutes et ils auraient été en parfaite sûreté. . . ."

(Trans.) "I hope that our friend Loppé will soon be in England. I saw him at Courmayeur in September and we went up together to the Glacier du Brouillard to see the crevasse where poor Fischer perished with Mr. Marshall. It was a very sad accident! Another five minutes and they would have been in complete safety. . . ."

(Extract from a letter by Sir Leslie Stephen to M. Millot, 10th March, 1875; *Alpine Journal*, Vol. XLVII, 1935.)

[11] A detail given by Dr. P. Güssfeldt in his book on Mont Blanc.

[12] The Coolidge papers in the archives of the Bibliothèque Centrale du Club Alpin Suisse at the Zentralbibliothek in Zurich include some unpublished evidence of this tragedy. It is nothing less than a letter from Ulrich Almer himself to the Rev. W. A. B. Coolidge. It is here reproduced exactly as written in English:

"Dear Mr. Coolidge!
     I received your letter and saw in it, that you wisch to know, how deep we had fallen into the cravasse, it was about fifthy feet. I spose they were killed by the fall, than Mr. Marschall was lying on his belly and has broken his forehead. Fischer has broken three ripp's on his right-side and his longue was spoild by those broken rippes. They must been killed by the fall than there was very little ice upon them, the rope was not broken between me and Mr. Marschall. I was hurt on my right side, and cagcht cold and the medician told me to take great care, because I could get a fever of the longue very easely.
     I think, if you will send something to Fischers widow, it would bee best to send it to herself. My father have not seen Jean Martin at Zermatt nore anywhere else, he did not know that they tried the Meije, and that they spended two nights there. My father sill send you a Telegram after Christmas when he finds that the snow is in good order.

Remain Yours
truly
Ulrich Almer."

(I have to thank Mlle. C.-E. Engel for having drawn my attention to this precious document, and the Commission des Archives, who have allowed me to publish it.)

[13] Ulrich Almer, whom the author of these lines met several times, died in his 92nd year in the autumn of 1940. Some ten years after his accident on the Aletschorn (with Drs. E. Jenny and Andreas Fischer, the latter losing his life, on the 21st July, 1912) he completely lost his sight. Thus it was that Ulrich Almer, who had been the friend and companion of the Fischers, father and son, saw both of them die at his side in the mountains. Of his four brothers—Christian, Hans, Rudolf and Peter—all famous guides —only Christian is still alive. Several of their sons were guides in their turn. At the present time, Hans, son of Peter and grandson of Christian, honourably maintains the name of this remarkable line of guides. (Personal communications of Dr. E. Jenny and the guide Steuri, senr., of Grindelwald. See also *Alpine Journal*, Vol. XLI, 1939.)

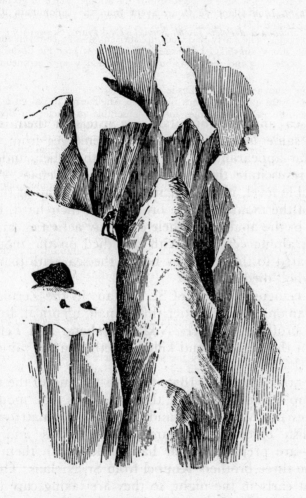

CHAPTER TEN

THE TREACHERY OF A CORNICE

*The death of W. A. Lewis, of N. H. Paterson, and of the guides
Niklaus, Johann and Peter-Joseph Knubel* (Lyskamm, September 1877)

T HE sea and the mountain are sisters in their immensity.
The same impression of eternity emerges from their dis-
similar appearances. The one and the other, under infinite
horizons, resuscitate the mystery of primeval chaos. And on a
more humble level, in the scheme of life, the man of the sea and
the man of the mountains are brothers: in their hard, hazardous
existence, in the analogy of their everyday activities, and even in
death. An alpine cemetery with its "died on the mountain" is
closely related to the cemetery beside the sea, with its memorials
to those who "died at sea."

Such a cemetery is that of St. Niklaus in the Zermatt valley,
where lie among others, under three small, identical, iron crosses,
the three brothers Knubel—Niklaus, Johann and Peter-Josef—
all three of them guides and killed together in the same accident
on the Lyskamm.[1]

On the 5th September, 1877, towards the end of the afternoon,
in the simple dining-room of the Riffelhaus, the mountain inn
which faces the Matterhorn and overlooks Zermatt on the east,
two English climbers—William Arnold Lewis and Noel H.
Paterson—are preparing their haversacks. With them are their
guides, the three brothers Knubel from St. Niklaus. They will be
setting out early in the night, so they are taking care to prepare
things and not leave them to chance at the last moment.

The evening is splendid. The autumn, just beginning, shades

with an amber-coloured patina the grassy expanses on the edge of which the inn, a roughcast limestone building, stands like a lighthouse on the shore of an ocean of mountains. Two hundred yards below it the surge of a forest of arollas, the last trees, beats like a dark tide against the foot of the cliff. All the summits of the massif, all the great "four-thousanders," the Breithorn, Matterhorn, Dent Blanche, Obergabelhorn, Rothorn, Weisshorn, Mischabels, and others, are grouped around. This astonishing chain, folded, carved and torn, throws up its resplendent peaks. In the background a craggy range loses itself in the cleft-like valley, tenuous in the misty distance. Everywhere are sunsplashed glaciers, and gilded rocks lined with very clear, very blue shadows, like the depths of jasper water. And carved at the heart of this sublime company, the Matterhorn, clothed in luminous shadows, bursts from the twilight, prodigious as the figment of a dream.

Nine years earlier, on this same terrace where Lewis and Paterson and their guides look for weather signs in the sky, Théophile Gautier, muffled in blankets, walked a hundred paces smoking his cigar and mutely admired "the desperate upthrust of the Matterhorn, the most magnificent spectacle it is given man to see." The evening draws in and the author of *Capitaine Fracasse* continues: "The sky, of an icy serenity, had the tint of blue steel, like a polar sky, and its edge was strangely cut by the dark silhouettes of the mountains forming a circle on the horizon. . . . The immense mass, violet-black, revealed its rugged arêtes against the void, raising its solitary pyramid. . . . Beside it, along its steepest flank, an enormous moon rose slowly, full, round and pale yellow."[2]

* * *

At two in the morning the door of the Riffelhaus slowly opens; the hinges creak. The lanterns cast their thin light upon the earth. One behind the other the shadows pass out; it is the Knubel party. The night is very dark and the stars glitter. It is cold.

After a long tramp along the path over the grassy slopes, the men reach the Rotenboden arête. Thence by day the eye embraces a wide glacier landscape. From the Breithorn to Monte Rosa a chain of peaks fills the sky, sixteen summits of over four thousand metres (about 13,000 feet). But in this moonless night only the colossal backbone can be descried, more obscure than a shadow, laid against the stars. A fragment of constellated sky is reflected in the little Riffelsee.

The climbers are now engaged upon the wide Grenz Glacier which runs gently down from these mighty acropolises to the plains, like a sacred road paved with alabaster. It is not yet day, but they can do without the lanterns. The night's limpidity, lingering with the grey-white of the snows, makes an uncertain dawn. Between Monte Rosa and the Lyskamm the rising glacier narrows, yet retains its ocean-like majesty. To the right the giant, ice-covered walls of the Lyskamm sweep upwards into space. With eyes raised the climbers contemplate this terrifying white mass, picked out with thin rocky lines as if to retain the mirror-like scales. In the pure silence and biting cold, which contracts the crumbling snow and the tottering séracs, at the summit of this tragic beauty, delicately raised against an ashen sky shaded with old rose, an exquisite dawn is about to break. And under a portico of golden shafts spreading from behind Monte Rosa, now immersed in violet shadows, the party reaches the Lyss Pass at a height of 13,800 feet.

A rest is called for and haversacks are dumped. A fine blue day is beginning on these snow-laden heights. They are alone in the limitless polar landscape, alone in a world adorned with dazzling whiteness, some lying softly in smooth curves like a woman's body, others raised in domes and cupolas, pale blue-green and glistening with iridescent light. Unknown horizons rise on the Italian side of the pass. Out of sight, beyond the valleys and folds of the foothills, the plain of Piedmont is lost in the mist-enshrouded distance.

The first avalanche shatters the bewitching silence. Somewhere a dull detonation rises and silences itself without an echo, smothered by the snows. And before the resting men the Lyskamm reveals in profile the icy covering of its northern flank like the gigantic keel of a capsized and stranded ship. This formidable rampart of inclined planes in rising steps, cut from the glaucous walls, glittering like steel and streaked with thin rocky lines, presents an almost symmetrical structure, massive and ethereal at once. It has the lightness of a wing and the solidity of a shield of brass. A single pediment, high up, touched by the dawn, lights the sky with the candour of a cherry-tree in bloom.

"Another British conquest, this Lyskamm," says Paterson.

"And what a conquest!" Lewis answers, smiling. "This mountain is marvellous, quite as fascinating as the Matterhorn or the Weisshorn."

"Whymper and Tyndall had great appetites, but they could not swallow everything," interposed Niklaus Knubel, laughing.

"Fourteen people set out to climb it the first time—eight Englishmen and six guides," says Johann. "There was one from St. Niklaus, Franz, the brother of Josef-Marie Lochmatter."

And Peter-Josef adds: "Almost all the Englishmen that have passed through the valley have tried to climb it or wanted to. Tuckett, Kennedy, Matthews. Do you know Mr. Stephen? He climbed it from the other end."

All five faces are now raised to the high slopes of ice where the party must pass. In front of them the arête makes one first spring, pitched against the rounded edge of a sun-splashed pinnacle, then, stretching itself out as if the better to gather its strength, rises again abruptly, springing up clear and hard like the flight of an arrow, to plant itself at the summit.

The men move off all on one rope, at long intervals, leaving behind them two unnecessary haversacks which they will pick up on their return. They silently ascend the steep roof of snow that overlooks the pass. From time to time the leading guide cuts steps in the smooth ice with his axe. The blows, the clearing of the step, and the dull grating of the falling fragments, are the only sounds in this basilisk-like calm. The bluish debris tumble furtively. And the climbers rise slowly with their shoulders to the wall of snow, its bitter breath upon their skin. After the long and monotonous hours on the Grenz Glacier, the décor has become severe, violent, almost terrifying.

The slanting light discloses a quite baroque architecture in the precipice of ice. Little glaciers, miraculously supported, incline their frail jade structures over the void. Blue arches, streaked with white frost, are supported on mutilated columns and pilasters of green marble. Partitions, gleaming piers, broken off from heavy upthrusts of ice, polished like piston-rods, here and there, in a single sweep, rejoin the glacier very far below: an indescribable tumult petrified by the frost. The sun, now high in the sky, clothes the silent mountain with an armour of gold. Several times the guides exchange words in their gutteral patois which cause them to look searchingly at the peak. The party makes a halt at the foot of the last slope, where the crest levels out for a short distance. The guides descend a few feet on the Italian side; there they stop and continue to scrutinise the heights, and with their arms outstretched seem to be discussing something. Menacing to the north, under its breastplate of ice, the Lyskamm to the south displays, by contrast, a wall of rock, a black pyramid standing some 2,000 feet up from the Lys Glacier. On the east of the pyramid a white edging is set upon the crest: an invasion of the snows from the north face. These snows accumulate, overflow the ridge and overhang, forming a sort of roof. Opposing winds clash on the arête. The south wind, dashing against the wall in furious waves, hollows the roof from below; while the northern winds, taking it in the rear, sweep over the top. Caught between these two eddies the ledge of snow lengthens, flattens and thins out. It transforms itself gradually into a thin, wide cornice, bent over the abyss. Such is the white décor in which the party moves forward, suspended between earth and sky, madly dangerous but very beautiful.

The guides have fixed landmarks on the cornice. Quite close to this point the elder brother, Peter, in 1871 just missed being swallowed up with his employers. A cornice had given way. Peter, without hesitation, had leapt to the other side (the north side), where he remained suspended on the rope, forming a counterweight for those who had disappeared. His heroism had saved the party.

So the three brothers are watchful. No step forward is made except on a taut rope, nor until the snow has been probed. They reach the foot of the last slope. Here the angle of the ascent steepens. And then, as frequently happens even with parties led by the best guides like the Knubels, in order to escape the now alarming steepness the party drifts towards the crest, where the slope is less acute and where the ice gives place to the less resistant hard snow.

They proceed along the crest. This crest is the precise limit, the point of rupture between the wall and the cornice. The skill of the leading guide, like a pilot steering his ship through a channel bristling with rocks, lies wholly in manœuvring along this arête between the solid mountain and the overhang, without encroaching too far upon this tempting balcony. The manœuvre can succeed; it often does. But it can also end badly. A hard climb may be likened to a battle in which a man's whole intellect is strained to conquer formidable obstacles while saving his skin; and as in war, courage and imagination are, together with prudence, the creative elements.

The Lyskamm is not a *terra incognita* for the Knubels. They have already climbed it repeatedly, and in the preceding year they had all walked in perfect ease along the narrow cornices, then as firm as concrete. But these cornices, a curious frosty growth, have a life as obscure as flowers. They fade; they are worn by the storms; they vanish by excavation; they are eaten away by certain eddies in the air; they are rotted by the sun and lacerated by the hail; and they grow up again. This season they are immense. Twenty-five to forty feet of snow clothe the arête with a sumptuous efflorescence. They blossom out, unfold themselves in elegant scrolls above the terrifying bluff.

The five men reach the arched surface in the following order, and penetrate into the region of the great cornices: Niklaus Knubel, followed by Mr. Paterson; Johann Knubel next, preceding Mr. Lewis, and Peter-Josef Knubel last. Niklaus advances cautiously. The danger is unseen, the more treacherous because it is present in every inch of progress. But it is always underestimated, which is only too human, above all on terrain which is already familiar. The icy slope on the right vanishes into its smooth and shining gulf, but no attention is paid to it now that this white pathway has been found rising tranquilly into the sky. To the left the convex curve of the cornice thrusts out into space.

The snow is good. They find it easy to place their feet, which bite into the crust of sparkling crystal. But are they not drifting too far from the crest? Last summer they passed this way safely; but last summer the cornices were more tightly packed, thicker set, more massive and stable. Johann and Peter-Josef can give no advice to their brother. To assess the thickness of the cornice and to estimate the extent of its overhang they should be below it, or lower down, at a point clear of snow. But they are above it.

Niklaus wields his axe automatically. Probing the snow, it sinks a yard into the surface before him, like a piston into a cylinder. So far the axe-shaft has not gone right through, and that is a good sign. Each step is thus protected, or at least it is supposed to be. But in such places it is not only the snow in front of the party that has to be watched; the flanks have a very great importance.

Now it is just at this point that very thin fissures begin to run parallel to the cornice at the edge of the crest, blue serpentine lines on the white snow. In a flash Niklaus has judged the situation and finds it very serious; in fact, terrifying. They are much too far to the left, completely above the overhang. He makes an abrupt change of direction to the right. Simultaneously, his two brothers, who have also seen the danger, shout and make the same move. The party, which has been advancing in Indian file, is now moving suddenly abreast, towards the crest, where safety lies. But new fissures, larger ones, tear the snow between the retreating party and the arête; they grow longer and longer, running forward silently, stretching to fifteen, then twenty yards, and farther still.

The five fleeing men never reach the edge. For them it is all over. For suddenly, some ten feet from the arête, the snow beneath them moves and slips away, like a ship sinking in the trough of a wave. Before and behind the party the cornice gives way with a dull sound: Niklaus, Paterson, Johann and Lewis are swallowed up in a flash and vanish into the abyss of the Italian side in a cloud of snow and ice.[3] Then the following heroic act ensues: Peter-Josef, the last on the rope, perhaps nearer to the crest than his companions, has time momentarily to escape the engulfment. Just as the snow collapses under him, he springs upon the arête and throws himself down the opposite side, the ice slope of the north face, in an attempt to check the fall of the other four by making a counterweight. But he cannot resist their combined weight. Taut as a steel rod, the rope hoists him up, drags him away from the slope and hurls him like a stone in a sling to the end of its six yards radius. Then Peter-Josef in this swift trajectory joins his two brothers and their English travellers in death.

*   *   *

That evening the Riffelhaus was seized with anxiety. The expected party had not returned, and that was even more unusual because the weather had been so fine and because the Knubel brothers were experienced mountaineers. Therefore, at six-thirty the next morning, the 7th September, a friend of Mr. Paterson, escorted by three guides from St. Niklaus—Peter Knubel (a brother of the missing men), Josef Imboden and J.-J. Truffer—set out with

94

the intention of solving the mystery. Light was quickly brought to bear and the truth was only too clear. At the Lyss Pass the two abandoned haversacks still lay on the snow, indication enough to fear the worst. With implacable logic, knowing perfectly well that the party was not in trouble on the summit, the guides searched below it. In tacit accord and without useless discussion, they descended the snows on the Italian side. The party arrived at the edge of the Lys Glacier, enclosed between the falling arêtes of the Lyskamm. And there, at the foot of the shining mountain, they discovered the five bodies. Poor Peter Knubel was soon kneeling beside his dead brothers.

Four of the victims were still attached to the rope, but between Peter-Josef and Mr. Lewis it was broken. Their injuries were terrible, especially Peter-Josef's;[4] they seemed to have been provoked by some unknown agency, additional to those brought about by the fall itself.[5] Great blocks of snow and ice, fragments of the fallen cornice, lay around the bodies. Directly above them, in the snow arête, a rent showed sauvely in the balcony of the cornice.[6] With the blue sky behind it, in this shadowed whiteness, it had the appearance of a rose-window high in a cathedral wall.

*　　　*　　　*

At two in the morning of 9th September the rescue party left Zermatt. It comprised about thirty guides and porters,[7] in charge of the guide Josef Imboden of St. Niklaus; H. Seymour Hoare, J. A. Hartley, W. E. Davidson, Josef Seiler and Dr. Gutz accompanied the guides. The transport of the bodies over the Lyss Pass (13,800 feet) and down the Grenz Glacier involved hours of wearing effort. Only at ten in the evening did the party re-enter Zermatt. Mr. Lewis and Mr. Paterson were buried in the English cemetery at Zermatt,[8] and the three brothers Knubel—Niklaus, Johann and Peter-Josef—at St. Niklaus, their native village. Their three graves can still be seen, grouped together and exactly alike.[9]

For the scene of the tragedy on the Lyskamm, see Plates 10 and 11.

---

[1] Cf. *Alpine Journal*, Vol. VIII, 1876–78.
[2] Cf. *Les Vacances du Lundi* (op. cit.).
[3] It is difficult to be certain whether the accident took place on the descent or ascent. The general opinion prevails that it was on the ascent. Some guides, as well as Mr. Davidson and Mr. Hartley, believed the contrary. The bad weather which set in

during the night of the 9th, the day the bodies were brought down, prevented these two English alpinists from climbing the Lyskamm themselves to verify the facts. On the 10th fresh snow covered the mountains. Peter Knubel, whom I was privileged to know well, always told me that he had no doubt at all that the accident took place on the ascent. The positions occupied by his brothers on the rope were also given to me by him: Nicholas at the head, Johann in the middle and Peter-Josef at the rear.

[4] The unfortunate guide had been decapitated.

[5] Hence the hypothesis of an attempt to prevent the catastrophe, as here described, and put forward by Mr. J. W. Hartley in his letter to the *Alpine Journal*, from Zermatt, 11th September, 1877. In the same letter the English climber declared that the fall had been from 350 to 450 metres (1,150 to 1,500 feet) deep. The fall was marked by two ice-axes retrieved by the rescuers, one planted in the snow, the other lying in the rocks.

The Sion correspondent of the *Echo des Alpes* (1876–77) gives the following details:

"The youngest Knubel was horribly mutilated. His head had disappeared, his trunk was almost cut in two by the rope. It might be supposed that this unfortunate man had fallen last, after having put up a desperate resistance."

[6] The cornice had collapsed through a length of close on 100 feet. A ten-foot projection of snow split the enormous gap in its centre, each wing having a spread of over 40 feet and a depth of nearly 50 feet. The tragedy had occurred at an altitude of about 14,430 feet.

[7] Among them were the famous guides Peter Rubi and Johann Jaun from the Bernese Oberland, and Alloys Pollinger *père* of St. Niklaus. Their attitude, like that of Josef Imboden, was particularly admirable.

[8] Their epitaphs:

"In loving memory of my beloved husband William Arnold Lewis, Barrister at Law of the Inner Temple and 20 Elsham Road, Kensington. Son of the late W. D. Lewis, Q.C., who lost his life on September 6th, 1877, by a fall from the Lyskamm, aged 30. 'Thy will be done.'"

"'At rest . . . Until the day break . . .' Noel H. Paterson, aged 33, September 6th, 1877."

[9] The crosses on the graves of the Knubel brothers bear metal tablets at the intersection, surrounded by heart-shaped medallions. On these tablets touching verses are written in Swiss-German dialect, which translate as follows:

(On the grave of Niklaus):

Oh! beloved mother! adored wife!
Here you find
A father and four sons
And the body of his wife.

Oh! weep not! Pray much
For me. You, well-beloved,
Will not have long to suffer
In this earthly valley!

Oh! have pity for mine!
As well as for the little ones,
In all their human sorrows,
Until we are united again in joy.
N. K.

(On the grave of Peter-Josef):

Hardly had I left the nuptial altar
And, loving, launched myself in life,
Than they brought me back home
In a coffin quite new.

Pray for me over my grave,
Pray long from the bottom of your heart,
So that one day it will be granted me,
Beloved wife, to find you again in eternity.

Take good care of all our living
With all your mother's love,
So that we might meet again
In holy reunion.

P.-J. K.

But from Johann's cross the storms have unhappily torn away both the tablet and the heart.

This chapter ought not to end without a few words concerning the terrible fatality which overtook the guide Peter Knubel.

Peter was the eldest of six brothers: Franz-Josef, Josef, Niklaus, Johann and Peter-Josef. The three last named, we have just seen, died together on the Lyskamm. Peter survived the other two, one of whom, Franz-Josef, died a violent death as a lumberman in the forest.

Peter was the father of four sons: Salomon, César, Rudolf and Josef. His wife died in 1896. Then he saw three of his sons die too: the eldest, Salomon, a very good guide, was carried away by an avalanche on the Wetterhorn on the 16th August, 1902[a]; César, a promising guide, died of a haemorrhage; Rudolf died in San Francisco.

Peter's brother-in-law, Johann Petrus, the guide, was killed in 1882 on the Aiguille Blanche de Péteret. (See Chaper 13, Part I.)

He himself died on the 6th April, 1919, at St. Niklaus, where he is buried.

His son Josef is one of the most remarkable climbers of our time, the guide and companion of the brilliant climber, Geoffrey Winthrop Young. They accomplished, among other numerous "firsts," the conquest of the Grépon-Mer de Glace, the Grandes Jorasses by the arête of the Col des Hirondelles, Mont Blanc by the arête du Brouillard, and the south face of the Taeschhorn. (Cf. Geoffrey Winthrop Young: *Over High Hills*.) Josef told me, in the winter of 1938–39, that four of the children of the victims of the Lyskamm accident of 1877 were still living; the eldest, the daughter of Niklaus, was then 72.

Frederick Gardiner wrote in the *Alpine Journal*, Vol. VIII, 1876–78, under the title "Expeditions Round Zermatt and the Riffel in 1876":

"Since I undertook this paper, the terrible catastrophe on the Lys Joch arête of the Lyskamm has taken place. Mr. Davidson, in writing of the brothers Niklaus and Peter-Josef Knubel, says that they were men 'sans peur et sans reproche,' able and experienced mountaineers, but that of Hans he could only speak of as a man and not as a mountaineer. While fully endorsing Mr. Davidson's handsome remarks about Niklaus and Peter-Josef, I gladly seize this opportunity of rescuing the memory of Hans from oblivion; that he was an able mountaineer in every sense of the word I have had many opportunities of testing, and as a worthy fellow I cannot speak too highly of him. While upon this melancholy subject let me most sincerely thank those friends who have so liberally responded to my appeal on behalf of the widows and children of those worthy men, assuring them that their liberality is well bestowed. There are three widows and six children; one of the latter has been a cripple since her birth. The application of the money subscribed will have been decided upon before these lines appear. I have also to acknowledge with many thanks the money received by me for Peter Knubel, whose property was almost entirely destroyed by an avalanche of mud and stones near St. Niklaus during the spring of 1877. Never again, I trust, may there be such sad necessity for testing the generosity of the Alpine public."

One last piece of evidence. It is an unpublished letter from Mrs. Ellen Abbott to the Rev. W. A. B. Coolidge, which figures in the Coolidge papers in the Archives of the Swiss Alpine Club library in the Zentralbibliothek at Zurich:

Sept. 14, 1877.

". . . I am so grieved about that sad accident on the Lyskamm. Three of the four Knubel brothers, killed at once—it is pitiable and they all leave widows. We know the wife and children of Nicolas. We took most of the Zermatt peaks with Nicolas and one or other of his brothers—and were up the Lyskamm with him and Pierre Joseph in 1875 the day after Mr. Lewis started for it and was tired or lazy (the snow on the Grenz glacier was heavy that day) and went up Monte Rosa by the *back* way instead, and *then* did not reach the Riffel till 9 or 9.30. Mr. Lewis has tried the Lyskamm again and perished—he was a heavy man for mountaineering. We wondered and asked Nicholas [*sic*] how he ever got him up the Dom! And they had three guides for only two travellers, I wonder how it was: I know the Knubels (as indeed all *good* guides) were very careful of snow cornices when they were with us. It *is* sad . . ."

(I have to thank Mlle. C.-E. Engel for drawing my attention to this valuable document, and the Commission des Archives for permitting me to publish it.)

(*a*) The party comprised Mr. J. H. Brown and Mr. Garden, and the guides Salomon Knubel and Théodul Imboden of St. Niklaus. It was caught by an avalanche during the descent and carried down a couloir over a distance of 1,300 feet. Brown and Salomon were killed at once; the other two were injured. Imboden was half insane and screaming. He completely recovered, however, from this terrible shock and died at St. Niklaus in 1914. (Cf. *Alpine Journal*, Vol. XXI, 1902–3.)

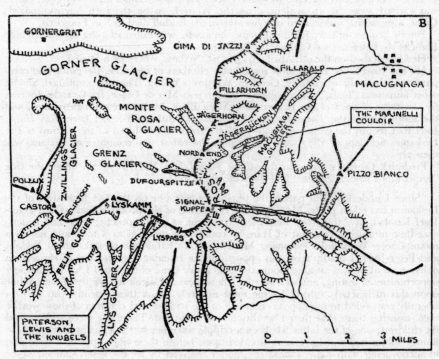

MONTE ROSA AND LYSKAMM

CHAPTER ELEVEN

THE GLORY AND TERROR OF THE MATTERHORN

I. A Boast that Ended Badly

The death of Dr. William Moseley (August 1879)

THROUGH the works of Gautier, George Sand, Maupassant and Daudet, the Matterhorn takes its place in French literature. Gautier, who saw it from close range, was fascinated by its beauty; a trembling lyricism pervades the pages he dedicated to it. As for the others, they had never seen it, but they did not forget the drama of its conquest and they were content to conjure up its tragic silhouette. As for Ruskin, he expatiated on the theme of *Mountain Glory* and *Mountain Gloom*, and that is more or less the theme of nearly all the writers of English alpine literature, from the first guidebooks of John Murray and Ball to the work of Whymper himself, when writing about the Matterhorn, so savage in its inviolate solitude. The glory and terror of the Matterhorn! That powerful rock, piercing the clouds, seems to have been sculptured by the gods for the chaining of Prometheus. But Zeus, alas, preferred the far-off Caucasus.

Since the tragedy of 1865 the Matterhorn had claimed no victim. It was fourteen years since Michel Croz, the Chamoniard, the valiant knight of the summits, without fear and without reproach, plunged with the three Englishmen down the formidable northern precipice. The snows of fourteen winters had covered their graves in the little cemetery of Zermatt, and fifteen times had the spring adorned them with flowers. Now, at the end of the fifteenth summer, death returned to haunt those rugged rocks.

Dr. William Moseley of Boston, U.S.A., a young man of twenty-six years, and his friend W. E. Craven, both accomplished climbers and members of the Alpine Club, arrived at Zermatt in the early days of August 1879.[1] Two of the best Oberland guides were with them; Peter Rubi and Christian Inäbnit of Grindelwald.[2] They had learned to know one another in the course of a long campaign. And this confidence in themselves, this deep knowledge of their own powers and those of their comrades, had given a sort of unified action to the party, a supple homogeneity. Their movements were sure, ruled by a collective instinct; their pace was fast. That summer they had not rested, and from the top of more than twenty peaks[3] they had been able to contemplate the wondrous gulfs beneath them and the skies above.

The Matterhorn was included in their programme. They had decided to make the journey from Zermatt to its summit and back again in one day and in a single stage. Though it is still not usual, such a journey is to-day accomplished several times each season; but at that time it was an innovation. In this way an uncomfortable night in a rock shelter, at 12,500 feet on the north-eastern face, could be avoided. And so it was that in the midst of general curiosity, of tourists, sightseers and villagers, the four men left Zermatt at 10.30 on the night of the 13th August.

The darkness was with them to the very foot of the first buttress of the mountain. At the Schwarzsee they passed close to the chapel of Notre-Dame des Neiges, guardian of a flock of stars herded in the dim waters. The slabs of the Hörnli grated under their boots. The glaciers glimmered palidly, the Furggen Glacier to the left, the Matterhorn Glacier to the right; and from this pedestal of ice rose the giant outline of the Matterhorn itself, surrounded by stars, vanishing into shadow.

It was a moonless night, and still too dark to extinguish the lanterns. Their thin gleams glimmered in the shadowy abyss where the party climbed among the cold rocks. Little by little dawn broke. Drifting breaths of wind, heralding the sunrise, came and went uncertainly. Space peopled itself slowly with an infinite succession of snowy peaks. The immensity of heaven adorned itself with delicately shaded clouds, while the distant crests of high and solitary mountains suddenly reddened. Then the rising sun embraced the Matterhorn and its light ran down the walls in glowing streams. A trembling life stirred in the mountain. Once again the world began to live.

The four men climbed strongly. When day broke Dr. Moseley, who turned out to be temperamentally a lone wolf, demanded liberty of action. He maintained that to untie himself from the rope would even further increase their pace.

"This damned rope," he said, "paralyses all my movements. You don't mind, Peter, if I untie it? It would be just splendid to climb this easy mountain alone."

"No, Mr. Moseley. Never! It's impossible. What a queer idea!"

The hut was soon passed. It raised its symmetrical walls at the foot of a precipice: a wooden roof, a door, a window—divine hospitality on a precipice swept by falls of stones. But the door and the window-shutters were closed. They passed on to the Shoulder, a rocky spur covered with frozen névé, overhanging two precipices, the sinister northern wall down which the bodies of Croz and the English climbers had plunged, and the eastern abyss, glowing with sunlight. Thence they passed to the Rochers Rouges, whose surface has the coppery tint of sails on the Venetian lagoon; and higher still, to the base of the Roof where, repelled by the steepness of the slope, climbers seek an outlet in the direction of the ice-encrusted surfaces of the north face, where Hadow precipitated the tragedy of 1865. There Dr. Moseley again asked that he be allowed to untie himself and finish the climb alone. But this untimely demand met with a categorical refusal from the guides. So, at nine in the morning of Tuesday, August 14th, the party reached the summit.

A few shattered stones; a mutilated pediment; a cushion of snow; a scrap of red cloth fixed to a stick and flapping in the wind. That was all. Around them in every direction lay the immense circle of the horizon, like the wide open sea. Blue the sky, blue the earth spread out below, and in every direction ranges of gilt-fringed mountains in ever-diminishing planes. Choughs called as they flew around the stones. Up and down they passed, rending the blue silence with their long shrill cries, their black wings cutting the light in swift arabesques.

Twenty minutes passed; then the guides gave the signal to leave. Once more they were on the move. Docile now, doubtless impressed by the extraordinary appearance of the descent, the young American was silent. They crossed the ice-covered Roof, then the Rochers Rouges, and let themselves carefully down the steps cut in the frozen slope of the Shoulder. Then they increased their pace, silent all the while. But when they reached a particularly difficult passage, where a chain had been fixed to the rock, Moseley again rebelled. The better to show his companions the contempt he felt for this precaution and to show also the complete uselessness of the rope, he cleared the *mauvais pas* without using the chain or the holds in the wall, displaying a quick judgement and a courageous will. But none remarked upon it.

The party was at this moment about three-quarters of an hour above the hut, involved in the precipitous rocks that support the arête. The difficulties were overcome. From this point, without exactly becoming a walk, the mountain provides only the smallest obstacles, but this does not mean that prudence can give place to carefree behaviour. Between 1,600 and 2,000 feet of sheer rock descend directly to the Furggen Glacier. This wide face is nothing but an immense ruin, ravaged by couloirs, an accumulation of black bastions and narrow, crumbling arêtes. No sooner does the sun rise on these rocks than the thunder of avalanches of stones and snow is heard.

It was in this area that the American resumed his complaints. Like a spoilt child, accustomed to everyone giving way to his demands, he stopped short and began to argue with Peter Rubi, who was at the head of the rope.

"Now, Peter. I've had enough of it. I'm going to unrope."

And Rubi replied: "Be patient, Mr. Moseley; in an hour and a half, two hours at most, we shall be at the foot of the arête, and there we can all unrope."

"But I tell you again, this damned rope annoys me."

"Do be reasonable, Moseley," Craven interposed. "What makes you want to unrope here? It's a stupid idea."

"Two more hours on this useless line. . . . Without it we could be down in an hour."

"And what good would that do you?"

"It's a bore, trampling around these rocks liked yoked oxen!"

Peter Rubi was angry. "No, Sir," he said. "What you say isn't true. We are getting down fast. You've only to look how high the sun still is . . ."

"The sun! To hell with the sun! This rope annoys me; I'm going to take it off."

He was already making a show of untying the rope, but Rubi and Craven vehemently intervened. They got the irascible American to agree to go as far as the hut, and there he could untie himself if he must. The party moved on.

An atmosphere of discontent troubled the climbers. Moseley's pretentions were ridiculous and tiresome. Since when has any member of a roped party decided suddenly to untie himself simply because the rope annoys him? How absurd, and what total lack of understanding of the moral and effective solidarity it expresses! Without considering his relation vis-à-vis the guides, whose responsibility was totally involved, his act was as unfriendly as it was incorrect.

A few minutes later, profiting by a moment when Rubi was examining the rock-face to find a route, he surrendered to his impulse and untied himself without a word. The enlarged noose slipped over his hips and fell to the ground. He stepped out of it and waited silently. Peter Rubi, his back turned, was about to take to the rock; he had seen nothing and believed himself perfectly secured by the rope. An exclamation from Craven stopped him. He turned round and saw the American untied, the rope on the ground in disorder.

"Good God!" he said. "What have you done? You might at least have warned me!" Rubi was furious. "What sort of manners are these? I was just going to move, relying on that rope. Don't you understand, Mr. Moseley, what might have happened? If I had fallen I would have dragged Mr. Craven and Christian with me. And it would have been all up with us, and all your fault."

Moseley made no response, but maintained an aggressive silence.

"You don't want to rope up again?" persisted the guide.

Moseley did not budge.

"Moseley, I implore you," begged his friend. "Don't be so obstinate. Do tie up again, please!"

Leaning against the rock, scowling and irritated, the American would listen to nothing. This tragi-comic scene, in a savage décor, had lasted long enough. Peter Rubi drew in the rope, since he could scarcely tie up his recalcitrant employer by force. With slow movements, trying to control his anger, he rolled up the abandoned line into a bandolier, making a normal interval (six or eight yards) between Craven and himself. And reduced by one member those on the rope prepared to move off.

"Mr. Moseley," the guide then declared solemnly, "what you have done is very serious. You engaged Christian and myself as guides, and we are responsible for your life. If we say that we must still use the rope, it is because we know that it is necessary, and you have no right to untie yourself. Your friend Mr. Craven is witness that it is against our will that you have done this and have thus renounced our assistance. If anything should happen to you, you have none to blame but yourself."

Craven, vexed by his friend's hostile attitude and stupid gestures, emphasised the guide's words: "Certainly, Peter; you are absolutely right."

And Christian Inäbnit, the watchful giant at the rear, perched on a rock thirty feet above and seized with admiration for the unaccustomed eloquence of his old comrade Peter, growled his agreement.

But Moseley did not deign to reply. He had an absent air and pretended to be watching a minute party on the Théodule Glacier. Those on the shortened rope moved on. The deserter, who could not be abandoned, also moved on, keeping his place between Rubi and Craven, but left to his own resources and carefully avoiding contact with the rope. Long minutes passed. No one spoke. The extraordinary incident that had just taken place seemed to give the climbers wings. They hurried down a relatively easy part of the mountain, each in his own mind turning over bitterly the words that had been spoken, each wounded at heart by the American's unfriendly gesture, blaming him for breaking both the sentimental and material harmony of the party. An ill humour poisoned the collective spirit of the caravan.

Suddenly a bright yellowish patch appeared among the brown rocks: the wooden roof of the refuge. In another twenty minutes they could push open the door and even have time to make some tea. But Peter Rubi stops and hesitates. A slightly overhanging slab bars his way. The holds are small and few. He inspects the rock, feels it, seems to test it and, his diagnosis made, he takes off. He advances very slowly, crouching, his body moulding itself to the shape of the rock. His hands grasp the tiny wrinkles, slide imperceptibly over the smooth surface. He stretches himself out, spreadeagled, his right foot like a sightless antenna seeking a point of support; he finds it, anchors himself there and, balancing with mathematical precision on that single square inch, the guide re-establishes his equilibrium and leaps onto a ledge. The *mauvais pas* is cleared.

He turns round at once. Moseley follows him. With perfect loyalty, forgetting the insult he has just suffered at the American's hands, the guide has no thought but to go to his assistance, to facilitate this difficult traverse by the isolated man who, despite all, is still his employer. He plants the point of his axe in a fissure so that the other man, lacking the rope's support, can find on it a sure footing. Moseley is already flattened against the rock. His first manœuvre succeeds. Now he is in the middle of the overhang; he searches for holds, he gropes, hesitates, then sees the axe held out to him as a step to facilitate the last and most acrobatic move. But rather than use it wisely, in a peevish voice he orders Rubi to take it away; he can do without it. Rubi obeys. Moseley stretches out his arm to seek a point of support as far forward as possible. Then he leaps. Unhappily his taking-off point gives way beneath him. He falls.[4]

A few yards lower down a small patch of snow, softened by the sun, receives his body. He has lost his axe and he falls on his back. The slope is steep. He slides. He has uttered not a word or sound, and he does not lose his head. With arched back, he brakes with all the strength of his elbows and heels. The glissade slackens and it looks as if he will be able to stop, turn round and reclimb the slope. Very swiftly Rubi has undone the extra length of rope and is preparing to throw it to Moseley's assistance when tragedy intervenes. The snow-patch ends in ice, and the unfortunate climber, caught by the slope once more, slides madly over the blue slab. Then he is seized by a patch of rock. Beyond is the abyss.

Now Moseley can see tragedy loom before him in all its horror. Though out of vanity he had wanted to abandon the rope, he has no wish to die. With a miraculous effort he succeeds in turning over. Now he slides on his stomach, his hands trying to grapple with the rock that flies very swiftly by. He succeeds only in tearing off the ends of his fingers. One pitiless wall repels his torn and bloodstained hands, then another receives the body, still furiously defending itself, reddening the rocks. At last the torture ends, and Dr. Moseley, through his wish to humiliate his guide, continues his hellish descent, rolls, bounds and rebounds, and finally disappears. Nearly two thousand feet below, on the Furggen Glacier, the last parabola ends.

* * *

The weather had deteriorated. On the heights it was snowing. After four days of storm the Matterhorn emerged, very white, from the grey clouds. A rescue party which included the guides Peter Knubel, Peter Gabriel and Josef Taugwalder, and the English climbers Craven, Vernon and Seymour Hoare, recovered the frightfully mutilated body of the unfortunate doctor. And, despite the American's repulsion for the rope, they were obliged to rope him for the last journey. Frozen solid, the body was drawn over the snow as far as the moraine.[5]

For the scene of Dr. Moseley's fall, see Plate 12.

[1] Cf. *Alpine Journal*, Vol. IX, 1878–80.

[2] On the 7th July, 1880, Peter Rubi and Christian Inäbnit were with M. Göhrs of Strassburg on the Jungfrau. While forcing a tunnel through the cornice in order to emerge upon the Rottalsattel arête (12,650 feet), on the Aletsch side, Inäbnit caused the collapse of a section of the snow some 60 feet long. The entire party was carried away as far as the bergschrund, where they were half submerged. Only Inäbnit was injured, but gravely; he fractured his vertebral column. Eleven days later, Peter Rubi was killed by a fall into the bergschrund of the Lauteraarsattel (10,351 feet). The snowbridge gave way under his feet; he fell into the chasm, dragging his companions with him, the guide F. Roth and his employer, Dr. A. Haller. All three disappeared for ever.

Peter Rubi accomplished some remarkable "firsts," one of which was Monte Rosa (Dufourspitz) by the Grenz Glacier (south-south-eastern arête) on the 20th August, 1874, with the guide Josef Mooser and the Englishman, Eustace Hulton. This arête bears the name of Cresta Rey, in memory of Guido Rey, who made the third ascent in 1886. Rubi also found a new itinerary on the Obergabelhorn (Mountet). Lastly, he was Leslie Stephens's "man with the ladder," referred to in the delightful story of the first traverse of the Jungfraujoch (21st July, 1862) in Stephens's *The Playground of Europe*. With his head between two of the rungs, Peter Rubi had carried a ladder over twenty-five feet long from Grindelwald to the Wengern Alp and thence to the Jungfraujoch, followed by a descent to the Guggi Glacier!

[3] Among others, they made the first traverse of the Viescherjoch, from the Aletsch Glacier to Grindelwald, and that from the Gross Doldenhorn to the Klein Doldenhorn by the arête.

[4] The name *Moseleyplatte* has been given to this place.

[5] My father, who was climbing that day to paint a picture, crossed the path of this lugubrious cortège. In his diary a moving sketch illustrates this unforeseen encounter.

II. A Solitary Agony

The death of the guide Josef Brantschen (August 1879)

GENEVA, city of international conferences since the days of the lake-dwellings, welcomed the International Congress of Alpine Clubs at the beginning of August 1879.[1] Among the papers presented to the Congress was an interesting one on Mountain Sickness by Professor Schiess of Bâle, a member of the Bâle section of the Swiss Alpine Club, and it was read by its author. Some days after this memorable event, Dr. Schiess and his friend, Mr. Lüscher, also from Bâle, arrived at Zermatt with the intention of traversing the Matterhorn—that is to say, to climb it by one side and descend by the other. They had come from Evolène by way of the mountains, accompanied by a guide of those parts, Pierre Beytrisson. At Zermatt they engaged two guides from St. Niklaus, one already well known, Josef-Marie Lochmatter (whose star shone beside those of his fellow-villagers, Aloys Pollinger, Peter Knubel and Josef Imboden), the other less known, but an experienced mountaineer and a great friend of Lochmatter. His name was Josef Brantschen.[2]

By way of the Théodule Pass, this caravan of two tourists and three guides arrived at Breuil in the afternoon of August 11th. It is a pleasant walk. The track stretches along the side of a declivity skirting the grassy slopes which overlook the Gorner Glacier. Monte Rosa and the Breithorn chain form a white wall along the southern sky ahead. Then the gentle rise of the Théodule Glacier, its surface broken at long intervals by timid crevasses, leads to the rock arête of the Théodule, the Italo-Swiss frontier, which is crossed at its lowest point, the Théodule Pass (10,900 feet). Far below lies the green hollow of Breuil, and from its pastures, where herds of cattle browse, rises the sonorous music of the cow-bells, muted by the wind. The deep, shadowy furrow of the Valtournanche stretches away to the valley of Aosta, and farther away can be seen the rugged relief of the Graian Alps under their sheet of eternal snow and bristling with great peaks. But above all, gigantic, and rising to an almost incredible height above the Théodule arête to which it is welded, is Saussure's "magnificent rock," the Matterhorn, terrifying in its *tête-à-tête* with the sky.

The north-eastern arête, known as the Zermatt arête, as regular as that of the pyramid of Cheops, rises in a straight line to the summit, then falls down the other side. But its fall on the south is broken at its first quarter. This immense drop outlines a large obtuse angle which fills the sky. Mists, in passing, wind themselves around those reddish rocks. Stones tumble down and rebound, invisible projectiles in the black ravines. A whole efflorescence of snow sprouts in the sinister depths, like trees of coral in the depths of the sea.

The Matterhorn dominates Breuil by over 8,000 feet. Stretched out on the cool and scented turf near the little Jumeaux Hotel, Dr. Schiess and his friend and their guides contemplate the splendid mountain. It is a perfect day. Mysterious forces seem to flourish in those rocks, clothed in a glowing golden patina, as if lit from within. Grandly carved, with tortured walls, streaked with deep shadows, the Pic Tyndall forms a first summit on its triangular pediment. Beyond is the peak itself, square as a turret. Seen from Zermatt on the Swiss side, the Matterhorn has slender lines, svelt in their lyrical sweep; it has an elegant aspect, something feminine, of a very pure loveliness. But from Breuil, on the Italian side, the impression is quite different, presenting an enormous rampart in all its massed strength.

At their ease upon the turf, the five men examine the mountain. They pass a small telescope from hand to hand, one borrowed from Jean-Jacques Carrel, that intrepid chamois-hunter, who in former times had had many a resounding struggle with the Matterhorn. Josef-Marie Lochmatter and Josef Brantschen, who have already climbed the Italian face, point out and explain the routes on this historic arête.

"Up there is where Mr. Whymper pitched his tent. Yes, just there, at the foot of that dark escarpment shaped like a tower. And Mr. Tyndall, with Bennen and the Carrels, climbed to that place, very high up, higher than that first sharp summit which bears his name, the Pic Tyndall."

"And where is the Cravate?" asks Dr. Schiess.

"The Cravate? Can you see, sir, that ledge of ice which crosses the mountain under the summit of the Pic Tyndall? It looks like a white ribbon tied around the rocks. That's the Cravate."

It is Brantschen speaking. He has the spy-glass to his eye.

"And is that where the refuge is?"

"A hundred yards from the arête, on the ledge. You can't see it from here. It's too small."

And Lochmatter adds: "That's where we can spend the night."

But in fact, abandoning their first project, which was to make the traverse in two days, bivouacing at the hut on the Cravate, at the suggestion of the St. Niklaus guides they are going to attempt it in one day, sleeping the same night at Zermatt.

* * *

The caravan left Breuil in the night (12th August) and early morning found the climbers on the flank of the Tête du Lion. They were moving along the edge of the snowy funnel where Whymper made his famous fall during a solitary attempt on the mountain. Dawn flushed the high and silent places and loosened the first stones. At the Col du Lion an immense vista was revealed; the Swiss Alps were visible as far as the Bernese massifs. At the foot of the col, on its farther side, the Tiefenmatten and Zmutt glaciers slumbered still, embedded in livid shadow.

The guides were glad to see again the mountains of their native valleys. The Dent Blanche, with its 4,000 metre cohort, stood before them like a cascade of light. Brantschen led with skill. At the foot of the Grande Tour the real difficulties would begin. The order of march was then reversed, and Josef-Marie Lochmatter took the lead. The climb was becoming aerial. Perilous passages now followed one another, end on end. The frozen slope of the Linceul stretched its glassy sheet between two barriers of rock. Josef-Marie cut a frail ladder of steps. The dull blows of his axe shivered the crust and shattered the solemn stillness.

Having joined the arête above the Tyndall rope, the climbers ascended the Crête du Coq, a series of shattered blocks. The precipices on either side of the mountain fell sheer away into gulfs of alarming depth. Suddenly, turning a rock, the summit of the Matterhorn took shape, proudly outlined upon a clear sky. Falsely presented by the ascending perspective, it seemed very near. The details of its architecture could be seen, the sharp angles of its rocks, the snow speckling the last ressaut. It looked as if an outstretched hand could touch the summit. Beytrisson set up a wild shout. But Whymper, Tyndall, the Carrels, the Maquignaz and all the obscure heroes, guides and porters, of all the years of struggle—they too had known this thrill at treading the forecourt of this sublime cathedral. And they had all, one after another, believed that it only remained to push open the door.

But Josef-Marie cruelly dispelled the old illusion that stirred their hearts, as it had done with those who had gone before.

"It's very late!" he said. "Another hour yet!"

He was holding his nickel watch in his hand. It was already quite problematical whether they could reach Zermatt that evening, or even the hut on the other side, the more so because the two men from Bâle were moving very slowly.[3] What were they to do? A brief council of war was held and the unanimous decision reached to spend the night at the Cravate. Twenty minutes later, by an easy passage along the snow-covered cornice which slantwise crosses the Pic Tyndall, the party reached the hut.[4]

It was a humble shelter: a vault discovered by Jean-Antoine Carrel and contrived by him and his men into a covered bivouac. They had built walls of dry stones, had constructed a roof end, a door and a window facing Breuil. Five sheepskins and some sloping planks to sleep on formed the entire furniture. But at this epoch this shelter, with its planks and sheepskins, was considered the height of luxury and comfort at 13,500 feet, higher even than the summit of the Aiguille Verte.

Despite their change of programme, the climbers were happy to drop their loads. The rope was hung out to dry in loops over the stones. They hung their axes on the wall. How strange a contrast this shelter was to the many rough hours among the rocks and the snow! And the smell of the refuge—the odour of damp wood, of sheepskins, of stagnant obscurity! To have hauled oneself up these inexorable walls where every movement has been a defence against death, to have freed oneself of the cruel void which has enveloped and pursued one, and suddenly to be here, in this peaceful refuge; a floor, walls, the quietude of these few poor things, were wonderful, almost fantastic. A board to sleep on, a sheepskin for covering.

In the afternoon Josef Brantschen was indisposed. He had drunk much water while climbing and he had slept a long time in the sun. Towards five o'clock he sat down on the doorstep, his face a little sad, his distant gaze stubbornly turned towards Breuil, nearly 7,000 feet below. His old friend Lochmatter was anxious. But his employers, convinced that it was only a passing attack of mountain sickness, did not regard the matter very seriously. As there was neither a stove nor any kitchen utensils whatever,

Josef-Marie constructed a rudimentary fireplace. An old tin box served as a saucepan, and Beytrisson chopped up some logs which he had found in a corner. Brantschen swallowed a mouthful of tea and went to lie down.

With twilight the air freshened. Although the sun still shone on the rocks they froze up. The climbers came in and closed the door. Wrapped in the heavy pelisses, they crouched around the hearth where the embers glowed redly. And they awaited the evening. It was then that Josef Brantschen began to groan. His groans, at first suppressed, became delirious, acquiring an almost regular rhythm, taking possession of the silence and the half-darkness. They became the disturbing master of the refuge, banishing every other preoccupation and the men themselves to a secondary plane. Josef-Marie and Dr. Schiess stood beside the sick man. He answered their questions with difficulty. He suffered an all-over malaise; a light fever consumed him, and his pulse was a little fast, though regular. Beytrisson had revived the fire; water steamed in the tin. Josef-Marie, kneeling beside Brantschen, held a mug of tea to his parched lips and, in the patois of St. Niklaus, was lavish with encouragement.

"To-morrow you'll be better," he said. "You'll see. We'll go very easily, tranquilly, gently. We shall be at Zermatt in the evening. You can get into bed as soon as we arrive. And the day after to-morrow you can go down to St. Niklaus by carriage."

Brantschen heard without replying. His groans, stilled for a while, began again as soon as Josef-Marie was quiet.

Evening came. The setting sun flamed on the window. Among the rocks the first winds breathed. The long cries of the choughs were shrill about the shelter. Through the open door—Beytrisson came in with a tinful of snow—could be seen the boundless earth below, stretched blackly under a still pale sky. In the distance Mont Blanc floated, a splash of gold which the shadows slowly conquered.

The candle, which was planted in a bottle, lit the refuge with a niggardly gleam. The men ate their supper without speaking. Possessively monotonous in their plaintive modulation, Brantschen's moans continued. In the refuge they created an atmosphere of vague terror and distilled an indefinable sickness of heart. With the night the wind rose, a wind born in limitless space, whose blows raged against the darkened rocks. Its ceaseless gusts whistled at the corners of the hut, withdrawing sonorously, while the five men lay motionless in their narrow box, so high up, very near to the stars, hemmed in by space and the wind.

The night was bad. The sick man's condition grew distinctly worse. An attack of pain seized him with a febrile trembling; he turned about ceaselessly. A frightening rattle tore at his throat, alternating with his groans. Stretched out beside him, leaning upon his elbow in the darkness, Josef-Marie spoke to him quietly, as he would to a child, as if watching a son gravely ill, Josef or Rudolf, or little Franz who was still in his cradle.

None slept. Thoughts and images passed swiftly and vividly behind closed eyes, a torrent of over-excited animation burning their brains. Outside the hut a stormy wind howled. Its long shrieks and its whines answered to the men's silent hallucinations, while they lay wrapped in their sheepskins. Distant thunder without lightning, or perhaps an avalanche on the Dent d'Hérens, growled for a long time, raising the echoes. Then, as the sky began to lighten, Brantschen gradually became silent. At last he fell asleep. And his companions slept too.

At dawn the party was on its feet. Roseate clouds were rippling among the flushing peaks. The night's threat of storm had gone, and a fine day opened its infinity to the dawn. Brantschen was becoming very much better. The short but restorative sleep and a cup of boiling tea produced happy results. He rose without help and answered sedately the questions they put to him. His strange sickness appeared to be entirely dispersed, but he was still very pale; his strength recovered very slowly. Would he have enough to follow the party? Would he have the energy to complete the climb and pursue the long descent to Zermatt? Brantschen was not after all a neophyte, and this was not the first time he had traversed the Matterhorn, so he knew exactly what awaited him, supposing he resumed his place on the rope. But would it be wise? Common sense and his still visible weakness conquered his desire to leave with the others. He decided therefore to stay at the refuge, and Josef-Marie approved his decision. They unanimously concluded that it would be best to reach Zermatt as quickly as possible, *making the traverse on the way*, and on arrival to despatch a rescue party at once.

At six in the morning of the 13th August the men roped up in front of the refuge and departed, Lochmatter leading, to reach the summit of the mountain. Josef Brantschen was on the narrow platform beside the hut. He watched his comrades vanishing along the snowy ledge. Josef-Marie turned round and called to him:

"Josef, don't stay all day inside. Come out on to the rocks in the sun. It will do you good!"

Brantschen smiled and assented, and the party disappeared. Brantschen was now alone. He contemplated for a moment the precipice in the middle of which he was placed like a gargoyle on a church wall. It fell perpendicularly before him and rose perpendicularly behind. Life began again at Breuil. Brantschen could see the smoke rising from its roofs, and with the ear of a mountaineer he could catch the musical sound of cow-bells as the beasts were driven out to grass. He heaved a sigh, entered the refuge, closed the door and unconsciously took stock of the worldly goods among which his seclusion was beginning. The inventory was quickly made: sufficient provisions to last until his deliverance, a little wood, so that he could make tea—the tin was filled with snow—and lastly the five sheepskins. Just then he was neither hungry nor thirsty. The best thing to do was to rest. He stretched himself out and, having become feverish again, pulled two or three pelisses around him. He fell asleep.

At ten-thirty Lochmatter's party arrived at the summit of the Matterhorn. After a brief rest they began the descent of the Swiss side and lowered themselves slowly down the precipices overlooking Zermatt. Only at five-fifteen in the afternoon did they reach the hut and send a message—by a guide relinquished by another party of climbers—requesting that help be sent to Brantschen as quickly as possible. They did not arrive at Zermatt until one-thirty in the morning of the 14th.

*   *   *

Nothing more is known of Josef Brantschen except that he died alone in that forlorn shelter, 13,500 feet up in the silent solitudes of the Matterhorn.

One could reconstruct this tragic end. One could, without much imagination, retrace hour by hour the concluding stages of Brantschen's life. Did this unfortunate and involuntary stylite ever awake? Did he fix his frightened gaze upon the little window that framed first the blue sky, then the sunset, and at last the stars? Had he heard the wings of silence weaving about the mountain? Had he heard, in this desert of perpendicular rock, the cries of the familiar choughs, or the wind beating against the walls of his refuge, or the many strange sounds which fill the high mountains with mystery? Had he suffered? Had he suddenly perceived, in this shelter so still and so dim, that he was not alone, that another presence was there, the presence of the dark wanderer? Had he seen him come? Had he felt his thoughts petrify with fear? Had he heard the stones roll down under the feet of a distant party on the arête of the Pic Tyndall?[5] Had he heard the men of St. Niklaus climbing to his rescue? Had their voices reached him? Or had he died peacefully at the end of a long sleep, without waking? When had he drawn his last breath?[6]

So many questions! Such curiosity! But it is not for us to disturb this good guide's spirit. When the rescue party, three men of St. Niklaus, pushed open the door of the hut in the afternoon of the 14th August, Josef Brantschen was already dead. They knelt and prayed.[7]

*　　*　　*

On the 20th August eight guides, having climbed again to the refuge on the Cravate, took the body of Josef Brantschen from beneath the stones where his friends had laid it, near the shelter. It was carefully wrapped, bound and precipitated down the Zmutt abyss to the west. A second party of guides, posted below in the Tiefenmatten Glacier, awaited the terrible package.

For the scene of Brantschen's death, see Plate 13.

[1] Cf. *Echo des Alpes* and *Alpina*, 1879.

[2] Cf. *Alpine Journal*, Vol. IX, 1880.

[3] The late arrival at the Pic Tyndall, the time taken to reach the summit of the Matterhorn on the following day, and the time taken on the subsequent descent to the Swiss Hut, and afterwards to Zermatt, abundantly prove it.

[4] On the 2nd September, 1865, Canon G. Carrel of Aosta, who had followed the conquest of the Matterhorn with passionate attention, submitted to the engineer Giordano the idea of constructing "a refuge near the Cravate, below the Pic Tyndall ... to excavate a grotto in the living rock." In the end the idea of the cave was abandoned and instead a small refuge of dry stones was erected under a vault with the rock for a ceiling. Jean-Antoine Carrel was entrusted with the work. This shelter, constructed in two weeks, was composed of three walls, a wooden door and a little glass window. The English climber, Leighton Jordan, provided it with twelve sheepskins (which Canon Carrel proposed should be called "the Jordan blankets!"). R. H. Budden provided a "good portable rubber mattress" and a small portable cooker which went to pieces in 1879—it was known as the "Rob Roy" cooker. On the 23rd August, 1867, the hospitable "Balme de la Cravate" was opened to climbers.

The Cravate refuge served until 1885. At that date the Italian Alpine Club (Aosta section) built the refuge at the Grande Tour. This was soon abandoned because of its rather exposed position; and in 1893 the Turin section constructed the present refuge a hundred metres (330 feet) lower down (at 12,759 feet). It was named after Luigi-Amadeo, Prince of Savoy, Duke of Abruzzi.

[5] On the 13th August a party comprising the Rev. A. Sloman and Mr. C. E. Freeman, with the guides Jean-Antoine Carrel and A. Supersaxo, left Breuil very early to traverse the Matterhorn in one day, just as Josef-Marie Lochmatter had reckoned to do. This party thus passed within twenty minutes of the Cravate, where Brantschen lay in agony, some hours after the departure of the Swiss.

[6] These lines were written when there accidentally came to my notice a note by Capt. Farrar concerning this tragic death:

". . . the first time, 1879, Daniel, then a porter, made the ascent of the Cervin (Matterhorn) with his uncle, J.-J. Maquignaz, the first thing they saw on reaching this hut was the body of a tall, black-bearded man lying across the door—Josef Brantschen." (Cf. *Alpine Journal*, Vol. XXXVII, 1925.)

[7] The circumstances of this solitary death aroused some violent polemics, as much in the general Press as in the Alpine reviews. It was nevertheless easy for Prof. Schiess to prove that he had never wished to abandon his sick guide, whose condition was far from suggesting a fatal conclusion, let alone one so rapid.

During this controversy all the combinations had been examined to find the arrangements that Prof. Schiess ought to have made and which would have best conformed to the situation and been the most humane.

There is no point in overloading this brief commentary with all the suggestions. Readers are free to imagine them and to decide for themselves. One fact remains certain: if Brantschen's comrades had been able to guess the seriousness of his sickness, they would not have left him as they did. Had they realised it, it seems that the best solution would have been to despatch the two guides to Breuil; these would still have been able to climb up again the same evening with a rescue party, while the two tourists remained to attend to the unfortunate Brantschen.

But all these mountain tragedies are easy to criticise from a distance and from down below. Give them back the atmosphere of their fantastic setting and the tune changes. The same fatality which orders the circumstances of life itself and of love is to be found again on the heights. Its inexorability is there disclosed the more sharply as the décor gives a tragic import to our poor human gestures, proclaiming everywhere the constant presence of death.

Some days after the tragedy my father, Albert Gos the painter, and a violinist of great talent, and my mother, an admirable pianist, both on holiday at that time in Zermatt, organised a charity concert for the benefit of Brantschen's family.

CHAPTER TWELVE

THE BLAST OF AN AVALANCHE

The death of D. Marinelli and of the guides Ferdinand Imseng and Battista
Pedranzini (Monte Rosa, Macugnana side, August 1881)

SOME four hundred years before a murderous avalanche drew attention to the splendid eastern ramparts of Monte Rosa, Leonardo da Vinci, the demi-god of the Renaissance, had already looked upon them. Fear and a sense of mystery mingled with his admiration. "There is no other mountain that has its base at so great an elevation," he writes. "This mountain towers to so great a height as almost to pass above all the clouds and snow seldom falls there, but only hail in summer when the clouds are at their greatest height. And there this hail accumulates, so that if it were not for the infrequency of the clouds thus rising and discharging themselves, which does not happen twice in an age, there would be an enormous mass of ice there."

In point of fact, this peak which "reaches beyond almost all the clouds" has never been exactly identified. But it is impossible to see of what other mountain da Vinci could have been speaking.[1] During the eighteen years which he passed at Milan, at the head of the Academy of Art, the immortal artist must each day have seen, emerging from its familiar skies, the sculptured mass of Monte Rosa, dominating the titanic frieze of the Alps. How, therefore, could he not have chosen, on that day in July 1511 or 1516, when he made his journey towards the snows which formed such a profusion of light in the sky, the most beautiful and the highest of all?

This Monte Rosa precipice is one of the mightiest in the Alps.

116

It shares its formidable glory with the Italian face of Mont Blanc. In one sweep the 9,400-foot wall rises to an altitude of 15,204 feet (Dufourspitz, the highest point of Monte Rosa and of Switzerland) and stretches to a length of over six miles. From the depths of the Piedmont plain its aery mass throws up the most noble of structures to the very limit of the Italian sky, and Ligurean fishermen, under a sail that glides over the Gulf of Genoa, can see its smooth whiteness flush in the light of dawn, like a lamp lit suddenly on the balcony of the sky.

The Macugnaga wall was conquered relatively early in the history of alpinism. Three climbers, English, as is fitting, and all of them members of the Alpine Club (the brothers Pendlebury and the Rev. Taylor), together with three guides of whom Ferdinand Imseng of Saas was the leader, succeeded in reaching the summit of the Dufourspitz in July, 1872, while opening up a route across the rough wall of ice.[2] But this magnificent climb, which had caused celebrated English alpinists, as well as guides like Christian Almer, Alexander Burgener, Franz Lochmatter,[3] Christian and Ulrich Lauener to hesitate, remained for a long time an isolated achievement. Eight years later (August, 1880) M. R. von Lendenfeld, an Austrian, and his guides had succeeded in climbing it a second time.[4] These were the only two ascents in eight years, and it is easy to guess from such infrequency the great prestige that was attached to this majestic rampart in alpine circles. It held the hearts of the mountaineers in suspense and the most foolhardy admired it in silence.

To view the eastern face of Monte Rosa in all its true splendour it must be approached by the Monte Moro Pass, on the Italo-Swiss frontier, from the direction of Saas. Suddenly, beyond the rent in the earth, in the wide splay of a succession of distant arêtes, symmetrically inclined, with their bases resting apparently on the horizontal line of the pass, surges this prodigious wall, etched in delicate lines like the long side of an ancient temple. Between its finely carved, lateral arêtes and the rocky ligatures of its flanks, gracefully modelled by the Creator, cataracts of ice precipitate their violent immobility, snow in vertical and rigid folds and glaciers full of blue waves. This ensemble adorns the rampart with astounding bas- and haut-reliefs, savage designs of inscrutable meaning whose lines, prolonged very low, plunge almost into the verdure of the Val Anzasca and give the mighty mass the easy freedom of a flower. One immense white scar divides the wall from top to bottom exactly in its centre, and looks rather like a shattered marble column still leaning its tragic ruin against the wall. This is the couloir, then without a name, followed by the only two parties which had crossed there, and to which Marinelli, by finding in it a dramatic death, was about to give civil status.

Damiano Marinelli, a brilliant alpinist and a pioneer of the Italian Alpine Club, is also a fervent patriot.[5] Jean-Antoine Carrel, the hero of the Italian Matterhorn, has already in the cause of patriotism sought to conquer his own particular mountain for the honour of his fatherland. The Englishmen who moved around the inviolate peak had the appearance of the suitors at the palace of Ulysses. And that could not be tolerated. The national sentiment of the Risorgimento stirs even in the depths of the alpine valleys. Thus, in the national cause, Damiano Marinelli also opens his heart to the stirring forces which reach him from the mountains of his homeland, and he is about to climb those which form its frontiers, perhaps the most beautiful and certainly the highest, by the sides which have their roots in Italian soil.

In this year, 1881, Marinelli has concentrated his activities on the Grisons-Italian summits. The peaks of the Bernina massif have seen him rise from their eastern cliffs, the Piz Roseg being the last. Thence he arrives at Macugnaga, fascinated in his turn by the famous wall. Three Englishmen have conquered it, then an Austrian. Four foreigners! And yet no Italian has inscribed his name in that glorious chronicle. How can he resist the challenge?

The guideless climbers of this epoch are rare; Marinelli is not one of them. He entrusts himself to Ferdinand Imseng, an intrepid mountaineer, a renowned Swiss guide belonging to the same region, even though a native of Saas in the Valais. But Saas, after all, is adjacent to Macugnaga, although a frontier wall of nearly 10,000 feet keeps them separate. Yet they are under the same sky, the same glaciers, the same rocks, and at the foot of the same mountain. And Imseng, moreover, is the daring guide who led the Englishmen to victory on the Macugnaga wall. He has other famous titles in addition;[6] but that one is enough, and Damiano Marinelli, who is no longer a novice, knows it well.

Marinelli arrives at Macugnaga at the beginning of August, 1881, with an excellent Italian guide, Battista Pedranzini of Santa Catarina, near Bormio; he will be the party's second. On

Sunday the 7th, after mass, the three men saunter out above the village along the tracks over the grassy slopes. Monte Rosa, all harmony and loveliness, streams with light. How high it is! Perhaps on that account Imseng explains a new plan of attack to his employer.

"I think that it would be best, Signor Marinelli," he says, "if we were to bivouac higher than where we passed the night with the Englishmen in '72. Can you see that rock to the right of the large couloir? No, not so far . . . there . . . yes, between the couloir and the Nordenspitz Glacier. . . . Yes, just there; that little terrace which seems to touch the couloir. That is where we slept. Well, I suggest that if we can bivouac higher up, as high as possible in the rocks of the crest which borders the couloir on the left, we shall save a lot of time. And we shall also be able to attack the large ice slopes very early in the morning, before the stones and the avalanches fall. The avalanches in that couloir! They are God's own thunder! Even as far away as the Monte Moro Pass the chamois run off when they hear them. Yes, I have noticed some places where we might bivouac. Not quite at the top, almost between the head of that black fissure . . . can you see it, Signor Marinelli? That's it! . . . between the head of the fissure and the summit of the escarpment. We could spend the night there."

At ten o'clock on the following morning (Monday, 8th August) the party leaves the little Macugnaga hotel. A porter, laden with blankets and wood, accompanies the three climbers. It is a lovely day, very lovely indeed, even overpowering. No breeze breaks the desperately clear sky. Under its implacable sapphire a baking heat hangs against Monte Rosa, which streams with the violent radiation of ice. At the Fillar Alp, where the party rests a moment, the master cheesemaker goes to fetch cream, which he offers them in a large, polished, wooden bowl with carved handles. He knows Imseng well and is proud to know him; throughout the Val Anzasca, moreover, they talk of Imseng's courage and daring. And they admire him. It is this same cheesemaker who in 1872 received the English party at the door of his hovel.

"You remember, Ferdinand? My cream brought you luck. Some more, signor? It will bring you luck too."

Marinelli smiles at these favourable auguries. He holds his bowl and drinks with slow pleasure. The enormous rampart sweeps up behind them in foreshortened flight. Oozing slabs and icy scales hang upon the light of the zenith. The torrents sing. In the direction of the grey moraine some lazy cows, lying on the cool grass, watch the party pass curiously. Then come the scorching solitudes of the Belvedere Glacier.

Towards four o'clock, after a climb that has been exhausting because of the abnormal heat, the party drops its loads upon the little terrace (approximately 10,000 feet) at the edge of the couloir.[7] Pedranzini uncoils the rope. The porter sinks down, the heavy load still on his back, and Imseng, happy to find himself again at this place, witness of his most glorious exploit, does the honours for Marinelli with childish delight. They can distinguish the remains of the little wall built against the rock, and stones blackened by fire.

"Here was the bivouac! Look! I was against this stone. I can still see the others' places. Here was Spechtenhauser, there was Oberto, and the Englishmen were in that corner. And this is where we made a fire of rhododendrons."

"And don't you think, Imseng, that we too . . .?"

But Imseng sticks to his project. Clearly, the crossing of the couloir obsesses and troubles him.

"The quicker we can cross that damned couloir the better. What's more, in an hour, or an hour and a half at most, we shall reach the site of our own bivouac, up there in those rocks."

The place where they now stand is severe with a somewhat frightening simplicity: only the perpendicular, blackish walls, streaked with snow. Very high, silhouetted against the sky, runs the metallic edge of the arêtes. And out of the silence, out of the flat radiance of the glaciers and the melting snows, emerges the litany of everlasting waters. But what gives a special character to this high mountain landscape—an unusual character, of almost sinister brutality—is the immediate proximity of the enormous, sharp-edged couloir of snow, lying there like a sword in a stone scabbard. Other spots in the Alps owe their fame to their view of some neighbouring peak, or to some other astonishing spectacle; but here, in this wall, it is the couloir which fascinates, which holds the eye and bends the mind to its violent imperative.

It is five o'clock. Not a cloud in the sky. Not a breath of air. The heat crushes the slopes under its formidable weight. It is as if there is danger in the air, but what that danger may be is not quite clear. Most of the avalanches have already fallen. And up there, at 15,000 feet, by five o'clock the frost has cemented everything that might have a tendency to move.

"Then why hesitate? It's ridiculous!" thinks Imseng.

The party, now roped, reaches the left bank of the couloir, which is more than seventy-five yards wide, and there descends, entirely vanishing, as if sucked into the gash. On the frozen surface they stand unsteadily. Imseng leads on a taut rope. Marinelli follows, then comes the porter, with Pedranzini bringing up the rear. Imseng advances a few yards; the splinters of ice fly in showers from his axe.

A black perpendicular track shows up on the sloping whiteness. Imseng raises his head, looks at the rising perspectives narrowly enclosed in their savage cliffs; his highly strained attention probes the secret of the heights whence death, like an eagle, can launch itself abruptly from its eyrie. But the heights are tranquil. Nothing moves. Not a stone whistles by, there is not the least movement of the snow. The couloir is still, like a slack sea. Imseng, quieted, moves on. The snow, too, is good, hardened, but soft enough to place the foot solidly after a few scrapings. Silently and attentively the party now finds itself involved in the midst of this dangerous passage. Before and behind them they are overlooked by the walls, while to their left is the swift channel which vanishes from sight and thrusts its delta into the Monte Rosa Glacier 2,600 feet lower down. Furrows which have been torn by the stones and opened up by blocks of ice display their delicate parallel flutings in the snow.

The climbers first descend, following the curve of the couloir, and then rise again. And in less than half an hour, the seventy-five yards being crossed, they reach the farther bank. Imseng, excited by this lucky crossing, his nerves at last relaxed, smiles at Marinelli, who is himself delighted, and assures him that in less than an hour they will reach the site of the bivouac; to-morrow's climb will thus be advanced at least a third. What remains to be climbed this evening is a reef of easy rocks, so easy that they can safely unrope.

Pedranzini coils the rope, fixes it to his knapsack, and the party resumes its climb. This triangular-shaped buttress, one of whose sides skirts the right bank of the couloir, extends southwards; briefly, it is the rock foundation uncovered by the retreat of the hanging glacier, whose séracs still overlook it. A slope of easy steps certainly, but terribly exposed; for besides the continuous menace of the hanging glacier above, it is precisely in the effective zone of the great avalanches detached from the semicircle of peaks tapering above to a height of over 15,000 feet. And against these attacks from on high the finest guide is but a toy easily broken. There are a few inclined rocks which can, at a pinch, protect the climbers, but they must be alert. It is in the shelter of one of those rocks that Imseng plans to set up the bivouac.

The party proceeds peacefully and has reached a height of about 11,150 feet, hardly half an hour from their proposed bivouac, when a fearful cry is raised: *"Avalanche! Avalanche!"*

The porter, who has remained behind to drink at a cascade slightly off the line of ascent, hears the terrible cry re-echo. He raises his head, terrified, and with dismay he sees his comrades flying before the whirling, roaring mass, and shot into space. Imseng is catapulted first, Marinelli follows him in his curve, then Pedranzini. Struck by the mass of air displaced by the avalanche —*la veura*—the three victims are hurled into the couloir and disappear.[8] Then, for a few seconds, perhaps five, the avalanche abates, engulfed in the couloir. But it overflows, thrown up by a rock obstruction and, like boiling surf, drowns and levels the reef. In its exasperated rage it fills the air with gigantic tentacles of snow and ice and rock, tormenting the earth with formidable blows, uprooting the boulders in its mad flight.

The wretched porter, stretched out at full length at the foot of a rock, is the terrified witness of the catastrophe.[9] Soon the tired mountain returns to its sleep. But 5,000 feet lower down, at the Pedriola Alp, a cloud of fine snow envelops the cattle.[10] Amused, the herdsmen smile.[11]

* * *

Ferdinand Imseng is buried at Macugnaga.[12] On his grave a cross, standing upon a broad pedestal of Monte Rosa granite, bears this epitaph:

A

FERDINAND

IMSENG

BON GUIDE ET

HONNETE HOMME

1881

THE BLAST OF AN AVALANCHE

For the scene of the Imseng-Marinelli-Pedranzini tragedy, see Plate 14.

[1] Cf. Charles Gos, *Alpinisme Anecdotique* (*op. cit.*).

[2] This caravan comprised the alpinists Richard and William Pendlebury and the Rev. Charles Taylor, with the guides Ferdinand Imseng, Gabriel Spechtenhauser and Giovanni Oberto, 22nd July, 1872.

[3] The uncle of the great guide of the same name who died on the Weisshorn in 1933.

[4] Robert von Lendenfeld, with the guides C. Imseng and Josef Knubel (one of the uncles of the guide Josef Knubel, living to-day at St. Niklaus).

[5] Cf. *Rivista Mensile del C.A.I.*, 1881.

[6] Among Ferdinand Imseng's conquests should be mentioned the ascent of the Matterhorn by the Tiefenmatten face (Zmutt) with W. Penhall and Louis Zurbrüggen, on the same day as A. F. Mummery's ascent with three guides of the Zmutt arête (cf. Chapter 13, Part II); the Zinal-Rothorn by the Mountet face; the Dom by the Domjoch; Monte Rosa by the Grenz Glacier; the Dent d'Hérens by the north-western arête; etc.

[7] For reasons of topography and toponomy, the name *Jägerrücken*, by which this rock buttress used to be known, has been given to another spot on this face; doubtless there are major topographical reasons for the change, but the result has been to falsify all the bibliography concerning the Macugnaga wall, if one is not warned of these cadastral fancies.

[8] To perpetuate the name of Damiano Marinelli in this locality the Italian Alpine Club in 1885 erected a hut on the north side (left bank) of the famous couloir, at a height of about 10,150 feet. The hut, the crest on which it is built and the couloir itself, all bear the name of this pioneer of Italian alpinism. As to Ferdinand Imseng, the conqueror of this formidable wall, his memory is more modestly recalled by the rock buttress which borders the couloir on the south (right bank), where death overtook him. It is called *Imsengrücken*.

[9] The porter reached Macugnaga terrified and gave news of the disaster. Only three days later, the weather having deteriorated in the meantime, did the search party recover the bodies on the Monta Rosa Glacier.

[10] The *Echo des Alpes*, 1880–81, gave the following details:
"The victims were not recovered until the third day. Marinelli's body was cut to pieces, the head was shattered and he was hardly recognisable.
"Damiano Marinelli, member of the Florence section of the C.A.I., came from Albano, near Rome . . . kindliness and energy showed in his amiable features in charming unity. He was strong and good, a knight without fear and without reproach, an excellent brother and a faithful friend, as prompt to comfort the unfortunate as to help with advice and encouragement the aspirants to the title of perfect alpinist. He was one of the most unsullied figures of the C.A.I."

[11] I take the liberty of recalling here a personal reminiscence. During a round of conferences in Italy in 1935, and having spoken in Rome, I had the signal privilege of being received in private audience by the Holy Father, Pius XI, who, as we know, had been a passionate alpinist in his youth, when he was only the Abbé Achille Ratti. The difficult conquest of the Macugnaga wall and the first traverse of the Grenzsattel (or Colle Zumstein, *c.* 14,600 feet), with Luigi Grasselli and the guides Joseph Gadin and A. Proment (July 1889), figure amongst his great climbs. In unforgettable terms the Holy Father told me about his night in a bivouac on the Monte Rosa arête (July 30th), which his party had reached rather late after traversing terrible slopes of ice. At his feet, in the shadows and under the stars, the first incurved lines of the couloir could be seen . . . After an interview which lasted an hour, the Holy Father, as he was about to dismiss me, moved towards one of the shelves of his bureau. He moved aside some holy objects and said to me simply: "Look!" I looked, and with surprise I saw, supported by a book, a little photograph of a stone refuge built against a rock. In the background the slanting whiteness of the couloir split the slope. "The Marinelli hut!" I cried. "The Marinelli hut," the Pope agreed. "One of my first nights in the heights, and one of my dearest, one of my most beautiful memories . . ."

I take this opportunity to clear up an error made by all the biographers of Pius XI. The Holy Father did not make the first ascent of Monta Rosa by the Macugnaga versant; he made the seventh. The ascents succeeded one another in the following order:

First ascent: Richard and William Pendlebury and the Rev. Charles Taylor, with the guides Ferdinand Imseng, Gabriel Spechtenhauser and Giovanni Oberto (23rd July, 1872).

Second ascent: Robert von Lendenfeld, with the guides Clemens Imseng and Josef Knubel and a porter (10th August, 1880).

Third ascent: Prof. Karl Schulz, with the guides Alexander Burgener and Clemens Perren (14th August, 1883).

Fourth ascent: Drs. Emil and Otto Zsigmondy and Ludwig Purtscheller, without guide (14th August, 1884).

Fifth ascent: Julius Prochaska, with the guides Matthias Zurbrüggen and Luigi Bonnetti (7th August, 1886).

Sixth ascent: Dr. Julius Kugy, with the guides Luigi Bonnetti and Josef-Marie Lochmatter (13th August, 1886).

Seventh ascent: The Abbé Achille Ratti and Prof. Luigi Grasselli, with the guides Josef Gadin and Alexis Proment (31st July, 1889). The abbé's party bivouacked on the arête between the summit of the Dufourspitz and the Grenzsattel, at about 14,760 feet. On the following day they made the traverse (the first) of the Grenzsattel (or Colle Zumstein, *c.* 14,600 feet) and descended to Zermatt.

[12] Capt. Farrar has devoted a most interesting study to Ferdinand Imseng, based on the celebrated guide's *Führerbuch.* Imseng was only twenty-seven years old when he led the English party to victory on the Macugnaga wall of Monte Rosa in 1872. The duration of the ascent was only twenty-one hours. Almost all the great English climbers employed him, including Tuckett, Kennedy and Passingham. Two particularly interesting testimonials have their place here, taken from Imseng's *Führerbuch:*

Ferdinand Imseng acted as chief guide to the Revd. C. Taylor, my brother and myself in the first ascent of Monte Rosa from Macugnaga, and in the descent from the summit to the Riffel Hotel. We had every reason to be satisfied especially with the judgement he displayed in the selection of what, in the state of the snow on the day, was probably the only moderately safe passage through the séracs and over the slopes of soft snow. Two days later Ferdinand Imseng acted as our assistant guide from Zermatt up the Matterhorn and down to Breuil. He also accompanied us (Mr. Taylor and myself) from Breuil to Zermatt over the Col Théodule.

W. M. Pendlebury,
Zermatt, 27th July, 1872.

The second of these testimonials is that written by William Penhall after the first ascent of the Matterhorn by the Tiefenmatten face:

Ferdinand Imseng acted as my leading guide in the first ascent of the Matterhorn from the Tiefenmatten glacier. He showed great judgement and intelligence in the choice of the route.

On the 6th Sep. he was my guide in the first ascent of the Nadelhorn. He is the best rock climber and the most agreeable guide to travel with that I know.

(Signed) Wm. Penhall, A.C.,
Zermatt, 7th September, 1879.

(Cf. *Alpine Journal,* Vol. XXX, 1916.)

CHAPTER THIRTEEN

MYSTERIOUS DISASTERS

I. The Deaths at the Aiguille Blanche
Professor F. M. Balfour and the guide Johann Petrus (July 1882)

IN his Cambridge laboratory the young scientist Francis Mait-land Balfour of Trinity College, Professor of Embryology, dreams of the mountains. Bent over his microscope, this young man whom Darwin has called the "English Cuvier" is unable to drive from his mind the obsessing vision of glaciers and peaks. He rises and walks to the window, gives an absent glance to the fields, and reads, for the third time since he received it not long ago, a letter written on rough squared paper. The writing is in large, childish, gothic characters, and the first line reads: *Eisten, Saasthal, Wallis, Schweiz*. It is from the guide Johann Petrus, who, from his distant alpine village, informs Mr. Balfour that he will expect him at Chamonix on the agreed date, but that his brother-in-law, Peter Knubel, is unfortunately not free; Knubel already has another engagement and in any case will not be able to join them for the first eight days at least. After that something might be arranged.

Professor F. M. Balfour is only in his third mountaineering season. He has been a devotee from the start, and he has found in Johann Petrus an admirable teacher and a friend. Relieved of the innumerable tiny troubles that hamper even the smallest party, so many things to weigh it down and slow its pace, the Balfour party forms the ideal outfit to bag the peaks. In the previous year, 1881, they had forestalled Mummery at the Grépon by fifteen days, and climbed the southern summit (Pointe Balfour), believing that they had reached the highest point of that famous aiguille.[1] As just consecration of his exploits Balfour has just been elected to membership of the Alpine Club.

Johann Petrus is proud of his pupil. For that reason, when the two climbers leave Montenvers on the morning of the 14th July, 1882, the guide climbs behind his employer, and watches him, almost moved, as he skilfully cuts the steps with one hand, some-times the right, sometimes the left, among the séracs of the Glacier du Géant. A hard apprenticeship, but Balfour's readaptation to the mountains will be the sooner ended.

Comfortably stretched out at the Col du Géant, with their hats shading their eyes, the master and his pupil happily admire the magnificent view spread before them. From the other side of the abyss where the Brenva Glacier lies like a slab of monumental marble, the Italian Mont Blanc (eastern face) rises in all its solemn majesty. The brilliant light shines upon it with a bluish tinge. It emerges from a circle of summits hollowed out into abrupt escarpments, and from its snow-covered, mitre-shaped peak, lost in regal isolation, a splendid arête runs off towards the east. This backbone, the longest and most beautiful in all the Alps, with its foot in the pastures at about 4,500 feet and its head in the summit of Mont Blanc at 15,771 feet, throws up a range of mighty summits. Its beginning in the summit snow is easy. Then, after its first surge upward (the Mont-Blanc de Courmayeur) it plunges smoothly but steeply, fashions a small snowy col, rises again, levels momen-tarily, stretches upward (the Aiguille Blanche de Péteret), resumes its accelerated fall, breaks up, bristles into a sheaf of slender aiguilles (les Dames Anglaises), falls, then climbs yet again, assumes the shape of a dark steeple (the Aiguille Noire de Péteret), then sinks to the valley, the Val Veni, close to Cour-mayeur, and there is lost. As the crow flies, this series of rises and falls must total something over three miles, but in reality it must be double that length. The Aiguille Blanche de Péteret (13,507 feet), sometimes known also by the lovely name of the Aiguille de la Belle Étoile, rises halfway between the savage spear of the Aiguille Noire and the high and noble summit of Mont Blanc. It is beautifully carved in hard granite and opal ice. Between its two summits, one of snow and the other of rock, is stretched a white and narrow arête of snow, slightly incurved like a tightrope under the dancer's weight. Then a dark gulf, a great wide gulf, opens its terrifying cliffs towards the Dames Anglaises. Alternately rugged and graceful in their modelling, its icy flanks retain the brightness of the day, and like the Matterhorn it arouses in the beholder a feverish exaltation of spirit.

"What a beautiful mountain, Johann!" Balfour observes, emerging from his contemplation.

"Very beautiful indeed, Mr. Balfour," Johann replies.

"Do you know if Emile Rey has begun again his attempts to climb it?"

"I couldn't say, sir; but all I know is that until now he has been disappointed. The Aiguille Blanche de Péteret is still virgin."

They are both silent awhile. Then the guide, looking fixedly at the mountain, concludes: "And so it will remain for a long time."

This peremptory conclusion only serves to bring to the lips of the young professor of embryology words which betray the thoughts spontaneously and tumultuously developed in his mind:

"You think so? Suppose we climb it ourselves!"

"Ourselves?"

"Yes, ourselves! . . . Why not?"

"But, sir," Johann protests, "how could we? Of course, if Peter Knubel were here, I wouldn't say . . . well, we could then see, but like this . . ."

"Very well! We will take a second guide at Courmayeur. Emile Rey, perhaps, will be pleased to come with us."

"Oh! That would be a different matter, certainly. But I am not at all certain that it would come off. Melchior Anderegg, when he was there in '65, on the day of the first ascent of Mont Blanc by the Brenva route with Mr. Moore—he examined this mountain closely, so he told me, and he thinks it's inaccessible."

"Perhaps Melchior was right—as regards this side, what with those ice precipices and those cliffs. . . . But what about the other side?"

* * *

In the evening of July the 16th Balfour and his guide arrive at the Hôtel Royale in Courmayeur. During the day they have ascended the Grandes Jorasses, an arduous climb which completes the apprenticeship of the Col du Géant. The young Englishman, yesterday still a little strange, his mind still a little preoccupied with the affairs of his Cambridge laboratory, is to-day another man. These few days have transformed him. His struggles amid the greenish ice and rust-coloured rocks, in the wind and under bombardments of stones, all this intimacy with the peaks, with infinite space and with silence—all this fills his soul with a strange music. A resolute eagerness carries him away. The high mountains, like faith, have rich powers. But the dazzling desires which they raise in the hearts of men often vanish, and Balfour has not yet experienced this uncertainty.

The next day, he meets in the hall of the hotel one of his friends of the Alpine Club, Mr. Carus D. Cunningham, a distinguished climber.[2] Emile Rey is his guide. They have just made the first ascent of the Aiguille de Talèfre from the Italian side. Emile Rey is the greatest guide in Courmayeur, and one of the finest climbers of his generation. Among his numerous "firsts" the most famous is the Aiguille Noire de Péteret (12,372 feet). Five years previously, in 1877, he guided Byron's grandson, Lord Wentworth, to its summit. Nor is the Aiguille Blanche de Péteret altogether unknown to him.[3] He has been examining it for a long time, has made attempts on it, but until now his efforts have failed. Its menacing grandeur, far from discouraging him, still attracts him, even as it attracts Balfour, so urgently seduced by its beauty. Balfour at once goes straight to the point.

"Shall we try it together, Emile?"

"But, Mr. Balfour," Emile expostulates, "it is impossible. I'm not free. You should know that I'm travelling just now with Mr. Cunningham."

Balfour brushes the protest aside: "It goes without saying that you will come too, Cunningham. What do you think?"

"Well, my dear fellow," says Cunningham, "your suggestion is terribly tempting. We had other plans, of course—Les Périades—the Calotte de Rochfort—but I'd willingly abandon them for the Blanche de Péteret. What do you think, Emile?"

Emile's manner is short, even a little stiff: "It shall be as you wish, Monsieur."

Cunningham is astonished. "Why this sudden ill-humour, Emile? Aren't you tempted? For my own part, I think this Aiguille . . ."

"I repeat, Mr. Cunningham, that it's for you to decide. I am only your guide."

"That is understood, but it isn't the question. What's upsetting you? If we should succeed, this victory . . ."

"Listen to me, Monsieur," Emile breaks in. "*We shall not succeed.*"

Surprised, the two climbers exclaim, "We won't succeed? And why not? What are you trying to say?"

"Monsieur, it is enough to look at the sky. The snow will be in very bad condition. The mountain will be dangerous."

"But, good God!" Balfour retorts, "that can change. We shan't be there this afternoon."

Cunningham is silent. He knows his guide's cool daring and experience. For him Emile's judgment is without question. If Emile declares that they cannot succeed because the snow is in a bad condition and the mountain dangerous, then they will not succeed. Feeling himself supported by his employer's silence, the guide continues urgently:

"I do not believe, Mr. Balfour, that it can change for some days. These days are scorching. The snow melts even at 13,000 feet. The other day, at the Talèfre, and at the Jorasses too, the avalanches were sliding off like spilt milk. They could be avoided on the Blanche, its true . . . But listen! On my last attempt it took me more than five hours to descend the eight or nine hundred feet of rock at the bottom of the couloir. I almost left my skin there! Besides, the couloir must itself be full of ice and snow just now. No, Mr. Cunningham! You take my advice: don't go there, at any rate not just yet."[4]

But Balfour is not convinced. So, on the morning of the 18th, he leaves Courmayeur with Johann Petrus and a porter for the Aiguille Blanche de Péteret.[5] The party ascends the Val Veni. It is a lovely day, all blue and gold. Optimism goes with them. They sustain their hopes by recalling their other victorious campaigns, but Emile's forthright warnings slightly darken their resolution. They have too much friendship, esteem and loyal admiration for this celebrated guide even for a moment to scoff at him. What he has said is incontestably true. But in the mountains things can change so quickly.

Balfour seeks Johann's support. "The Aiguille Blanche should be in splendid condition to-day, don't you think, Johann?"

"Yes, of course, Mr. Balfour. But we'll see better to-morrow," the guide concludes with a laugh.[6]

So here they are on the Alp de Fresnay. From the chalet roof the bluish smoke curls upwards. Some pigs, wallowing in the mire, grunt at their approach. The sound of cow-bells can be heard rising from a grassy fold. An old black cross is silhouetted against the sky. The party stops and the master cheesemaker comes out for a gossip. He does not climb the mountains himself, but he cannot forget his one and only experience of a glacier.

"Do you remember when the English gentleman fell into the crevasse on the Brouillard. It isn't so long ago. Six or eight years, perhaps. He had two Swiss guides, and one of them died with him. Ah, well! I went up with the rescue party. I was there when they took them out of the crevasse."

This recollection of the Marshall–Fischer–Almer accident,[7] which happened in this locality in 1874 does not affect the morale of the party in the least. Such things can happen to others; never to oneself. In the evening, after a march over steep grass and rock, the climbers drop their packs at the foot of a stony combe. They are going to bivouac there on those still warmish slabs. To the right is the rock buttress indicated by Emile Rey, and to the left is the Aiguille du Châtelet; between the two lies the rocky crest that leads to the Col de l'Innominata, and from there to the Glacier de Fresnay. Very high above them, the summit of the Aiguille Blanche lifts its snowy arête like a slender, polished wave. Mont Blanc, directly above it, envelops the aiguille in its immense shadow. Lower down, its slopes are already lost in depths dissolving in the violet light of evening.

A fire is soon blazing. The porter lays out the blankets. And the sweet peace of the stars ensues.

*   *   *

The porter was the last man to see the young scientist, Francis Maitland Balfour of Cambridge and his guide, Johann Petrus of Eisten, near Saas, alive. Towards two in the morning Petrus revived the fire and boiled water for their chocolate. A little later the climbers got themselves ready and left by lantern-light, disappearing into the darkness. At the first light of dawn the porter bundled the blankets, tied the pot to his pack, and went down into the valley.

At Courmayeur they expected the party's return on the evening of the following day, or, at the latest, on Thursday the 20th in the afternoon. The climb is not only very dangerous, but, having never been done before, the men would find themselves at grips with unforeseen obstacles which would slow up their progress considerably and make them hesitate over their route. So it was by no means impossible that they would spend a second night on the mountain.

But on Wednesday nothing had been seen of their return, nor, to the anxiety of everyone (for the new attempt on the Aiguille Blanche had aroused the deepest feelings in the village), on the Thursday evening either. In such cases there is nothing more human than to search for extenuating circumstances before believing the worst. In this particular instance the alternatives were these: either Balfour and his guide had succeeded in their climb and (as suggested by Emile Rey) "they have gone on to Mont Blanc by Mr. Eccles' route and have descended to Chamonix," or else, having exhausted their provisions and wishing to continue their efforts, they had gone to replenish their supplies at the Cantine de la Visaille, on the other side of the valley, opposite the Alp de Fresnay. In either case they could not return before Saturday. Nevertheless, every heart was overwhelmed with anguish.

To solve the mystery, M. Bertolini, the proprietor of the Hotel Royale, despatched a messenger on Saturday morning to the Cantine de la Visaille, and simultaneously telegraphed to Chamonix. Some hours later both replies reached Courmayeur, and they were both in the negative. At la Visaille nothing was known, and at Chamonix no party had been reported as having traversed Mont Blanc by the Aiguille Blanche de Péteret. Moreover, Balfour and Petrus would not have passed unnoticed at Chamonix, for their victory on the Grépon in the previous year had made them popular at the Priory. So from that moment no new hypothesis was possible, no equivocation. They were face to face with misfortune. A single hope remained: that of finding the men still alive.

A rescue party under the orders of Emile Rey was organised at once; an English clergyman went with it, the Rev. H. Verschoyle. The same evening (Saturday) they rested at the site of Balfour's bivouac, where they found the provisions left for his return. And early on Sunday morning (August 23rd) they arrived at the Fresnay moraine, whence the view over the glacier and the Aiguilles de Péteret is disclosed in all its magnificence. Above the fearfully enclosed and crevassed glacier the complicated wall of the aiguilles rose heavily against a pale sky. It had snowed the day before and the high crests were finely sprinkled.

This forlorn and greyish glacier is strangled towards its top by a contraction of the rock walls forming its two banks. In order to pass this narrow gullet—a precipice of livid ice, split into yawning gaps and encumbered by chaotic séracs—one has to climb some very difficult *rochers moutonnés* which serve as a base for the Aiguille Blanche. Further on one reaches the upper névés of the Fresnay glacier, a little below the Col de Péteret. These *rochers moutonnés* are cut into two by a wide couloir, filled with ice and snow, which vanishes into the top of the wall. Tempting at first, it ends in a hopeless impasse. Emile Rey knew this better than anyone, for it was there that his own attempts had failed.[8] It was down there, therefore, towards the mouth of the couloir that he turned his eyes at once.

His features contracted immediately. He could see two black objects at the foot of the couloir which could not be stones. Their shape was impossible to mistake. The rescue party hurried along, crossing the glacier by a convenient route. The bodies were already frozen, partly covered by fresh snow and still roped together. There were no signs of an avalanche. One of the climbers must have lost his footing on the glazed surface and dragged his comrade down. They had fallen while descending. Their tracks could be seen in the snow towards the summit of the couloir. Up there they had been forced to surrender, like Emile Rey before them, repulsed by the hostile walls and by the ice, and to undertake a desperate descent. But judging by their relatively light injuries, apart from the fatal fracture of their skulls, it was possible to infer that the accident had taken place at the bottom of the couloir. Their clothes were scarcely torn, their hands were injured only superficially, as if, sliding on their backs, the victims had not been able to turn over or attempt to recover. The large side nails of Balfour's right boot-heel were missing on one side, suggesting that they had given way to a sudden and violent strain. Finally, a rappel rope had been abandoned in the rocks. It was believed that this rope had perhaps broken, having been worn through by friction against the stone. A slip on the ice, or a rope worn through by the rocks, the cause will never be known.[9] There were no witnesses to this mysterious tragedy, not even the yellow-billed choughs, the familiar spirits of the high rocks.[10]

For the scene of the Balfour tragedy, see Plate 15 (also Plates 8 and 9).

[1] At this epoch the Grépon and the Grands Charmoz were regarded as one group, designated at Chamonix the "Aiguilles des Grands Charmoz." On the 15th July, 1880, the Mummery party (A. F. Mummery with the guides Alexander Burgener and Benedikt Venetz) made the first ascent of the northern summit of the Aiguilles des Grands Charmoz (11,302 feet), present summit of the Grands Charmoz. But the southern summit (to-day the Grépon), consisting of two teeth of rock of almost equal height, passed for the highest. On the 19th July, 1881, the Balfour party (Francis Maitland and his brother Gerard William, with the guides Peter Knubel and Johann Petrus) set out to climb it. On the Glacier des Nantillons the party hesitated, undecided whether to ascend the couloir as far as the gap (the present Col Charmoz-Grépon) and afterwards follow the northern arête (to-day the classic Mummery Route) or, on the other hand, to traverse the Col des Nantillons in order to climb the south-east wall. In the end it was the latter solution which prevailed, especially because the altitude of the rock tooth farthest south (the Pointe Balfour) seemed to them to exceed that of its neighbour (the real summit of the Grépon) from which it is separated by a gap now known as the Brêche Balfour. The climbers reached the Col des Nantillons, traversed the C.P. (point reached earlier by the guides J. E. Charlot and Prosper Payot) and, after a hard climb, ascended the southernmost summit of the Aiguilles des Grands Charmoz, which they forthwith baptised Pointe Balfour. Nevertheless, they ascertained that the summit of the neighbouring tooth (the real summit of the Grépon) surpassed them by a few feet; they then strove to construct a cairn whose height would bring them to the level of their rival. But stones were lacking, and they abandoned their amusing project and descended. (*Alpine Journal*, Vol. X, 1880-82.)

Thus it was that, fifteen days before Mummery, the Balfour brothers set out to conquer the Grépon and, by a regrettable error of judgement, mistook the true summit. Similarly they preceded by four years the well-known French climber, Henri Dunod, who, with the guides François and Gaspard Simond and Auguste Tairraz, conquered the Grépon by the south-eastern face on the 2nd September, 1885. Dunod, in fact, except for the seventeen metres (approx. 56 feet) of chimney which bears his name, only followed the Balfour's route. It can be taken for certain that if the Balfours had decided to take the northern arête, as they had at first intended, rather than climb the south-eastern wall, they would on that day have made the first ascent of the Grépon. Their guides were not men to retreat.

In Peter Knubel's *Führerbuch* this brief commentary on the climb may be read:

Peter Knubel and Johann Petrus have again accompanied us as guides this year, in the following expeditions:

Col du Géant to Courmayeur;
Aiguille du Midi and down the Col du Midi to Chamonix;
Col de Telèfre to Courmayeur;
Over Mont Blanc from Courmayeur by the Aiguilles Grises;
The highest peak of the Aiguilles des Charmoz (first ascent ever made);
Jungfrau;
Finsteraarhorn.

We can fully confirm what we said of Knubel last year. We are thoroughly satisfied with him in every single respect. Both as guide and servant he leaves nothing to be desired.

This *führerbuch* is to be found in the library of the Alpine Club in London.

Shortly after the accident to his brother, Gerald W. Balfour tendered his resignation to the Alpine Club. Later elevated to the peerage (the second Earl of Balfour) and a distinguished statesman, he died in 1945.

[2] Author, in collaboration with Capt. Abney, of the famous book *The Pioneers of the Alps*, 1888.

[3] See Chapter 19.

[4] Besides his attempts on the Aiguille Blanche by this couloir, Emile Rey had traversed it in its lower part on the occasion of his variant to Mont Blanc by the Péteret arête, on the 11th to 13th August, 1880, with Georg Gruber and the guide Pierre Revel.

[5] Cf. *Alpine Journal*, Vol. XI, 1882-84.

[6] It is interesting to recall that Johann Petrus was one of the Mummery party on the occasion of its conquest of the Matterhorn by the Zmutt arête with the guides Alexander Burgener and Augustin Gentinette, 3rd September, 1879.

[7] See Chapter 9.

[8] Emile Rey succeeded, on the 31st July, 1885, in making the first ascent of the Aiguille Blanche de Péteret by the Glacier de Fresnay and the Col de Péteret, with Mr. H. Seymour King and the guides Ambros Supersaxo and Aloys Anthamatten. The first ascent by the Fresnay side was made on the 16th August, 1909, by Mr. H. O. Jones, with the guides Laurent and Alexis Croux, father and son. They followed the rock arête which bounds the left bank of the couloir where Mr. F. M. Balfour died.

[9] In England the tragic end of this young Professor, Francis Maitland Balfour, produced a veritable state of stupefaction. Queen Victoria herself caused the Prime Minister, Mr. Gladstone, to be asked if she could not intervene to prevent so many mountain tragedies involving British citizens. At Cambridge especially, no one ever remembers a like emotion at the death of a member of the University. (In this connection, see note 2 to Part III of this chapter.)

[10] In August 1912 the celebrated climber and author, Geoffrey Winthrop Young, (one-time President of the Alpine Club), accompanied by his faithful Josef Knubel, while seeking a passage among the séracs of the Glacier de Fresney with the following day's expedition in view, found the debris of an old ladder. According to the Courmayeur guides, it must certainly have been the remains of the ladder which had served the rescue party on the occasion of the Balfour accident. (*Alpine Journal*, Vol. XXVII, 1913.)

II. The Deaths on the Wetterhorn

William Penhall and the guide Andreas Maurer (August 1882)

MR. WILLIAM PENHALL, a student of medicine and one of the younger stars of the Alpine Club, was killed on the Wetterhorn at the age of twenty-four, together with his guide, Andreas Maurer, of Meiringen. Penhall saw the Alps for the first time when still at college, and he was at once captivated by their splendour and by their alluring dangers. It came upon him in a flash, and he was overcome by the desire to climb them. His impetuous desires were quickly realised and his conquests soon classed him among the élite.[1] Three new ascents in particular made his name illustrious in climbing circles and among the inhabitants of the valleys: in 1878 the Zinal Rothorn (13,855 feet) from the west, and the Dom (14,942 feet) by the Domjoch; in 1879 the Matterhorn by the Tiefenmatten-Zmutt side, though Mummery and his guides reached the summit by way of the arête a few hours before him.

Coming straight from England, Penhall joined his friend, Mr. F. J. Church, at Grindelwald on the 1st August, 1882.[2] To accom-

pany them in their wanderings across the Bernese Alps *en route* for
Zermatt, they had chosen two famous guides, Andreas Maurer and
Rudolf Kaufmann.

The first of August is the day of the Swiss National Fête. In the
evening the village was filled with merriment; fires were lit on the
tops of the hills despite the clouds which enveloped the heights;
patriotic songs were sung to the accompaniment of accordions.
Delighted with the festival, the two young Englishmen participated, sauntering in the lanes where the lanterns were swinging,
talking with their guides. In the immensity of the night the barrier
of high peaks could be seen as massive silhouettes truncated by
cloud. Penhall was quickly recaptured by this mountain atmosphere. He was eager to leave for the heights as soon as possible,
to feel the rough rocks under his feet, to breathe again the wind
that is keen with the savour of snow.

As a beginning he therefore suggested to Maurer that they
climb the Wetterhorn by the classic route, direct from Grindelwald, but without a sleep on the way. They might start the next
night. Meanwhile Church and Kaufmann might climb slowly to the
Schwarzegg hut, where they would all meet in the evening, and on
the following day they could cross the Finsteraarjoch together.
Maurer was pleased with the plan and Church agreed to it.

Next day it could be seen that snow had fallen quite low. The
weather improved, but this inopportune snow would have to melt
quickly before it could freeze, and for a day or two the summits
would be dangerous. Mr. Church decided to wait at Grindelwald.

On Thursday, August 3rd, half an hour after midnight, Penhall
and Andreas Maurer passed out of the Bear Hotel. As he crossed
the threshold, Maurer made an unusual gesture. He took his pipe
from his pocket, retraced his steps and, holding the pipe out to
Emile Boss, the hotelier, he said:

"Take it! I shall probably never ask for it back."

And he went out. Thus, obedient to some obscure presentiment,
the reflex of a subconscious whose antennae had sensed the direction of his fate, the good guide bowed to his sentence and offered
his pipe to his friend with prophetic words of whose real meaning
he was not fully aware.

The night was very black, broken by swirling gusts of lukewarm
wind. Only for a while can we in our thoughts follow Penhall and
his companion along the tracks over the fields and through the

woods, then over the stony slopes of the moraine. It was the first time they had travelled together. The daring and the charm of the young Englishman were pleasing to the Oberland guide. Penhall, moreover, had chosen his man well, and he was not unaware of Maurer's fine qualities. At the Alpine Club in London one is better informed than anywhere else about the virtues and faults of the guides; the brief recitals of striking adventures or heroic failures have many times sung the praises of these rugged and loyal friends of the distant mountains. Thus it is easy, without exaggeration, to imagine the words that were exchanged in this warm night between Andreas Maurer the guide and William Penhall his employer.

They recalled their great "firsts," they spoke of their mutual friends—Middlemore, Whymper, Kennedy, Mummery—and of the guides they both had known. They remembered Ferdinand Imseng, Penhall's guide on the Matterhorn from Zmutt, who died with Marinelli on the Macugnaga wall of Monte Rosa just a year ago,[3] and poor Johann Petrus, who was killed with Balfour on the Blanche de Péteret[4]—he too was one of the "firsts" of Zmutt, though he was in Mummery's party.

"How royally you prepared the way for Mr. Mummery by cutting those steps in the whole of that arête of snow the day before! Alexander Burgener couldn't help laughing as he put his feet into your fine big steps!" Maurer laughs heartily.

"Poor Imseng!" Penhall replied with a sigh. "That was the heaviest blow of my life. For two years I had been thinking about that climb and I was convinced that it was feasible, in spite of Whymper's pessimism, which was shared by the Zermatt guides. But Imseng leapt with joy at the idea. We had explored the Zmutt and Tiefenmatten base of the Matterhorn for a long time. We had even climbed the Zmutt arête as far as the third gendarme, cutting steps in the crest of ice. Nobody had ever been there before us.[5] But the weather broke up. We bivouacked on a stone in the middle of the arête, firmly hoping we could resume the climb the next day. But the filthy weather continued in the morning, so we had to resign ourselves to returning to Zermatt. On the way we met Mummery and Burgener and their men. The weather got more and more gloomy. I dined at Zermatt, and in the evening the sky cleared up; so we left again at ten o'clock. We plodded on all night, only to discover on reaching the Tiefenmatten Glacier that

Burgener's party had already left their bivouac. And our tracks were in the ice! With their help they would quickly be on top. So, in order to shorten the route and get in front of them, Ferdinand decided that he would climb to the right. We then took to a frightful couloir which we had avoided some days earlier, but we were beaten all the same. 'Thanks to our tracks! . . . Thanks to our tracks! . . . Ah! if I had only known!' poor Imseng repeated endlessly. He was pitiful, I can assure you."[6]

"He was quite right: thanks to your tracks! Alexander Burgener himself said so," said Maurer, who well knew what daring and endurance such expeditions involve.

"How about your Aiguille Verte by the Argentière side: that was also a very difficult climb, wasn't it?" the Englishman asked.

"Yes, Mr. Penhall. A couloir less dangerous than yours undoubtedly, but a cursed couloir all the same, and all ice. But not so tough as that expedition with Emile Rey to the Aiguille du Plan by the north face."

"What a fearful night that was! Why, you even had to sing to keep up your employer's spirits!"

"Ah! you know all about that, do you?" exclaimed the guide with a happy laugh.[7]

"Yes, Andreas, I know all about it. Mr. Oakley Maund told me. It's a wonderful story. . . . You were very tactful. But, for Heaven's sake, how were you able to stick it?"

"Oh! it was not so bad." Maurer's modesty was startling. He replied evasively: "Emile Rey is a fine guide, you know. At six in the morning the sun warmed us up and we were able to begin the descent."[8]

Thus contact was made. These reminiscences of adventures and difficult climbs threw a mystic bridge between the minds of the two men. Now they knew one another as if at 13,000 feet, in the wind and the snow, or under summit skies of profound blue, unforgettable bonds had been forged between them. They had a mutual esteem for one another. The pride of climbing together excited them both. They were happy to be alive.

It was in this state of contentment that they reached the last névés on the moraine. A cold wind now blew. In the pale dawn Maurer extinguished the lantern, as together they attacked the Upper Grindelwald Glacier.

* * *

At Grindelwald they expected to see the climbers return in the afternoon of the same day. But at nightfall neither had been seen. Anxiety seized the minds of those who waited, the more so because both climbers were known for their speed. Further, the sky had been overcast the whole day; the weather had not been exactly bad, but long tangles of cloud had obscured the summits, giving the impression that snow was falling on the higher places. Down below it had been sultry.

It was human for those who waited to delay with conjectures the moment when they must realise that the worst may have happened.

"They may have gone down into Rosenlaui; who can tell?" suggested one charitable soul. "With fellows like that anything is possible."

But a native of Meiringen, close to Maurer's own home, who was sent at eight-thirty in the evening to the Rosenlaui hotel, returned to Grindelwald at four-thirty in the morning. "They don't know a thing over there," he said.

"Nothing? This is awful! But that doesn't mean that all is lost. Perhaps they've been caught by the mist and forced to bivouac. Perhaps they've run out of provisions; we'd better take them some."

So, two hours after the messenger's return from Rosenlaui, a party—not exactly a rescue party, but one made up, shall we say, of anxious friends—left in search of the missing men. This little company comprised the guides Ulrich and Rudolf Kaufmann, Kaspar Maurer, Peter Baumann and Johann Tännler, and an English doctor on holiday in Grindelwald, Dr. Howard Barrett. By way of the Milchbachloch and the Upper Glacier they followed the route taken by Penhall and Maurer. To clear their consciences, they explored the crevasses in passing and examined the snowbridges. In vain. They began, therefore, to throw off some of the anguish that had weighed upon their hearts; but on entering the Gleckstein hut, the first objects they saw were Maurer's knapsack, some of their provisions on a corner of the table and a few other articles belonging to the missing men. Decidedly, this looked bad.

Dr. Barrett had taken the precaution to bring with him a powerful spy-glass, and accompanied by Johann Tännler he installed himself some thirty yards from the hut, and from that observation post he examined the Wetterhorn. Tännler pointed out the presumed route of ascent, but in fact the tracks of the two climbers could be seen in the snow. The slender line of footprints rose steadily, then made a hook to the right, and finally entered a couloir of snow overlooked by a rock wall known as the Willsgrat. The tracks could be seen to reach some rock and disappear,[1] but they were to be seen again, quite clearly, leaving the north bank of the Krinn couloir, describing a right angle to the south and boldly swerving back again into the couloir, where the snow seemed terribly steep—to the mind's eye, almost vertical. Then came something which made the doctor rub his eyes. He wiped the lens and peered again with strained attention, and then in a tense voice, passing the instrument to his guide, he said:

"Look, Tännler. The tracks seem to vanish into an avalanche, don't they? And I can't see them on the other side."

Tännler looked, and his verdict was immediate.

"Yes, they do, sir; you are right. The tracks have been effaced by an avalanche."

He lowered the instrument in silence. Then Barrett ventured: "Perhaps they turned about in their tracks?"

"If they had turned around, sir, they would be in Grindelwald, and we should not be here."

Dr. Barrett took up his spy-glass again. A large furrow tore the couloir throughout its length, and all around the surface was smoothed and beaten down; in the vicinity of the track, as if projected under pressure through a narrow channel higher up, rocks and blocks of ice were scattered about. The mountain itself thus loudly proclaimed the news of the tragedy.

While Rudolf Kaufmann hurried down to Grindelwald to raise the alarm and to organise help, Dr. Barrett and his guides reached the heights. The day was very warm. The avalanches were frequent, raising the echoes with their thunder. As there was no point in following the tracks of the missing men, the party left them and manœuvred diagonally towards the foot of the couloir. After some hours of exhausting and dangerous progress, they arrived at the edge of an immense basin of snow. Very high above them the gash plunged its head into the Willsgrat, while below them the track of the avalanche buried itself in an accumulation of great masses of snow, some twisted into spirals like monstrous shells, others crushed and broken: the debris of a fallen peak.

Carried down by this glistening tide, two bodies lay quietly on a beach of lonely névés. They were close together, the guide and his traveller, like two men sleeping on the grass. They were almost touching; their clothes were rumpled, but hardly torn, and the rope was twisted between them. They must have been surprised by the avalanche and snatched away; but instead of sinking, the current had brought them to the surface. Death had struck them while crossing a reef of rock which cut the couloir in two, and the flood had carried them away like wrecks. It could be seen at close quarters that Maurer's attitude was that of a fighter: an attitude of combat, with arms bent partly back, with mangled fingers, with chest drawn up. Everything suggested that, in a supreme hand-to-hand struggle with the mountain, the guide had tried to arrest the disaster and save his young employer. But the mountain had prevailed. Mr. Penhall's watch had stopped at 4.10, but was not wound up; Maurer's had stopped at 6.30, and that was probably the time of the disaster.

The victims were temporarily buried in the snow beyond the range of the avalanches, and the rescuers silently regained the hut. On the morrow, with the help of the company that had arrived in the night, the bodies were taken down into the valley, wrapped in sacking and lashed to poles.[9]

*   *   *

At nine in the morning of Tuesday, the 8th August, the bells of Grindelwald began to toll. A solemn procession was slowly following the road which led from the schoolhouse to the cemetery, after divine service had taken place. Guides carried the two coffins. Some British alpinists, in a moving gesture, a symbol of the close bonds uniting British alpinism to the Swiss mountaineers, shared in carrying Maurer's bier. A joint service, conducted by the Rev. H. W. Majendie, a member of the Alpine Club, had brought Andreas Maurer the guide and William Penhall the young and ardent climber together in their final seclusion. So perished two great conquerors of the Alps, the one the victor of the Tiefenmatten face of the Matterhorn, the other the victor of the north face of the Aiguille Verte. A stone from the Wetterhorn covers their common grave.

*   *   *

Some years later, the English climber Mr. J. Oakley Maund, a distinguished member of the Alpine Club, and his guide, Johann Jaun of Meiringen, both of them companions of Maurer in his great conquests,[10] were together at the summit of the Dossen-horn.[11] The rays of the sinking autumn sun were lighting the high façades of the Wetterhorn. Together, the two men watched the slow vanishing of the light from the snows, and when the shadows had invaded the peak, Johann Jaun turned to Maund and said, his eyes filled with tears:

"I loved Andreas so much."

And the Englishman replied, "And so did I."[12]

For the scene of the Penhall tragedy, see Plate 16.

[1] Capt. Farrar writes that at Cambridge, in physical culture and sport, Penhall had been the pupil of G. S. Passingham, one of the most remarkable climbers of his day: "We can well imagine the steady purpose with which master and pupil strove to prepare themselves for the great mountains." (*Alpine Journal*, Vol. XXX, 1916.)

[2] Cf. *Alpine Journal*, Vol. XI, 1882–84.

[3] See Chapter 12.

[4] See Chapter 13 (Part I).

[5] This was on the 2nd September, 1879. Route taken by Mummery on the following day.

[6] On the 3rd September, 1879, the Matterhorn by the Zmutt arête, and by the Tiefenmatten (north-western) face, was conquered by two parties: (1) A. F. Mummery with the guides Alexander Burgener, Johann Petrus and Augustin Gentinetta, by the arête; (2) William Penhall, with the guides Ferdinand Imseng and Louis Zurbrüggen, by the face.

[7] In the summer of 1880 Emile Rey and Andreas Maurer, with an English climber, were surprised by a violent snowstorm during an attempt on the Aiguille du Plan by the north face. The climbers spent a terrible night, standing on a narrow platform excavated with an axe, their backs against a wall of ice. Beneath them the great ice-slope sank towards Chamonix. Maurer, almost naked to the waist, clasped his benumbed traveller to his own body to protect him from the cold.

[8] Cf. *Alpine Journal*, Vol. IX, 1880; also Cunningham and Abney, *op. cit.*, p. 164.

[9] Ed. de Freudenreich, an excellent Bernese mountaineer, reckons that if Penhall had had two guides the accident would not have happened. This is a quite gratuitous hypothesis. Numerous alpine tragedies run counter to his supposition. (*Echo des Alpes*, No. 1, 1884.)

[10] Especially the Aiguille Verte by the north face, les Courtes by the north face, and the first ascent of les Droites in 1876. This victorious party was composed of the following: J. Oakley Maund, Henri Cordier and Thomas Middlemore, with the guides Andreas Maurer, Johann Jaun and Jakob Anderegg. In 1880 Maurer had taken part in an expedition to the Himalayas with the well-known Hungarian climber de Déchy.

[11] A small summit of 10,300 feet, overlooking the Rosenlaui Glacier from the east.

[12] Maurer left a young widow and an infant.

III. The Deaths on the Dent Blanche

The death of W. E. Gabbett, of the guide Josef-Marie Lochmatter and his son Alexander, porter (August 1882)

A T the edge of the cemetery of St. Niklaus in the Valais, against the white, rough-cast wall of the church, there stands a stone bearing two small crosses of bronze. On this stone are two little hearts with the initials J.-M. L. and A. L. Its inscription is dedicated to the memory of an Englishman, Mr. W. E. Gabbett,[1] and recalls a mysterious tragedy in which three men died on the Dent Blanche in August 1882.[2] An old and blackened fountain is fitted into the wall beside the stone, and not far away, above the fantasia of the flowers, rise the three crosses of the brothers Knubel.[3] The graves of other mountain dead, of other guides, are scattered about this peaceful retreat, filled with the scent of flowers and the murmur of insects.

Even the little church seems to watch over them with attentive tenderness, standing between them and the wild couloir in the mountain above; and they that lie there, victims of glaciers, of rocks, of treacherous cornices, will never know the destruction of their graves by an avalanche. Their sleep will be respected. For the mountains have scarcely spared this church. Three or four times an avalanche from the Sparrhorn has struck at it fiercely; but when the masses of snow have melted with victorious spring the white walls have resumed their place in the valley's skies, and the broken belfry and the cracked nave still extend their protective shadows over the dead.

*　　*　　*

At the beginning of August 1882 an Englishman, Mr. W. E. Gabbett, from the University of Durham, arrived at St. Niklaus. He ascended the valley on foot with the supple and regular pace of a man accustomed to walking. He had just completed an intensive training in the Dauphiné, and had now been attracted to the Valais. But when the gilded bulb surmounting the belfry shone before him in its rustic décor, the vision of another church, the cathedral at Durham, crossed his mind. Not that there was the slightest similarity between the two buildings, but the church reminded him that his vacation was coming to an end. And beyond the shining bulb there slowly appeared the imposing silhouette of an earthen cathedral, the Dent Blanche, a mountain of 14,318 feet, and one of Zermatt's great "four-thousanders." This mountain was in the Englishman's programme, and in order to climb it he had secured one of the best guides in St. Niklaus, Josef-Marie Lochmatter, who had guided him the preceding year.[4]

It was Lochmatter who, in 1868, with Peter Knubel and the Rev. J. M. Elliott, had dared to attack the Matterhorn from Zermatt and accomplish the first ascent since the catastrophe of 1865.[5] To conceive this ascent by the Whymper-Croz route, and to effect the fatal passage again, called for a strong will and a quiet strength. The exploit at once established Lochmatter's repute, and his name from that time took its place beside those of the most renowned guides of his village—Peter Knubel, Aloys Pollinger, and Josef Imboden. Güssfeldt, the celebrated Prussian climber, had travelled with him, as well as Mr. Leighton Jordan, Captain Utterson-Kelso and others. And when in 1874 Whymper reclimbed the Matterhorn from Zermatt, the mountaineers he chose to accompany him were Josef-Marie Lochmatter and Jean-Antoine Carrel.

*　　　*　　　*

In front of the Hôtel-Restaurant Monte Rosa in St. Niklaus a number of people are busy about a carriage. Two men, a woman, and ten children are there. While the driver loads the packs and stows them under the seat, Mr. Gabbett watches the Lochmatter children with amusement. There are six boys and four girls. Alexander, the eldest, is twenty-one; he is making a start as a porter, and is about to leave for the Dent Blanche with his father. His brothers, Josef, Rudolf and Raphael, surround him with admiration and envy. Franz, who is only five, is drawing pictures in the dust with his father's ice-axe. Gabriel is still in his mother's arms.[6] The guide leans over his children to embrace them, then seats himself at the back of the carriage with his employer, while Alexander sits in front with the driver. The whip cracks, the bells tinkle, and the cart moves noisily over the stones. Josef-Marie turns round, smiles behind his beard, and waves farewell. And St. Niklaus, the patron of the village, standing vividly painted within his latticed niche above the old fountain, watches them pass, the two men and the boy who will never return.[7] The valley

143

of Zermatt opens before them, and in the distance the large, snowy back of the Breithorn chain.

Now the Gabbett party moves slowly along the sinuous moraine of the interminable glacier of Zmutt. The last arollas, bowed by the wind, look in their defensive posture as if awaiting the attack of approaching blasts. The completely grey glacier stretches out under a chaos of stones. Near to a tiny lake where a *névé* lies mirrored, black-faced sheep with twisted horns are browsing; the climbers drop their packs and stretch themselves out with delight on the warm grass. Before them the Matterhorn, now very close, springs from its pedestal of ice and splits the sky with its sharp crests. Rising from three wide tiers of ice, each like a glistening step, the solitary peak seems to climb and climb again to seek the light, as if drawn up to it like an ancient oak reaching above all the trees of the forest. Shadows of the deepest blue flood its feet or hang in thick branches down its precipitous walls. The day is cloudless; there is not a breath of wind; and the climbers are seized by a blissful serenity, touching upon ecstasy. The tragedy that stains this northern face is forgotten in the light of its aerial grace, rich with sunlight, vivid against an infinite sky.

Josef-Marie breaks the wondrous pause and points to a black streak below the summit. "Mr. Tyndall," he says, "wanted an iron spike planted up there, and he sent me to Geneva to buy a thousand yards of rope. And, tied to the end of it, I was to explore the precipice to try and find the little Englishman, Lord Douglas, who had disappeared, though he wasn't perhaps dead. He might still be rescued. It was three days after the accident. And then, as we were taking the material up . . . My God! So many coils of rope! . . . a storm broke. See, Mr. Gabbett; we had just got to that point up there, at the foot of the arête, opposite the buttress. We had to stop and come down again."

"And didn't you go up again the next day?" asks Mr. Gabbett.

"No. It snowed for two days. The Matterhorn was as white as a sheet. If Lord Douglas was not dead before that, he certainly was afterwards. Mr. Tyndall abandoned his plan and left for Macugnaga. That's how the affair ended."

A silence ensues, broken only by the collapse of some unseen séracs. Then the party resumes its march.

It is Friday, the 11th August. That evening they arrive at the hut on the Stockje. This refuge lies close to the far end of the

Zmutt Glacier, on an island of rock encircled by the glaciers. It is passed on the way to the Col d'Hérens. Behind it the arête of the Dent Blanche, hidden by some slopes, stretches itself out, rises steeply, supported by the ramparts of the Wandfluh, and ends by falling sharply to the north-east after describing a gigantic irregular triangle in space. Facing the Stockje, on the other side of the Tiefenmatten Glacier, split by wide horizontal crevasses succeeding one another like the lines in a stave of music, the Zmutt face of the Matterhorn fills the heavens like an enormous spear of bronze. This immense black rampart, curved like a pillar and tapering in proportion to its rise, is encrusted with a delicate filigree of snow. Its Italian arête stretches to the south in a great hump, and from its heights unlit hangings of snow, dim as a tarnished mirror, fall heavily down and lose themselves in the blackish rocks below. The Penhall couloir lies obliquely across this sinister face, and the debris of avalanches, littered with rubble and stones, weld the glacier to the wall in heavy, unsubsiding waves.

In the rising night Josef-Marie Lochmatter and his son are seated with their backs to the wall on the bench in front of the hut. This is Alexander's mountain baptism, and he watches the peaks die in the starry sky with amazement and curiosity. A faint roseate light still lingers on the high, shattered lines of the earth —the only peaceful feature in this violent, this impassioned land-scape, where ice and snow and rock combine to preserve the geological effervescence of a force so tragic, so majestic, so august, that it pierces and unsettles the spirit.

"You see, Alexander," the father says, breaking the silence, "how beautiful these mountains are. The more you know them, the more you will love them. But one thing you must never forget, that they are always stronger than you. . . . Be watchful, too; be watchful always. These mountains are like our little black d'Hérens bulls: one day they are quite gentle, quite peaceful, then suddenly they tumble you over just when you are not expecting it. Look how the Matterhorn seems asleep. . . . But apart from those who died there in '65, three of those who climbed it by the Zmutt arête three years ago have already been killed: Mr. Penhall only the other day;[8] Josef Knubel's uncle, Johann Petrus, last month;[9] and a year ago Ferdinand Imseng.[10] . . . And you see that point to the right, in the angle of the Breuil arête, below the Pic Tyndall? It was down there that we slid my poor friend Brantschen when he died at the Cravate refuge and I had to go on with the climbers from Bâle. . . . You remember it, don't you? . . . Poor old Brantschen![11] . . . Come on, my boy, let's get some sleep now. And go quietly, so as not to waken the Englishman."

At eleven-thirty that night a sudden cry is raised, guttural but joyful, rousing Lochmatter from the peace of his first sleep. He leaps from his palliasse and strikes a match. The voices of a belated caravan can now be heard approaching, and when the door opens a giant, bearded silhouette can be seen in the combined light of the match and of a candle stuck in the bottom of a broken bottle, serving as a lantern. It is Aloys Pollinger, Lochmatter's brother-in-law.

"You! Aloys?"

"No," the figure replies gravely. "The first of four asses; the three others are behind me."

A noisy party of exhausted men invades the hut: two English climbers, Mr. G. P. Baker[12] and Mr. J. Stafford Anderson, members of the Alpine Club, with their guides, Aloys Pollinger of St. Niklaus, and Ulrich Almer of Grindelwald. They have just accomplished the first ascent of the Dent Blanche by the Zinal arête, which they have named the "Arête des Quatres Anes"[13] —the "Arête of the Four Asses." Both Gabbett and Alexander have risen at hearing the noise, and conversation becomes general. Almer revives the fire; Pollinger hugs the brandy-flask and solemnly declares, "*Nur schmecken, nicht trinken*" ("Only to taste, no drinking"), which sets them all laughing. As the new arrivals are very hungry and have run out of provisions, Mr. Gabbett generously offers his own surplus victuals; and Mr. Stafford, eating them all up, answers the questions of the Durham professor who will be leaving in a few hours for the same mountain.

"Yes, the mountain is in an excellent condition. Quite exceptionally good. The rocks are dry; no ice; not the least bit of snow. In fact, no difficulty at all beyond those inherent in the climb itself."

"And, given the same weather, you will be up there quickly."

"Josef-Marie," Aloys Pollinger interrupts, "you will have to descend by our arête, and that will make six asses in two days, and one young ass, since there's the youngster."

146

Awakened by an alarm clock, the Gabbett party is quickly up at three in the morning of Saturday, August the 12th. Just as they are about to leave, while Alexander lights the lantern and Gabbett adjusts his gaiters, Josef-Marie Lochmatter quietly stretches their now unwanted blankets over the exhausted climbers.[14] They leave the hut. The night is cold, but divinely clear. A bright star, hanging upon the arête of the Dent d'Hérens above the Col Tournanche, resembles a bivouac fire. Enshrined in darkness, the mountains have lost their savage appearance; they are but great nameless downs lost in the enchantment of the stars and the blackness of the night. Then the still uncertain dawn begins to stretch a greyish veil across the heights of Monte Rosa.

* * *

While the Baker–Stafford–Anderson party early that morning descended to Zermatt, the Gabbett party was toiling up the arête of the Dent Blanche by way of the Col d'Hérens. The delay attending the return of the first party (they had been expected on the previous evening) had put Zermatt into a flutter, and the victors of the Arête des Quatres Anes learned there with some surprise that a rumour had been circulating which reported them as having perished on the Dent Blanche. It was just when the good news of their arrival reached the village of St. Niklaus that Josef-Marie Lochmatter, his son Alexander, and Mr. W. E. Gabbett fell on the same mountain. So death was there after all; only a change of names was needed.

The Gabbett party was expected at Zermatt on the evening of Saturday the 12th. When, at midday on Sunday the 13th, the party was still reported missing, two guides from St. Niklaus, together with Mr. F. J. Church, who had just arrived from Grindelwald after the burial of his friend William Penhall,[15] left for the Stockje hut. Mr. Church returned to Zermatt the same evening with valuable information: Gabbett's knapsack was still at the refuge—a sinister omen. What last hope could there be? If they had descended to Zinal or to Evolène, the fact would have already been reported by telegraph.

A rescue party was formed at once of seven guides and an English climber; Josef Imboden was its leader. It left Zermatt at two in the morning of Monday the 14th. By five-thirty they had reached the Stockje hut, and their number was there increased by the two St. Niklaus guides who had come up the day before, as well as by a party which had arrived over the Col d'Hérens, consisting of two English climbers (the Wilson brothers) and their guides. The total strength was now fourteen, eleven guides and three English climbers. Josef Imboden immediately prepared his plan of campaign: it seemed most probable that the accident had occurred on the east (Wandfluh) side. Three ropes, comprising ten men in all, were to explore the Schonbuhl glacier at the foot of the precipice, and one party of four men, crossing the Col d'Hérens, was to make for the Ferpècle Glacier; then, if the Wandfluh parties discovered nothing, they would cross the arête near the saddle (about 12,500 feet) and join the Col d'Hérens party near the upper Ferpècle névés. No mistake was possible.

Contrary to expectations, the disaster had occurred on the western (Ferpècle) side. About midday the parties rejoined as arranged, and the long column made for the base of the Dent. During the morning the sky, which had been wonderful the day before, had clouded over. A stormy heaven drowned the summit of the mountain, and its giant rampart, furrowed by rock couloirs, vanished into the clouds. A fine snow began to fall, quickly whitening the rocks. The wind broke loose.

The searchers followed the *bergschrund*, the long gap which festoons the edge of the glacier. They explored its surroundings, but nothing suspicious could be seen. But at two o'clock, at the foot of the buttress in front of the Ferpècle arête, separated from it by a glacier bay slightly below the *bergschrund*, the three bodies were found. There they lay, partly covered already with snow and sleet. Separated from each other by about sixty yards, they formed an equilateral triangle: at the bottom, Alexander; to the right, higher up, Mr. Gabbett; to the left, Josef-Marie Lochmatter. They were atrociously mutilated, hardly recognisable, and almost naked. From the young porter's middle there still hung a knotted fragment of rope, but that was all they found of it. The wrists and chests of the other two men were cruelly scarred, as if by a sudden and terrible constriction of the rope. They had fallen about 2,600 feet.[16] Their axes and watches had disappeared.

By this time the storm had become violent. Josef Imboden had the bodies brought together. He motioned his thirteen men to form a circle about them and kneel. Kneeling himself, he began to chant the prayer for the dead.

The howling wind and the snow swept over the motionless group in squalls. The hail showered its arrows upon the living and the dead. Whirls of snow smoked at the lips of the *bergschrund*. Tearing themselves to pieces on the rocks, the clouds now revealed and now submerged a sombre rampart already sheeted in snow.

Kneeling on the glacier, the fourteen men continued their prayer for the dead, looking like penitents in white. The three bodies were now only vague shapes under their canopy of snow.

The same evening the bodies were brought, not without difficulty, as far as the moraine of the Ferpècle Glacier, and were there abandoned for the night. The rescuers slept at a neighbouring alp, and a messenger, despatched to Evolène, telegraphed to Zermatt for a second party to be sent as soon as possible to the Col d'Hérens, there to relieve the first, laden with the dead.

On Tuesday, August the 15th, in the morning, the two parties met as arranged at the Col d'Hérens (11,418 feet), and the same evening, at seven o'clock, the column entered Zermatt with its mournful burden.[17] On the morrow they buried Mr. Gabbett in the English cemetery at Zermatt,[18] and on the 17th Josef-Marie Lochmatter and his son Alexander were buried at St. Niklaus. A grey stone, surmounted by two small bronze crosses, and bearing two little hearts with the initials J.-M. L. and A. L., lies at the edge of the cemetery against the white roughcast wall of the church, close to the old blackened fount.

For the scene of the tragedy on the Dent Blanche, see Plate 17.

[1] This inscription is a replica of the epitaph on Mr. Gabbett's stone at Zermatt. The text will be found below, note 18.

[2] This accident, the third of the summer of 1882, in which three well-known English intellectuals lost their lives in less than a month, aroused a curious reaction on the part of Queen Victoria, which can be judged by these two letters:

From Sir Henry Ponsonby to Mr. William Gladstone.

24th August, 1882.

"Dear Mr. Gladstone,—The Queen commands me to ask you if you think she can say anything to mark her disapproval of the dangerous Alpine excursions which this year have occasioned so much loss of life.—Henry F. Ponsonby."

From Mr. William Gladstone to Sir Henry Ponsonby.

25th August, 1882.

"My dear Sir H. Ponsonby,—I do not wonder that the Queen's sympathetic feelings have again been excited by the accidents, so grave in character, and so accumulated during recent weeks, on the Alps. But I doubt the possibility of any interference, even by Her Majesty, with a prospect of advantage. It may be questionable whether, upon the whole, mountain-climbing (and be it remembered that Snowdon has its victims as well as the Matterhorn) is more destructive than various other pursuits in the way of recreation which perhaps have no justification to plead so respectable as that which may be alleged on behalf of mountain expeditions. The question, however, is not one of wisdom or unwisdom; but viewing it, as you put it, upon its very definite and simple grounds, I see no room for action." (Signed) W. E. Gladstone.

(Extract from *The Letters of Queen Victoria*, second series, Vol. 3, 1879–95. Edited by G. E. Buckle. Murray, London, 1928. See also *Alpine Journal*, Vol. XL.)

[3] See Chapter 10.

[4] Mr. Gabbett and the guide J.-M. Lochmatter were not unknown to one another. They had travelled together in 1881 in the Dauphiné and, in particular, had made the first ascent of the Râteau (12,313 feet) on the 25th August. The party comprised W. E. Gabbett and W. M. Baker, with the guides J.-M. Lochmatter and Aloys Pollinger.

[5] See Chapter 6.

[6] All the Lochmatter sons became celebrated guides, especially Josef and Franz. The latter, the most famous of them, perished on the Weisshorn in 1933 (see Charles Gos, *Alpinisme Anecdotique, op. cit.*). In 1947 only Rafael and Gabriel were still living, and the sons of Josef and Rudolf maintain the honour of this race of great guides.

[7] Alexander Lochmatter (like Andreas Maurer, p. 135) had had the clear presentiment that he would not return. "We were at Jungenalp," Aloys Pollinger told me, "and in parting Alexander said to his brothers, to my brothers and to me: 'I bid you adieu, for I shall not see you or the Jungenalp again.'"

[8] See Chapter 13 (Part II).

[9] See Chapter 13 (Part I).

[10] See Chapter 12.

[11] See Chapter 11 (Part II).

[12] Cf. G. P. Baker, "Mountaineering Memories of the Past" (*Alpine Journal*, Vol. LIII, 1942).

[13] "Our first proceeding, [on reaching the summit]," said J. Stafford Anderson, "was to shake hands all round, then Almer, grasping the situation in its entirety, exclaimed in a loud and solemn manner, '*wir sind vier Esel* (we are four asses)', a sort of concentrated summary of the day's proceedings." (Cf. *Alpine Journal*, Vol. XI, 1882–84.)

[14] This touching gesture impressed Mr. Stafford Anderson. He recalls it in his story of this memorable expedition. (Cf. *Alpine Journal*, Vol. XI, 1882–84.)

[15] See Chapter 13 (Part II).

[16] It is almost certain that the accident happened while crossing some slabs on the east face a little below the arête, about twenty minutes from the summit. This is a bad passage; the rock there is rotten for about ten metres. Mr. Stafford Anderson, who had traversed it the day before, says the water issuing from a névé above had moistened the rock. It is thus possible, if not certain, that the slabs were coated with ice at the time the Gabbett party was there.

My father, Albert Gos the painter, told me that some years later there was found, very near the slabs, or at the middle of the passage, a flask which had belonged to Josef-Marie Lochmatter. Hence the hypothesis, developing logically from the words of Mr. Stafford Anderson when he mentioned the stream of water at this place: had one of the climbers stopped to drink?—an abrupt movement, a second's inattention?

[17] My father, who was at Zermatt at the time, knew Josef-Marie Lochmatter very well. He still remembers the sad return of the rescue parties. In his sketch-book for that summer I discovered a hasty drawing, done from life, of stark realism. "It was no more than the debris of a human body," he told me. And, he added, one curious fact impressed two doctors who were present and remained inexplicable: "Alexander Lochmatter's jaw-bones were intact, but all his teeth were missing both in the upper jaw and the lower. As for Gabbett, one leg had been torn away, severed at the middle of the thigh."

[18] Mr. Gabbett's epitaph reads as follows:

"W. E. Gabbett, aged 32. Fell from the Dent Blanche, August 12th, 1882. In the midst of life we are in death. I am the resurrection and the life."

Mr. Gabbett, after studying classics at Lincoln College, Oxford, had entered Durham University with a tutorship. Gabbett made his appearance there in October 1880. Less than two years later he perished in the Alps. To commemorate him at Durham, two annual Gabbett prizes were created, which still continue; one for a philosophical essay, the other for the best oarsman.

A bronze plaque was placed in the University chapel; on it one may read:

"In affectionate remembrance of William Edward Gabbett, M.A., tutor in this University, who died on the Dent Blanche, August 12th, 1882 A.D., aged 33. Erected by members of University College."

CHAPTER FOURTEEN

THE BRIGHTNESS THAT WILL
NEVER FADE

The death of Dr. Emil Zsigmondy (Meije, south face, August 1885)

I N 1879 Emil Zsigmondy, a Viennese student of medicine, was only eighteen years of age.[1] The University of Vienna had just closed its doors; the summer term was ended. In the deserted lecture halls the dust settled on the desks. This summer the brothers Zsigmondy,[2] Otto and Emil, and their friend Julius Kugy, had surprisingly engaged a guide to explore the Dolomites.[3] Judge, then, the surprise of Michel Innerkofler[4] at seeing his chalet invaded by the enthusiastic youthfulness of these three impenitently guideless young climbers, who between them all did not total fifty-four years.

"We intend to prove our capacities to Michel," wrote Emil Zsigmondy. But on the Zinnen and on Piz Popena[5] their prowess almost came to catastrophe and elicited a volley of imprecations from the good guide. Two years later, in 1881, Julius Kugy was still one of the company, but at the Bachern hut on the day before they returned to the plains this short dialogue took place:

"My dear Emil," said Kugy, "I think this will be the last time we shall be together."

"Really!" said Emil, surprised. "Are you going to abandon the mountains?"

"No. Not the mountains, but you. And you know why. I have already told you repeatedly."

"But look here, old man, you're not serious. Why should we

separate because you find me too daring? How can you hope to do the big climbs without a certain degree of temerity?"

"Temerity, yes. But imprudence, no. And you, Emil, know better than anyone that you are imprudent."

"People always exaggerate," sighed Emil grudgingly. "This isn't because of my slip the other day . . .?"

"Yes," replied Kugy honestly. "Just because of that. Three times during our climbs you've fallen before my eyes, and you've had the luck to escape. But you won't always escape. Your luck will tire, and at the rate you're going you'll leave your skin on the mountains one day."

Zsigmondy scoffed at him amiably. "I can see you haven't forgotten the words we read in that visitors' book at the hut the other day: 'Every climber falls sooner or later, the victim of his own passion.' I saw how deeply it impressed you."

Kugy was serious. "There's nothing to laugh at. I'm too fond of you and I think too highly of you not to speak quite frankly. I'm not at all anxious to take part in the final disaster. I don't want to see you die, and I've no wish to die with you."[6]

* * *

Four more years had passed when, in February 1885, Emil Zsigmondy, who had just graduated as doctor of medicine, went to spend eight days in Trieste with his friend Julius Kugy,[7] who had just graduated as doctor of law. These two young men, despite their alpine disagreement, remained closely attached. They had scarcely resumed contact when Emil Zsigmondy confided to Kugy:

"I've some big news for you, Julius!"

"Big news? This looks serious!"

"Yes; very serious!"

"You're going to get married?"

"No, old man, worse than that."

"You're going to give up mountaineering?"

"You're getting warm."

"Well, you've decided to stop climbing without guides?"

"Not yet. But you're still warm."

"Ah! I know! You're going to be careful!"

Zsigmondy beamed. "Yes. If you like. Almost. I've thought a lot about what you said to me one evening at the Bachern hut some years ago. . . . You remember? . . . And I'm finishing a book, which will give you pleasure, about the dangers of the Alps and how to avoid them. (He laughed.) My manuscript is almost finished. . . . You'll read my book. Julius, you'll be pleased with me. Yes, I admit it : I'm now of your opinion. Boldness is necessary in ideas, but not over-confidence, not false vanity. The impossible exists for all of us and it mustn't be forgotten. You disapproved of my imprudence. I'm going to try and correct myself."[8]

A month after this conversation the young doctor wrote the conclusions of his book, and amongst them we find these quasi-Nietzschean considerations : "Success . . . in mountaineering . . . is the triumph of man's will over the forces of nature. . . . Who-ever has once succumbed to the impress of these solitudes will always return to the luminous regions of the high mountains." The work appeared in July,[9] and some weeks later—sinister irony!—Emil Zsigmondy was killed on the Meije.

So many pages have been written about that catastrophe, beginning with the accounts of the two survivors, Dr. Otto Zsigmondy[10] and Professor K. Schulz, that it would be puerile to attempt to romanticise those stories. While numbers of alpine tragedies are sealed in an hermetic silence and one is obliged, in order to reconstruct them, to have recourse to the inductive method, passing afterwards to the deductive, here everything has been told and everything is clear. My rôle is limited, therefore, to retelling the tragedy that has been described by its witnesses.

* * *

On the 4th August, 1885, two parties occupy the refuge of la Bérarde : one consisting of five Austrians, the brothers Otto and Emil Zsigmondy, Professor Karl Schulz, Professor T. N. Kellenbauer and Herr Ludwig Purtscheller, all first-class climbers ; the other of four Frenchmen, MM. Joseph Lemercier, Georges Leser, P. Engelbach and Felix Chancel. The Zsigmondys and Herr Purtscheller have just climbed the Meije by a new route (26th July), by the eastern arête, a splendid exploit which makes quite a stir in climbing circles. Professor Schulz has been unlucky ; an injury to his hand prevented him from participating in that remarkable climb. And because of bad weather he has just failed to reach the summit by the classic route, accompanied by the guides Pierre Gaspard *fils* and J. B. Rodier. But his comrades have promised that before they leave the massif they will take him to this lovely peak, whose height and prestige make it the Matterhorn of the Dauphiné and one of the most splendid mountains in France. Otto Zsigmondy favours the orthodox route, for the difficult ascent of the eastern arête has been happiness enough for him. But his younger brother Emil has mysterious plans of his own.

On August the 3rd, from the summit of the Aiguille du Plat, Emil has closely examined the wide south face of the mountain, which reveals itself like a saw above the Etançons Glacier: of blackish rocks, gashed with couloirs, and traversed by an almost entirely snow-covered ledge.

On August the 5th the Austrians and the Frenchmen climb the easy Tête de la Maye together, and from its summit the Zsigmondys examine their mountain afresh. Then Emil, a man of dreamy and sensitive nature, having settled his plan of attack, puts down his axe, takes from his pack a block of paper and a box of colours, and paints a water-colour of the scene. This is his last poetical gesture, for those which follow will be rougher, occupied with more prosaic considerations—combative and violent movements, dictated by the rocks and the ice.[11]

In the afternoon of the 5th the Frenchmen and their Austrian comrades are back at la Bérarde, and the same evening the two Zsigmondys and Professor Schulz sleep at the Châtelleret hut in the Etançons valley.

At two in the morning of August the 6th the climbers leave the hut by lantern-light and cross the Glacier des Etançons.[12] By six they are at the foot of the rocks directly below the Pic Oriental. Their plan is to ascend the southern face diagonally by the snow-filled ledge in the direction of the Grand Pic, then to try and force the terribly steep rock couloir from the point where the ledge dies out, below the gap between the Grand Pic and the last of the teeth on the arête of the Pic Central.

The day begins badly. A storm and falls of stone overtake them in the midst of considerable difficulties which have persisted since the beginning of the attack. But though the dark clouds withdraw, the difficulties increase. The climbers succeed, however, in overcoming these defences and, having assumed their crampons, they set foot on the verglas-covered rock cornice which stretches like a path above the abyss and skirts the ascending lane of snow. At ten-thirty they are grouped on the last névé. The snow and the ledge have come to an end and it is impossible to continue the traverse. One way out remains: to climb straight up the wall and attempt to join the arête near the second of the great teeth from the Pic Central.

Using a ribbon of ice in which they are obliged to cut some steps, they are soon involved in the wall. A vertical ascent of 130 feet brings them to a narrow horizontal terrace. They are now firmly implanted in the precipice. Around them in every direction is the inexorable wall. The lower edge of the Carré Glacier looms whitely to the south. It is eleven o'clock. Should they go on?

An enormous pillar of rock, united to the wall and looking rather like the corner-tower of a fortress, bars the way. Behind it lies the couloir through which passes the route they have hoped to follow. Emil Zsigmondy, leading, climbs the pillar, lengthily examines the terrain, and calls out:

"It doesn't seem to go!"*[13]

His brother and Professor Schulz are resigned to a retreat. But Emil unropes so as to be freer in his movements;[14] he loops the rope to a projecting piece of rock and disappears. At this Otto, too, sets out on reconnaissance and, holding the rope in one hand, he circles the pillar. The two brothers have now succeeded in turning the bastion and reaching the bank of the couloir, raised like the edge of a wound. Leaning over the edge, they look into its depths, examine it closely. It is impossible to pass this way. How, in fact, can they cross those smooth, steep slabs which are, moreover, coated with ice? Emil himself, despite his zeal and daring, has to admit that he is checked.

They return to the foot of the pillar whence they started and where Schulz is waiting. An hour has passed without progress. They rest awhile. They hold council. The sky is very blue; the sun is ablaze at its zenith. Showers of ice fragments and stones whistle by. It is very hot. Exhaustion of mind begins to follow the weariness of the flesh. It is midday. Schulz urges that the attempt be abandoned here and now and that they descend. Otto has no clear views and is content to question his brother.

"What do you intend to do?" he asks.

Emil lifts his head towards the rock against which they are leaning. His eyes caress the precipice, which is furrowed by little couloirs.

156

"Try up there," he answers. "It would be a pity to give up because the large couloir is impossible."

So saying, he takes to the rock and quickly climbs some thirty feet without the rope. But his effort is so obviously futile that his two comrades call on him to come down again. He does so, and they are once again all together at the foot of this unfortunate wall. Emil's heart becomes a gulf where clouds of bitterness are slowly spreading, a state of mind which can easily become dangerous and lead to complications.

How hard it is to admit defeat! How hard to form the syllables of those few positive words: "We can do no more; we must go down." Emil dismisses them roughly, but one voice gives them expression, though they make no impression on his mind. It is Otto who speaks; he is convinced that it is now impossible to reach the summit by this route, and he insists that they should abandon the attempt and turn about. Emil does not answer. Time passes. It is one-thirty in the afternoon, and according to their aneroid they are at a height of about 12,000 feet.

"Now, Emil, what do you think?" asks Schulz. "Haven't you yet given up all hope?"*

"What would one have if one hadn't some hope?"* Emil replies, rising again and tying one end of twenty metres of manilla rope to his middle.

Then, turning abruptly to the wall, he seizes the rock and begins to climb straight up. A slab turns him straight into an impasse. He extricates himself and takes to a very steep chimney with polished sides. He expects to find a ledge of rock a hundred feet higher, and it is clear that the young climber's efforts are directed there in order to see what is beyond it, whether they might not find there, *in extremis*, a last way out towards the arête. He arrives half-way up the chimney. Sixty feet of rope have already run out.

Suddenly his panting voice is heard: "It doesn't go any farther!"*

"Come down! Emil! Come down!" the other two call out together.*

Painfully and slowly Emil lowers himself a few yards. Stones roll noisily down. Otto and Schulz huddle against the rock to avoid them. After a while they raise their heads and see, to their surprise, that instead of coming down as they had thought, Emil has resumed his climb. With incredible daring and magnificent strength he has succeeded in mastering the passage which had forced him to recoil and admit defeat. And he is still going forward. The rope wriggles in the chimney. Breathless and muted by distance, the voice is heard again:

"I can get on farther; have you any rope left?"*

"Yes. Schulz's twenty-metre silk rope is still here," his brother replies. "If you really wish it, we will tie ourselves to it."*

"That's all right!" the voice above joyfully responds.*

Otto knots the two ropes, and inch by inch, yard by yard, the frail silk line unwinds and rises up the wall. Three . . . five . . . eight . . . ten yards. God! how long it is! Will he never arrive at that cursed terrace? It is already an hour and a half since he started.

The two men watch what happens. They see their comrade flattened out against the perpendicular rock. Three feet above him is the coveted edge, but they end in an overhang. Then . . . Good God! No, Emil! . . . Exactly at the end of his hundred feet of rope the following incident occurs. An arm stretches out and a hand succeeds in passing the overhang. It feels and tests the rock—a little feverishly—then draws back. One wavering leg makes a sidestep and hastily returns to its place. Stubbornly the arm begins again, then the hand. But how can that one hand which, like a hesitant bird, cannot decide to settle, possibly draw up the weight of the whole body over a slab without purchase? At the slightest displacement, at the slightest tension on that raised arm, now lightly outthrust as if signalling a halt, the body, losing contact with the wall and forced back by the projecting rock, would re-establish itself automatically in the perpendicular . . . but in empty space.

"I'm afraid that something may happen," Otto murmurs.*

Schulz does not reply. But their eyes, momentarily turned away, are again fixed up there, where a wordless tragedy is being performed between one man and three feet of overhanging rock. Emil, feeling that he will not pass and that his resistance is weakening, is preparing to descend. He can be seen to lift the hanging rope with one hand. His movements are very slow, very cautious, almost gentle, as if trying not to waken the terrible brute that slumbers in every rock. Once again the arm rises, but this time it is in a reconciled gesture, not a gesture of attack, but one which seeks to seal the peace with the impossible. The hand no longer tries to find a grip; it simply encircles the lip of the over-hang and passes the rope gently above it, placing it on the rock above like a halter on the neck of a beast. Gripping the doubled rope in his hands and abandoning his foothold, Emil has allowed himself to slide out about a yard, entirely suspended. From fear of stones, Schulz moves and flattens himself against the rock. Otto continues anxiously to watch, then he too takes shelter.

"If only nothing happens to him," says Schulz.*

Simultaneously with these unhappy words, which cut like light-ning into the minds of the two watching men, the tragedy unfolds. "In this moment," states Otto, "there first came into my head the idea that Emil might fall. And almost at the same time the fall took place."

"I suddenly heard an uncanny noise," continues Schulz; "caught the low cry 'Oh!' and the next moment poor Emil fell on the ledge above us."[15] Moved by a sudden reflex action, Otto twists the rope around his right arm and clings to the rock with his left hand, while beside him Schulz seizes the end of the rope in his right hand and clings to the earth. "Swift as a shadow Emil's body flew over our heads," says the Professor.

Several seconds passed, filled with swift tumult, with incoherent movements, with violence and blood. And when the two men recovered their lucidity they saw between their wounded hands a five-yard fragment of rope hanging down. Otto had first been thrown down upon Schulz, who had taken the strain, and was then drawn to the very edge of the precipice, where he lay clinging to a stone. Forty yards below them Emil's bloodstained body, with thirty-five yards of rope floating behind it, fell upon the last slope of ice (the one crossed at about eleven o'clock). This hard blue slab received the body and, like a terrifying springboard, sent it ricocheting into the profusion of light which expanded in a burning corolla from the Glacier des Etançons 2,300 feet below.[16]

The two men on the narrow terrace looked at one another dumbly. Otto raised himself painfully. Blood was running down his face; his left thumb was broken; his arms and hands were deeply cut when the rope tightened as it leapt; his right side was badly contused. Schulz, too, had severe cuts on his hands.

It was two-fifteen. What was to be gained by delaying on these reddened stones? Tied to three yards of rope, the defeated men began the formidable descent.[17] They lowered themselves slowly, mutely, with broken hearts. They lowered themselves towards the glistening snows, lying below them like a lake of light, where the body of Emil awaited them.

Schulz led; Otto remained in the responsible position behind, despite his wounds. The sun had softened their steps and the torment of cutting new steps in the descent was forced upon them. Stones fell whistling by. And, unknown to himself, taking up the words spoken by his brother when he set out to attack the chimney where he had perished—"What would one have if one hadn't some hope?"—there where Dante himself had abandoned hope, Otto descended, sustained by the wondrous illusion of finding alive the young brother who had been so beloved of men and gods. At seven o'clock, in the splendour of the twilight, the tragic pair reached the glacier. Their last hope was extinguished with the last roseate light on the summits. There was nothing left but to weep.[18]

* * *

In the night, at nine-thirty, these two men, still tied to one another by three yards of rope, arrived at the Châtelleret hut. On the following day (August 7th) they rejoined their two friends, Purtscheller and Kellenbauer, at la Bérarde. Purtscheller left at once, with a rescue party of seven men, to retrieve the body. They brought it down to the moraine, and on the 8th to la Bérarde.

The curé of St. Christophe, M. l'Abbé Vallier, was deeply sympathetic, and was infinitely kind to the foreign climbers, and he authorised Emil's burial in the little cemetery of his parish although the dead man was a Protestant.

The funeral took place on the 10th August. The four Austrians surrounded the coffin; the village dignitaries and most of the inhabitants rendered honour to the dead, and a Dutch pastor, on holiday at Venosc, said the prayers. Ludwig Purtscheller's rope, which had so often tied him to his friend on arduous climbs, was used to lower the coffin into the grave.[19] Kellenbauer gave a short funeral oration and laid the broken rope and a wreath of edelweiss on the grave.[20] Seven weeks later a stone was raised with this simple epitaph:

DR EMIL

ZSIGMONDY

VIENNE

AUTRICHE

11 AOUT 1861

MEIJE

5 AOUT 1885

EXCELSIOR

*　　　*　　　*

Some time after this tragedy, the Rev. W. A. B. Coolidge, then editor of the *Alpine Journal*, a well-known climber and alpine historian, published the following letter in that journal. It was written by a climber of the first order, the surgeon Dr. Clinton Dent, conqueror of the Aiguille du Dru, later President of the Alpine Club.

"Concerning the recent terrible accident by which Dr. Emil Zsigmondy lost his life, you will have information enough from other sources, and I have no intention of discussing its details. I trust, however, that you will allow me in a few words to speak of the man and not of the mountaineer. Dr. Emil Zsigmondy was not a member of our Club, but I had the pleasure of his friendship as a fellow-member of the Austrian Alpine Club and of my own profession. The loss has been great to the brotherhood of climbers and mountain lovers; but the loss has been no less signal to science and the medical profession. No one could fail to recognise the energy, the enthusiasm and the thoroughness that distinguished Zsigmondy's mountaineering exploits. A smaller circle, perhaps, knew how these characteristics were but part of the man's nature, and, as such, brought to bear on all that he undertook. A brilliant career seemed to be assured for him, for though not quite twenty-four years of age he had already attained a high position in the scientific world. But it was destined, we know not why, that he was only to furnish yet another instance of a bright nature suddenly called away, and of great promise abruptly checked. There remains to us but the example of a man who was possessed of strength of character beyond his years, and of intellectual gifts developed and fostered by rare individual perseverance. Well might it be said of him

Thou madest man, he knows not why;
We think he was not made to die.

"In May of this year Zsigmondy paid a brief visit to England.[21] Some of us are not likely to forget the slight figure, the keen face, the bright, enquiring expression; nor can those who knew him more closely fail to recall his genial disposition, his nature as simple and affectionate as that of a child, happily blended with the gentle courtesy and refinement so characteristic of his native city of Vienna. There is a beauty in the dignity of an honoured old age drawing slowly to its close, but there is no less beauty perhaps in contemplating a life whose brightness was never permitted to fade."[22]

Three weeks after Emil Zsigmondy's death the International Alpine Congress, meeting at Turin, expressed the wish that his work, *Die Gefahren der Alpen*, should be translated and published as soon as possible. The French translation appeared the following year.

Finally, in 1889, Professor Schulz published a very remarkable book dedicated to the memory of his young comrade, and comprising twenty-three accounts of climbs written by Emil Zsigmondy himself, *Im Hochgebirge*.[23] It is enough to run through its vibrant and poetic pages, overflowing with his love for the mountains, to grasp better the sense of Clinton Dent's words when writing of the young climber who died on la Meije: "The beauty of a life whose brightness was never permitted to fade."[24]

For the scene of Zsigmondy's death, see Plates 19 and 20.

[1] Born on the 11th August, 1861.

[2] They were four: Otto, the eldest, doctor of medicine; Emil, doctor of medicine and surgeon; Richard, doctor of science, Nobel prizewinner in physics and chemistry; Karl, professor of mathematics at the Polytechnicum of Vienna. They were the sons of Dr. Adolf Zsigmondy of Pressburg (now Bratislava). The first three were brilliant alpinists, but the youngest did little mountaineering. The four brothers Zsigmondy are to-day all dead.

[3] In his very fine book, *Aus den Leben eines Bergsteiger*, translated and published in English under the title *Alpine Pilgrimage*, Dr. Julius Kugy, the Guido Rey of Austro-German mountaineering, devotes several picturesque and moving passages to his expeditions with Otto and Emil Zsigmondy.

[4] Michel Innerkofler perished on Monte Cristallo some years after this expedition with the Zsigmondys and Kugy.

[5] See Emil Zsigmondy's *Die Gefahren der Alpen*, Leipzig, 1885, pp. 106 and 120. (See also note 9.)

[6] It is sufficient, in fact, to run through the pages of *Die Gefahren der Alpen* to be convinced that Emil's excessive daring verged upon imprudence. Between 1875 (when

he was fifteen) and 1884 the author had had fifteen accidents, and his party, or the members of it, seventeen. "Otto," Dr. Kugy told me, "was much more prudent than Emil."

[7] Honorary member of the Alpine Club. Died at Trieste on the 5th February, 1944.

[8] This dialogue and the earlier one are not purely imaginary. Their substance was provided by Dr. Julius Kugy in personal conversations.

[9] This work had been indirectly inspired by a meeting called by the Swiss Alpine Club in 1884 to discuss the subject: "The dangers of excursions in the Alps." Dr. Emil Zsigmondy did not participate, but he wrote his book to rectify some mistakes and preconceptions, whereby beginners in the Alps might benefit by the experience of their forerunners. In April 1885 Emil wrote his preface and conclusions, and in the same month sent his manuscript to the publisher. The work appeared in July, only a few weeks before its author's tragic end on the Meije, under the title *Die Gefahren der Alpen, Praktishe Winke für Bergsteiger* (*The Dangers of the Alps, Practical Hints for Climbers*).

[10] In the *Bulletin Mensuel du Club Alpin Français* (No. 12, Dec. 1885) a brief account of the catastrophe, written specially for that publication by Dr. Otto Zsigmondy, will be found. The stories of Otto and of Prof. Schulz will also be found in the *Alpine Journal*, Vol. XII, 1884–86.

[11] Emil, very cultured, discriminating and artistic, was a charming character; in his person the flame of a noble ideal burnt brightly. There was an astonishing spiritual resemblance between the four brothers. (*Personal communication from Dr. Julius Kugy.*)

[12] Cf. *Alpine Journal*, Vol. XII, 1884–86.

[13] The phrases marked with an asterisk were actually spoken and are taken from original texts.

[14] The Zsigmondys advocated rock-climbing *without* ropes. This method, proposed and defended in *Die Gefahren* (Chap. 8), was confirmed to me by Dr. Kugy. "In 1879 and 1881," he wrote, "every time we had rock walls to climb we did it without a rope." This was also Emil Rey's principle. (See Chap. 19.)

[15] It may be regarded as certain that the cause of the accident was a slip of the rope from the rock over which it had been passed. Dr. Otto's opinion, and Prof. Schulz's too, is categorical on this point. This might, furthermore, explain the sudden sinking of the rope an instant before the climber's fall. The great guide Franz Lochmatter perished in the same manner on the Weisshorn in 1933.

[16] The famous Austrian climber, Guido Lammer, in an article published on the fortieth anniversary of the death of Emil Zsigmondy, went so far as to regard Schulz as almost directly responsible for Emil's death. The disagreeable remarks that he made during the climb might have wounded Emil so deeply that in bitterness of heart he rushed blindly forward to the assault of the wall where he perished. This sort of accusation, for which one finds no foundation in the accounts of the accident given by Dr. Otto, straightway appears both arbitrary and excessively violent. (Cf. Lammer's *Emil Zsigmondy* in the *Donauland Nachrichter, Zeitschrift des Alpenverein Donauland*, Vienna, No. 50, 1925.)

[17] The route which the Zsigmondy–Schulz party intended to follow, after having defied several attempts, was successfully climbed in July 1912 by a party consisting of G. and M. Mayer with A. Dibona and L. Rizzi. (Cf. Emile Gaillard, *Les Alpes du Dauphiné, Guide pour l'Alpiniste*, Vol. II, Part 1. Chambéry.)

[18] Professor Schulz says: "It was a terrible meeting. Otto sank into my arms, sobbing loudly. . . . Otto wished to carry down the body on his back, and it was only my repeated representations that induced him to go on."

[19] Purtscheller died in 1900 at Berne from the unfortunate results of a fall on the Aiguille du Grand Dru.

[20] It is interesting that during his last nine years of alpine climbing (from his fifteenth to his twenty-fourth year) Emil Zsigmondy made more than one hundred ascents above 3,000 metres (or about 10,000 feet), only six of them being guided. Almost all the great summits of the Alps figure in this impressive list, the greater part being con-

quered by routes either quite new or particularly difficult. Circumstantial details of the tragedy will be found in the following publications:

    (a) *Oesterreichische Alpenzeitung*, 28th August, 1885.
    (b) *Mitteilungen des Deutschen und Oesterreichischen Alpenvereins*, 1885.
    (c) *Rivista Mensile del C.A.I.*, 1st September, 1885.
    (d) *Alpine Journal*, Vol. XII, 1885.

[21] As house surgeon in a London hospital.

[22] Cf. *Alpine Journal*, Vol. XII, 1885.

[23] Prof. Karl Schulz, *Im Hochgebirge, Wanderungen von Dr. Emil Zsigmondy. Mit abbildungen von E. T. Compton*, Leipzig, 1889. In the opinion of Dr. Julius Kugy, this remains one of the most beautiful books on mountains ever published.

[24] The *Echo des Alpes*, No. 1, 1886, published this touching verse from the pen of an anonymous admirer:—

EMIL ZSIGMONDY

La nature t'avait prodigué ses faveurs,
Elle t'avait donné richement en partage
Tous les biens qu'ici-bas cherchent les noble cœurs:
Jeunesse, dévouement, force, santé, courage.
Mais le destin jaloux, qui marche sur nos pas
Pour ravir une proie à la vie trop féconde,
T'a brisé, pauvre enfant, de son robuste bras
Et ne t'a pas permis de rester en ce monde.

Mais ton ame vivra. Dans le ciel des héros
Tu verras se dresser des cimes bien plus belles,
Tu pourras t'illustrer par des exploits nouveaux
Et fouler sous tes pieds les Alpes éternelles.
Laisse-les te blâmer, ceux qui voudraient restreindre
Cet intrépide instinct qui brave le danger.
Le lâche et le méchant pour nous seuls sont à plaindre
A toi la récompense; à nous de te pleurer.

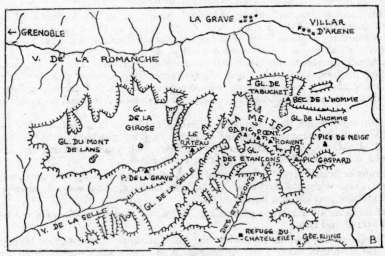

LA MEIJE

CHAPTER FIFTEEN

NIGHT ON THE MATTERHORN

The death of F. C. Borckhardt (Matterhorn, 1886)

WHAT an extraordinary fate befell the Matterhorn! Twenty years after its conquest at the cost of nine years of struggle, eighteen attempts, the combined strength of about forty men, and the deaths of four men at the end, to climb it has now (1886) become the fashionable thing. Anyone climbs it who wants to—or nearly anyone. The terror which it inspired is now no more than a dream. Its shadow which alone in former times would cause men to tremble with fear, now falls upon numerous comfortable hotels, on tennis courts, on tea-rooms and dancing salons. It is, in fact, the attraction of the valley. Guides are born for it—or almost; it breeds them, just as Mont Blanc does at Chamonix. And when, on Saturday, 14th August, 1886, John Davies and Frederick Charles Borckhardt[1] arrive at Zermatt from Central Switzerland, their first thought, after curiously examining and admiring the beautifully carved silhouette, is to climb it. So they make enquiries.

"You wish to make the ascent of the Matterhorn? Nothing, sirs, could be easier! How many of you? Two? Very good! There will be parties on Monday. However, women and youths, everybody climbs it."[2] Rather like the Pont d'Avignon, except that they don't dance there in a ring, but vertically!

"It was," Mr. Davies concludes, "a regular thing to go up the Matterhorn, and we accordingly determined to make the ascent."*[3]

The Englishmen engage two young guides, two good Zermatt guides whose *führerbucher*[4] give every confidence: Fridolin Kronig and Peter Aufdenblatten. On their side, these two mountaineers are careful to find out what experience their "clients" have, to make certain that they are able to undertake the expedition.

"For, after all, even if the Matterhorn is relatively easy of access on good days, it can have freakish moods, and not always comfortable ones. And up there that can very quickly become serious, you know."

Davies reassures the guides. He has lived since infancy among the English hills, he has clambered up several Pyrennean peaks, he has travelled in the Engadine and has made a few excursions there. Only last week he climbed the Titlis. As for Mr. Borckhardt, his oldest friend, he is a very hardened walker.[5] So the business is concluded; they will set out on Monday. The next morning the two friends amuse themselves watching climbers on the Matterhorn through a telescope.

"How tiny they are, those climbers! How slowly they move! . . . But what enormous precipices! Isn't it possible to go another way? . . . Anyway we shall see. . . . It's all terribly exciting, isn't it?"

On Monday evening, August the 16th, four parties occupy the Hörnli hut at the foot of the north-eastern arête of the Matterhorn. The first consists of an Englishman, Mr. J. B. Mercer, and his two guides from Saas, Franz Anthamatten and Josef Furrer; the second of two Dutchmen named Walter, with the guides Josef Mooser of Taesch and Peter Taugwalder of Zermatt; the third, of two Italians, Sig. A. de Falkner and his son, with the three guides Jean-Pierre and Daniel Maquignaz of Valtournanche, and Angelo Ferrari from Pinzolo in the Italian Tirol; the fourth is the Davies–Borckhardt party, with the guides already named.[6] "We were," writes Mr. Davies, "in capital spirits."*

The magnificent weather changes in the night and suddenly becomes angry. The south wind rises and the *foehn* begins to bellow about the mountain. It shakes the hut and tears at its corners in long-drawn howls. But at about three o'clock the sky is clear, despite the wind, and filled with moonlight. It is so transparent and beautiful that the several parties set out without lanterns towards the foot of the promontory-like arête. They disappear one after the other into the archipelago of shadows and light. And while the sixteen men rise among the rocks a distant sheet of mist invades the valley of St. Niklaus, repelled from the Rhone by the rising air, unfurling slowly over Zermatt. A south wind and dense mists like these are bad signs at such an hour. The guides, of course, have seen them; hence their rapid pace.[7]

The Mercer party is leading, followed by the Dutchmen. Near the old hut, where they take a snack, they are joined by the Davies–Borckhardt party, very formally. The Italians are behind. Day is here. There is no sunrise. A wan dawn has paled the moon and absorbed the rising sun. It is an unrelievedly sombre Matterhorn which lifts its precipices towards a sky of uniform grey. But the climbers are not dispirited by this sullen landscape; they continue the ascent, each party at its own pace.

At eight-fifteen, in the middle of the terminal slope, known as the Roof, where rock-strewn snow leads to the summit, three parties come together. Those from below, the Davies–Borckhardt party, can see, by raising their heads, foreshortened bodies black against the white surface of the mountain, their big boots raised, the rope in the sky like a telephone wire on the posts of their axes, and as background the grey wastes of space. Those from above, the Mercer party and the Dutch party, can see, looking down, equally black against the white surface, hats and hands and axes, and a rope like a hand-rail, and as background the valley, nearly seven thousand feet below, enclosed by the mists.

The parties cross. With perfect courtesy each gives way to the other, stepping cautiously a few inches to one side. They graze one another in passing. They stop. The guides exchange a few words in patois.

"Is it far to the summit?" asks one of the travellers.

"No, not very far. You will be there in twenty minutes."

"What's the weather like up there?"

"Not at all good. We didn't stay there very long. No view at all. Everything is obscured. The mist is everywhere."

"And it's getting worse, you know."

"*Vorwärts jetzt, meine Herren!*" the guides then order.

"*Au revoir* . . . good luck."

"Be seeing you soon, down at the hut. A good descent!"

The parties move off. The intervals increase rapidly. Descent. Ascent. Descent. Ascent. Nothing can be seen but moving black spots in the immense sloping solitude.

A little before nine o'clock the Davies–Borckhardt party, followed closely by the Italians, arrive at the summit. The two Englishmen are not at all tired.[8] All is well.

"What a wonderful mountain this Matterhorn is! What a surprise if our families could see us!"

"What! Is this the summit? This crest of snow? These stones? Really! I had expected something quite different. Didn't you?"

The sky is uniformally grey, a twilit sky stirred up like a demented sea. From south to north it rolls, heavily and forcefully. Or is it the Matterhorn itself that heaves? In passing from one side to the other, from the Italian side to the Swiss, the dense mists, as they drift between two enormous cliffs, tear themselves to pieces on the long icicles which hang from the arête. The falling extremities of the wide summit are drowned in spray. And the peak itself is sombre: it has the likeness of a ship's bridge battered by the seas and submerged by a gigantic wave. And this gloomy opacity is suddenly filled with hail.

The parties are on their feet again. The ropes are checked. Knapsacks are adjusted. At nine-twenty the windswept summit resumes its isolation.

Five minutes later, while descending the Roof, a first squall, lurking behind a projecting rock, assails the party with fury. The disordered air suddenly becomes cold, bitterly cold. The hail pours down with violence. The mountain at once becomes white, gripped in a huge cap of frost. A slope that had loomed blackly in the mist mysteriously vanishes. The tracks are effaced. But in these snow-covered rocky slopes, despite the storm, the danger of lost tracks is less than on the wide glaciers of Mont Blanc. The precipice itself is a signpost. Landmarks force themselves on the mind. So, despite the thick bed of hail, the Rochers Rouges, fitted with ropes and chains, are passed without trouble.

The two parties arrived almost together at the Shoulder (14,008 feet), a steep slope of ice covering the arête and overhanging both precipices, the north and the east. This passage is perilous. The least slip will go a long way, a very long way. In fact, into eternity. The Davies–Borckhardt party, leading thus far, gives way to the Italian party and waits patiently until the Italians have cleared the passage. The Italians set foot upon the ice which vanishes into the fog and are soon swallowed up. The blows of their axes can be heard.

At this instant a veritable hurricane is let loose. Snow mingles with the hail. A brutal wind wheels about the rocks with the roar of an express train on a steel bridge. And when the Englishmen's turn has come to venture upon the ice, the steps just cut by the Italians no longer exist. The Swiss guides remake each step with minute care. The violence of the squalls, the frenzy of the snow, the hail which blows into their eyes, the frozen rope, the deathly cold, the steps which fill up at once and have to be cleared or remade—the sum of all these torments, constantly increasing, is such that this unhappy party takes two hours to cross this frozen slope which would normally occupy ten minutes. Rock is reached at last. The climbers find themselves on a firmer footing once more.

Despite the storm the Englishmen's spirit is still perfect although they are only novice climbers.[9] This incredible fact gives us the impression that until now they have not in the least realised the extent of the dangers through which they are passing. Like Tartarin on the Jungfrau or Mont Blanc, these novices know for certain that all will be well, and that this evening, at the hut. . . . Ah! the joy of a cup of boiling tea, and the warmth of the blankets. So why make a fuss? This serene confidence, this unshakable faith in the illimitable powers of the guides is almost too touching.

However, an apparently insignificant incident has just disturbed these ingenuous souls:[10] in the dense mists and the masses of snow, voices, broken by the wind, rise from mysterious depths— "Where are you?" they can be heard to say. "What is there? What are you saying?"

The voices are those of the Italians who have strayed in the storm and have come to an abrupt halt on the edge of a precipice. The two parties join up once more. The Swiss and Italian guides argue amongst themselves and point in opposite directions.[11] Those from Valtournanche hesitate to go on.

Now the darkness begins to fill the hurricane. It is six o'clock. The Italians have started off again. In a short while they call out that all goes well; they have found the track. The Englishmen follow. The snow settles on the viscous rocks, melts, settles again, and melts once more with unwearying meekness. The hail streams down and rebounds; its noisy fall mingles with the soft rustle of the snow. And above them passes the great wild surge of the wind.

It is now, for the first time, that anxiety strikes at the hearts of the English climbers like a ravening beast of prey, and will not let them go. "It now seemed impossible to make our way to the cabin that night."* Their courage collapses. They can no longer think. They are automatons, led by their guides on a leash. They turn to the right in the snow and are slapped in the face by the wind; snow gets into their mouths, their eyelashes and eyebrows; their moustaches are thick with it. They cross a couloir, they turn left. Their backs are to the snow and are whipped by it. Now they cross the Moseley-Platte.[12] Leaning over a ravine they stop short, start again, stop once more, hesitate.

"Certainly not . . . no . . . it can't be done. . . . Fridolin, Peter . . . What do you want us to do? . . . Must we really? . . . You find it difficult too? . . . Ah! Good! . . . You are such nice fellows."

At about 12,800 feet, beside a rock and on the edge of a precipice, under a slight projection of rock offering terribly illusory shelter, the party awaits the night, blockaded by the hurricane and the invading darkness. It is seven o'clock. These men have been on the move for sixteen hours, with no more rest than the twenty minutes spent at the summit. Ten hours have so far been occupied by the exhausting descent. They are broken with exhaustion and numb with the cold. Their ice-stiffened clothing burns where it clings to the flesh. In this fearful bivouac the cold is everything.

The mountain is very quickly enveloped in darkness, a darkness streaked with the snow, a wall of hail on the move. It is too cold to eat; a little brandy is passed around, but it is already frozen. Three hundred feet below them the Italians too have been forced to halt, and their voices can be heard through the holes in the wind. Now and then they shout from one bivouac to another, as if the vocal link can create a tangible and strengthening solidarity between these two remnants of humanity, lost in the savagery of the night.[13]

* * *

An atrocious night; a night of torment. "We were chilled to the bone and too exhausted to stand. The wind rose and each gust drove the hail into our faces, cutting us like a knife."[14] The guides faced misfortune with courage. They "did everything that man could do to save us."

Peter Aufdenblatten tried to reassure his travellers: "Only

keep yourselves warm," he said; "keep moving, and we shall go down all right to-morrow, when the sun rises."

"It is of no use," Davies replied, "we shall die here."

"They chafed our limbs," Davies's own account continues, "and did their best to make us stand up; but it was in vain. I felt angry at their interference. Why could they not leave us alone to die? I remember striking wildly but feebly at my guide as he insisted on rubbing me. Every movement gave me such agony, I was racked with pain, especially in my back and loins—pain so intense as to make me cry out."

As a precautionary measure the guides tied the rope to a rock to make the party fast; and it served them as bars in a gymnasium, leaping up and down to maintain their circulation.

*"They brought us to it, and made us jump twice or thrice. Move we could not; we lay back prostrate on the snow and ice, while the guides varied their jumping by rubbing our limbs and endeavouring to make us move our arms and legs. They were getting feebler and feebler. Borckhardt and I, as soon as we were fully convinced that death was imminent for us, did our best to persuade our guides to leave us where we lay and make their way down the hill. They were married men with families. To save us was impossible. They might at least save themselves. We begged them to consider their wives and children and to go. . . . They refused. They would rather die with us, they said; they would remain and do their best.

"Borckhardt and I talked a little as men might who are on the point of death. He bore without complaining pain which had made me cry out from time to time. We both left directions with the guides that we were to be buried at Zermatt. Borckhardt spoke of his friends and his family affairs, facing death with manly resignation and composure. As the night wore on I became weaker and weaker. I could not even make the effort necessary to flick the snow off my companion's face. By degrees the guides themselves began to lose hope. The cold was so intense we crouched together for warmth. They lay beside us to try and impart some heat. It was in vain. 'We shall die! . . . We are lost!' we said. 'Yes,' said Aufdenblatten, 'very likely we shall.' He was so weak, poor fellow, he could hardly keep his feet; but still he tried to keep me moving. It was a relief not to be touched. I longed for death, but death would not come.

"Towards half-past two on Wednesday morning—so we

171

reckoned, for all our watches had stopped with the cold—the snow ceased and the air became clear. It had been snowing or hailing without intermission for eighteen hours. It was very dark below, but all was clear above, although the wind still blew. When the sun rose we saw just a gleam of light. Then a dark cloud came from the hollow below, and our hopes went out. 'Oh, if only the sun would come out!' we said to each other I don't know how many times. But it did not, and instead of the sun came the snow once more. Towards seven, as near as I can make it, a desperate attempt was made to get us to walk. The guides took Borckhardt, and between them propped him on his feet and made him stagger on a few steps. They failed to keep him moving more than a step or two. The moment they let go he dropped. They repeated the same with me. Neither could I stand. I remember four distinct times that they drove us forward, only to see us drop helpless after each step. It was evidently no use. Borckhardt had joined again with me in repeatedly urging the guides to leave us and save themselves. They had refused and continued to do all that their failing strength allowed to protect us from the bitter cold. As the morning wore on, my friend, who during the night had been much more composed and tranquil than I, began to grow perceptibly weaker. We were quite resigned to die, and had, in fact, lost all hope. We had been on the mountain from about 3 a.m. on Tuesday to 1 p.m. on Wednesday—thirty-four hours in all. Eighteen of these were spent in a blinding snowstorm, and we had hardly tasted food since we left the summit at nine on the Tuesday morning.

"At length (about one) we heard shouts far down the mountain. The guides said they probably proceeded from a search party sent out to save us. I again urged the guides to go down by themselves to meet the searchers and to hurry them up. This they refused to do unless I accompanied them. Borckhardt was at this time too much exhausted to stand upright, and was by now in a helpless condition. The guides, although completely worn out, wished to attempt the descent with me, and they considered that by so doing we should be able to indicate to the searchers the precise spot where my friend lay, and to hasten their efforts to reach him with stimulants.

"Since early morning the snow had ceased falling. We began the descent, and at first I required much assistance from the guides, but by degrees became better able to move, and the hope of soon procuring help from the approaching party for my poor friend sustained us. After a most laborious descent of about an hour and a half, we reached the first members of the rescue party, and directed them to where Borckhardt lay, requesting them to proceed there with all haste, and, after giving him stimulants, to bring him down to the lower hut in whatever condition they found him."*[15]

At five in the evening of Wednesday, 18th August, thirty-eight hours after having left the Hörnli hut, Mr. John Davies and his guides recrossed its threshold. Simultaneously the rescue party reached the desolate bivouac.[16] Stretched upon the rock, his terrors stilled at last, Frederick Charles Borckhardt, his eyes wide open, seemed to be watching the plumes of snow which were swept from the arête by the wind and took flight with the beat of an angel's wings. The frost had clothed him in a shining garment. He was dead.

*   *   *

The desertion of the unfortunate Borckhardt by his guides and companion aroused a passionate controversy. Eminent British, Austrian and Italian alpinists then in Zermatt, and the whole of the Alpine Club, joined in. The cantonal government of the Valais conducted a judicial enquiry, and a new Code was worked out for the guides. But the enquiry ended with insufficient grounds for legal action: the culpability of the guides in the Davies–Borckhardt party was not recognised. It is sufficient, however, to read Mr. Davies' account of the night at the bivouac, as given above, to convince oneself immediately that these guides did everything, or almost everything, to save their employers. And again, in this tragedy, as in the 1871 catastrophe on Mont Blanc[17] and in others, because of argument and conjecture one tends to lose sight of what in my view are the essential elements: the strength of the storm at such great altitudes and the tragic nature of the bivouac. The drama which slowly develops is thus no more than the out- come of a succession of physical facts whose inexorability ends by enclosing a man's mind and exhausting his energies. The mis- takes that are made and the blameable deeds—they are always to be found—are clearly determined by external circumstances and not by a pre-existing psychological inferiority. To which one other factor, the physical condition of the victims, must be added.

For my own part, the most logical conclusion concerning this fatality is that given by Guido Rey with clarity and simplicity: "The guides descended too late to be able to hope to bring help to their traveller in time, and too soon, since they did not remain long enough beside the dying man to close his eyes."

This is the epitaph to be found in the English cemetery in Zermatt:

IN MEMORY OF FREDERICK C. BORCKHARDT

SAINT-ALBANS HERTS.

WHO PERISHED ON THE MATTERHORN DURING A TERRIBLE

SNOWSTORM, 18 AUGUST, 1886, AGED 48

For the scene of the Borckhardt tragedy, see Plate 18 (also, for the principal features of the Swiss side of the Matterhorn, plate 12).

[1] He was the youngest son of the Rev. Borckhardt, vicar of Lydden.

[2] This authentic statement exasperated Whymper. He quotes it in his *Guide to Zermatt.*

[3] All the quotations marked with asterisks are taken from Mr. John Davies's story, more vivid and human than any literary effort.

[4] Every Swiss guide is furnished with an official booklet (*Führerbuch* or *livret*) by the cantonal authority, and it is annually inspected. In it a traveller notes the climb or climbs he has made with an appreciation of his guide, his capacity and behaviour.

[5] Puerile evidence and of no value whatever.

[6] Cf. *Alpine Journal*, Vol. XIII, 1886–88.

[7] The same night, and at the same hour, an English climber, the Rev. T. A. Lacey, slept at the Riffelhaus with the intention of climbing Monte Rosa the following day. But seeing the weather deteriorate, his party decided not to set out. Two parties which persisted, nevertheless, returned late in the day, Monte Rosa being obliterated and badly battered by the storm.

[8] Davies notes: "Both Mr. Borckhardt and myself were quite fresh, although we had made the summit before the Italians, who started together with us from the second hut."

[9] "We were still in good spirits," writes Davies, "nor did we feel any doubt that we should reach the bottom."

[10] On this point Davies's statement, disconcertingly naïve, is revealing: "Had the weather remained favourable, we could have made the descent with ease." Doubtless! But the true climber should be able to carry out his descent whatever the weather—or at least try to. Whoever is able to make an ascent only in calm and fine weather presumes too much on his physical and mental powers; his place is not on the heights—he should remain in the tea-room or not venture beyond the huts.

[11] Such hesitation in thick mist, in the storm and at nightfall, while descending the Swiss side of the Matterhorn is quite natural. I have found myself in similar conditions, perhaps worse, in this locality at the end of September 1923. We had traversed the Matterhorn from Breuil towards Zermatt with a squad of the best guides of St. Niklaus and Zermatt, in order to complete the filming of my book *La Croix du Cervin*. At five-thirty in the afternoon a storm swept the summit just when we were undertaking the descent—snow, hail, cloud and wind. Night overtook us at the Shoulder. We pursued the interminable descent in raging darkness, arriving at the Hörnli hut without a hitch at two in the morning. We were clothed in ice and snow, as white as ghosts.

¹² See Chapter 11 (Part I).

¹³ The fate of the other two parties—Mr. Mercer's and the Dutch party—was less tragic. The former, very quick, had already returned to Zermatt by four-thirty in the afternoon; the latter just avoided a bivouac and reached the hut at eleven at night. Neither party could guess the drama that was being played out in the rocks they had just left.

¹⁴ In the admirable paper dedicated to his guide Daniel Maquignaz, Capt. Farrar said: "It was in great measure due to his sangfroid and example that his party in 1886 survived that awful night spent on the Cervin (Matterhorn) which proved fatal to Mr. Borckhardt. He has often told me how the cold was so intense that the snow froze on them as it fell, clothing them in a sheet of ice, till life seemed insupportable." (*Alpine Journal*, XXV, 1910.)

¹⁵ Cf. *Alpine Journal*, Vol. XIII, 1886–88.

¹⁶ This party comprised the following guides, all from St. Niklaus: Peter Knubel, Chanton, Brantschen and Imboden.

¹⁷ See Chapter 8.

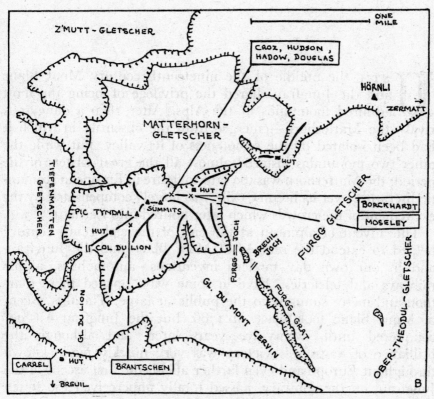

THE MATTERHORN AND SURROUNDING GLACIERS

CHAPTER SIXTEEN

TRAGEDY ON THE JUNGFRAU

The death of the six guideless climbers: Dr. Alexander Wettstein, Heinrich
Wettstein, Gottfried Kuhn, Wilhelm Bär, Karl Ziegler and Gustav Bider
(Jungfrau, south-east side, July 15th, 1887)

UNTIL the middle of the nineteenth century Mont Blanc
and the Jungfrau shared the privilege of being the most
admired mountains in the Alps. After 1860 a dangerous
rival—the Matterhorn—emerged from the obscurity in which it
had been isolated by the remoteness of its valley. But while the
other two mountains inspired almost all the great writers of the
period, the Matterhorn was too late to figure in European Romantic literature; yet its literary exile was largely compensated by the
excitement of the crowds which later poured into Zermatt.

The advent of alpinism at the end of the eighteenth century
helped to extend the renown of Mont Blanc and the Jungfrau,
and in our own day modern inventions—automobiles, alpine
railways and teleferics—have in some ways opened these four-
thousand-metre summits to the public at large. The first ascent
of Mont Blanc took place in 1786, but the Jungfrau was not
conquered until twenty-five years later, and although the
brilliance of Saussure's victory was very quickly made known
throughout Europe and even farther afield, the first ascent of the
Jungfrau, on the contrary, passed totally unperceived—so much
so that ten, twenty, thirty and even fifty years afterwards, eminent
travellers in Switzerland (to name a few at random: Mme de
Staël, Byron, de Musset and Lamartine) continued with imper-
turbable innocence to excite themselves about this Virgin, who

had not been virgin for a long time. "We perceived in the distance," writes Mme de Staël, "the mountain which bears the name 'The Virgin' (Jungfrau) because no traveller has succeeded in climbing to its summit; it is not so high as Mont Blanc, but it inspires more respect because it is known to be inaccessible."

This definition sets the tone. The symbolical name "Jungfrau" alone, in fact, led all these artists and thinkers into error, and their lyrical fervour took fire at the Jungfrau's spurious virginity. Twenty years after the first ascent, Alfred de Musset, unfaithful to his tender muse of *Nuits*, took up his lute and, turning to his new flame, struck up this paean:[1]

AU YUNG-FRAU

Yung-Frau, le voyageur qui pourrait sur ta tête
S'arrêter, et poser le pied sur sa conquête,
Sentirait en son cœur un noble battement,
Quand son âme, au penchant de ta neige éternelle,
Pareille au jeune aiglon qui passe et lui tend l'aile,
Glisserait et fuirait sous le clair firmament.
Yung-Frau, je sais un cœur qui, comme toi, se cache.
Revêtu, comme toi, d'une robe sans tache,
Il est plus près de Dieu que tu ne l'es du ciel.
Ne t'étonne donc point, ô montagne sublime,
Si la première fois que j'en ai vu la cime,
J'ai cru le lieu trop haut pour etre d'un mortel.

However, on 3rd August, 1811, exactly eighteen years before these lines were composed, the Jungfrau (13,670 feet) was conquered by two honest citizens of the Canton Aargau, the brothers Johann-Rudolf and Hieronymous Meyer,[2] sons of a rich Aarau merchant. And in 1887, many years after the publication of the poem, which in all good faith glorified the innocence of the virgin of Interlaken, a terrible accident occurred on its exciting snows. Six men died there and, with the exception of the Mont Blanc catastrophe of 1871,[3] it was the greatest of all alpine disasters. Between the first ascent in 1811 and the occasion of this great tragedy, the mountain had been ascended many times from almost every side and by the most renowned climbers of those days—Hugi, Agassiz, Forbes, Studer, Winkworth, Tyndall, Stephen, Moore, Hornby, Fellenberg, Mathews, Coolidge, Walker, to name but a few—and their guides. But with touching blindness, although this élite of the climbing community had made their rendezvous "on a place too high for mortals," the mass of tourists, inheriting the romantic tradition, continued to tremble before this magnetic mountain to whose magic was added the prestige of its wild virginity. The six men who died there in 1887 must almost certainly have put a prosaic end to this too beautiful legend.

*　　*　　*

The chalets of the little village of Lauterbrunnen cower at the foot of the high cliffs which support the village and the high pastures of Mürren. It is the kind of deliciously poetic spot the Romantics loved, first for the echoes raised by the sad notes of the alpine horn, and second for its cascade, the Staubbach, which three illustrious sponsors—Goethe,[4] Wordsworth[5] and Byron—introduced into German and English literature. Goethe dedicated an enchanting poem to this fascinating waterfall, with a kind of imitative harmony, the fluid verses recalling the music of its waters. And Byron, contemplating "its lines of foaming light . . . like the pale courser's tail, the Giant steed, to be bestrode by Death . . ." makes it appear in *Manfred* as the genius of the place in material form. Nothing less!

But besides its inspirational role, Lauterbrunnen (the name alone is a delight—"Clear Springs") also holds a prominent place in mountain history. Its guides, like those of Grindelwald or Meiringen, played their part in the conquest of the Alps.[6] In the period which follows the heroic age of alpinism, when the peaks were climbed with the aid of immense alpenstocks and long-handled axes, when rope technique was still little understood and the guide was king, the years from 1876 to 1890 roughly mark a notable change in the art of climbing and exploring mountains. It would be false to say that the guides' star was waning. Far from it! But the change which then took place and the feature which then developed was the increasing body of simple alpinists attempting to do without guides at all. Until 1876 the parties that dared to free themselves from the paternal commands of a guide were in fact extremely rare;[7] in the valleys through which they passed fingers were pointed at them. But from about that time the idea developed rapidly and made recruits in increasing numbers. The alpine clubs argued the matter heatedly, the public joined in, the Press examined the

178

matter, censured or approved, and the *Alpine Journal* attempted gravely to establish an essential difference between the mountaineer and the tourist and the accidents assignable to each category. The cruel death of young Emil Zsigmondy on the Meije in 1885, one of the first notorious "guideless" accidents, attracted much controversy, and the terrible tragedy on the Jungfrau in 1887 seemed to give commanding proof to the defenders of guided climbing. But since alpinism is above all the product of a clearly psychological process, how could the march of ideas be halted?

On Wednesday, 13th July, 1887, a happy band of six young climbers, all of them German Swiss, arrived at Lauterbrunnen from Wengeralp. On the way they had ascended the Mänlichen, the classic Wengen excursion. The highway from Interlaken, after passing through half-shadowy woods where mossy rocks are massed, emerges at last into the crystalline light of the meadows and joins the road from Wengen at the entrance to the village. The church stands out above the chalets; the valley's cliffs rise on both sides to form a romantic Turner-like décor; the Staubbach fall drapes its shifting veil over the wall; while the aery glaciers of the Jungfrau and of the Breithorn chain lose themselves in the vaporous distances of a quiet blue sky.

Neat and prepossessing, like one of those little Swiss chalets made in the workshop of some local woodcarver, with gilded walls and windows filled with scarlet geraniums, the Staubbach Hotel was an attraction to the traveller. Bursting into the village street, this noisy band of climbers gathered in front of the inn, while the deep notes of an alpine horn were heard afar off.

"Come in, won't you?" Gretchen, the courteous maid in Bernese costume, asked them. And the inn-keeper put in an appearance too: "Yes, yes," he said, "we have room. Come in, sirs. Please be good enough to enter."

The corridor resounded to their nailed boots, and soon all these young men were installed in little rooms still smelling of resin, while articles of climbing equipment and clothing piled up on the floor—ropes, alpenstocks, ice-axes, flasks, geological hammers, knapsacks, field-glasses. Lively voices mingled one with another; occasionally a song broke out. Then, while the young men made their round of the shops, Gretchen and the inn-keeper, both intrigued by these merry companions, leaned over the visitors' book and read the following names:

Dr. Alexander Wettstein, geologist, S.A.C., Uto section, Küssnacht.
Heinrich Wettstein, Divisional Chief, Federal Department of Commerce
and Agriculture, Bern.
Wilhelm Bär, schoolmaster, Hottingen.
Karl Ziegler, schoolmaster, Zurich.
Gustav Bider, pharmaceutical chemist, Bern.
Gottfried Kuhn, schoolmaster, S.C.A. Tödi section, Glaris.

"So, so," says the inn-keeper. "*Feine Herren!*"
The oldest of the party was only thirty-four years of age.

* * *

In the evening the six men met around the big table where the
soup tureen was steaming. There with animation they discussed
their plan to climb the Jungfrau from the Rottal;[9] but they
changed the subject the moment a third party appeared. The
most diverse topics were discussed, concerned with yards of rope,
with alpenstocks, with the superiority of alpenstocks over ice-axes,
with four-spiked crampons, with hard snow in couloirs and verglas
on rocks, with geology and marmots, with the effects of lightning
on rock, with botany and with wood for their bivouac, with
blankets and with beds of rhododendron, and with the strange route
taken by the Meyer brothers on their "first" on the Jungfrau. All this
talk, thrown into the air and caught in flight, all this exuberance
continued to intrigue the inn-keeper, who was curious to know
his guests' plans. He approached the question cautiously:

"The gentlemen are undoubtedly preparing to cross the
Petersgrat? M. de Fellenberg, from Bern, slept here too when he
crossed the Tschingelgrat in 1868, but it was my father who
owned the inn in those days."

The young men fell silent, apparently impressed to know that
celebrated Swiss climbers had also slept at the Staubbach Hotel,
and the eldest of the party, Dr. Alexander Wettstein, was the
first to reply:

"We are only going to explore the mountains," he said. "It's
a change for us after the city air."

"After the air of a laboratory, too," added the chemist.

There was a general babble of irrelevant conversation, but the
inn-keeper, guessing that something was being hidden from him
and scenting a major expedition, concluded:

"Be careful, my dear sirs! If you are planning to climb a big mountain, do not hesitate to take a guide. There are sufficient here in Lauterbrunnen, and they would be happy to accompany you. Accidents happen so easily. Remember Mr. Penhall on the Wetterhorn in '82 and Andreas Maurer. Andreas was a good fellow, too. I was in Grindelwald on the day of the funeral and I saw Peter Baumann in tears."

Hardly had the inn-keeper left them when one of the company, impressed by these reflections, openly suggested engaging a guide. A general hue and cry followed.

"Take a guide? In heaven's name, why? . . . If you're afraid, don't come with us. . . . A guide? What's the use of a guide? . . . And what about us? I suppose we don't count!"

Before this overwhelming majority, indignantly rejecting such an absurd suggestion, the dissentient voice was silent, and calm returned.[10]

That night, on reaching his room, one of the tourists scanned the sky from his window and was addressed by a guide who was leaving the café: "You're setting out for the glaciers, sir?"

"Yes, to-morrow."

"Without wishing to be indiscreet, may I ask where?"

"Oh! We don't exactly know. Over that way, in the Rottal direction."

"Then be careful! The weather is changing. Look at that small cloud over there on the summit of the Breithorn."

On the following day, Thursday the 14th, the unknown guide's prediction was clearly fulfilled. The sky, still very blue the day before, but of that hard blue too beautiful and heavy to last, grew dull, became heavy with grey cloud. "The precursory signs of a prolonged storm struck the gaze of all the inhabitants of the country."[11] But heedless and youthfully headstrong, the guideless climbers prepared to leave. On the terrace of the Staubbach Hotel they filled their packs,[12] adjusted their loads, picked up their ice-axes and alpenstocks,[13] exchanged farewells with the inn-keeper, his wife and Gretchen, and off they went.

"Well, sirs," said the inn-keeper in parting, "I hope you have a good journey. But, once again, do be careful."

*　　　*　　　*

The caravan left Lauterbrunnen for the Rottal hut[14] at two in the afternoon. As they left the village and took the Stechelberg route, a guide, returning from the fields with a rake over his shoulder, addressed them rather harshly. "See to it," he said, "that we don't have to come and pick you up in the Rottal." But these prophetic words, which might in ancient times have caused an army to turn back, were without effect. They were brushed aside with jests, and they struck up a students' song.

On their way to the Stufensteinalp a brutal storm broke loose. The climbers plodded on through dense rain and reached the alpage soaked to the skin. Among the grey hovels the little band indolently suffered the teeming rain. The master cheesemaker was stirring his milk, a large bright fire crackling under the caldron, and the weary and sodden group invaded the cabin and pleasurably swallowed the café-au-lait that was offered them. But when the herdsman tried to dissuade them from continuing their expedition and invited them to spend the night on the hay, he met with a vigorous refusal. His hospitality was brushed aside, like the words of the prophetic guide down in the valley that same afternoon.

In the evening they reached the Rottal hut, where they were to sleep. The south wind blew in squalls. The dark clouds tore themselves to pieces on the peaks. The air was almost lukewarm. But soon, in a starless night, there was only a flickering light in the window of the hut and happily grouped around it these six young men who were about to die. Then the gleam was extinguished, and the damp shadows took possession of the night, deadening the creaking of the glaciers.

At five o'clock on Friday morning, the 15th—relatively late— the climbers were again on the move. Gustav Bider and Karl Ziegler were the last to leave. As they closed the door, someone thought it would be a good idea to leave a note of the party's passage. Bider handed one of his visiting cards to Ziegler, and on the back of it were written the names of the six climbers, with these laconic words: "On the way to the Jungfrau."

An uncertain dawn, alternately concealed and revealed by the movement of the clouds, fell by luminous patches on the peaks. Areas of shadow and light ran irregularly over the glaciers, but the horizon remained dull. On the heights it had been snowing. And the sounds of the party as it tramped over the moraines were very quickly lost in the heavy gloom of a too warm dawn.

They were just leaving the last of the grass when a volley of whistles pierced the fluidity of the morning silence. Not far away some marmots ran off. But a little marmot, curious and disobedient, stayed to watch these strange animals, never seen before, climbing towards him. When he tried to flee it was too late. He was seized from above. Touching, because of his wild looks, his childlike eyes, his thick fur and his moustache, the captive achieved a quick success. One of the young men decided that the marmot should also make the ascent and that they should take him home and train him. At this there was much laughter, and the happy proprietor gathered a handful of grass, placed the marmot in the middle of it, rolled it up in his handkerchief and carefully slid the whole bundle into his knapsack. At that moment Ziegler and Dr. Wettstein rejoined the party, well satisfied with their researches; Ziegler had discovered numerous traces of lightning on the rocks, and Wettstein had gathered certain specimens of stone for his mineralogical collection.

The marmot hunt, the search for rock specimens and for the marks of lightning on the rocks being finished, the climbers unwound their rope, tied up and slowly took to the rocks above. These diversions had somewhat delayed them and bad weather was threatening.

In the valley the secrecy of the expedition had not failed to arouse considerable curiosity. Quite early some chamois-hunters at Trachsellauenen and Schilt were watching the Jungfrau through telescopes, and between six and seven o'clock the six climbers had been located, still quite low on the south-east face. The fresh snow and the uncertainty of the weather alone could justify such a late departure. "They are just imprudent," said some. "They have been delayed by geological investigations," said others. But here, as in many other tragedies whence none came back, we are reduced to conjecture. Be that as it may, the six young men on the arête rose quite quickly, as if they sought to regain the time they had lost. But lost time, Virgil's *irreparabile tempus*, is never recovered, above all in the high mountains, where every minute holds within it the seed of so many occurrences whose repercussions on the plane of reality can very quickly become formidable. At midday gloomy signs appeared in the depths of the sky. Squalls of wind rushed in and became colder; the clouds piled up, becoming more dense, obscuring the summits. But these portents, heralding the storm, did not break the enthusiasm of the climbers; on the contrary. They had surmounted all difficulties and had now reached the last névés flanking the culminating arêtes. At that moment a sooty cloud capped the Jungfrau; it remained there a moment, hesitating; then, over-balancing, it suddenly submerged the caravan. It was then two o'clock.

Simultaneously a flood of rain fell upon the whole valley of Lauterbrunnen. This mass of water, falling from a livid ceiling, was soon ablaze with lightning. The thunder roared and rolled, rebounding against the valley walls; it was taken up again and amplified by the echoes which, thanks to the strange acoustics of these mountains, reverberated infinitely like the great voice of an angry god. Tattered by the wind, rent by the spurs of rock, the clouds momentarily opened and snow could be seen lying white upon the slopes to the upper limits of the grass.

*　　*　　*

On the summit arête, in the howling wind, in the assaults of the snow and the clouds, the six climbers pursue their way. They are tied to a single rope, and thus united against the storm, these six young men face a hostile fate and all its snares with quiet confidence. Their common lot increases their courage. Exhaustion cannot destroy their strength.

"Is it still so far to the summit? We've been climbing a long while."

Nobody answers Karl Ziegler, who does not repeat his question. Some minutes later, however, overwhelmed by the monotony of the snow, Ziegler stops and breaks the order of the column. The taut rope drags on those in front, while those who follow run foul of each other. They stop, surprised. Exclamations are heard. Ziegler, exhausted, declares he has had enough and points out, among the stones bordering the crest to the east, a corner pro-viding some shelter. He will wait for his comrades there. A brief discussion ensues, rendered incomprehensible by the wind. One voice asserts that the summit cannot be far off. Ziegler is not convinced. He releases himself from the rope with difficulty and carefully makes his way to the platform.

The summit is, in fact, no more than twenty yards away. But twenty yards in such a storm, at a height of over 13,000 feet, can suddenly transform themselves into miles.

The summit? It is no more than this volute of snow in the midst of a whirlwind. The surge of the wind, like conflicting currents of water which end by neutralizing each other, thereby reaching almost complete immobility, has fastened a platform of cloud to the northern parapet, almost as if the arête itself is prolonged into a floor. But under a more violent gust of wind this platform of cloud half opens above a bottomless abyss of black and white, which reeks like a perspiring beast.

They stay there at the summit for a minute, long enough to congratulate themselves on their victory by smiles and nods, signs which in their way express the supremacy of mind over the brute force of the hurricane.[15] They begin the descent forthwith. Behind them the storm tears at the summit and plays on its fringe of icicles a series of syncopated whistles of barbaric beauty.

* * *

The tracks on the arête were already covered. Like blind men the climbers groped their way through the snow. The ridge of this frozen roof was their guide, forbidding them to venture towards the depths of demented whiteness from which a deafening uproar rose.

A rope of five men is a long one. The last two were still treading the summit when those in front had already reached the place where Ziegler was waiting. It was a narrow space, a stony platform slightly below and to the east of the crest and problematically protected from the wind by the parapet of snow. Ziegler, to avoid catching cold, had occupied himself in clearing away the snow with his feet and piling up the stones. His returning comrades caught him at work. There was a brief exchange of words, and very quickly, one after another, the climbers left the arête, slid down the snow and landed on the platform. A few yards in front of them lay the edge of the enormous precipice which plunges to the Jungfraufirn in a single flight.

In this relatively calm spot, leaning on their sticks, with their packs still on their backs and the rope in disorder about their feet, the climbers held council whether to continue their descent, and if so, by what route. Should they follow the way they had come up? It had never been done before, and they might quickly lose direction in a storm like this.

"Will you be able," one of them asked, "to find the way again?"

The man who was questioned remained silent. But since it was impossible to reach Concordia that evening should they not bivouac on the glacier, where they would at least have some idea of their position?

"These storms never last very long, you know. In the morning we can be on our way to the hut; there will be plenty of blue sky, you will see . . ."

On this they agreed. The rope was untied, they dropped their packs and Ziegler, improvised chief mason, expounded his plans. The wind was piling the snow up quickly down there; so, by building a shelter of four small walls, two good paces wide by about five feet long and about twenty-seven inches high, they should be able to pass a relatively good night.

"What about the roof?" someone asked. "You've brought no joists or tiles!"

"The roof! Oh, that's quite simple: we'll do without one."

"That damned Ziegler thinks of everything, doesn't he?"

"He'd certainly make a better success as a builder than a teacher!"

"My goodness! I'd swear he came here to look for a site."

"He has foreseen everything."

"Gentlemen; book your rooms by telegram!"

"One or two beds?"

"Prompt and attentive service!"

"Heating is extra!"

Such pleasantries revived their slightly flagging spirits, and the six young men set to work. A feverish activity soon prevailed on the platform and the foundations quickly took shape. But when at the end of some thirty or forty minutes' work the walls were completed, the workers found themselves suddenly face to face with sinister idleness; there was nothing then to do but wait— wait for the evening, wait for the night, wait for dawn, wait for the moment when they could rope up again and be on their way. But that could scarcely be for a few hours yet.

Thus, confusedly obedient to the instinct of self-preservation, they used the strength and warmth regained by their building activities in preparing themselves to endure their isolation as comfortably as possible. But the snow was so dense and the wind so fierce that they had not the courage to take off any of their clothes, and they contented themselves with putting on their sweaters and spare shirts over their waistcoats, then buttoning their jackets again over the lot. They tied up the ends of their sleeves with string and resumed their gaiters. They turned up their collars, tied scarves round their necks and knotted others under their chins and over their hats. Then they put on their gloves and were ready, laughing rather thinly as they looked at one another thus bundled up and already shrinking a little from the touch of the snow and from the wind which cut at the backs of their necks. Then they stepped over the walls, cleared away the snow for the last time, and sat down on their packs or on the rope in two ranks of three, leaning upon one another, close together, as if dovetailed one into the other. Then one or two of them lit their pipes, and for a moment the storm was softened by the aroma of tobacco.

Not far from the bivouac the wind raged at the summit with the roar of the sea against a jetty. Blankets of snow followed one another relentlessly in the gloomy emptiness of space. They could hear the rumble of distant thunder as it travelled along the valleys far below.

Night fell swiftly, without twilight. Abruptly, almost without transition, came the shadows which thickened the showers of snow and intensified the force of the wind.

The six climbers very quickly became white. The snow stuck to their woollen clothing, moulding itself to sloping backs, to the bowed heads and to the arms which were pressed firmly to the climbers' sides. They began to look like six abandoned plaster-casts. And in order to dispel the insidious distress of this wretched shelter, and to hold discouragement in check, the more lively men exchanged amusing and ridiculous talk:

"Gentlemen," said one of them, "I have the honour to inform you that it is still snowing." He stretched out an arm and brought back a handful of snow.

"That's what Noah did during the flood, to see if it was still raining!"

"Yes; but he had all sails set for Ararat! While we . . ."

"The first by boat to the summit of Ararat! Seventeen thousand feet by boat! That's an adventure unique in all the history of climbing!" There was a burst of laughter.

"While we, thirteen thousand feet up in the air are pleasantly motionless on these stones."

"Don't make a fuss. If this wind continues we shall be able to fly to Concordia!"

"Why not? Don't you remember old Dollfus-Ausset and the balloon he was going to use to reach the top of the Matterhorn?"

"Perhaps Cathrein will use a balloon to tell us if he has sent the provisions to Concordia."

"Good God!" someone sighed. "What wouldn't I give for a slice of bread and butter and honey!"

"Rather! But while we're waiting, what about some supper? We can begin with an omelette."

A knapsack was opened, the gigantic "omelette for six" appeared and was quickly divided.[16] But the wise man of the party observed that it would be wise to keep a bit for the next day.

"As for desert, it is still snowing."

"Still snowing?"

"Not even a blade of grass for the dove to bring us."

"A dove? No! A marmot!"

In the hurry of the ascent and the torments of the storm they had in fact completely forgotten the animal's presence. He who had charge of it drew a bundle out of his pack and unwrapped it with motherly gestures. The little marmot appeared in its wrapping of grass, hardly larger than a kitten. It opened its round eyes, casting a terrified glance around, and with its fur in disorder and its ridiculous little face it amused the company. They passed it from hand to hand, each one caressing its plump body, and addressing it with tender and stupid words. The marmot suffered it all, completely amazed, bringing to the sinister bivouac the mysterious charm of its wild young life, snatched from the peace of the grassy slopes and fallen rocks.

"And if any burglars should come near, you whistle. See?"

"After the omelette I suggest we have stewed marmot," a sepulchral voice proposed. A protesting murmur muffled this infamous suggestion.

"Gentlemen; it is time to put out the fires."

There was some forced laughter. Their reactions were growing less, as if the collective spirit which until then had animated the party, giving it a sort of unity, was falling apart and the six men were becoming insidiously exhausted. They sat there tightly crammed together, all undergoing the same martyrdom, but each individually assuming his freedom and isolating himself in

his dreams, foundering in a kind of stupefaction. In the terrors
of that cruel night a new psychological state was born in which
all thought was extinguished. After that there was nothing but
the enormous complaint of the angry wind, and on this maddened
sea of air this frail raft of shipwrecked men.

*   *   *

In the café of the Staubbach Hotel the guides were drinking.
Anxiety kept them silent. Near them, standing under the oil-
lamp which hung from the ceiling, the inn-keeper was saying:

"What's more, I strongly recommended them to be careful,
and at any rate to take a guide. One guide for six men—it isn't
much."

One of the guides spoke up. "Listen," he said; "I passed them
when I was coming back from the fields about two o'clock. The
weather was breaking up, and I said to them: 'See that we don't
have to come and pick you up in the Rottal.'"

"Well, you were wrong their, Gottlieb," another guide replied,
"since they actually reached the summit."

"Granted, I may have been mistaken, but only partly," the
prophet sententiously concluded.

"After all," said another, "whether they reached the top or
not, they are certainly on the arête, very high up, and the best
thing they can do is to stay there. And to-morrow . . . we shall see."

"But how can they get down?" ventured the inn-keeper.
"Listen!"

Sheets of rain were beating on the roofs. A torrent was pouring
over the stones. And above it all was the terrifying music of a
maddened wind.

When they left the café the guides halted on the threshhold
of the night. They had their backs to the light and their faces to
the darkness, turning towards that black and roaring wall. They
looked before them, their eyes raised. They looked towards the
invisible Jungfrau, which raised the perfection of its contours
into the storm. And somewhere at the summit of this surge of
rock and snow were six men.

*   *   *

Penned in their enclosure were six men like plaster casts. Over
them the hours unrolled like raging water over a rock, levelling

it and wearing it away. One by one, at the beginning of their heavy watch, they had sunk into a blissful coma; and in that period of suspense, whose brevity had sufficed to abolish all their sufferings and to efface the storm, the sweetness of their dreams was enchanting. But then they had to come back, abandoning the luxury of oblivion, to return to reality, exhuming themselves painfully from their brief but miraculous peace.

They slept no more. A sullen silence constricted their spirits. But behind the closed eyes, and under the torment of the persistent snow, the stridently clamorous wind and the icy darkness —a vast nocturnal agitation that seemed coeternal with the world itself—six watchful spirits defied their fate. In this fashion the hours of the night passed slowly one by one, like the beads of a chaplet in the unsteady hands of misfortune. Within the shelter of one man's jacket the flame of a match, ephemeral as a spark, illumined the face of a watch: it was ten o'clock!

It was eleven o'clock.

Then it was midnight.

Nothing changed. Everything persisted in a perpetual sameness of cold and wind and clamour. From the depths arose a solemn and powerful uproar, like the sound of a gigantic cataract.

It was one o'clock.

It was two.

It was three. Then four.

The frozen minutes slowed their march, refused to go on, upsetting the order of the hours. And under the turned-down brims of frosted hats the snow moulded a mask of dumb misery upon the shrunken faces and closed eyes.

Fragments of the grey dawn shortly began to drift in upon the wind. This half-light, mingling with the unrelenting snow, revealed a group of strange silhouettes on watch about the bivouac, emerging gradually from that immense monotony, resuming their age-long place in the undulating murk: a black rock, the arête, the shattered balcony edge above the precipice, a rocky pediment. Day was thus born.

At six o'clock—it was Saturday, the 16th of July—Kuhn and A. Wettstein, the most experienced of the party, put their heads together to decide whether or not they should start. Must they really try to move, to break this immobility and assume the guise of living men, tear themselves away from this common

grave where their bodies had already assumed their final posture?
Even the most daring of them hesitated, and the rest, corroded
by fatigue, overwhelmed by the merciless night and numbed by
the cold, remained on the margin of renewed life, half-immersed
in nothingness like Dante's damned. But the deadly halt could
not be prolonged, so they decided to hold themselves in readiness
for the first lull in the storm.[17] Then they would descend to the
Rottalsattel, whence it should be easy to reach the Concordia hut
over the Jungfraufirn with the aid of a compass, even in the dense
fog. At the Concordia—ah, yes!—they could linger under the
blankets, stretch themselves and yawn, turn over and go to sleep
again. And there would be Cathrein's box of provisions, the
crackling fire and the aroma of tea.

They began at once their preparations for departure. They
rose painfully; their stiffened limbs rebelled, and wherever a
little warmth remained on their bodies their frozen clothing had
the touch of fire. Human shadows stumbled about, moving slowly
with the curious motions of automatons, wordless and thoughtless.

Then a voice broke the lugubrious silence, saying almost with
indifference: "The marmot is dead."

"Dead?"

"Yes. Frozen."

"Ah! If you had only listened to me, we should have had a
better supper last night."

None laughed. The jest fell flat. Scarcely a pitying look was
given to the already stiffened carcase, and each in his inner being
mused obscurely on the decrees of fate. Then they forgot. From
their heavy boots, their gaiters and all their equipment they drew
a faint feeling of security and gradually rebuilt a vestige of their
former strength and courage. The rope had to be tied; but it was
as stiff as a rod and the knots were difficult to tie. But eventually
the intervals were measured and the order of march reformed.
Towards eight o'clock the squalls seemed to space themselves
out, like the waves of the sea when the wind has eased, and a
vague lightness, rising from the depths below them, thinned the
mists. The snow thinned, and the flakes grew heavy, large and
gentle like feathers.

Kuhn and Wettstein consulted once again and decided to start.

"We shall be at the saddle in half an hour," one of them said,
"and by twelve-thirty we should be at the hut."

One by one they emerged from their grave and ascended the slope of snow above them; they spilled out like drops from a pipette, progressing clumsily, heavily, with the motions of men entangled in a bog. The nearer they approached the arête the fiercer they found the wind. For a while they struggled with this terrible and invisible adversary, tottered, recovered their balance, and then resumed their places in the column. Quickly camouflaged by snow the phantom caravan now advanced with cautious steps. The frozen rope hung between them in heavy arcs, swollen with frost. Under their feet the powdery snow drifted over the seams of the lateral slabs, its light wrinkles indicating clearly that they were keeping to the crest; but when they thrust their alpenstocks into the moving surface they found no support. Everything seemed unstable and unreal. Mountain and sky merged into one another, mingling their clamour and their cataclysmic elements.

After a little while the man in the lead stopped. He closely examined the terrain before him; but in front, as well as behind and to right and left, there was nothing to see, nothing but the total madness of the elements. The second man came up, and with their heads together they shouted words which the wind tore from their mouths in syllables, like dead leaves. An axe pointed in one direction; an alpenstock pointed in another. But the axe persisted; doubtless they had reached the saddle, and since they had their backs to the Rottal, all they had to do was descend at a right-angle, facing south-east. As soon as the bergschrund was crossed and they were in shelter, they would consult again. The leader then resolutely left the arête and moved off to the left, the second man following in his footsteps. But the slope steepened sharply. It swept down like a flying buttress, razor-backed; then it incurved further and further, and vanished.

"God! Stop!" the leader shouted. "Stop . . . We can't go on . . . We must go back. . . . It goes straight down. . . . Hold me! . . . Hold me! . . . Hold . . ." But the wind carried his words away.

It was too late. The snow collapsed. The leader, losing his foothold, carried the second man away with him in his fall, and the third man was swiftly dragged into the gulf. The three last men, still on the arête, completely ignorant of the tragedy which was unfolding beneath them in the dense mists, isolated from one another by the roar of the wind and blinded by the whirlwinds, found themselves suddenly whisked away. The fourth went off and, overthrown in their turn, the fifth and sixth; they were engulfed rapidly, without realising what was happening, tumbling down, torn to pieces, mutilated by the relentless rope that plunged away into the void.

Rapidly remoulded by the wind, the arête resumed the innocence of untrodden snows. One gust of wind, as it rose from the glacier below, carried with it, in the soft rush of an avalanche of snow, a succession of dull thuds, curiously irregular like an arrested fall, later suddenly resumed, then arrested again, then resumed. Then, but for the shrill clamour of the wind, there was a final silence.[18]

* * *

As soon as it was clear that an accident had occurred, the post office at Lauterbrunnen informed the President of the Commune that on Thursday, the 14th, a telegram had been sent to M. Cathrein, manager of the Eggishorn Hotel, asking him to despatch a box of provisions to the Concordia hut. This was valuable information. The six climbers might have reached there on Friday the 15th. Therefore the first reaction at Lauterbrunnen was to telegraph to the Eggishorn Hotel for information (Saturday the 16th). But at the Eggishorn nothing was known, except that the provisions had been duly transported to the Concordia in the name of Dr. A. Wettstein. Moreover, no caravan had been seen on the glacier. A telegram was despatched simultaneously to the Grimsel Hospice, to which the party might have been able somehow to find its way by the passes in the Finsteraarhorn massif, presuming it had succeeded in reaching the Concordia, which was not the case. It would be madness to admit for one moment that anyone could find any pleasure in facing such a hurricane for the sake of an excursion across those oceans of ice. But from the Grimsel also the reply was negative; nothing was known.

On Sunday the 17th a further telegram was sent from Lauterbrunnen to the Eggishorn, with the same negative response. The terms of this message silenced the last hopes and a first search party left Lauterbrunnen for the Jungfrau. The column of seven men set out at one in the afternoon; it comprised the following mountaineers, von Almen (President of the Commune), and the guides Adolf Graf, Hans Graf, Christian Brunner, Konrad Gertsch, Fritz Steiner and Ulrich Lauener. The column reached the Rottal hut in the evening and there passed the night. On Monday the 18th, the bad weather persisting, the searchers could not leave until eight in the morning. They ascended the steps of the Jungfrau's south-east face, but were soon obliged to interrupt their search under the menace of renewed squalls. At four in the afternoon they had returned to Lauterbrunnen without discovering a thing.

The same day (Monday), but on the other side of the massif, at the extreme end of the gigantic Aletsch Glacier, Cathrein learned from a reliable source that the box of provisions sent by him to the Concordia on the 14th was still there and unopened. Thus five days had passed since orders to forward it had been given. Five days is a long time. So the manager of the Eggishorn Hotel decided to send a search party of his own (the second, but the Eggishorn's first) of seven men, and this one left the Concordia between seven and eight o'clock. From Berne, and from other places where the families and friends of the missing men were becoming anxious, telegrams poured in, and the most heart-rending enquiries multiplied. But to these anxieties there was no answer but the assumption that the caravan had fallen in the storm into the abyss of the Rottal, or that it had been struck by lightning, or that the six climbers had slipped into the bergschrund of the Rottalsattel (on the Jungfraufirn side), which that year was enormous.

On this Monday, the 18th, very far from the scene of the tragedy, in another valley, at the foot of other glaciers and under other summit skies—of the Matterhorn and its surrounding four-thousanders—Herr F. Oertly-Jenny, a friend of the vanished climbers and Vice-President of the Tödi section of the Swiss Alpine Club, was informed of the presumed catastrophe. He was on holiday in Zermatt. We read in his report: "Ten o'clock was striking at the Zermatt Church on the night of the 18th July; in the hotel they were dancing happily and I was reading the proclamation of the Alpine Club which recommended the assistance of an experienced guide for big climbs as the best guarantee of success,[19] when a despatch was suddenly brought to me, informing me that Kuhn and five comrades had perished while crossing from the Rottal hut to the Concordia hut. The despatch was sent to me by the committee of the Tödi section and begged me, if I was able, to proceed to the sinister spot. I did not hesitate, and the next day, at five in the morning, I left in haste to catch the train calling at Viége at one-twenty."

In the afternoon of Tuesday, the 19th, the parents of the missing climbers arrived at Lauterbrunnen. Their grief only added to the common anguish. They were pitied and consoled, but all such sympathy could effect nothing. Officials of the Swiss Alpine Club, neighbouring magistrates and local clergymen also assembled in the village.

A new search party (the third, Lauterbrunnen's second), composed of the same guides as before, with the guide Johann Feutz in addition, set out again for the Rottal. The hypothesis set the pace. Presuming that the missing men had found it impossible to descend on the Rottal side and had fallen into the bergschrund while passing from the Rottalsattel to the Jung-fraufirn, the Eggishorn had been requested to prepare a long ladder with which to explore the crevasse. This third party had therefore the purpose, apart from continuing the search in the precipices between the Rottal and the Sattel (12,713 feet), of making contact with the forces sent with the ladder from the Eggishorn. But they had just left when Cathrein announced the check sustained by the party he had sent the day before:

Guides returned. Nothing found. Necessary continue search Rottal. Impossible send ladder. No guide available. Cathrein.

On receiving this news, Lauterbrunnen decided to use the Rottal hut as a base camp for the search parties in the event of subsequent searches. During this time, and despite his pessimistic telegram, Cathrein was hastily constructing a large ladder, and he succeeded in forming a further rescue party (the fourth, the Eggishorn's second) which left with the ladder.

At Lauterbrunnen, late in the night, the President of the Commune, von Almen, sent two mountaineers to the Rottal hut, laden with provisions. They were also to join in the efforts of the third party.

A dull day broke that Wednesday, the 20th. The weather had never completely cleared up after the storm which had descended on the chain several days earlier, but on that morning it was thought that it might turn fine. The parents of the missing men, with a few curious persons, some villagers and Herr Strasser, the famous "Pastor of the Glaciers," the good shepherd of Grindelwald, had gone—some to Trachsellauenen, some to Obersteinberg, and some to the wild heights of the Schmadribach —to watch the progress of the rescue parties through field glasses. But the nonchalant mists, which alternately veiled and disclosed the mountains, hindered observation. The greatest perplexity reigned everywhere. It was now five days since the climbers had disappeared, and since then not the least news had come to lighten their hearts.

That evening the Eggishorn began again to show signs of life. But without tangible result. Its telegram announced laconically that the Valaisian party—the one carrying the ladder—had explored the crevasse in vain. A new party of porters left for the Rottal hut to reprovision the ten men already there.

At eight in the morning Oertly-Jenny, who had arrived from Zermatt by way of Lausanne and Berne during the night of the 19th, set out with the guides Fritz Graf, *père* and *fils* (the fifth party, Lauterbrunnen's third). At the Stufensteinalp, where the six young men had halted on the 14th, he questioned the old herdsman, the last person to have seen the victims and to have spoken with them. Oertly reached the hut to find it fully occupied by the mountaineers, guides and porters, of the second Lauterbrunnen party.

The same evening Grindelwald informed Lauterbrunnen that a party (the sixth, Grindelwald's first) composed of the guides Peter Kaufman, Peter Egger, Hans Brawand, Christian Bohren, Gottlieb Meier and Hans Kaufmann, which had left Grindelwald at eleven on the night of Tuesday the 19th, had climbed to the Mönchjoch (11,870 feet) by way of the Bergli hut on the 20th, had been forced by bad weather to turn about and had returned to the hut, remaining there with a view to resuming the search later.

The same bad weather was thwarting the Lauterbrunnen guides too, and they, having explored the mountain, regained the Rottal hut to avoid a new catastrophe.

Thus, until that moment, despite the combined efforts of six search parties (about fifty men), leaving by turns from the Valais, from Lauterbrunnen and from Grindelwald, having scoured the heights of the Jungfrau and explored the Rottalsattel bergschrund, nothing had been found—not the slightest sign, not the least prognosis. The mystery remained complete.

On Thursday the 21st blue sky was born again in the cloudy chaos which had lasted for many days. The Grindelwald party, which had slept at the Bergli hut, left again for the Mönchjoch; while on the other side, at the Rottal hut, the Lauterbrunnen parties (the third and the fifth, the second attempt of the third) also got moving.

At Mürren, the Lauterbrunnen, and as far away as Interlaken, telescopes were brought to bear on the mountain. Suddenly, at about nine in the morning, human silhouettes were seen against the blue sky at the summit of the Jungfrau.[21] A slow surge of disappointment passed through every heart, for this seemed categorical proof that once more the efforts of the valiant rescuers had led nowhere. And out of weariness this handful of brave men was left to the eternal snows. Then, at two in the afternoon, a dramatic event developed: two guides—Fritz Steiner and Hans Graf—of the third rescue party, arrived breathless at Lauterbrunnen, bringing this time a definite message, terrible in its laconicism though all hopes had for a long time been extinguished:

"The six men have been found dead on the glacier at the foot of the south-east face of the Jungfrau."

These mountaineers (those in fact who had been seen that morning on the summit of the mountain), had descended at a mad pace, taking only five hours by a new route from the summit to the village.[22] The main point of their account was this: the tracks of the vanished men were clearly visible on the snow and ice, both on the Rottal side, on the slopes below the summit, and on the summit itself. In places the wind had swept away the fresh snow without touching the footprints.[23] This was the report which the two men drew up:

"Yesterday we searched the 'Kessel'[24] (the well-known couloir exposed to avalanches and stone-falls) and, despite the unfavourable weather, we climbed it. It was impossible to complete the ascent of the Jungfrau, for the wind would have swept us off. And as that would have been certain death, we did not wish to worsen the catastrophe.

"At three o'clock this morning we left the Rottal hut. We followed the tracks of the vanished men continuously; they were still quite clear. They had chosen the correct route; sometimes they deviated a few steps, but they always returned to the right route. We were quite astonished that these men had been able to follow the correct road without a guide. 'These were first-rate climbers,' we said to ourselves, 'who know the mountains well.' We were surprised to be able to follow the tracks right up to the Jungfrau. On the summit of the Jungfrau the footprints were wholly visible. They could not be those of other climbers. The guide who was last on the Jungfrau, with a photographer, said that their tracks were quite different. So those that we had seen could not be other than those of the six gentlemen.

"The guides split up. I (Fritz Steiner) and Hans Graf, as well as Brunner and Konrad Gertsch, turned left at about ten minutes from the summit in order to take a look at the Aletsch Glacier, when we noticed very far below us, on the Aletsch Glacier (Jung-fraufirn), two caravans: one of three men and, further ahead, another of four.[25] We shouted; they stopped and replied, shouting also. There was a short silence, then someone cried: 'They have been found!' . . . 'All six?' . . . 'Yes!' . . . 'Where?' . . . A man stretched out his arm in the direction of the foot of the precipice below us, towards the right: 'At the Kelle.'[26]

"As we were returning to report, the guide Graf, Herr Oertly's companion, called out to us from above that they had found various objects near the summit. Evidently the six men had bivouacked at the summit. Then we came down as quickly as possible to make our report.

"We feel it necessary to assert that the six gentlemen had found the route to the top of the Jungfrau perfectly well. The bad weather alone had caused the catastrophe. We must say that. In the weather that was prevailing at the time they could not do otherwise than spend the night up there in order to wait for good weather, perhaps on the following day. We know what it's like up there! If they had tried to descend by the Rottal in such weather they would have fallen. No; these men could not have done otherwise. We certify this in exact accordance with the truth, and we guarantee every word, even if others say differently. We have told everything. There is nothing more to add."[27]

On their part, the Oertly-Jenny party, a moment before the discovery of the bodies by the Grindelwald guides, had come upon the remains of the bivouac, quickly identified.

"Arriving at the crest, near the summit," writes Oertly, "judge our surprise at finding, twenty yards below it, a kind of shelter, formed by a rectangle of four small walls some sixty or seventy centimetres high, where we found a pocket handkerchief enclosing, wrapped in hay, the body of a young marmot; a box containing the remains of some preserves; the debris of an omelette in paper; and lastly, some playing cards dispersed over the surface. But no trace of a written document."[28]

In the evening of this dismal day a telegram from Grindelwald, sent by Pastor Strasser, confirmed the discovery:

"Two of our guides who were at the Rottalsattel close to the victims have returned. They say the disaster must have taken place not far from the summit. Instant death."

On the other hand, the Eggishorn telegraphed the harrowing news. Like the Rottal messengers, two guides detached from the Grindelwald party had in five hours of forced march descended the Great Aletsch Glacier from the Kelle to the Eggishorn.

On Friday, the 22nd July, a column of seven guides (the seventh party, the Eggishorn's third), ascending the Aletsch Glacier, was able to reach the place where the men lay. The fall had been about 650 feet. The six victims, partly covered by fresh snow, lay grouped over about fifty feet, at the foot of a snow couloir. All of them had fallen head downwards, and all of them suffered fractures of the skull on the left side, apart from numerous other injuries. They were all still tied to the rope which, though badly torn in places, had not been broken.[29] None of the victims could have survived this terrible plunge into the abyss.

The temperature was singularly high, and masses of snow were running down the walls. A soft rustling sounded in the chasms, punctuated by the buzz of flying stones and the sound of breaking icicles. An ice-axe belonging to one of the dead men, which had become stuck in a fissure, was struck by a falling stone and, leaping from the couloir, it fell only a couple of paces from one of the rescuers. An instant later an alpenstock described a parabola through the air. The guides' heavy task was constantly impeded and menaced by such dangers. Thick mists were settling on the peaks. Then the prelude of a storm raised its long lament, and the ceaseless south-west wind soon released its showers of hail. The clouds fell and it began to snow, and to escape death themselves the guides interrupted their dismal task. Abandoning the bodies in the middle of the glacier, where they had been brought together from the crevasses of the Kelle, they were forced to flee to the Concordia, pursued by the storm. A reinforcement of seven men (the eighth and last party) was in the evening sent by the Eggishorn (its fourth) to the succour of the seventh party.

*   *   *

On Saturday, the 23rd of July, in dull weather, an imposing column of twenty-two guides descended the Great Aletsch Glacier,[30] that gigantic blue-grey causeway. The mountaineers were harnessed to six heavily laden luges. They made slow progress. Their heavy, rhythmic efforts, the combination of their posture and movements, gave them the appearance of haulers towing a barge along a leaden canal. The thick mists were clinging to the mountainsides; the summits remained invisible. Through the rifts fresh snow could be seen very low down. At the end of the day the silent haulers and their cargo of the dead reached the edge of the tiny Marjelen-see. Under the taciturn sky its waters retained a forget-me-not blue.

As day fell the setting sun broke up the mass of cloud. Golden furnaces were lit above the sombre troughs of valleys still chilled with rain. The earth and the appeased heavens began to live again after breathless days. And the vanished men, now refound, were on their way to the fields where they would sleep. On the terrace of the Eggishorn Hotel six biers, covered with blankets and strewn with rhododendrons, stood in line. The guides of the later rescue parties, with their axes raised, formed a guard of honour. On the two central biers the Swiss flag was unfurled. Pastor Rossé, from Bienne, invoked divine mercy, and the lawyer Klausen spoke in the name of the cantonal government of Valais. The same evening the bodies were carried by lantern-light to the valley.[31]

For the scene of the tragedy on the Jungfrau, see Plates 21 and 22. For portraits of the victims, see Plate 23.

[1] *Poésies*, Vol. 1, 1867.

[2] This Meyer family played a prominent part in the beginnings of Swiss alpinism. Not only did J.-R. Meyer, the father, provide the funds for the publication of the Weiss atlas (Weiss, the Swiss geographer) which, according to Coolidge, was a marvel of its time so far as the High Alps are concerned, but his own exploits in the Alps, and those of his sons and grandsons, place those pioneers in the front rank. For this fact is very little known, an historical truth obscured by legend, but one which must be re-established: the Swiss were the first conquerors of the Alps, a half-century, moreover,

before the English. From 1744 (the first ascent of the Titlis) until 1865 (the first ascent of the Matterhorn) the Swiss climbed more than fifty important virgin summits. It was only after 1855 that the English surpassed all their rivals and took the lead in the conquest of the High Alps. And to the brothers Meyer of Aarau, as we have just seen, goes the honour of the Jungfrau's conquest.

We are badly informed about the earlier history of these climbers. Without doubt they were not exactly beginners, but from the tone of their story we might almost infer that until then they had not passed the snowline. On the other hand they were animated by the scientific spirit; alpine science, brought into fashion by Saussure, remained until near the end of the eighteenth century the larger preoccupation of the greater number of noted alpinists.

[3] See Chapter 8.

[4] *Gesang der Geister uber den Wassern.*

[5] *Memorials of a Tour on the Continent,* 1820, Poem XII.

[6] The Laueners, von Almens, Schluneggers, etc.

[7] When, in 1876, a party of three Englishmen—Cust, Cawood and Colgrave—made the first guideless ascent of the Matterhorn, their expedition, although perfectly successful, let loose a Press campaign in England. The *Globe,* in particular, regarded this exploit as imbecile recklessness. We might mention the following as the great guideless climbers of the period: Charles Hudson, T. S. Kennedy, the brothers Zsigmondy, Girdlestone, etc. The first guideless ascent of Mont Blanc took place in 1855, of the Finsteraarhorn in 1865, of the Matterhorn in 1876, of the Meije in 1879 and of the Jungfrau from Wengeralp in 1881.

[8] All these young men were first-class intellects. Alexander Wettstein (born 1861) took a doctorate in science at Zurich. He was a distinguished geologist, specialising in the research of marine fossils. He had been a pupil of the great Albert Heim, who devoted a moving article to Wettstein in the *Neue Zürcher Zeitung.* Heim considered him already an authority on geology.

[9] This route (the south-western spur of the Jungfrau) had been followed for the first time by a caravan of Lauterbrunnen guides: H. von Almen *fils,* Fr. Brunner, Graf *fils,* K. Schlunneger, J. Stäger and the younger F. von Almen, on the 20th September, 1885.

[10] Alexander Wettstein and Gottfried Kuhn were strong climbers. As the party's leader, Kuhn had to his credit a respectable number of serious climbs; on the other hand, the rest were more or less novices. Ziegler wrote a card to his family from Innertkirchen, saying that he was "in the company of very reliable comrades."

[11] Quoted in the Report—that is to say, in the brochure containing the three reports of the tragedy: *Das Unglück an der Jungfrau vom* 15 *Juli,* 1887. Cf. also *Echo des Alpes,* 1886–87; *Alpine Journal,* Vol. XIII, 1886–88.

[12] The Staubbach inn had provided a part of the provisions, including "an omelette for six," the remains of which were found at the bivouac. The caravan carried only few provisions, reckoning on arriving at the Concordia hut the next day and finding there the box of victuals ordered from the Eggishorn.

[13] Only two ice-axes and four sticks. The axes belonged to A. Wettstein and Kuhn.

[14] With the intention of climbing the Oberaarhorn besides the Jungfrau.

[15] The well-known English climber, Mrs. E. P. Jackson (who, amongst other climbs, accomplished the first ascent of the Dent Blanche by the Ferpècle arête, with Karl Schulz and the guides Aloys Pollinger *père* and J.-J. Truffer, on the 29th July, 1889) was at the Jungfrau on the 22nd January, 1888, with the guide E. Boss of Grindelwald. At the summit the party discovered a bottle containing a card with the names of five of the victims of the 1887 catastrophe inscribed upon it: (Trans.) *A. and H. Wettstein, Kuhn, Bider and Bär, guideless ascent in a violent storm,* 15 *July,* 1887.

[16] See note 12 to this chapter.

[17] For their return the climbers had the choice of three routes:

(*a*) to retrace their steps, but that would be a "first" in a raging storm. It was accomplished five days later, on the 21st, by the guides Fritz Steiner and Hans Graf, who carried to Lauterbrunnen the news of the discovery of the bodies.

(*b*) The Rottal couloir, known as the *Kessel,* a dangerous route, swept constantly by avalanches and scoured by falls of stone. The guides Bischoff and von Almen died there on the 24th July, 1872.

(c) The normal route: a descent to the Sattel and from there, via the Jungfraufirn and the Aletsch Glacier, to the Concordia hut. But how were they to cross the berg-schrund at the Sattel in such terrible weather? Yet it was to this solution that the caravan was won over. We know what followed. And supposing the exhausted caravan, half-frozen and famished, had succeeded in reaching the Jungfraufirn, how would they have managed on that immense glacier—a monotonous ocean of snow, streaked with crevasses—in that frightful storm?

[18] The first ascent of this south-east face was carried out by M. D. Lewers and the guide Adolf Rubi on the 3rd August, 1933. This party seems either to have climbed the bottom of the couloir down which fell the victims of 1887, or, as appears more exact, the first couloir farther to the north. They then followed to the north the large ledge of snow and reached the summit by a vertical climb. (Cf. *Alpine Journal*, Vol. XLV, 1933.)

[19] This proclamation was signed by Eugène Rambert, Central President of the Swiss Alpine Club, and W. Cant the Vice-President.

[20] There were four parties engaged that day in the same search; two from Lauter-brunnen, one from the Eggishorn and one from Grindelwald.

[21] These two parties left the hut at three in the morning.

[22] The descent of this south-west arête had never, in fact, been done before. These two brave mountaineers, in doing their duty so magnificently, at the same time achieved an admirable "first."

[23] The easy discovery of the tracks of the vanished men is readily explained: none of the preceding search parties had yet reached so high into these localities because of the bad weather. The persistence of tracks in ice or hard snow for days or even weeks, despite heavy falls of snow, is frequent at heights. The wind sweeps the snow away as it falls, without touching the imprints, which are obliterated much more slowly.

[24] South-western side.

[25] These were: (a) The Grindelwald search-party (the two other guides having descended to the valley the day before to give news and probably to get provisions); and (b) The English climbers H. Nankivell and J. Wilson and their two guides Peter Baumann, jr., and Ulrich Kaufmann, also from Grindelwald.

The Times of the 26th July, 1887, published the following letter:

"The sequel to the late accident on the Jungfrau, in which a party of six Swiss gentlemen, unaccompanied by any guide, lost their lives, may be of interest to your readers.

"We spent the evening of the 20th instant at the Bergli Club Hut with our guides Peter Baumann (the younger) and Ulrich Kaufmann. There was present also a search party of six Grindelwald guides who had been unable on account of the stormy weather to proceed that day towards the Jungfrau.

"We left the hut at 1.30 a.m., the morning being fine and the snow firm, and reached the final bergschrund at 6 a.m. to find the bridge broken and the schrund apparently impassable. We were soon joined by the search party, some of whom commenced bravely cutting a pass round the western termination of the schrund. After an hour's work their efforts succeeded, but as a heavy fog had then formed over the summit of the mountain, and as the pass, being cut under an ice cornice, was by no means free from danger, we decided at 7 a.m. to descend. Half-way down the long snow slope Peter Baumann saw an alpenstock fixed in a ledge of snow about 500 yards to our left, under the abrupt eastern precipice, and on proceeding to a patch of snowfield about 120 feet below, we found the half-buried remains of the unfortunate victims, all lying in an area about fifty feet square.

"Word was passed at once to the search party, and we returned without delay to the Club Hut, and reached Grindelwald at 5.45 p.m. ...."

(Signed) Herbert Nankivell; J. Wilson.

[26] The name locally given to the base of the eastern wall of the Jungfrau where it plunges into the Jungfraufirn (south-eastern aspect).

[27] The guides' report (in translation) has been allowed to retain its original rough simplicity.

[28] See note 11 to this chapter.

[29] The eminent English climber, Clinton Thomas Dent, conqueror of the Grand Dru (amongst other conquests), declared in the *Alpine Journal*, Vol. XIII, that the rope had broken in sixteen places. This must be a mistake. Oertly-Jenny, who was on the spot that very morning when the bodies were found, states that it was only frayed (*zerrissen war*), which is different.

[30] The party included, among others, the Valaisian guides Sittler, Burgener, two Günterns, Bürcher, Einholzer, Holzer, Biederpost, two Inhasslis, Minnig, Preter, etc., and six Grindelwald guides in addition. It should be added that the two Grindelwald guides who had descended to Grindelwald had rejoined their comrades in the evening of the 21st or the morning of the 22nd.

[31] This tragedy had, from the 17th to the 23rd July, required that eight search-parties should be constantly on their feet. Until the transport of the bodies to the Eggishorn, these parties had made eleven reconnaissances (including two complete ascents of the Jungfrau from the Rottal). Altogether about sixty men were thus mobilised.

CHAPTER SEVENTEEN

THREE WHO VANISHED

The disappearance of Count Humbert of Villanova and of the guides Jean-Joseph Maquignaz and Antonio Castagneri (Mont Blanc, Italian face, August 1890)

TRAGEDY, brief and brutal, wrapped in silence; a tragedy over which mystery stretches its serene and sorrowful shadow. Well might we ask whether we would rather see our loved ones again as tortured bodies on the bloodstained snow or rock, or weep their disappearance for ever, swallowed up in the depths of a glacier. For through the screen of spiritual contemplation, the image of the most cruel mountain ends by adorning itself with a sad sweetness, and its alternating manifestation of menacing grandeur and limpid beauty soothes every pain. Those who have not returned will go with it into eternity, vanished in the magic of high places, their disappearance beautified thereby. Such a death was that which befell two great guides, Jean-Joseph Maquignaz[1] and Antonio Castagneri,[2] and their traveller, the young Count Humbert of Villanova.[3]

On Saturday, 16th August, 1890, Guido Rey[4] left the train at Chatillon, near Aosta, en route for le Breuil and the Matterhorn by the Furggen arête.[5] In passing the Hôtel de Londres he saw two men seated on a bench in the courtyard. "One of them was strongly built, stout, bronzed in face and rough in aspect, while the other was an aristocratic-looking man, with delicate features, a fine white skin, and a somewhat palid countenance. They were smiling at me, and seemed as surprised to see me as I was to see them. They were Antonio Castagneri, the guide, and Count Humbert of Villanova, the climber, both of them my friends."

They were waiting for Jean-Joseph Maquignaz, before going on to Aosta and Courmayeur to attempt a great ascent. This ascent, however, they did not describe, which was a little surprising and straightway placed the tragedy which was to follow in a curious atmosphere. Guido Rey continued on his way, and near Moulins he encountered the third of the men summoned to die in the next forty-eight hours: the guide Jean-Joseph Maquignaz, "pipe in mouth, freshly shaven and cleanly clad. He looked as if he were going to a fête. . . . This was the last time he was to descend his native valley."

On the Sunday afternoon (17th August) the Villanova party leaves Courmayeur to spend the night at the Cantine de la Visaille, not far from the barren moraines of the Glacier de Miage, at the foot of the Val Veni. Opposite, on the other side of the narrow valley where the brawling Doire carries its quivering reflections along, Mont Blanc raises its imperious rocks above the glistening terraces. The edges of the Brouillard and Fresnay glaciers overlook the valley like two clenched and menacing fists. Further to the left the Glacier de Miage, a wide highway strewn with stones, curves between the promontories of the Monts de Brouillard and the Aiguille de Combal, and then ascends towards the distant regions of the south-east face of Mont Blanc. Precipitous glaciers, damned up by secondary chains, overlap its flanks. It is there, in those wild and lonely places, between the cliffs of the Aiguille de Bionassay (13,287 feet) to the south-west, and the giant spines of Mont Blanc, that the Villanova party intends to make its way. This side of Mont Blanc is closed to the east by the gigantic arête of the Monts de Brouillard (10,997 feet), which joins the valley below the Jardin de Miage in the vicinity of the Cantine de la Visaille.

But do we know if the climbers' real plan lies there? For if they wish to climb Mont Blanc by one or the other routes on this face, either by the Italian Glacier de Bionassay or by the Glacier du Dôme or the Glacier du Mont Blanc, the three principal basins, there is no need to make such a mystery of it. These routes, though not exactly excursions, are far from being comparable with the formidable slopes of the Brenva, of Péteret or of the Brouillard. Nor are they exactly novelties; all three have already been traversed repeatedly[6]—notably, that mentioned by Maquignaz to the chief guide of Courmayeur, Séraphin Henry, known as the "route du Dôme," which joins the Mont Blanc arête between the Col de Bionassay and the Dôme du Goûter at about 13,100 feet. Three parties have already followed it this same summer, one of which comprised three Italian priests, including the Abbé Achille Ratti, later Pope Pius XI. Jean-Joseph Maquignaz himself, with Emile Rey, acted as guide to the four brothers Sella on this route to Mont Blanc in January 1888.

Perhaps the Count of Villanova and his guides have another plan. In this connection we may enumerate several points: when a man secures the company of two great guides to whom he entrusts the secret of his climb; when he maintains a discreet silence, even towards climbing friends—the Count of Villanova has not, in fact, informed anyone of his plans;[7] when by accident he meets in the mountains a man like Guido Rey, whose friend he is, and still keeps silent; when, finally, he spends a day and a night at Courmayeur, where Maquignaz and Castagneri have nothing but old and trusted comrades, where he is fêted, where he drinks and smokes and talks of climbs, and where he recalls memories, where he discusses this or that ascent of long ago or yet to be accomplished, and where, in this simple and loyal intimacy, he continues his silence—is there not really something surprising, something mysterious in this attitude, this voluntary secrecy?

"Well," asks Séraphin Henry, "where are you going?" He is the chief guide in Courmayeur, and he, at least, has the right to be informed.

"Oh! You will see. We intend to climb Mont Blanc by the Glacier du Dôme," Maquignaz honestly replies.

But an intention is not a certainty. And does this ostensible and rather vague plan not hide, perhaps, a more ambitious purpose, some more hazardous, more reckless expedition? For instance: Mont Blanc by the Glacier du Brouillard, or Mont Blanc by the Glacier de Mont Blanc. These are certainly hypotheses, but if you approach them from a distance, they seem at first sight to conform more closely with reality. Quite definitely, Maquignaz has not lied. He has maintained a careful reserve, since his employer has enjoined discretion. But again—and it must be emphasised—is it not curious to have engaged two guides of this quality for the south-east routes on Mont Blanc? What reason can there be for such precautions?

The Brouillard face is still inviolate. Since the accident in 1874[8] and the four earlier failures, only one attempt has been made, and that one equally unsuccessful.[9] Here, certainly, there would be good work for a Maquignaz who has conquered the Aiguille du Géant! It is understandable that the support of two such guides should be secured to overcome such a rampart, and that the expedition might be kept secret.

There are other possibilities: Mont Blanc by the Glacier du Mont Blanc, by a variation of the 1872 route, or better still, Mont Blanc by the Brouillard arête. These are *terrae incognitae*. But in these two cases the Cantine de la Visaille is not indicated, although from this inn you could quite well reach the Glacier du Brouillard by a counter-march, avoiding the chalets and herdsmen of Fresnay, just as you can avoid the Sella hut if you wish to bivouac and to climb in those localities.

The engineer Montalti meets these three climbers between Courmayeur and la Visaille during a walk on the Sunday afternoon; they greet one another in the mountain fashion and exchange a few words, but there too no information comes to light.

Then at three-thirty on the morning of Monday, 18th August, Count Humbert and his two guides, Jean-Joseph Maquignaz of Valtournanche and Antonio Castagneri of Balme, take their leave of the Cantine de la Visaille. They vanish into the black night; their lantern hovers, the only gleam in the starless darkness. The inn-keeper, who has wished them *bon voyage*, closes the door and returns to bed; he is the last person to see them. *From that moment nothing is ever heard of them again.* No other party crosses their path. No person in these sequestered regions, except a party at the Sella hut, will see them again.[10] Nothing more is known, nothing will be known, ever.

From that moment there is nothing but a sequence of facts, almost without comment. For the understanding of this narrative, and also in order to show the courage, the energy and unlimited devotion of the Courmayeur guides, virtues which are common to all true mountain guides, the facts are as follows.

* * *

A day passes: *Monday the 18th.* The weather breaks abruptly in the afternoon. Towards five o'clock a storm blows up. In the evening the storm develops into a hurricane, a veritable cyclone, and in the night it seizes the chain of Mont Blanc with terrifying violence.[11] Two days pass, then a third and a fourth. On the fifth day, *Friday the 22nd*, a telegram reaches Courmayeur from the Countess of Villanova, the young climber's mother. Addressed to Sig. Ruffier, the manager of the Hôtel de l'Union, it asks for news of her son. The distressed mother's message suddenly fills the village with confusion. The reply is difficult. According to calculations, it is possible that the climbers, having arrived at Chamonix or St. Gervais on the 19th or 20th, would normally return to Courmayeur by Thursday the 21st or Friday the 22nd. But they have not done so. And, having decided to postpone a reply until nightfall, when evening comes the climbers are still missing.

Séraphin Henry, the chief guide, organises the first search party under the orders of the guide Julien Proment, and sends it out to patrol in the direction indicated by Maquignaz. It leaves by night, and on the *Saturday evening (the 23rd)*—the sixth day— it has already returned. Its report is more or less negative. At Chaux des Pesses, the junction of the Italian Glacier de Miage and the Glacier du Dôme, at approximately 10,100 feet,[12] tracks were picked up, but they vanished in the glacier. Thence the searchers made the traverse to the Sella hut, on the right bank of the Glacier du Mont Blanc. The bad weather then suspended operations.

At this stage Francesco Gonella, an Italian climber, takes charge of the search, and with Séraphin Henry he decides on the following plan: an exploration of the two faces of the sector of Mont Blanc indicated by Maquignaz, that is on the Italian and on the French side. (1) One party, in charge of the guide Julien Proment, will explore the Glacier du Dôme and the Italian Glacier de Bionassay, traversing the Aiguilles Grises. (2) Another party, under the orders of the guide Laurent Proment, will explore the French Glacier de Bionassay, in the supposition that the Villanova party has vanished on that side. According to information reaching Courmayeur at the last moment, it appears that the Count had actually told some climbers (!?) that he was proposing to reach the south-eastern arête of Mont Blanc by way of the Glacier du Dôme and, from the point marked as 4,003 metres (13,130 feet), follow it to the summit, passing over the Dôme de Goûter, the Vallot refuge and les Bosses. The mission thus conforms to the presumed aims of the vanished party.

But the two parties, which have been ready to leave since the evening of Saturday the 23rd, are still held up by the raging storm. On *Sunday the 24th*, the seventh day, the Countess of Villanova arrives at Courmayeur. Her mortal anxiety lends so pathetic an eloquence to her prayers that the guides can only bow to her sorrow and depart. At midday, braving the howling wind, Julien Proment's party sets out for the Aiguilles Grises. The second party awaits the night.[13]

The eighth day, *Monday the 25th*. Leaving Courmayeur at three in the morning, Laurent Proment's party has crossed the Cols de la Seigne (Franco-Italian frontier) and du Bonhomme, and by evening has reached the chalets of Nant Borrant above les Contamines, where the searchers spend the night. The mountains are evil. The wind has been blowing without respite, driving the snow very low. Through St. Gervais its leader immediately establishes telegraphic communication with Courmayeur and asks: "Must we carry out the search despite the enormous quantity of new snow?" And Courmayeur answers: "Yes!"

During the night of Monday to Tuesday reinforcements reach Courmayeur: a contingent from Valtournanche, comprising four Maquignaz, Alexandre and Anselme (Jean-Joseph's sons) and Daniel and Antoine (his nephews). They halt awhile, then resume their melancholy journey. Somewhere in the neighbourhood of the Glacier de Miage or the Aiguilles Grises they join up with Julien Proment's party. Eight days have now passed since the disappearance of the old head of their family. Eight days! No hope is possible. Yet there are miracles. Notre-Dame des Neiges, pray for them!

The ninth day, *Tuesday the 26th*. Julien Proment's party returns to Courmayeur before midday, forced back by the storm.[14] Fresh snow is so abundant that it is impossible to search the mountains. In the evening, with signs of good weather beginning to take shape, Julien Proment decides to set out once more. Meanwhile, the Laurent Proment party continues its work. By way of Contamines and a flanking traverse of the mountain-side, the party reaches the Alpe de Miage and pitches camp. Closing the valley to the south, the Dôme de Miage and the Aiguilles de Tricot and de Bionassay are lost in dark clouds.

The tenth day, *Wednesday the 27th*. The Julien Proment–Maquignaz party has left again. Gonella has taken charge of it.

It has scarcely departed before the storm returns. Its violence is such that the men have no option but to take refuge in the chalets at Arp Vieille, above the Cantine de la Visaille, not far from the Combal Lake.

At three in the morning the Laurent Proment party leaves the Miage chalets, crosses the Col de Tricot and sets foot on the Glacier de Bionassay, ascending it as far as the precipice of the Aiguille de Bionassay. Thence the searchers explore the frozen slopes which converge towards the glacier from the Col de Bionassay and the Dôme du Goûter. Then they reach the foot of the crests (10,627 feet) buttressing the Dôme du Goûter, discover nothing and undertake at once the ascent of the Aiguille du Goûter, in order to spend the night at the hut there. But some 600 feet from the summit, at a height of nearly 12,000 feet, the storm breaks out afresh. The searchers descend again and reach the Pavillon de Bellevue above les Houches at nine in the evening. There they sleep.

The eleventh day, *Thursday the 28th*. Profiting by a lull in the bad weather, the Julien Proment party leaves the chalets at Arp Vielle and ascends the Glacier de Miage. They make their way as far as la Chaux des Pesses, the point already reached on the 23rd. But white compact snow is everywhere. Towards four in the afternoon the party abandons its search because of renewed squalls and returns to Courmayeur. The four Maquignaz themselves declare "that it would be madness to pursue the search." Threats of avalanches loom on every side.

The Laurent Proment party, too, returns to Courmayeur, over the Cols du Bonhomme and de la Seigne.

Thus, at the end of twelve days, despite a strong combination of efforts, the mystery is established as unfathomable, completely sealed. After this long seclusion, after this interminable storm, the snowy cover of a crevasse closes over the victims; or, perhaps, somewhere in the gigantic Brouillard ramparts, three broken bodies are fixed unseen.[15]

*   *   *

Before they returned to their distant valley at the foot of the Matterhorn, before abandoning their father to his endless solitude in the murmuring darkness of a lonely glacier, the four Maquignaz, resigned and stoical, talked with their comrades of Courmayeur.

Together these saddened guides re-examined the facts of the tragedy. Their conclusions were these: *Jean-Joseph Maquignaz and Antonio Castagneri could not have fallen.* It was not carelessness, let alone incapacity, that caused the catastrophe. The responsibility lay entirely with the storm, the cyclone which thundered against the summits on Monday the 18th and Tuesday the 19th August. If at that time the Villanova party was really in the vicinity of the 4,003 metre point on the arête between the Col de Bionassay and the Dôme du Goûter—steep, narrow, snow-covered crests, heightened by cornices—it is by no means impossible that a gust of wind had carried the party off.

Two or three days after the news of the tragedy had been carried from valley to valley, Francesco Gonella received the following telegram from the Abbé Chanoux, rector of the hospice on the Petit Saint-Bernard. "Catastrophe Villanova-Maquignaz-Castagneri due solely to the cyclone reaching the Alps 18–19 August. In similar circumstances all the guides of Courmayeur would have been carried off into some abyss like feathers. Carelessness, a new route, ordinary accidents are impresumable."[16]

And so the Countess of Villanova returned to Turin without her son, and the Maquignaz re-ascended the Valtournanche without their father, and the President of the Balme Commune made his way to Castagneri's chalet with a saddened face.

* * *

The Courmayeur guides did not consider themselves beaten. Up on the mountains were the dead. At all costs, as on the battle-field, they must go to pick up their fallen comrades. It was a duty, but at the same time a mission, a sacred mission. And the self-sacrifice of the guides is infinite, as infinite as the beauty of the mountains themselves. In September the weather eased a little and the search was renewed.

On the 10th a party, comprising the guides Julien Proment and Joseph Petigax and the porters Laurent Truchet and César Ollier, bivouacked in the ruins of the old miner's hut at Cellere (about 9,900 feet) at the foot of the Col Infranchissable. On the 11th these men ascended the Dôme du Goûter (14,118 feet) over the Glaciers du Dôme and de Bionassay, passing from one to the other by the Col des Aiguilles Grises (12,493 feet) and joined the crest of the ridge (Franco-Italian frontier) at the Col de Bionassay

(12,762 feet). They explored all suspected places, crevasses, bergschrunds, séracs and the feet of the couloirs, picking up some old tracks on the col in the névés which had been swept clean by the wind. Were these the vestiges of the Villanova party? The men leaned over the snowy precipices of the French side and went down again to their bivouac.

On the 12th the party crossed the Col de Miage (11,073 feet, the Franco-Italian frontier) and slept at the Pavillon de Bellevue above les Houches. While climbing to the Col de Miage, exactly at the axis of the Glacier de Bionassay, they discovered tracks in the ice and wind-blown snow, clearly visible when seen from a distance, rising towards the Col de Bionassay and appearing to have been a variation of the 1889 ascent.[17] And the haunting question arose again: was this the route of the Villanova party? To these searchers it was a certainty: *the tracks were those of the Villanova party*.

On the 13th the French Glacier de Bionassay was explored, especially the bay overlooked by the slopes and couloirs of the Col de Bionassay, of the Aiguille and Dôme du Goûter. Avalanches of snow and ice seriously complicated the search. The party regained the Pavillon de Bellevue, traversing the Tête Rousse. They had discovered nothing. On the 14th they descended to St. Gervais and telegraphed Courmayeur for orders.

On the 15th Courmayeur replied, instructing them to continue. They went up again to the Bellevue. At St. Gervais they had met the guide Frédéric Payot of Chamonix who, on the morning of the 18th August, the day the Villanova party disappeared, had reached the Vallot refuge by way of the Grands Mulets, together with the French scientist Janssen and other guides and porters. Payot had stayed at the refuge from the 18th until the 22nd August: *no other party had passed that way between those two dates*. Thus it was clear that Jean-Joseph Maquignaz, Antonio Castagneri and their employer, Count Humbert of Villanova—supposing that the mysterious tracks on the Italian Glacier de Bionassay were theirs—had not passed over the Col de Bionassay or its immediate environs.

On the 16th the mountaineers left the Bellevue at three-fifteen in the morning, and at ten they arrived at the summit of the Aiguille du Goûter (12,382 feet). There was no sign of the missing climbers at the hut. They set out again at ten-forty-five to explore minutely the crests and slopes of the Aiguille and Dôme du Goûter. At two o'clock they were at the Dôme (14,118 feet), already reached on the 11th by the Italian face, and scrutinised afresh the whole of the arête as far as the Col de Bionassay, but this time on the descent. The results were still negative. They then reclimbed the Dôme and descended thence to Chamonix by way of the Grands Mulets. They arrived there at ten in the evening.

On the 17th and 18th they made their way back to Courmayeur through Nant Borrant and over the Col de la Seigne.[18]

* * *

"More than ten years have passed since then," wrote Guido Rey, concluding his narrative. "I do not know why it is, but the figures of these men are as indelibly impressed on my mind as are the troubled figures we see in dreams, and every time I enter the courtyard of the Hôtel de Londres I seem to see those two brave men sitting on the bench and smiling at me. . . . And whenever I walk up to Valtournanche, in fancy I meet old Jean-Joseph at the same spot with his pipe in his mouth, serenely descending his native valley for the last time, with all the vigour of a second youth.

"And now, when I compare the reality of what I saw with the imagined details of the subsequent tragedy, it feels to me as if the two I met were the ghosts of my friends, and as if the guide's smile contained at the time a touch of bitterness, whilst the pale, refined face of the climber expressed resignation to fate; as if old Maquignaz's grave salute was that of a wise man who knew that he was starting for a place whence there was no return."

* * *

More than fifty years have passed since then. No gleam whatever has come to lighten this secret tragedy. Nothing has changed. Nothing has moved. The mystery has continued as inaccessible as on the first day. Three bodies, up there, are entangled in the blueness of a glacier and the innocence of the snow. Or, somewhere in the giant ramparts of Brouillard, the three skeletons hang captive.[19]

This inscription at Valtournanche recalls the memory of Jean-Joseph Maquignaz:

GIOVANNI GIUSEPPE MAQUIGNAZ DA VALTOURNENCHE
GUIDA ALPINA
PER INTREPIDEZZA E PRUDENZA
DEGNA DEL MASSIMO ELOGIO
IL 18 AGOSTO MDCCCXC
SUI GHIACCIAI DEL MONTE BIANCO
NON LUNGI DAL DENTE DEL GIGANTE
CH'EGLI PRIMO VINSE
CON ALPINISTI ITALIANI
DA IMPERIOSA BUFERA TRAVOLTO
SPARI
IL CLUBO ALPINO ITALIANO
ANDAVO DI LUI SUPERBO
LA SEZIONE D'AOSTA CON ORGOGLIO
LA ADDITA AD ESEMPIO
CON QUESTO RICORDO
2 AGOSTO MDCCCXCI[20]

While at Balme d'Ala one may read the following epitaph:

ANTONIO CASTAGNERI
GUIDA VALENTE
DELLE ALPI ARDITO ESPLORATORE
COMPANO DESIDERATO DAGLI ALPINISTI
SUI GHIACCIAI DEL MONTE BIANCO
SORPRESO DA VIOLENTA BUFERA
IL 18 AGOSTO 1890
PERI VITTIMA DEL DOVERE
A PIE DELLE BALZE NATIE
OVE SI ADDESTRO A PIU ARDUI CIMENTI
LA SEZIONE TORINESE DEL CLUB ALPINO ITALIANO
QUESTO RICORDO POSE
ADDI 24 MAGGIO 1891[21]

For the scene of the Villanova disappearance see Plates 2 and 24.

[1] Jean-Joseph Maquignaz, born at Valtournanche in 1828. His first exploit made him famous. With his brother Jean-Pierre he discovered a new route on the Italian Matterhorn (September 1867), by which he reached the summit directly from the Breuil side, while Carrel's route made use of the top of the Tiefenmatten face and joined the Zmutt arête in its upper sector by a passage known as Carrel's Gallery. In 1868 he accomplished the first traverse of the Matterhorn from Breuil to Zermatt with the celebrated English climber Tyndall, and five days later he made the first traverse in the

opposite direction. But the glory of his life was the first ascent in 1882 of the Aiguille du Géant (13,166 feet) with his son Jean-Baptiste and his nephew Daniel, in company with some brothers and cousins, Sella Corradino, Alfonso and Gaudensio.

Maquignaz was, furthermore, a specialist and pioneer of winter alpinism. Together with Vittorio Sella he accomplished the first winter ascents of (amongst others) the Italian Matterhorn, Monte Rosa, the Lyskamm and the traverse of Mont Blanc by the Aiguille Grises; ski were unknown in the Alps at this time. Jean-Joseph Maquignaz, with Jean-Antoine Carrel, his best friend, takes his place as one of the most illustrious Italian guides of his time. It is tragic to note that these two splendid mountaineers perished in the mountains within a week of one another (see Chapter 18 for the story of Carrel's death).

[2] Antonio Castagneri, born at Balme in 1845. An admirable figure; with Carrel and J.-J. Maquignaz, he was one of the greatest Italian guides of the day. He specialised in the conquest of the Graians. His record totalled forty-three first ascents, including Monte Viso by its eastern face, the Gran Paradiso by the Noaschetta Glacier, the Bec de la Tribulation, the Charbonel, and the Jaegerhorn by its south-east face.

[3] Member of the Turin section of the C.A.I.

[4] A great mountaineer and writer, born at Turin 1861; he died in 1935. One of the best writers of contemporary alpine literature. Author of several remarkable works, of which the best known is *The Matterhorn* (new English edition published by Blackwell, Oxford, 1947), the magnificent homage of a poet and a historian to that wonderful mountain.

[5] Cf. Guido Rey, *The Matterhorn*, Chap. VI.

[6] (*a*) *By the Italian Glacier de Bionassay*. Followed for the first time in 1864 by A. Adams Reilly and John Birbeck, with the guides Michel Croz, Michel-Clément Payot and Marc Tairraz. Improved in 1889 by an Italian party comprising A. E. Martelli, Francisco Gonella, B. Graziadei, G. Luzzati and E. Scifoni, and the guides Joseph Gadin, Joseph Petigax and J. Melica.

(*b*) *By the Glacier du Dôme (called the "Route du Pape")*. Followed for the first time in 1865 by F. Crauford Grove, E. North Buxton and R. J. S. Macdonald, with the guides Jakob Anderegg, Jean-Pierre Cachat and Peter Taugwalder *fils*. Improved in 1890 by the party of the Abbés Achille Ratti (later Pope Pius XI), Grasselli and Bonin, with the guides Joseph Gadin and Alexis Proment.

(*c*) *By the Glacier du Mont Blanc (called the "Route du Rocher du Mont Blanc")*. Followed for the first time in 1872 by T. S. Kennedy, with the guides Jean-Antoine Carrel and Johann Fischer.

[7] See, however, paragraph 2 on page 208.

[8] See Chapter 9.

[9] See note 1 to Chapter 9.

[10] The Italian climbers Césare and Pietro Timosci, with the guides Alessio and Laurent Proment and the porter Laurent Bertholier. "At 2.45 in the afternoon," these climbers record, "the weather was already bad; at five o'clock it had completely deteriorated; and at nine in the evening a violent storm broke out which lasted all night, thus forestalling all hope of climbing the next day (19th August)." (See also note 11.)

[11] As it happens, the celebrated French astronomer Janssen, of the Académie des Sciences, and director of the Meudon observatory, was climbing Mont Blanc by way of the Grands Mulets on the 18th August. He and his guides were surprised by a storm just as they reached the Vallot refuge, where they were blockaded for several days. This is what he records:

"We thought we should resume the ascent the following day and arrive at the summit early. But in the evening (of the 18th) the weather suddenly broke up and in the night the tempest was terrible. In these high regions we felt the effects of the cyclonic whirlwind of the 19th August, which began its ravages at Oyonnax (Ain), afterwards passing through St. Claude, les Rousses, les Brassus, and ended them at Croy (a station of the Lausanne-Pontarlier line).

"During the night of the 18th to 19th, the day of the 19th and that of the 20th, except for certain lulls we had no respite from the tempest. I fully recognised in the speed and sound of the gusts of wind that we were experiencing the features of the great typhoon which we suffered in 1874 in the Hongkong Roads, when I was leading the French mission to Japan to observe the transit of the planet Venus—a typhoon which destroyed a part of the city and ravaged the China Sea.

The violence of the gusts was so great that it was dangerous for our guides to go outside when they were blowing, and everything which we had been obliged to leave outside, even of considerable weight, was lifted up and carried off as far as the Grand Plateau." (From J. Janssen: *Comptes rendus de l'Académie des Sciences*, Vol. CXI, No. 12.)

[12] Near where the Gonella refuge is situated to-day, known as the Dôme hut, constructed in 1891.

[13] The party comprised four men: the guides Laurent and David Proment and the porters Alessio Fenoillet and Luigi Musillon.

[14] It was this same tempest (24th to 26th August) which blockaded Jean-Antoine Carrel's caravan at the Italian refuge on the Matterhorn and brought about the death of that great guide at the foot of the Tête du Lion (see Chapter 18).

[15] The news of the discovery of three bodies on the Glacier de Bionassay had been falsely announced by the *Oesterreichische Alpenzeitung* on the 19th September.

[16] "It was the 18th August, 1890," writes the Abbé J. Henry in his book *Alpinisme*. "I was at the Petit Saint-Bernard. The Abbé Chanoux, the rector of the Hospice, and I left shortly before midday to take the air. From the Hospice plateau we could see Mont Blanc all smoking. Chanoux looked at it through his binoculars and then said to me, 'If anyone is on Mont Blanc to-day, he is lost.' As it happened, Count Umberto di Villanova was on the mountain with the two guides Castagneri and Maquignaz. It was related at Courmayeur that the widow di Villanova had only two sons: one died at sea, the other had extracted from her permission to climb Mont Blanc once more before ending his mountaineering career. In order to reassure his mother he had engaged the two best guides of the time, Maquignaz and Castagneri. Despite search after search, lasting several weeks, on the Glacier du Dôme and on the two sides of the arête de Bionassay, nothing was found of the three bodies. They had been carried away by the storm."

[17] See note 6(*a*) to this chapter.

[18] Concerning the accident and the searches, see the *Rivista Mensile del C.A.I.*, Nos. 8, 9 and 10, Vol. IX, 1890.

[19] In July, 1938, I was at le Breuil. In looking for Ange Maquignaz, the old guide and Guido Rey's factotum, I came upon his brother Jean-Baptiste. Sole survivor of the party which conquered the Aiguille du Géant, and son of Jean-Joseph, he still belonged to the (one might say "heroic") generation of the old guides of Valtournanche; legend had already glorified him, like his father. Having suffered the loss of all ten toes and the soles of his feet in a storm-bound bivouac on Mont Blanc de Courmayeur, which he was climbing in 1893 by way of the arête de Péteret (in the company of his cousin Daniel Maquignaz and Capt. Farrar—cf. *Alpine Journal*, Vol. XXXIII), he continued to climb the great peaks for another thirty years. I turned the conversation to his father's disappearance and to my surprise, before I had expressed my own views, Jean-Baptiste showed that he had like me the very strong impression that the vanished party had not been in the places where the search had been made, but had been on the Brouillard side. Will we ever know? We chatted, seated on a bench against the wall of Guido Roy's chalet. This chalet is to-day closed up and I had been the last guest in September 1934. But I seemed to see Guido Rey, enveloped in his black cloak, joining in our conversation and recalling to Jean-Baptiste the memory of his father descending his native valley, never to return.

[20] (*Trans.*) "Jean-Joseph Maquignaz of Valtournanche, Alpine guide, worthy of the highest praise for his boldness and prudence, on the 18th August, 1890, on the glaciers of Mont-Blanc, not far from the Dent du Géant, which he was the first to conquer

with Italian mountaineers, was carried away by the hurricane and disappeared. The Italian Alpine Club is proud of him. The Aosta section proudly commemorates his example by this memorial, 2nd August, 1891."

[21] (*Trans.*) "Antonio Castagneri, a brave guide, a daring explorer of the Alps, much-sought companion of mountaineers, was caught by a violent hurricane on the 18th August, 1890, on the glaciers of Mont Blanc. He perished, a victim of his duty. At the foot of his native rocks, where he put himself to a hard test, the Turin section of the Italian Alpine Club dedicates to him this memorial on the 24th May, 1891."

JEAN-JOSEPH MAQUIGNAZ

CHAPTER EIGHTEEN

CARREL THE GREAT

The death of the guide Jean-Antoine Carrel (Matterhorn, August 1890)

IN 1849 Jean-Antoine Carrel, the bersagliere,[1] saw the conquest of his country by the Austrians at Novara. The Italian
army beat a retreat, its regiments decimated. And when
Carrel reached his native Valtournanche, at the foot of the
Matterhorn, the young soldier carried with him a little of that
heartbreak, at the thought of the ravaged fatherland, which then
ennobled the whole Italian nation.

His period of service ended, Jean-Antoine Carrel, the conscript
who began his career with a battle, became an ardent patriot
in his love for his native mountains.

The heights called him. The chamois and marmot called him
too, but above all he was moved by an intense love of his native
soil. From the heights Carrel looked down and dreamed.[3] Before
him he could see the valleys and the little villages, stretching out
into the distance. Afar off he could hear the church-bells ring,
and the bells of the cattle too. A hazy light encompassed this
sonorous swarm of confused harmonies, while above the glaciers
the clear outlines of the great peaks thrust their summits into the
azure sky. One of them, beautiful above all others, a massive and
solitary rock with snow-spangled ramparts, dominated these high
places and helds Carrel in thrall. This was the Matterhorn. No man
had ever climbed it. In the mystery of the evening it crouched
there like a god-like hero. Carrel gazed at it with fascination.
He could not take his eyes from it. It troubled him with a secret
exaltation. And when, as in a dream, the soldier from Novara

returned to his chalet, his future was settled; it had been fixed by fate. The Matterhorn was the constant theme of his life. But it was also his death.

In 1857, eight years after the battle of Novara, Carrel made his first attempt on the Matterhorn. In 1859 he fought at Solferino, where a brilliant victory revenged the humiliating defeat of ten years before, and Carrel was promoted Sergeant on the battle-field. Returning thereafter to Valtournanche, Sergeant J.-A. Carrel exchanged his rifle for an alpenstock and began to think of the Matterhorn once more; the struggle for his native land being ended, the struggle for the Matterhorn continued with ever-increasing intensity.

A young Englishman, Edward Whymper, almost a greenhorn, hardly twenty years of age (1860), had designs on Carrel's mountain; it was enough to measure his cold tenacity to know that he intended to be its conqueror. But Carrel had that intention too. Thus began, just as in one of those antique tragedies revolving around a woman, the chain of suitor's intrigues, the frequently dramatic clash of impassioned rivalry. Alternately, Whymper and Carrel entered into alliance and opposition. Other suitors arose. The years passed and the Matterhorn still raised its inviolate splendours above the valleys and above the paltry designs of human beings.

From Novara and Solferino Carrel had brought back a heart drenched in patriotic joys and sorrows. Soldier and patriot, this humble peasant intended to conquer the Matterhorn, not for his own glory but for the honour of his fatherland, his own valley and his native village.

In 1865, on the 14th July, Whymper reached the peak from the Swiss side, from Zermatt. Three days later, Jean-Antoine Carrel reached it too, but from his own side, from Breuil.[4] At least, he had not compromised. Edward Whymper was the victor, but Carrel remained unconquered, for there, where Whymper and Tyndall had retreated, he passed, snatching victory with one supreme and magnificent effort.

*   *   *

Twenty-five years elapse. Carrel forges a glorious career. Paladin of the peaks, he is one of the unsullied glories of Italian alpinism.[5]

On the 21st August, 1890—three days after the mysterious disappearance of the Villanova party, and before anyone even suspects a tragedy[6]—Jean-Antoine Carrel arrives at Courmayeur, descending Mont Blanc by the Rocher route, of which he had made the first ascent in 1872 with the Swiss guide Johann Fischer, and the Englishman, T. S. Kennedy.[7] In Courmayeur a young law student, Leone Sinigaglia[8] of Turin, asks Carrel if he will guide him to the Matterhorn. The old guide accepts.[9] On the 22nd they leave Courmayeur, passing through Aosta and Châtillon, and reach the Valtournanche in the afternoon. Carrel stops at his own chalet to reassure his wife and to embrace his grandchildren, then continues with Sinigaglia to Breuil. A second guide, Charles Gorret,[10] a brother of the Abbé Gorret, one of the priests who took part in the conquest of the Matterhorn, joins them.

In the evening of the 22nd the climbers sleep at Breuil, at the little Hôtel des Jumeaux.[11] Their intention is to traverse the Matterhorn in one day from Breuil to the Hörnli hut (on the Swiss side), a long and fatiguing undertaking. But Carrel knows that he can count on the endurance and skill of Sinigaglia. Moreover, the conqueror of the Italian Matterhorn always feels a secret happiness at finding himself once again on his own mountain. A day or two ago, on the summit of Mont Blanc, turned in this direction, he had admired its lonely silhouette in silence, the bold lines describing a great geometrical figure in the sky, the acute angle of a belfry on a rectangular pediment. Thus in his heart he rejoices to find himself again on these honey-coloured rocks, climbing once more these precipitous walls.

On the 23rd, at two-fifteen in the morning, in a night of glistening starlight, the party leaves Breuil and, crossing pastures wet with dew, makes its way towards the Matterhorn, massive as it crouches there in the shadows. The sunrise is splendid; an entrancing day is about to begin. But this is the last time that Jean-Antoine Carrel leaves for the Matterhorn.

To the climbers' surprise a patina of verglas covers the rocks of the Tête du Lion, and they lose a great deal of time. At the Col du Lion the rocks are fortunately dry. So there they are on the Matterhorn arête. Above them, at the foot of the Grande Tour, where the refuge is situated, there is a trail of smoke.[12] They will not be alone, for some men can be seen in front of it. On arrival at the refuge they are received with jovial cries from the three

Maquignaz (Daniel and two Antoines) and Edouard Bich. They have passed the previous day among the rocks of the Matterhorn examining the condition of the fixed ropes, and now, their duties completed, they are preparing to return to Valtournanche.

"You are going to climb the Matterhorn *now*?" they ask.

"*Diable!* It's a bit late for that, isn't it?"

"We had to go slow on the col. . . All over verglas, you'll find. It needs care."

What should they do? Make a forced march, or put into port here?

It is ten-thirty. The weather is already badly broken. There is no time for hesitation. Carrel, Gorrett and Sinigaglia are not beginners and they know the mountains too well to argue for long. They agree quite readily to put off until to-morrow the plans which the weather has changed. Whitish plumes have invaded and dulled the resplendently blue sky. Carrel, moreover, is not upset by this halt; he is overcome by a strange lassitude and he falls asleep on a mattress. When, rested, he rises two hours later, the weather is completely threatening: clouds are massing in the direction of Mont Blanc, while above the Dent d'Hérens and the Dent Blanche inky storm-clouds are hanging like curtains agitated by the wind. At three o'clock the Maquignaz and Bich take advantage of a clearing—a northern squall which checks and repels the storm—to decamp. And the Sinigaglia party, henceforth alone at the refuge (12,837 feet) quickly shuts the door upon the precursory winds of the storm which prowles about afresh and seems to be coming slowly to a head.

The wind changes. The refuge, a wide wooden box, moored to the mountain with steel cables, pitches and quivers like a ship on a demented sea. All its angles creak and groan; the cables vibrate stridently like shrill flutes. The hail begins to hammer upon the iron roof. Snow dims the windows. Within the hut are a few cubic yards of calm silence in the midst of the uproar, and every object, every detail of the furniture and its construction, even to its shape and placing, invites the spirit to quietude. All these rough things take possession of one's eyes and propagate in the heart a delicious feeling of security and comfort. The fire crackles. The men are seated around it, idle and silent. Jean-Antoine Carrel smokes his great pipe. He listens to the commotion of the hurricane without. He loves these disordered forces; they speak to him and charm him. Thus in his day-dream memories arise.

"The first attempt in '57. . . . How astonishing it was to see this Matterhorn from the top of the Tête du Lion, so big and high, immense and inaccessible. We were eating dried meat and looking at the mountains without saying a word. . . . What a plucky little Englishman that Whymper was! . . . And his fall in the couloir below the col! Three days later, *nom de Dieu!*, he set out for the Matterhorn again."

The snow settles against the windows with the rustle of angry bees.

"And there were Tyndall and Bennen, too. . . . What a strange idea it was to bring that ladder up amongst these rocks. . . . Ah! that day, upon my word! We were jolly near the summit. . . . Uncle Jean-Jacques and I, if we had wished. . . . And those bivouacs under the tents or in the rocks . . . how stiff with the cold we were in the mornings on those whitened rocks!"

Between the gusts the wind, like a hand, feels at the corners of the hut. A little smoke, driven back down the flue, mingles its acrid odour with the tobacco from the climbers' pipes.

"Michel Croz; he had to come for a look too. And that sad Giordano affair. Those five days and four nights on the Matterhorn, only to see Mr. Whymper's white trousers suddenly on the summit . . ."

The half-darkness slowly takes possession of the refuge. Through the flue a gleam falls upon the floor and moves. Outside, the angry commotion continues without respite.

"Then our turn arrived, and Bich and I up there beside Croz's blue shirt. We fixed a stick in the snow and tied my red handkerchief to it. It was fine, that summit, all alone in the sky. . . ."

All these memories! One might think, as each of them passes through the mind of the old mountaineer, that they are all here, all these memories, the things and the shades of vanished men, motionless, silent, entering and filling the refuge.

A blaze of lightning abruptly lights the half-darkness and the three men turn round. An enormous roar of thunder shakes the mountain, and the precipices clamour raucously. The lightning flashes again and again, without interval. "The air was so charged with electricity," writes Leone Sinigaglia, "that for two consecutive hours in the night one could see in the hut as in broad daylight. The storm continued to rage all night, and the day and night following, continuously, with incredible violence. The temperature in the hut fell to three degrees.

"The situation was becoming alarming, for the provisions were getting low, and we had already begun to use the seats of the hut as firewood. The rocks were in an extremely bad state, and we were afraid that if we stopped longer, and the storm continued, we should be blocked up in the hut for several days. This being the state of affairs, it was decided among the guides that if the wind should abate we should descend on the following morning; and, as the wind did abate somewhat, on the morning of the 25th (the weather, however, still remaining very bad), it was unanimously settled to make a retreat."

At nine o'clock the climbers closed the double door of the refuge behind them and launched themselves into the tempest.[13] They at once encountered such difficulties and such great dangers that it took them $5\frac{1}{2}$ hours to reach the Col du Lion.[14] "The ropes were half frozen; the rocks were covered with a glaze of ice, and fresh snow hid all points of support. Some spots were really as bad as could be, and I owe much to the coolness and prudence of the two guides that we got over them without mishap.

"At the Col du Lion, where we hoped the wind would moderate, a dreadful hurricane recommenced, and in crossing the snowy passages we were nearly suffocated by the wind and snow which attacked us on all sides. Through the loss of a glove, Gorret, half an hour after leaving the hut, had already got a hand frostbitten. The cold was terrible here. Every moment we had to remove the ice from our eyes, and it was with the utmost difficulty that we could speak so as to understand one another.

"Nevertheless, Carrel continued to direct the descent in a most admirable manner, with a coolness, ability and energy above all praise. I was delighted to see the change, and Gorret assisted him splendidly. This part of the descent presented unexpected difficulties, and at several points great dangers, the more so because the tempest prevented Carrel from being sure of the right direction, in spite of his consummate knowledge of the Matterhorn. At eleven at night (or thereabouts—it was impossible to look at our watches, as all our clothes were half frozen) we were still toiling down the rocks. The guides sometimes asked each other where they were; then we went forward again—to stop indeed would have been impossible. Carrel, at last, by marvellous instinct, discovered the passage up which we had come, and in a sort of grotto we stopped a minute to take some brandy.

"While crossing some snow we saw Carrel slacken his pace, and then fall two or three times to the ground. Gorret asked him what was the matter, and he said 'nothing,' but he went on with difficulty. Attributing this to fatigue through excessive toil, Gorret put himself at the head of the caravan, and Carrel, after the change, seemed better, and walked well, though with more circumspection than usual. From this point a short and steep passage takes one down to the pastures, where there is safety. Gorret descended first, and I after him. We were nearly at the bottom when I felt the rope pulled. We stopped, awkwardly placed as we were, and cried out to Carrel several times to come down, but we received no answer. Alarmed, we went up a little way, and heard him say, in a faint voice, 'Come up and fetch me, I have no strength left.'

"We went up and found that he was lying with his stomach to the ground, holding on to a rock, in a semi-conscious state, and unable to get up or to move a step. With extreme difficulty we carried him up to a safe place and asked him what was the matter. His only answer was, 'I know no longer where I am.' His hands were getting colder and colder, his speech weaker and more broken, and his body more still. We did all we could for him, putting with great difficulty the rest of the cognac into his mouth. He said something, and appeared to revive, but this did not last long. We tried rubbing him with snow, and shaking him, and calling to him continually; but he could only answer with moans.

"We tried to lift him, but it was impossible—he was getting stiff. We stooped down, and asked in his ear if he wished to commend his soul to God. With a last effort he answered 'Yes,' and then fell on his back, dead, upon the snow.

"With broken hearts we cut the rope that tied us to our valiant companion and pursued the descent. We arrived at le Breuil at five in the morning of the 26th August, after a descent of twenty hours without stopping or eating, a descent which would require only four or five hours in normal conditions.[15]

"Carrel died, like a good and brave man, on his own mountain, after having summoned up all the energy he possessed in order to save his employer.[16] He died after bringing him out of danger to a place of safety, exhausted by the supreme effort of sixteen hours of assiduous work, amid continuous struggles and difficulties, in a snowstorm which several times appeared irresistible. I shall never think of him without infinite emotion and gratitude."[17]

Whymper, steely and cold of aspect, and with a heart that seemed inaccessible to tenderness or pity, adds: "It was not in his nature to spare himself, and he worked to the very last. The manner of his death strikes a chord in hearts he never knew. He recognised to the fullest extent the duties of his position, and in the closing act of his life set a brilliant example of fidelity and devotion. For it cannot be doubted that, enfeebled as he was, he could have saved himself had he given his attention to self-preservation. He took a nobler course; and, accepting his responsibility, devoted his whole soul to the welfare of his comrades until, utterly exhausted, he fell staggering on the snow."

In the summer of 1900 Guido Rey, descending from the hut at the Grande Tour, having climbed the Matterhorn the day before by the Zmutt arête, passed close to the rock where Carrel died. The morning was very threatening under an overcast sky. He wrote:

"On a morning drear as this, but far more terrible, Carrel, the Bersagliere, had left the hut at the Tower for his last descent, which came to an end not far below the Col, after a night and a day of fearful struggle, near a rock by which there now stands a cross. Ten years have passed since then. The pilgrims of the Matterhorn stop reverently before that rock. It was there that the old soldier, weary after his last desperate battle, his strength all gone, was laid by his comrades; it was there that he died. Perhaps in the visions of his last moment he heard once more the trumpets sounding on the Colle di San Martino,[18] and the shouts of victory on the conquered Matterhorn; these were the two glories of his life. Or perhaps his mind grew suddenly dark, and he was not even conscious of his own heroism which had saved his companions on that last descent. Such was the end of the long contest between the mountaineer and his mountain; a contest that lasted thirty years, full of ardent deeds of daring and of passive defence, of hard-won victories, and of defeats that were as glorious as any victory. Carrel had ceased to conquer; his weapons were worn out by long use, blunt with age, and no longer served the valour and experience of the ancient warrior. The Matterhorn watched its opportunity and dealt him his death-blow. But popular rumour immediately lent a noble shape to the image of the first of the Matterhorn guides: 'Carrel did not fall; he died,' they said in his native valley."[19]

*   *   *

On the 26th of August, the same afternoon as the Sinigaglia party returned to Breuil, a company of eight men, comprising the guides Alexandre and Elie Pession and Victor Maquignaz (of Valtournanche), Adolf Schaller (of Randa), Aloys Pollinger (of St. Niklaus) and three shepherds, brought Carrel's body back to Breuil. His mortal remains were deposited in the chapel of Notre-Dame des Pélerins. The funeral took place on the 29th at the little cemetery of Valtournanche.

*   *   *

Three years after his heroic end a small iron cross was erected by Leone Sinigaglia at the very place where Jean-Antoine Carrel drew his last breath, not far from the place where the Rionde hut now stands. Charles Gorret, the guide, and Leone Sinigaglia, his former employer, some friends, some climbers, guides and mountain folk participated in this moving ceremony (July 1893). To the centre of the cross a metal heart is fixed, bearing these words:

ICI EST MORT L'INTREPIDE
GUIDE JEAN-ANTOINE CARREL
LE 26 AOUT 1890 AGE
DE 62 ANS UNE PRIERE
POUR LE REPOS
DE SON AME[20]

And this inscription may be read on the wall of the town hall in Valtournanche:

GIOVANNI ANTONIO CARREL
DETTO IL BERSAGLIERE
DA VALTOURNANCHE
GUIDA ALPINA
PER INTREPEDEZZA ED ABNEGAZIONE
SUPERIORE AD OGNI ELOGIO
CHE FIN SULLE ANDE D'AMERICA[21]

FECE RIFULGERE

LA FAMA DELLE GUIDE ITALIANE

MORI VITTIMA DEL SUO DOVERE

IL XXV AGOSTO MDCCCXC

SCENDENDO IL CERVINO

CHE PRIMO IL XVII LUGLIO MDCCCLXV

AVEVA SUPERATO DAL VERSANTE ITALIANO

E RISALITO DI POI PER LIII VOLTE

IL CLUB ALPINO ITALIANO ANDAVA DI LUI SUPERBO

LA SEZIONE DI AOSTA CON ORGOGLIO

LO ADDITA AD ESEMPIO

CON QUESTO RICORDO

IL AGOSTO MDCCCXCI[22]

And Leone Sinigaglia once confided to me: "I think he should be called 'CARREL THE GREAT.' "

For the scene of Carrel's death, see Plate 25. See also Plates 26 and 27.

[1] As a soldier of the corps of Bersaglieri, Carrel, when in uniform, wore the cock's feather in his hat, the insignia of this élite formation. Hence the name of that part of the Italian arête of the Matterhorn between the Grande Corde (13,464 feet) and the Pic Tyndall (14,008 feet)—the "Crête du Coq"—a point which Carrel was the first to reach.

[2] The exact date of his birth is unknown. He was baptised at the church of St. Antoine at Valtournanche on the 17th January, 1829.

[3] G. W. Prothero, an experienced English climber, notes that Carrel was the only guide he had ever met who felt a real admiration for the beauty of mountains. One day when they found themselves together at the summit of Monte Rosa, Jean-Antoine Carrel never wearied of admiring the landscape. On another occasion, at a summit, he could not refrain from exclaiming, very much moved: "*O la bella Italia! La bella Italia!*" And elsewhere he described a beauty-spot with a truly artistic joy. (Cf. *The Pioneers of the Alps*; also *Alpine Journal*, Vol. XXV, 1910–11.)

[4] With his comrade, Jean-Baptiste Bich of Valtournanche.

[5] Carrel "was the finest rock-climber I have ever seen. He was the only man who persistently refused to accept defeat, and who continued to believe, in spite of all discouragements, that the great mountain was not inaccessible, and that it could be ascended from the side of his native valley." (Whymper: *Scrambles Amongst the Alps*, Murray, London.)

[6] See Chapter 17.

[7] See note 6(*c*) to Chapter 17.

[8] Leone Sinigaglia early abandoned law for music. He achieved a prominent place in the modern Italian school of music, especially in Piedmont. He died tragically in 1944, a victim of the war.

[9] It was only on the 22nd that the fate of the Villanova party began to cause alarm at Courmayeur. Otherwise it can be taken for granted that Carrel, a great friend of J.-J. Maquignaz and of Castagneri, the vanished guides, would not have hesitated for an instant in leaving with the search parties.

[10] The guide Charles Gorret was one of the party of three mountaineers chosen by Carrel to attempt, at the instigation of Giordano, to reach the Matterhorn before Whymper. It was this party which passed five days and four nights on the mountain

from the 10th to the 14th July, 1865. His brother, the Abbé Aimé Gorret, had taken part in the first attempt in 1857, with Jean-Jacques and Jean-Antoine Carrel, and in the climb (on the 16th and 17th July, 1865) which ended in victory. In order to gain time, the Abbé Gorret and his comrade Jean-Augustin Meynet did not go further than the northern extremity of the Gallery, where they awaited the return of Carrel and Bich.

[11] Until 1938 it was kept by one of Guido Rey's old guides, Aimé Maquignaz, who died in December 1938.

[12] The old hut. The new and present hut, constructed in 1893, bears the name of Luigi-Amadeo of Savoy, in honour of that renowned climber of the Italian royal family. This refuge was built some 300 feet below the first hut which is described here.

[13] Throughout the 25th a party of guides held itself ready at le Breuil to go to the assistance of the Sinigaglia party. But the violence of the storm was such that they were obliged to give up.

[14] A distance which in normal weather can be done in an hour, or in an hour and a quarter.

[15] Published by Whymper in the *Alpine Journal*, Vol. XV, 1890–91, and translated from Sinigaglia's account in the *Rivista Mensile del C.A.I.*

[16] Sinigaglia wrote to a friend : "I will not try to tell you what immense pain the death of Carrel has caused me. He fell after having saved me and no guide could have done more than he did." In a letter to Whymper the guide Charles Gorret adds : "We would have given our own lives to have saved his."

[17] This paragraph, also by Sinigaglia, is quoted by Guido Rey in *The Matterhorn* (*op cit.*, p. 277, 1946 edition).

[18] San Martino is the name of the sector of the Solferino battlefield, 1859, held by the troops of Piedmont, Carrel among them. Tyndall remarks, in the testimonial which he wrote in Carrel's *livret* (1862), that the military discipline which Carrel had acquired in his two campaigns was useful to him in his profession as guide. (Quoted by Guido Rey in *The Matterhorn, op. cit.*, p. 269.)

[19] Cf. Rey, *The Matterhorn, op. cit.* pp. 186–7.

[20] The French text was composed by Leone Sinigaglia himself. (*Trans.*) :
"Here died the intrepid guide Jean-Antoine Carrel on the 26th August, 1890, aged 62 years. A prayer for the repose of his soul."

[21] An allusion to his campaign with Edward Whymper in the Cordilleras of the Andes (1879–80) where, with his brother Louis as second guide, he made eight great first ascents, among them Chimborazo (20,498 feet) and Cotopaxi (19,613 feet). (Cf. Edward Whymper, *Travels Amongst the Great Andes of the Equator*, Murray, London.) Whymper opened a subscription in England for Carrel's family, which produced 10,000 francs, with assurances of more.

[22] *Trans.*: "Jean-Antoine Carrel, the Bersagliere, of Valtournanche, Alpine Guide, beyond all praise for his fearlessness and self-sacrifice. He made the reputation of Italian guides to shine as far away as the American Andes. He died, a victim of his duty, on the 25th August, 1890, while descending the Matterhorn, which he was the first to conquer from the Italian side on the 17th July, 1865, and which he afterwards climbed fifty-three times. The Italian Alpine Club is proud of him. The Aosta section proudly commemorates his example by this memorial. August 11th, 1891."

CHAPTER NINETEEN

WHEN LUCK RUNS OUT

(The death of the guide Emile Rey (Aiguille du Géant, August 1895)

O N the terrace at Montenvers, an English tourist, equipped *à la Tartarin*, approaches a guide who stands there looking at the mountains. In an off-hand manner the tourist points to the Mer de Glace and asks "How much?" The guide courteously takes off his hat, then indicates a group of individuals on the watch for tourists: "Those are the guides for the Mer de Glace," he says simply. "As for myself, I am only for the high mountains." Proud words, but spoken without vanity by a man who knows his worth; they have dignity and simplicity.

This man is an eminent guide, one of the greatest among the greatest: Emile Rey of Courmayeur. The profession is of little consequence, for genius is not exclusive to one category of men. This man escapes all classification, and at his heart the ardent flame burns with the purest light. The Golden Age of alpinism, the age of the conquest of the Alps, brought men of genius to light among the mountain dwellers, in their characters, in their intelligence, by the very radiance of their presence; qualities which, allied to physical strength, made such magnificently outstanding figures of such men as Christian Almer, Melchior Anderegg, Michel Croz, Aloys Pollinger, Jean-Antoine Carrel, Jean-Joseph Maquignaz, Emile Rey, Franz Lochmatter and two or three others.

Emile Rey the carpenter[1] began his career as a guide very late. He was thirty when he undertook his first big climbs. But he was called to a high destiny and at once revealed himself as a virtuoso.

And when he abandoned the hunter's gun for the ice-axe, he scarcely changed his terrain, only passing beyond the solitudes where the chamois had so often drawn him, leaving the stony glacier and the mossy rocks for the white plateaux and the pointed, sky-crowned summits. His first employer, Lord Wentworth, Byron's grandson, was of his own stamp. The carpenter of Courmayeur and the British aristocrat got on well from the start. They had no need to try each other out; they understood one another and agreed. The guide's nature, a blend of passion and of slightly haughty frigidity, went well with Wentworth's sensitive nature, a byronic lyricism transformed into a love of high places. Wentworth trod the mountains which his poet-grandfather extolled from below, and proved by experience the impressions which the grandfather presented by divination. "All that expands the spirit, yet appals, gather around these summits."

For this descendant of Manfred, the romantic hero, Emile Rey became the ideal "chamois-hunter," the initiator to the mysteries of the peaks.

MANFRED: *The mists boil up around the glaciers; clouds rise curling fast beneath me, white and sulphury, like foam from the roused ocean of deep Hell, whose every wave breaks on a living shore . . . I am giddy . . . .*

CHAMOIS-HUNTER: *. . . Away with me—The clouds grow thicker— there—now lean on me—Place your foot here—here, take this staff . . . Now give me your hand, and hold fast by my girdle . . . Follow me. . . .*

Their first conquest (1877) revealed a severe and refined taste: the Aiguille Noire de Péteret (12,372 feet).[2] The years passed and the exploits of Emile Rey accumulated, composing with a masterly brilliance the great unity of his life, this royal gift of moving with consumate ease on narrow crests of ice and on perpendicular rock in the splendour of the sky and the snow.[3] In 1885 he conquered the Aiguille Blanche de Péteret (13,507 feet),[4] the last summit of the Mont Blanc chain to have remained inviolate. Ten years after this memorable victory Emile Rey was killed on the Aiguille du Géant. He was not yet fifty years old. "I have always been lucky, monsieur," he once said to an employer. But on this occasion he was not.

* * *

In the evening of Thursday, 23rd August, 1895, a camp-fire flames at the base of the grassy slopes which overlook the Mer de

Glace and stretch towards the Couvercle track, at about the same level as the Egralets. Three men are seated around the flames among the rough undergrowth and rhododendrons.

This is an unusual site for a camp; for generally, when making an expedition either to the Verte massif, or to the regions of the Cols du Géant and du Midi, or even farther afield, the bivouac is sited under the Couvercle rock itself, an hour higher up, or near the little Lac de Tacul. But this party, apart from the porter, has climbed the Petit Dru during the day,[5] and—an extraordinary circumstance—Emile Rey feels a little tired and has no appetite. He finds it comfortable down here; so why climb up to the Couvercle? Emile's employer, Mr. A. Carson Roberts, assents, and the three men are soon stretched out beside the glowing embers. Before them, on the other side of the Mer de Glace, against a sky in which the setting sun gives way before the first stars, rises the sombre array of the Aiguilles, Dante's "flames of rock." The glaciers glimmer vaguely. Above their confused palor enormous mountains mass themselves distantly, and from their mass a sword stands out, planted at the heart of the invading darkness. It is the Aiguille du Géant.

To-morrow it is the climbers' plan to ascend the Aiguille Verte by the arête du Moine. But the guide's fate has another love. When morning comes nobody stirs at the bivouac before four o'clock, and then Rey, who has always accepted the views of his employers and has never recoiled before the most strenuous task, modifies the plans first adopted. For a man like him this is a curious act.

"No, monsieur; it is too far to the Verte by the Moine from here, and it is late. We shall have to abandon it."

"Abandon it? Then where shall we go, Emile? It's going to be a fine day. Let's do something."

"The Aiguille du Géant?" suggests Rey.

"The Géant? If you like. Why not?"

"Then let's go to the Géant."

"And let us take a close look at the north face," adds Roberts. "Maybe we shall try it one day."

At five o'clock Roberts and Emile Rey leave for the Aiguille du Géant, while the porter descends to Montenvers. They cross the séracs to the east and set foot on the rocks of the Aiguille Noire. Thence, climbing all the while, they examine the northern precipice from top to bottom; it is still immersed in shadow and embedded in the bluish air. From higher and closer they will be able to complete their examination and verify their impressions. Then they reach the rock promontory which supports the mountain on the south in the direction of the Aiguilles Marbrées.

At one-ten they reach the foot of the giddy rocks of the gigantic Dent. This Dent is like an arrow fitted into its drawn bow, marking the initial movement of its flight. Along its inclined slabs and its very steep walls, and without being roped (the rope is still in a coil on the guide's pack), the climbers rise rapidly and with confidence. Not that Emile Rey should treat a fundamental climbing principle in this way, but a "gentlemen's agreement" has been reached between the guide and his employer. "We had talked this matter over," writes Mr. Carson Roberts, "and agreed that, unless one is so much weaker a climber as to need support from the other, two are safer on rocks, as well as quicker, without the rope, and time and again in discussing the subject we came to the same conclusion."[6] Two days earlier, at the Petit Dru, they had not used the rope except to traverse the glacier. Robert's project had been to find a route from the Petit Dru to the Grand Dru, but without using the rope left behind at the Grand Dru by another party, which was the custom. Further, he wished to try the Aiguille du Géant by a new route, by the north face or the north-east arête.[7]

Pushing the trial of this method of climbing to its farthest limit,[8] at the Géant Emile Rey allows his employer to go in front at the most risky passages, with a view to seeing how he will manage between the pitons fixed by Maquignaz[9] and the holds in the rock. This dizzy peak has, one might say, nothing but the vault of the sky to support its isolation in space and the strange magnificence of its soaring four-thousand-metre peak, like a gigantic leaning tower of Pisa.

At two o'clock the climbers reach the summit (13,166 feet). Emile Rey is happy. He slowly surveys the great, glittering, blue-enhanced circle which the Alps and their valleys form around him. And there, quite close, are his first three conquests: Mont Blanc by the Péteret arête, and the two Aiguilles de Péteret, the one black and all angles, the other white and harmonious, both of them fascinating and terrible. The one with its sombre ramparts, the other with snows like rigidly folded linen. Emile Rey points to a spot on the arête de Péteret and says, laughing:

"That's where I had to sing!"

"To sing!"

"Yes, at the bivouac, with M. Güssfeldt. I sang *La Lisette* to warm us up. There was no other way!"[10]

"*La Lisette?*"

"Yes, *La Lisette*. What! You don't know *La Lisette?*"

He laughs at this recollection and hums Béranger's song, which evoked so gentle a vision in that frightful bivouac:

> *A Notre-Dame de Liesse*
> *Allons, me dit Lisette un jour.*
> *J'ai peu de foi, je le confesse;*
> *Mais Lise, malgré plus d'un tour,*
> *Ferait tout croire a mon amour.*
> *Ma Lisette, prenions-nous donc,*
> *Pour mener l'amour a l'auberge,*
> *Ma Lisette, prenions-nous donc*
> *Coquilles, rosaire et bourdon?*

* * *

But now, behind the arête de Péteret, bad-weather clouds, already veiling the great bulk of Mont Blanc and lying like smoke in the south wind, encumber the horizon and break the charm. A moment before leaving, the two men examine the smooth gulf facing north. There, undoubtedly, one might open up an interesting route. But there is also a route to trace on the Aiguille de Rochefort, of which Rey has long been dreaming. While they delay the weather deteriorates still further. In the depths of a trough opening in the clouds above the Val Ferret, Rey can glimpse a white spot in the midst of the verdure, the chapel of Notre-Dame de la Guérison, where many times he has been to pray, and which, from high up on the rough summits, has seemed so many times so pleasing to his eye and spirit.

The thick mists already trail over the glaciers. It is three-twenty. There is not another minute to lose in day-dreaming on these rocks, if they are to reach the hut on the Col du Géant before the storm breaks. Unroped, just as they had climbed, the two climbers scramble down and are quickly involved in the precipice. In a patch clear of cloud, while they halt for breath between two clefts, Emile Rey points to the hut on the rocks of the col. When they reach the foot of the Aiguille (at 4.05), there where they leave the rock in order to return to the south and gain the top of the promontory, the guide, at the request of his employer, unrolls the rope and the two men tie up. In this region there is a dangerous névé. They had roped to cross it on the ascent. The crossing does not last more than a few minutes, but "neither of us," Mr. Roberts insists, "dreamt of using the rope for the easy descent thence to the snowfield."

So Emile Rey then rolls up the rope and fixes it to his pack. They set off once more, the guide a few yards in advance. Shortly after having worked their way past the two small spurs which crown the promontory, Rey notices a crystal. He bends down to pick it up, examines it and, seeing that it is nothing unusual, is about to throw it away when, changing his mind, he holds it out to Roberts and says, "Here, monsieur; keep it. It might perhaps be a souvenir."

Those are his last words. Less sybilline, certainly, than Maurer's at Grindelwald, when a few hours before his death he handed his pipe to his friend in almost complete certainty that he would never smoke it again.[11] But might we not find in them a mysterious meaning? Why that strange word "perhaps"? Might this not have been a breach in the inexorable wall of destiny? Might it not convey obscurely some dread decree? When Emil spoke those words it was 4.15. One minute later, at 4.16, he fell.

When the mishap occurred Rey was involved in a small chimney.[12] A few yards above him, standing at the edge of the same chimney, Roberts was watching his guide descend, awaiting his own turn. Suddenly the climber heard a quiet exclamation, an "ugh!" suggestive of disgust or pain, and he saw his companion, as he reached the bottom of the chimney, let himself drop about a yard, feet first. A sloping slab, covered with broken stone, received him; he tottered and fell to one side on the hardened snow.

"Emile . . . Emile . . . What's the matter? . . . hold on . . . *Emile* . . . Ah!"

Almost simultaneously with the beginning of the fall and with Roberts's cries, and before the slide had acquired speed, the mountaineer grazed an outcrop of rock; but it is curious that he made no attempt to lay hold of it, which might still have saved him. He ran against it, leaving there his hat and axe. The snow carried him off. The slide accelerated, became swifter and swifter. Then, flung into space, the body disappeared "like a cart-wheel in the air."[13]

Overwhelmed, Roberts hurried down the chimney. Instinctively he recovered the axe and hat in passing, the jettison of the vanished man. And as far as he could go, he descended the fatal north slope, following the line of Emile's fall. A cliff more than three hundred feet high brought him to a halt. He leaned over it and descried the body below, on a quiet, rounded beach of snow, with one leg doubled up under the back. He called, he shouted, but only the echoes replied.

"Emile," he cried, "if you can hear me wave your hand. . . . Can you hear me? . . . Move a hand! . . . *Emile!*"

But Emile heard nothing, and the hand which lay on the snow had already acquired the immobility given to it by eternity.

* * *

The thunder rolls and draws nearer. Mont Blanc, the Péterets and Mont Maudit vanish into the massing and boiling mists. The solitary climber has scarcely time to take the direction of the hut by his compass before the shafts of hail assail him. He tries vainly to approach the body from another side. But another wall bars his way and almost tumbles him down. The snow begins to fall: a blinding snow, thickening the already dense mists. High above him the wind breaks with dull blows against the slabs of the invisible Géant.

Then Roberts abandons his plans and, with the help of his compass, and despite the numerous crevasses and the swirls of snow, arrives at seven o'clock at the Col du Géant. In the darkness of the storm he descries the rectangular outline of the hut; he is safe. But to his great surprise the door resists his thrust. He bangs on it loudly and shouts. In a few moments the door half opens to reveal two haggard faces. They are those of two young French-Swiss climbers,[14] arrived from Montenvers during the day. Frightened by the violence of the storm, they had shut themselves up in the refuge, and now are frightened to death to see this ghost, sheeted in snow and ice, emerging from the angry night.[15]

Roberts tells the young men about the accident and asks them to come with him at once to the help of Emile Rey, perhaps still alive. Because of the late hour (7.30), the storm and the risk of a further accident, they refuse. The argument they set up and raise to the level of a dogma is that it would be better "to search for the living rather than the dead," and the Englishman at last understands that a caravan of twelve persons, six Dutch tourists (three men and three women) and six guides, which had set out from Montenvers, has not arrived. At this very moment they are perhaps astray in the storm.

The men hesitate no longer. They equip themselves and, abandoning the poor corpse to the snow and the clouds, leave in search of the living. Twenty minutes below the col they run into the Dutch party. Soon these weary and half-frozen people fill the hut. Roberts's further attempt to reach Emile Rey fails, for the leading guide of the Dutch party, to whom he makes his request, answers that his men can do no more; above all, no word of the accident must reach his already disordered caravan or it will, from fear, never arrive at Courmayeur intact. Discreetly consulted, the least exhausted of the tourists declares that the most they can do is to send a guide to Courmayeur early in the morning. Resigned, Roberts can do nothing but wait. He sits down near the fire to pass the night. He dozes, then falls asleep, wakes up with a start, sleeps again, and dreams time and again that Emile has succeeded in dragging himself to the hut, that he walks in, looks at him and sadly reproaches him for his desertion.

Early the following morning (Sunday 25th August), the two young climbers make a new approach to the leading guide, suggesting that he instruct one of his comrades to accompany them and Roberts to the scene of the accident. But the guide coldly ignores the question. To solve the problem the Swiss address themselves to the tourist who was informed of the tragedy, in the hope that he will hand one of his guides over to Roberts. The tourist agrees to the suggestion, but not one of the guides is accommodating. Not one of them moves. One of the mountaineers agrees to go ahead of the rest of the caravan, if necessary, and inform Courmayeur.

At 7.45 the Swiss climbers, reckoning that they can do no good —to act alone with Roberts would be imprudent because of the continuing bad weather—then record their stay in the hut-book[15] and leave the refuge for Montenvers, bearing a message from Roberts.[16] Thus, towards midday, the alarm is raised at Montenvers. Two rescue parties are formed and leave at once; one of them of guides under the orders of Alfred Simond, a famous Chamonix guide, and the other of British climbers, Spencer and Stutfield,[17] accompanied by the guides Hans Almer, Christian Jossi and Perruquet.

Meanwhile, at the Col du Géant, the timid Dutch tourists and their faint-hearted guides prepare to leave. At nine o'clock the snow ceases. The weather clears up. The caravan gets under weigh. Roberts, now alone, draws up an account of the accident in the hut-book,[18] which he decorates with a black frame, then stretches himself out on a palliasse to sleep. He is awakened towards four by the advance-guard of the rescue-party (two men) despatched from Courmayeur. He leaves with them immediately to try to reach the body of his guide; but during the ascent he changes his mind and makes off for Montenvers. At Rognon he meets the two Montenvers parties, sends the two Italians back, and joins the French caravan, which now turns back, their services no longer necessary since the arrival of the rescuers from Courmayeur.

*   *   *

The same evening, Sunday the 25th, the rescue-party of guides and porters from Courmayeur, numbering twelve men under the orders of the guide Joseph Gadin,[19] arrived at the Col du Géant. The men slept at the refuge and on Monday the 26th made for the foot of the slope down which Emile Rey had fallen; there they discovered the body half-buried under the snow. Death had been instantaneous, as witnessed by two fractures, one of the skull and the other of the vertebral column. The mountaineers took the remains down to the valley the same day and left them at Rey's chalet in the hamlet of La Saxe. The eminent Italian climber, the chevalier Giovanni Bobba, who was there, writes: "Emile Rey had no injuries to his face. One might say that he slept, deaf to the shrill lamentations of his wife and cherished sons."[20]

The funeral took place on Tuesday the 27th. There was no work that day in Courmayeur. Leaving la Saxe, the long procession made its slow way to the parish church of Courmayeur. The great guide's axe lay on the coffin with two large wreaths on either side, one from the Club Alpino Italiano, the other from the

English climber, C. D. Cunningham,[21] a distinguished member of the Alpine Club, employer and friend of Emile Rey. Giovanni Bobba spoke in the name of the Club Alpino Italiano, and M. Philippe Fouque for the Club Alpin Français. And when the Abbé Clapasson, curé of Courmayeur, recalled the noble figure of the guide, those present were profoundly moved.

Then, just as the procession was about to enter the cemetery, a party of four climbers, exhaustion showing in their sunburnt faces, their axes in their hands and the rope over their shoulders, came out of a lane and joined the cortège. They were Mr. Carson Roberts and Mr. Schintz who, with their guides, Aloys Pollinger *père* and *fils*,[22] had come direct from Montenvers.[23]

And in the presence of that magnificent and mighty chain of very high mountains, those which had already carried off two great hearts, Maquignaz and Castagneri, in the charm of a miraculous morning and the dazzling radiance of the snow, the remains of Emile Rey were consigned to the earth.[24]

* * *

From the preceding story the three following points emerge:

1. *The Causes of the Accident.*—Roberts has made it clear that the death of Rey was not due to a false step. In his view—and it is equally the view of Dr. Paul Güssfeldt, one of Rey's principal employers during eight seasons—that his fall was the result of a sudden seizure, an organic crisis or congestion, a giddiness which completely paralysed his powers of control. We might recapitulate, in fact, that sequence of strange symptoms which occurred during the two days which Rey and Roberts spent together in the mountains.

(*a*) On the 23rd August, at the summit of the Petit Dru, Emile Rey abandoned the idea of going on to the Grand Dru and of searching for a new route farther to the north[26] (although he would have been the first to accomplish the traverse in both directions) alleging that he did not feel in a good enough condition to make so great an effort.

(*b*) On the evening of the 23rd the party, which for the next day had designs on the Aiguille Verte by the arête du Moine, abandoned the ascent to the Couvercle and bivouacked instead near the foot of the track, at about the height of the Egralets. Emile Rey said he felt tired and that he had no appetite.

(*c*) Instead of waking, as he should, towards eleven or midnight and leaving for the Verte, Emile Rey slept deeply until about four. It was very late to make the proposed ascent.

(*d*) The climbers then left for the Géant. Roberts notes: "In spite of the fact that he had eaten very little since we left the hotel and had been troubled by continuous thirst, he was in excellent spirits."

(*e*) Rey, once more, had not fallen, he had not made a false step; he had let himself drop, giving voice at the same moment to a sad "Oh!" Had he been conscious, had he been in full possession of his powers, he would have easily been able to lay hold of the stones where he had abandoned his hat and axe, even as his companion had begged him to do. Roberts had the impression that he had made no attempt to stop himself, that he had not handled his axe forcefully when he tottered on the slab and fell into the snow. What, in fact, did he do? He lost his axe almost at once, which was quite extraordinary for a man of his calibre. Is it not reasonable, therefore, to suppose that he was actually unconscious at the moment when he collapsed in the chimney, the only place in the least dangerous in the whole ascent of the promontory between the base of the Aiguille and the glacier?

2. *The Matter of the Rope.*—Roberts has been reproached for neglecting to rope up. But we have seen above why, by common accord, Emile Rey and his traveller had not done so. However, it is possible to argue that, if at the moment of the fall Rey and Roberts had been roped, the accident would not have occurred. Roberts would easily have been able to hold the man who had lost his feet. Theoretically that might be so. "But," the Englishman replies with good sense, "had we been roped I would have been below and in snow steps." And then . . .

3. *The Abandoning of the Body.*—Without in any way wishing to dramatise this aspect of the accident, one cannot help being surprised at the attitude of the parties at the hut on the evening of the 24th.

Roberts made two solitary attempts to reach the body of his guide. The storm and the precipices prevented him from doing so. Then on arriving at the hut at seven in the evening, Roberts declares: "I had a mad notion that Rey might still be alive and I was aching to reach him." The first party to which he addressed himself, the two young Swiss climbers, took refuge behind a philosophical argument and refused to accompany him. The second party, that of the twelve Dutch tourists and Chamonix guides, was exhausted, and Roberts was requested not to speak of the accident in front of the tourists for fear they might collapse with fright. So much for the 24th.

On the 25th one of the Savoyard porters went down at dawn, it is said, to carry the news of the accident to Courmayeur. Very good. But one might well ask if this messenger really left.[26] According to the report which appeared in the *Rivista Mensile*, the news did not reach Courmayeur until midday.[27] One might think that the morning of Sunday the 25th would be the long-awaited moment for all the guides shut up in the hut to rush up there to the glacier to retrieve the poor broken body. Nothing of the kind! Let us emphasise, moreover, the fact that Roberts and the two Swiss made two futile approaches to the Chamonix guides. At 7.45 the Swiss returned to Montenvers. At nine the weather cleared. The party of twelve hastily got ready—yes! but in order to descend to more hospitable regions. And one feels a shock of surprise that neither the chief guide of the Chamoniards nor the tourist approached the night before, nor any one of the five other guides—not a single person, in fact—thought for a second of the unfortunate Rey. Or rather, what is sadder but more true, each in his innermost heart did think of him, but none spoke of it and none had the courage to act.

It is clear that, alone, Roberts could do nothing. When the first two men of the rescue-party arrived at the hut, he left with them at once "across the high snowfield to where Emile was lying under his shroud of snow." But suddenly he turned around in his tracks and went down to Montenvers! At Montenvers, on the 26th, it was his English climbing friend Schintz who informed him that Rey's funeral was to take place on the 27th, and Roberts left again in a hurry for Courmayeur. He left Montenvers shortly after midnight with Schintz and the Pollingers,[28] recrossed the Col du Géant,[29] and arrived too late to attend the burial service, but just in time to see the coffin vanish into the grave. So much confusion confounds us! It is all incomprehensible.

*   *   *

Several days after the interment, the famous German climber, Dr. Paul Güssfeldt, whom Emile Rey had often led to victory (notably on the Aiguille Blanche de Péteret from the Brenva side, Mont Blanc by the arête de Péteret, the traverse of Monte Scerscen from the Italian side and by the Tschieren Glacier, the Grandes Jorasses in January, the Grand Paradis in a winter storm, and many others) placed a wreath on the tomb of his indomitable guide, broken at last. This was the inscription:

A LA MEMOIRE D'EMILE REY
MON VAILLANT ET INCOMPARABLE GUIDE
A JAMAIS REGRETTE
EN SIGNE D'AMOUR ET DE DOULEUR[32]

And on the stone above his grave these moving and restrained words may be read:

IN MEMORIA
DI
EMILIO REY
GUIDA ILALIANA VALENTISSIMA
AMATO DAI SUOI ALPINISTI
IN LUNGA SERIE D'IMPRESE
MAESTRO LORO
DI ARDIMENTI DI PRUDENZA
FATALMENTE CADUTO
AL DENTE DEL GIGANTE
IL 24 AGOSTO 1895[33]

For the scene of Rey's death, see Plate 28.

¹ Emile Rey loved his craft and he constructed, with masterly skill, the huts on the Col du Géant, the Grandes Jorasses, the Aiguilles Grises and the Gran Paradiso.

² On the 5th August, with the guide Jean-Baptiste Bich of Valtournanche, Carrel's comrade and companion in the conquest of the Matterhorn.

³ One might quote here some of his famous remarks. To one of his travellers, Maurice de Déchy, he said: "You shall see Emile Rey at work when a great summit demands it." And Dr. Paul Güssfeldt records that one day, on a formidable slope of ice which required a desperate effort, Emile Rey turned round at the end of the rope and spoke these challenging words: "I have never beaten a retreat in my life, and I will not do so to-day." And straightening his back he began again to cut at the ice after the manner of a wood-cutter chopping a tree-trunk to pieces.

⁴ On the 31st July, with the English climber H. Seymour King and the Swiss guides Ambros Supersaxo and Aloys Anthamatten.

⁵ This is an occasion to recall that Emile Rey had made the second ascent of the Grand Dru and the Petit Dru, and was the first to traverse from one to the other in both directions. At the Grand Dru he accomplished the ascent without the aid of either the ladder or the fixed ropes left in the walls by their conquerors. In four days he ascended the Grand Dru three times—the third, fourth and fifth ascents of the mountain. One of them he did directly from Montenvers, without a bivouac, returning there in the afternoon.

[6] Mr. A. Carson Roberts was a very experienced climber. In 1893, at the Grépon with Joseph Simond as guide and Joseph-Aristide Simond as porter, he led the party after agreement with his guide. He seems to have been the first tourist, after Mummery, to climb the famous fissure at the head of the rope.

[7] Cf. *Alpine Journal*, Vol. XLVIII, 1936.

[8] In this connection see note 14 to Chapter 14. Already in 1881, on the famous Mitteleggi arête of the Eiger, Rey had stupefied his companions by his audacity. Without the rope he had succeeded in crossing alone the dizzy and terribly difficult overhang against which all previous attempts had been shattered. Thus he reached a point so far untouched.

[9] In this connection see Note 1 to Chapter 17. The Maquignaz took four days to prepare the conquest of the Aiguille du Géant, laying out their itinerary in the wall, blazing the trail with pitons and fixed ropes.

[10] On the 14th and 16th August, 1893, with Dr. P. Güssfeldt, the guide Christain Klucker and the porter César Ollier. "At one in the morning," writes Güssfeldt, "Emile Rey struck up Béranger's *Lisette* in a clear voice, and it has become our warsong since the January ascent of the Jorasses. This sudden appearance of the female element in our icy bivouac warmed us all despite the persistent frost." (Cf. Paul Güssfeldt, *Le Mont-Blanc*.)

[11] See page 135.

[12] Cf. *Alpine Journal*, Vol. XVII, 1894–95.

[13] The length of the fall was estimated at about 300 metres (or nearly 1,000 feet).

[14] In his first version (Cf. *Alpine Journal*, Vol. XVII, 1894–95) Mr. A. C. Roberts says that they were Swiss; in his second (Cf. *Alpine Journal*, Vol. XLVIII, 1936) that they were French. They were definitely French-speaking Swiss.

[15] A translation of this entry is as follows:

"*25th August*, 1895; *John Jaccottet, S. A. C. Geneva and Diablerets; Aug. Baumann, S. A. C. Geneva.*

"*Coming from Montenvers on the 24th in order to spend the night at the Géant hut, at seven in the evening we encountered Mr. Roberts, who had made the ascent of the Dent du Géant with Emile Rey. On arriving he declared that 'Emile Rey has been killed.' This news caused us the greatest surprise and the greatest sorrow; but in view of the abundant snow that was falling furiously, and above all because of the night, we could not follow Mr. Roberts, who said that the body lay at the foot of the great couloir, two and a half hours from the hut on the Chamonix side. We relinquished the responsibility of searching for it to the guide Tournet (?), who will do everything necessary at Courmayeur as soon as the caravan, composed of six ladies and gentlemen and seven guides and porters, are safely there. Because of the snow we are leaving for Montenvers and will also do what we can.*"

(Extract from the *Livre des Voyageurs* of the old Géant hut, now in the archives of the Turin section of the Italian Alpine Club, and kindly communicated by its President, Sig. Felice Arrigo.)

[16] It is interesting to read the story of what happened at the refuge, as told by one of these two young men, Aug. Baumann, in the *Echo des Alpes* (1896, No. 1). He throws light on many of the points in Mr. Roberts's story.

I summarise the preamble: On the 24th August, 1895, about four in the evening, two young Genevese climbers, J. Jaccottet and Aug. Baumann, coming from Montenvers, ascended the last snow-slope to the Col du Géant. Examining the Aiguille they perceived, clinging to the slabs, a party of two men. These were Mr. Roberts and Emile Rey, as they later learned. The two Genevese raised a shout, to which Emile Rey gave a prolonged and joyful response. They reached the refuge, made some tea there, and when a violent storm broke out they were seized with anxiety at the thought of the party on the Géant:

"Spontaneously," writes Baumann, "our thoughts turned to the party enduring the storm, for it had been snowing for half an hour. The silence of death had followed the only living being of the preceding hour—a chough perched on a stone—and everything in the hut seemed to us fantastic. Outside the snow, driven by violent squalls, raged furiously and produced a very distinctive and lugubrious rustling on the roof.

Then the night, which fell very quickly, gave to the whole landscape the most melancholy and least encouraging appearance.

"It was seven o'clock and nobody had arrived! The caravan on the glacier ought to have been near us a long time before and the party on the Dent de Géant ought not to be so late. Oh! how long the minutes were at such a dreadful time, as we suffered the agony of waiting!

"The snow fell thickly all the time, compact, and nobody came. . . . Suddenly the door opened and a man appeared. . . . Mr. Roberts (climbing companion of Rey, the guide) . . . covered with snow, his hair disordered, his eyes haggard, his jacket torn, pronouncing in the saddest possible voice the words: 'Oh! Emile Rey has been killed!'

"Knowing Rey by reputation, we were terrified and stupefied, and at once the funereal portent of the chough's appearance came back to our minds.

"Recovering from our emotions, we offered Mr. Roberts a cup of tea and then asked him to tell us about the accident."

Roberts quickly told the young men his story, and Baumann goes on:

"Mr. Roberts, who seemed to us to have a quite special love for the guide Rey, with whom he had just succeeded in climbing Mont Blanc and the Petit Dru, grieved in a corner of the hut. Outside the squalls redoubled their rage; from time to time we went out and called as loudly as possible, so that we might be of some use to the travellers whom we impatiently awaited. Many times we came in again without hope. The snow had already reached several centimetres in depth and the night advanced apace. It was certainly impossible that they had gone down again by the séracs, for the guides would never have assumed such a responsibility. The minutes of waiting seemed to become centuries.

"An extraordinary fever took possession of us! Our temples burned, the blood boiled in our veins and, despite our wishes, we could not be of the slightest use to the tourists who, so joyful in the morning, were now pushing their way through the soft snow, under the falling snow and hail. We went out for a last time; the weather, more frightful than ever, became sinister. We went up towards the Col and raised a long cry.

"But, oh! A miracle! A voice in the distance answered and soon the longed-for tourists appeared out of the thick and penetrating mists like veritable phantoms. What a difference between the gay and carefree company of the morning and these beings, certainly living but almost mentally and physically dead! Not a word; not a look! On all their faces was nothing to be seen but grief, sorrow and great frozen tears that hung down their cheeks.

"Happily everyone was there. . . . We slipped across to the guides to tell them of Emile Rey's accident and to ask them what they reckoned to do. At once there was no question of going to search by night, for the snow was still falling and it was preferable to wait until the morning. Moreover, Mr. Roberts, who spoke little French, had given us to understand that the accident had occurred on the Italian side. In that case it was useless to attempt a rescue, for the mountain is not approachable at night without running very great risks.

"We then requested the chief guide (whose name we suppress) to be good enough to search at an early hour in the morning and we put ourselves entirely at his disposal. As the travellers were exceedingly tired, they could not leave before nine or ten in the morning, and that interval should permit us to proceed with the search for Rey in company with Mr. Roberts and several guides.

"After several fruitless efforts we went to lie down and left the continuance of the discussion until the morning. As soon as we rose (Sunday the 25th) we asked the chief guide once more to spare us one of his guides, for we could not go à deux on the glacier to search for the guide Rey, who perhaps was not dead, despite Mr. Roberts's conviction. Further, during the night ten centimetres of fresh snow had fallen; it continued to whirl in great compact flakes and we would have to hurry or everything would be covered up.

"Then, on receiving a very evasive answer from the chief guide, we begged the travellers to release one of their guides, whom Mr. Roberts would engage. We received this favour and thought that the deal was arranged, but none of them would come. They preferred to remain at the hut, to descend to Mont-Fréty or Courmayeur and thus leave this arduous task to the Italian guides, whom one of the porters would be released to forewarn.

"On the guides' refusal and in view of the impossibility of undertaking this search alone in such bad weather, with our consciences at rest, for we had done our duty, we entered what had just happened in the hut register and prepared to descend. At the moment of leaving, Mr. Roberts gave us a letter which he addressed to his parents, who were on holiday at Montenvers. He would remain at the hut to await the guides from Courmayeur and direct them in their search. We left the hut at 7.45 in the morning, and slowly, solemnly, ascended the few metres which separated us from the Col, and then, on a taut rope, we descended rapidly to Chamonix.

"Arriving at Montenvers, we delivered the letter which had been confided to us and went down to Chamonix, where we arrived at one o'clock, and finally announced to the chief guide the catastrophe which had occurred at the Aiguille du Géant."

This story provoked violent reactions in alpine circles. Le Revue Alpine (Lyons), especially, set on foot an enquiry into the strange attitude of the Chamonix guides at the Géant refuge. But this enquiry had only imperfect and contradictory results and was never published. The affair was buried; it was clearly too simple and nobody cared!

On the other hand, in its issue of November 1895, the same journal published the following:

"On the 24th August the death of the guide Emile Rey brought surprise and consternation to the alpine world. Shortly afterwards, a letter from Mr. Matthews, published in The Times, gave us the official version of the facts, according to the explanation of Mr. Roberts, the sole eyewitness of the accident. Various Italian papers have on their part recounted the event as having occurred in their region. That the great guide was killed *at the foot* of the Dent du Géant, which he had ascended many times, seems incomprehensible. So his death remains, as the former President of the Alpine Club has said, an 'inexplicable disaster.' Consequently, what is the good of seeking afresh the causes of the accident and recounting here its vicissitudes? As we have had the honour of making numerous expeditions with this master of alpine science, we wish only to try and give a portrait of he whom the Italians, in their picturesque language, have called 'the prince of guides. . . .' (Here follow some thoughts on the career of Emile Rey and a list of his principal ascents.)

". . . Emile Rey died of a strictly professional accident. The ascent was finished; he had just untied the rope which had linked him to his traveller and, feeling himself free of all responsibility, he lightly leapt the last obstacle, slipped on some rolling stones, lost his footing without uttering a cry, and in three bounds fell to the glacier. We are of the firm conviction that the rope would have saved him. . . ." (Here follow some thoughts on the use of the rope and the hope that Rey died without suffering.)

(Signed) Mary Paillon; Katherine Richardson.

[17] Personal communication from Mr. Sydney Spencer.

[18] The text is as follows:

"IN MEMORIAM. EMILE REY, R.I.P. 24 *Aug.* 1895. *A. C. Roberts—alone—my poor guide Emile Rey having fallen from the top of the steep couloir on the North West of the Dent du Géant right at* 4.30 *p.m. After trying in vain to reach his body on the snow below, I made my way here in the snow and dense cloud. Here I found two gentlemen who have written above (no guides) they were of the opinion that it would be worse than useless to attempt to find Emile on such a night. Half an hour later* (7.30 *p.m.*) *a party of* 12 (*six guides*) *arrived.*

"*They had started from the Montenvers at* 5.00 *a.m. and appeared very glad indeed to reach the shelter, the guides said nothing could be done.*

"*When the accident occurred, we were unroped having descended from the Aiguille itself. Emile was in front. I was standing at the top of a small chimney waiting for him to get through (about* 200 *feet above the little snow col which one traverses on the ascent). Emile dropped himself, the foot on a small stone plateau sloping slightly and dusted with very small pebbles, his foot slipped away and he fell the whole length of the long couloir in three bounds.*

"*We two had left the Montenvers on the* 22d *and had climbed the little Dru on the* 23d. *The good time made on that ascent was mainly due to the inimitable guiding of one of the best Guides who ever climbed. We started from a gite on the Couvercle slopes at* 4.40 *on the* 24.

"*25 Aug. The snow continues. It is now* 10 *a.m. and I am alone, awaiting a party of guides and porters from Courmayeur.*"

(Extract from the *Livre des Voyageurs* of the old Géant refuge, now in the archives of the Turin section of the C.A.I., and obligingly communicated by its President, Sig. Felice Arrigo.)

[19] The favourite guide of the Abbé Achille Ratti (Pope Pius XI)—see the end of Note 11 to Chapter 12; also Note 6(*b*) to Chapter 17.

In the month of March 1938, during a brief stay at Courmayeur (Cf. "A Winter's Day at Courmayeur," *Alpine Journal*, Vol. XL, 1938), I was able to talk about the accident to Emile Rey, with his sons Henri and Adolphe and some old guides of his generation, one of whom was another Emile Rey, with Cyprien Rey the sole survivors of the rescue party. The rescue party comprised the following mountaineers: Joseph Gadin, Laurent Bertholier, César Ollier, Felix Ollier, Louis Musillon, Cyprien Rey, Emile Rey (son of Joseph-Marie), Alexis Brocherel, Joseph Brocherel, Ferdinand Melica and Eléazard Mochet.

[20] Henri, Jules and Adolphe. Henri and Adolphe, continuing their father's tradition, have become illustrious guides. Henri, since 1936, has been chief guide in Courmayeur; his brother Jules, the Abbé Rey, was canon of Aosta and died in July 1939. (See also *Rivista Mensile del C.A.I.*, No. 8. 1895.)

[21] The author, in collaboration with Capt. Abney, of *The Pioneers of the Alps*, Sampson Low, London, 1888.

[22] The guide Aloys Pollinger *fils*, who died in September 1945, wrote to me on the 27th December in response to my question whether he remembered the episode:

"*On the day of Emile Rey's accident I was with father and Mr. Schintz at the Aiguille de Talèfre. The same evening a violent storm broke out. On the following day two parties arrived at Montenvers from the Col du Géant. I cannot remember if Alfred Simond was among them. Some guides and porters surrounded Mr. A. C. Roberts in front of the Hôtel du Montenvers. I drew near and they told me that Emile Rey had fallen from the Géant.*

"*On the following day Mr. Schintz, Mr. Roberts, father and myself, went to Courmayeur for the funeral. We arrived just as the procession left the church. Mr. Schintz and Mr. Roberts afterwards left again for Mont-Frety, and father and myself a little later.*

"*On the next day we went up again to the Col du Géant and from the Col we went to the place where Rey died.*"

This summary differs in several respects from Mr. Roberts's story. However, as the funeral of Emile Rey took place on Tuesday the 27th, it was not the second day after the accident (Monday 26th) that the Schintz–Roberts–Pollinger party went to Courmayeur, but a full two days afterwards.

[23] They had left in the night, near midnight, and had crossed the Col du Géant.

[24] On Sunday, 13th March, 1938, being at Courmayeur, Henri Rey introduced me to one of the two survivors of the rescue party which, on the 26th August, 1895, had recovered Rey's body. This old guide (it is a curious fact that he too was named Emile Rey) was the first to touch the body of the celebrated mountaineer. "He must have died at once," he said to me, "his jacket was drawn up over his head, his right leg was broken and bent under his back, and furthermore, the ends of his ten fingers were torn away as if he had tried to grip wherever he could." This detail is interesting. It corroborates Mr. Roberts's impression, and also Dr. Güssfeldt's, that Rey was the victim of an attack of vertigo; coming to himself he would then have tried desperately to check his fall. But it was too late.

[25] The route which Mr. Roberts had contemplated in 1895 was accomplished for the first time by the eminent French climber Emile Fontain, with the guides Joseph and Jean Ravanel, on the 23rd August, 1901.

[26] According to Baumann's story he had not done so at 7.45! However, he must have set out a little after the departure of the Swiss climbers, "for," Henri Rey told me in 1938, "about 10.0 or 10.30, just before Mass at Courmayeur, a porter arrived from the Col du Géant and informed me that my father had been killed the day before, while descending the Aiguille du Géant, and that I must send a rescue party quickly. It was thus that we learnt the news."

[27] According to my personal enquiries at Courmayeur, the messenger left about eight o'clock and arrived at Courmayeur at ten.

[28] In the *Führerbuch* of the guide Aloys Pollinger *père*, which is in the library of the Alpine Club, this evidence from Mr. Schintz may be read concerning the rapid journey to Courmayeur by the Col du Géant. It could not be more precise:

"*For the 10th year in succession, Alois Pollinger has climbed with me. During the month of August we accomplished the following:*

Les Périades traverse;
Les Charmoz;
Chardonnet;
Tour Ronde;
Taléfre;
Grépon, traverse N.-E.-S.;
Mont Mallet;
Les Droites;
Col du Géant and return."

These last six words apply to the 27th and 28th August, 1895; that is to say, Montenvers—Col du Géant—Courmayeur—Rey's funeral—Col du Géant—ascent to the place where Rey was found—return to Montenvers.

[29] Mr. C. E. Matthews, author of *The Annals of Mont Blanc*, ascended with the Schintz–Roberts–Pollinger party as far as the point below the Col du Géant with the object of inspecting the site of the accident. Mr. Matthews published a letter about the tragedy in *The Times*.

[30] Mr. Roberts died on the 12th November, 1944.

[31] In December 1895 the Turin section of the C.A.I. opened a subscription for the erection of a monument to Emile Rey at Courmayeur. It was unveiled on the 29th August, 1896. It is the work of the sculptor Biscarra. It is a marble pyramid recalling the shape of the Aiguille du Géant. It is decorated with the attributes of a guide: the rope and the ice-axe. An inscription recalls the name and virtues of the brave mountaineer.

[32] (*Trans.*) "To the memory of Emile Rey, a brave man and an incomparable guide, for ever lamented, as a sign of affection and sorrow."

[33] (*Trans.*) "To the memory of Emile Rey, Italian guide of the greatest skill, loved by his travellers during a long series of climbs, their master in daring and in prudence, who fell fatally at the Dent du Géant on the 24th August, 1895."

JEAN-ANTOINE
CARREL
(*see Chap. 18.*)

CHAPTER TWENTY

THE ANNIHILATION OF AN
ENGLISH FAMILY

The death of John Hopkinson and his three children, John, Alice and Lina
(Petite Dent de Veisivi, August 1898)

T HE delights of the mountains have attracted the romantic
painters. As background to charming and patriarchal pictures rises a décor of glaciers and peaks. But into this para-
dise of alpine divinities man has rapidly penetrated and put the
genii and the nymphs to flight. And so, from the contact of the
human spirit and the eternal serenity of high places, a new poetry
is born, and a new kind of death at the same time. Very soon all
these mountains, whose snows are so lightly suspended in space,
were to have their tragedies.

The skyline into which the Dents de Veisivi—which are to be
the scene of the cruellest and the saddest of all mountain tragedies
—thrust their angular outlines is not one of any great fame. In all
directions they are overlooked by the great four-thousand-metre
peaks, but they themselves are lost in the movements of secondary
planes. Nevertheless, their lines, as in some old master, collaborate
obscurely with the general harmony; they point to the heavens;
they catch the eye, and, prolonged by the outstretched arêtes
behind, they find their consummation in illustrious summits,
glittering above the fugitive clouds.

The Val d'Hérens begins at the foot of the Dents de Veisivi,
which plunge into the valley like the stem of a ship into the sea,
hollowing out the Ferpècle valley to the east and the Val d'Arolla
to the west. Above the glaciers the Dent Blanche and the Dent

d'Hérens raise their burnished snows and their beautiful rock-girt profiles, while between them can be seen the sombre spearhead of the Matterhorn. Towards Arolla the forests of arollas unroll to the very moraines of the glaciers. The fury of the winds has tortured the last trees, and they display their wasted limbs against the icy brilliance of the snows. When the wind passes over its forests the valley of Arolla sings like a viol; aromatic exhalations hover among the trees, mingling with the luminous foam of the cascades and the music of the cow-bells.

It was at the beginning of August, 1898, that the Hopkinson family arrived at Arolla.[1] Ever since the far-off day when Mlle. d'Angeville, known as the "fiancée du Mont Blanc," began the fashion of climbing among the ladies, they too have made their conquests among the summits. And the two Misses Hopkinson, Lina Evelyn, aged nineteen, and Alice, twenty-three, quite naturally accompany their father, Mr. John Hopkinson,[2] a distinguished climber and member of the Alpine Club, and their young brother John, only eighteen years old but an experienced climber. They all adore the mountains, both for their beauty and for the joys of the climb. They have spent a number of summers together in the Alps and more than one peak has seen their radiant faces. The mountains are for them a family affair, and this affectionately united family, which has found its natural climate in the heights, prolongs and maintains its passion under English skies by its memories and hopes.

This summer its hopes have been materialised in a fine harvest of climbs. The Bertol hut and the surrounding massif, the Aiguilles Rouges d'Arolla, le Pigne and Mont Collon, have all seen this proud and happy family rise to their summits. And their youthful laughter and gay chatter, still tinged with just-discarded adolescence, has been heard in that wondrously limpid air. The local guides who have met the Hopkinsons on their climbs have admired the competence and sureness of Jack,[3] the party's leader. As for Alice, the elder daughter, her assurance is no less astonishing, and her father's words—"as good as any man"—class her at once. But alas! time flies so swiftly. Already the enchanting days of their holiday pile up like dead leaves, and into the visions of forthcoming climbs—the Aiguille de la Tsa and the Petite Dent de Veisivi—strange pictures furtively slip: a ship, the water, an immense stretch of green and black water, the short and choppy waves of the Channel, the Dover jetty, the lighthouses, the return. . . .

The Aiguille de la Tsa, by the western face, directly above Arolla, was accomplished nine years earlier (26th July, 1889) by a great English climber, a woman, Miss Katherine Richardson. Supported by two celebrated guides, Emile Rey and Jean-Baptiste Bich,[4] with an excellent local guide as reinforcement— Antoine Maitre, Miss Richardson succeeded in conquering this pyramid-shaped pinnacle by this wall. Climbed several times subsequently, this fine feat has just been brilliantly accomplished by the Hopkinsons, led by Jack. And some days later, after exquisite saunters among the arollas and beside the tiny, dreaming pools, set in flowering meadows, the family is ready to leave again for the summits.

* * *

It is Friday, August the 26th, at the Hôtel du Mont-Collon at Arolla, after dinner. It is a perfect evening. The guests are out for a stroll, their eyes raised towards the high places where the day dies and the moonlit night is born. A soft peace passes over the valley. Surrounded by their friends, the Hopkinson family is involved in a discussion.

"Aren't you going to accompany your husband, Mrs. Hopkinson?"

"Mother in our party!" Alice maliciously replies. "Dear Mother! What a complication you would be!"

Mrs. Hopkinson is content gently to smile agreement.

"Me? No. I love the mountains, but I do not climb them any more. To-morrow I shall be satisfied to play tennis with my younger son."

The conversation becomes general.

"Yes, I think the weather will be magnificent."

"Is it true that you're taking a guide?"[5]

"A guide?"

"Why take a guide?" asks Jack.

"No," says Lina, "we shall not."

"It's an easy ascent."

"A family excursion!"

"Then take me," suggests the youngest Hopkinson boy, who has been relegated to a game of tennis.

"Veisivi will probably be our last climb."

"Really?"

"Yes, we must think about our return."

"So you're going to make a sort of family visit to take leave of the mountains?"

"Exactly, a last courtesy visit to our old friends."

"So we'll go peacefully by the normal route, Col de Zarmine and the arête."

"And when we get to the top we can slip our visiting-cards between two stones."

Everyone laughs. The air freshens. A puff of wind blows from the livid glaciers. The chairs empty.

*   *   *

The Hopkinsons' projected climb, the Petite Dent de Veisivi, is neither a long expedition nor a very high peak. It is only 10,465 feet high. It is the classic course in this area, combining the exhilarating pleasures of a rock climb with the charms of a delightful walk. In five or six hours the party can reach the summit. Thus it is not until 7.30 in the morning of Saturday, 27th August, that the English family leaves the village. Certainly, it is a late hour to start. But as there are no glaciers to cross, and therefore no sun-softened snowbridges or séracs to fear, to leave at a comfortable hour is a luxury in which they can safely indulge.

By way of the Lex chalets, the Mayens de Satarma and the Alpe de Zarmine—all the loveliness of the mid-mountain region, of woods and meadows—the family party arrives at the edge of a vast névé which stretches its fresh beauty like a field of narcissi to the foot of the Petite Dent de Veisivi. There the Hopkinsons halt and examine their mountain. The morning is perfectly serene, blended of silver and palest blue, softening the hard shadows of the valley. Le Pigne and the rising tiers of the glaciers are as if carved in ivory. The sound of avalanches a long way off and of the torrents produce in the silence a murmur like two or three low notes of an anthem.

From where the climbers stand the rising arête of the Petite Dent is seen in profile; from the Col de Zarmine to the summit it rises in a broad and sustained movement, in a succession of rocky waves, broken by a heavy swell. In proportion as it rises and falls, only to rise again, this rampart, between the arête and the almost

250

horizontal line of the névé, widens out, forming a rock face some 1,000 to 1,300 feet high, which from the summit falls sheer into a stony combe covered with patches of snow. The sunlight strikes it in the face. The amber-coloured granite is impregnated with warmth and light.

Nothing moves. From this perpendicular, motionless landscape a very real beauty emerges. The Hopkinsons succumb to its charms; they abandon the Col de Zarmine and the arête, the normal way, in order to attack the southern wall itself.[6] Jack and his father examine its folds; they dissect the wall and settle on an approximate direction. Between those fissures, those steps and those cliffs a way might be found. A notch to the left of the summit, slightly to the south-west, might be used as a landmark.

Jack buckles up his haversack while his father uncoils the rope. As they are not used to climbing in two parties, and still less un-roped—contrary to the method which has brilliant defenders[7]—the head of the family measures the intervals and ties the knots. They are so close to the wall already that it will be better to rope up here at their ease. Soon they are ready: Jack leading, then Lina (the younger daughter), followed by Mr. Hopkinson, ready to support his son or to guard against the mistakes of either of the first two. At the rear comes Alice. They deploy over the névé on a well-stretched rope.

The sky clings to the snow, shading the shining crystals with a gentle bluish light. And over the Hopkinson family, now at grips with the rock, falls the shadow of a bulging slab. The sound of friction against the rock can be heard, and the rasp of heavy steel-shod boots. A breath of wind passes like a wing, drawing with it, like the bursting of a bubble inflated with sound, the echo of the bells of the Zarmine herd.

*   *   *

Dinner is being served in the large dining-room of the Hôtel du Mont-Collon at Arolla. The waitresses bustle around, their arms laden with trays. The late-comers reach their places. There is a clatter of crockery and glass, and a babble of conversation. But a table with six places laid remains unoccupied and it attracts attention.

"No, no. There's no need to be anxious. How do you know they haven't already returned?"

A moment later Mrs. Hopkinson enters with her younger son. The same looks which took in the empty table now fasten upon the lady. People look at these two as if seeing them for the first time. Mrs. Hopkinson passes through the room, greets those to the right, nods to those on the left, smiles, exchanges a few words with her friends, and sits down with her boy beside her. The four unoccupied chairs surround them. A neighbour says pleasantly:

"Climbers, madame, are like artists; they can never return in time for their meals! We just have to excuse them. Isn't that so?"

Mrs. Hopkinson smiles graciously, then scolds her inattentive child. But throughout the meal she remains face to face with the four empty chairs. Glances are still cast in her direction, glances which are already unconsciously inquisitive. A belated climber enters abruptly; against the light, in the door's recess, he is for a moment mistaken for Mr. Hopkinson. Minds relax. At one table a voice exclaims:

"Ah! Here they are!"

Mrs. Hopkinson, hearing it, sharply turns her head. But the diversion serves only to intensify the atmosphere and to create a general feeling of uneasiness. Then the room is quickly emptied. Mrs. Hopkinson leaves with some friends. An old and sentimental lady approaches the table with the four untouched places and in front of the empty chairs deposits a bowl of gentians which had been decorating her own table. "That," she says to the waitress, "is to wish them a warm welcome."

Then a band of young men and women set out to meet the missing climbers on the valley road. Meanwhile night draws slowly in.

This prolonged absence is disquieting. Mrs. Hopkinson and her friends encircle the manager. A sign is made to some guides who are idling nearby, and the group talks the matter over. The guides agree and go out; a moment afterwards, equipped, they move off. This is, without doubt, the best solution; in this way something can be discovered. Towards ten o'clock, the anxiety increasing, a second party sets out, comprising some guides and a few climbers staying at the hotel. Finally, at midnight, Mrs. Hopkinson, consumed with anguish, decides to take part in the search herself and she leaves the hotel with her friends. For an instant, framed in the jerky light of the lanterns, we can see the silhouette of the stricken woman vanishing into the darkness.

*   *   *

On Sunday, 28th August, in the grey light of dawn, one of the parties,[8] passing along the base of the wall which faces the Mayens de Satarma, ran suddenly upon the bodies. The candles had just been extinguished. There was no need to light them again; enough could be seen, alas! to be certain of calamity. Still roped (the line was not broken), the Hopkinson family lay there in the order of their climb: Jack above, then Lina, then the father and Alice. The father was still holding the rope in his clenched fist, as if he had tried to keep either Jack or Lina from falling, perhaps both of them together, one having dragged the other down. But his efforts having failed, he had been carried away in his turn and had dragged the elder daughter with him. They had fallen while climbing a point slightly to the south-west of the summit, and the guides estimated the depth of the fall as from 500 to 650 feet. A watch had stopped at eleven o'clock, and that was probably the hour of the tragedy. The bodies were already stiff and cruelly broken. On Jack lay an enormous stone.

The rising sun reddened the rocks. It was the beginning of a radiant morning.

All day and during the whole night two guides stood guard over the bodies.[9] Before authority to move the bodies could be given, they had to await the completion of the Evolène commune's inquiry. What a vigil it was, up there, in those rocky solitudes, close to the snow, at the foot of the mountain wall! What a vigil beside those two shattered young women, those touching girlish forms stilled for ever, and the boy beneath the stone, and the father close by! The taciturn guides smoked pipe after pipe. Vaguely they heard the angelus ring at Evolène. In the evening they lit a fire of dry rhododendron and juniper, little branches that blazed like bines. The night was warm, glittering with stars, streaked with faint trails of vapour. The two mountaineers, seated on stones close to the fire, mused as they gazed distractedly at the mountains enshrouded in shadow; and when the night wind fanned the flames they could see, in the fugitive gleams, the four Hopkinsons outstretched upon the rock, almost like sleepers beside their bivouac.

Then in the paling dawn the world slowly built itself up. The fire died out. In ripples the bluish smoke ascended towards the Col de Zarmine. The hard outlines of the mountains began to take shape, but the whitish surface of the glaciers still showed a neutral tint. Very far away, very high in the sky, a sudden roseate light caught fire in the depths of the utter silence; thus, in a mottling of gold on sculptural snows, Mont Blanc was lit by the rising sun. The light of day soon ran from peak to peak. The valleys brightened. But in this resurrection of all things the Hopkinsons slept on.

During the morning of Monday the 29th the secretary of the commune and the gendarme brought up the requisite documents.[10] Other mountaineers had preceded them. The bodies were carried to the alpage of Satarma where the coffins, hastily fashioned by the Evolène carpenter, awaited them. There the Rev. George R. Thornton, before the four biers decorated with leaves and mountain flowers, read the prayers and performed the service for the dead. Then a column of guides and porters carried the sad burden to les Haudères, where they were left in the schoolhouse.[11] On Friday, 2nd September, the unfortunate father and his three children were buried at Territet. On their common grave stands a stone on which you can read:

IN

LOVING MEMORY

OF

JOHN HOPKINSON, M.A., D.SC., F.R.S.[12]

BORN IN MANCHESTER JULY 27 1849

AND OF HIS THREE CHILDREN

ALICE AGED 23

LINA EVELYN AGED 19

JOHN GUSTAVE AGED 18

WHO WERE KILLED BY A FALL FROM

THE PETITE DENT DE VEISIVI

AUGUST 27 1898

LOVELY AND PLEASANT

WERE THEY

IN THEIR LIVES AND IN THEIR DEATH

THEY WERE NOT DIVIDED

For the scene of the Hopkinson tragedy, see Plate 29.

[1] The Hopkinsons were habitual visitors at Arolla. For eight years they had regularly spent their summers there.
[2] Born in Manchester, he lived in London. He was a brilliant science student at Trinity College, Cambridge, and a doctor of science at London University. He specialised in electrical engineering.

[3] Jack's eighteenth birthday had been celebrated on Thursday, the 25th August.

[4] Of Valtournanche. Friend of J.-A. Carrel and his companion on the occasion of his conquest of the Italian Matterhorn on the 17th July, 1865.

[5] According to the guide Pierre Georges of Evolène—who as porter took part in several of the Hopkinson expeditions and in the searches of the party which recovered the bodies—Mr. Hopkinson had engaged one of the best Evolène guides, Jean Maitre, for certain climbs. Then, as it happened, on Saturday the 27th, the day of the catastrophe, Mr. Hopkinson had freed his guide for the day. (Personal communication from Joseph Georges, known as the "Skier," of La Sage, near Evolène.)

However, in a letter to the *Alpine Journal* (Vol. XIX), Prof. J. A. Ewing positively declares that the Hopkinson family climbed without guides.

[6] The route of descent when the Dent is traversed. This route was followed for the first time by H. Seymour King and Howard Barrett, with the guides Ambros Supersaxo and L. Anthamatten, on the 29th August, 1885.

[7] See note 14 to Chapter 14; also Chapter 19 page 232.

[8] According to the proceedings of the Département de Justice et Police, this party comprised two English tourists, Mr. Travers and Mr. Walker, and four guides, among them Pierre Maître, Joseph Quinodoz and Martin Pralong, all from Evolène.

[9] Joseph Quinodoz and Martin Pralong.

[10] The proceedings of the Département de Justice of the Canton Valais, held at Sion on the 31st August, 1898, and signed by the examining magistrate Ribordy, and by P. Bourdin, record (*trans.*):

"1. *The Petite Dent de Veisivi forms the north end of the chain of Dents which separate the valley of Arolla from that of Ferpècle.*

2. *It forms a conical arête from east to west, showing to the south a more or less vertical wall 300 metres high (approx. 1,000 feet).*

3. *From this towards the east hangs a large couloir; to the west, a second couloir, scarcely visible, starts from the foot of the wall and ends three-quarters of the way to the summit.*

4. *At the foot of this latter couloir lay four bodies, tied together by a rope, in the following order:* (1) *a young man;* (2) *a young girl;* (3) *a man of mature years;* (4) *a young girl.*

5. *Beside them the guides Martin Pralong and Joseph Quinodoz kept watch.*

6. *The rope was intact.*

7. *The victims bore numerous traces of violent blows. The limbs were broken and the skulls shattered.*

8. *Near the bodies, and above them in the western couloir, traces of blood were found, fragments of human remains and the debris of articles belonging to the victims.*"

[11] Cf. *Alpine Journal*, Vol. XIX, 1898–99; *Gazette de Lausanne*, 29th, 30th and 31st August and 1st September 1898; *Alpina*, 1898.

[12] In an address to the Alpine Club, Mr. Charles Pilkington, its President in 1896, expressed himself in these terms:

"Dr. John Hopkinson, one of our finest rock climbers, with two daughters, and a son who promised soon to be an ornament to our Club, perished on the Petite Dent de Veisivi. You all know what little there is to know of this, the saddest calamity in the annals of climbing, and we all deeply regret the loss his family, this Club and the country has sustained by his premature removal from that world of science which he so much adorned." (*Alpine Journal*, Vol. XIX, 1899.)

CHAPTER TWENTY-ONE

THE COLLAPSE OF A BAS-RELIEF

The death of Owen Glynne Jones and of the guides Elias Furrer, Clemenz Zurbriggen and Jean Vuignier (Dent Blanche, August 1899)

TWICE in his literary career Maupassant ventured to write about the mountains,[1] but Daudet attempted to do so only once. Daudet was well documented, for he had corresponded with Edward Whymper and Sir Martin Conway, one-time President of the Alpine Club, and even later entertained these two celebrated climbers at his table; he speaks with elegant nonchalance of Kennedy's crampons,[2] the Alpine Club manilla rope, of Whymper's tent and Chamonix ice-axes, almost as if his entire life had been spent among these strange and dangerous objects. All this, of course, to equip and arm his Tartarin. And in order to give atmosphere to his ideas of mountaineering, to compose his pictures, to adjust their parts, and construct their aerial architecture, the gentle dreamer of *Etoiles* had journeyed to Chamonix and Grindelwald, had crossed one or two of the glaciers given up to the crowds, and had levelled his telescope at the summits. All this explains in part his astonishingly accurate but delicately poetic descriptions.[3] Few climbers returning from the Jungfrau or Mont Blanc have evoked with such charm and accuracy the climbs which Alphonse Daudet, without having actually done them, depicts with virtuosity.[4]

But Maupassant failed. Some twenty years earlier, Théophile Gautier had produced dazzling pictures of the Matterhorn. From the very first there was a subtle harmony between the summits and the author of *Emaux et Camées*. But when Maupassant faced the mountains he felt ill at ease; they were beyond his comprehension, they astonished him. The author of *Boule de Suif* looks at them, examines them, admires them, but cannot enter into their spirit. His mountain folk are conventional, their gestures puerile, their words false. It is more the psychological situation in the framework of high places which attracts him rather than the landscape itself. Thus, face to face with the four-thousand-metre peaks, Maupassant, otherwise the delicate painter of the hours, the seasons and the beautiful places, finds himself awkward. Anonymous definitions, stripped of all lyrical quality, attached (often falsely) to the name of a summit, and of which no decorative feature helps to evoke the hallucinating outline, convey his perplexity: the Matterhorn is "the mankiller," and the Dent Blanche, quite banally, "a monstrous coxcomb."[5]

*　　*　　*

The Dent Blanche (14,318 feet) is one of the boldest peaks in the Zermatt massif.[6] Its ice-encrusted ramparts, and the arête hewn from its rock and enhanced with snow, reach into the brightness of the heavens with one imperious sweep. Few mountains in the entire Alps—the Matterhorn excepted—have had the power to hold minds in thrall by their wild beauty, to impress themselves on the imagination and to exalt the spirit, as the Dent Blanche has done. This it achieves neither by the solemn serenity of Mont Blanc as seen from Chamonix, nor by the romantic poesy of the Jungfrau from Interlaken. The Dent Blanche imposes itself brutally and the beholder submits; it takes possession of his feelings. And following these reactions, there is nothing to do but cross its threshold of glaciers and leave for its summit. The Zinal and Ferpècle aspects, notably, with their prodigious ice-emblazoned walls, have a splendid violence. Like the Tiefenmatten precipices or the northern face of the Matterhorn, they exhale a kind of mystery, which intoxicates the beholder with its treacherous perfume.

Ever since he had first breathed this heady perfume, Mr. Owen Glynne Jones, a young and able British climber, had coveted the Dent Blanche from the Ferpècle side. A remarkable rock-climber, having specialised in the English and Scottish mountains, and one of the finest mountaineers among the younger members of the Alpine Club, Jones had become familiar with the Alps during the previous ten years.[7] At Chamonix, Zermatt and Grindelwald he had climbed and explored very nearly everything. He had climbed the Schreckhorn in January and the Dent Blanche in April,[8] and was thinking of higher peaks beyond the Alps, far away in the Caucasus. Big, muscular and resolute, his rapid pace and cool daring were well known among the guides. More than one of these quiet mountaineers, disconcerted by such toughness, had refused to accompany him.[9]

In the middle of August, 1899, Jones was at Arolla with his guide, Elias Furrer of Stalden (close to St. Niklaus). His friends, Mr. and Mrs. F. W. Hill, joined him, coming from the Binn valley. As yet the two British climbers had only vague plans, at least so far as Mr. Hill was concerned, and the rain confined them to their hotel during the first few days. While the thick mists brushed past the windows there were long talks before the fire and discussions with the guides. Then, the sun having reconquered the snows and dispersed the clouds, the two men and their guides —Hill had secured the services of the guide Jean Vuignier of Evolène—submitted themselves to intensive training. No day but saw them rising to a neighbouring summit, on the rocks, the crests of snow, the slopes of ice and the glaciers; so that towards the end of the month they found themselves in admirable condition and ready to try their physical and mental mechanism elsewhere than on secondary peaks.

One day, while descending the Aiguilles Rouges d'Arolla, Jones opens his heart to his friend. The two ropes have halted on rocks sheltered from the wind. The afternoon is of unparalleled clearness; above the glaciers the mountains, their flanks steel-grey and armoured with blue-green ice, rise calmly into the blue air. And rooted in the centre of this landscape, very close, fascinating in its cruel immensity, is the Dent Blanche. Its arêtes, fortified with sharp pointed rocks and snowy furrows, stretch out, curving a little, like giant tentacles ready to close on their prey. It is a stirring moment, propitious for confidences.

"See how beautiful it is, this Ferpècle arête!" says Jones. "What terrible power sleeps in its devastated walls!"

"Yes, truly, it is very beautiful."

"For a long time, Hill, I've wanted to climb it."

"Really?"

"Yes, for a very long time. But it was necessary to wait for the

most favourable moment, and I think the present conditions. . . .
Don't you, Furrer?"

"*Jawohl, Herr Jones*!"

"Yes, we've studied it minutely, Furrer and I. And Furrer's
had a word about it with Aloys Pollinger[10] . . . You know Pollinger
of St. Niklaus? He made the first ascent, and he's in the know."

"And what had Aloys Pollinger to say?"

"He says it's a very fine climb. . . . We're impatient to do it,
Furrer and I. . . . Will you come with us, Hill? I'm sure Vuignier
would be delighted."

"Ah! Yes indeed, Monsieur Jones. Just think of it! A fine
climb like that!" exclaims Vuignier.

Jones and his guide have travelled together for five years;
they know one another as only two old climbers can. And Jean
Vuignier has led Hill to the conquest of almost all the high
mountains in the Zermatt region, including the Dent Blanche
by the normal route; while last summer the four climbers who are
now comfortably ensconced in the rocks of the Aiguilles Rouges,
climbed the Taeschhorn together by the Teufelsgrat. So it is an
old party which finds itself together again and elaborates its
splendid hopes.

Jean Vuignier is enchanted. The Dent Blanche is somewhat
to Evolène what the Matterhorn is to Zermatt. From his chalet
windows he can see the mountain throughout the year; it is part
of his familiar skyline. Furthermore, no Evolène guide has so far
climbed this formidable arête de Ferpècle, which runs down
into the Val d'Hérens. The glory will be his. But Hill decidedly
lacks enthusiasm. Not that he does not fully value the marvellous
climb offered him, but he has already fixed his departure for
Zermatt. Other arrangements, more difficult to change, have
been made; among them the crossing of the peaceful Col d'Hérens
with Mrs. Hill. A change of programme will condemn her to a
long solitary journey through the valleys of Hérens and St.
Niklaus. Decidedly, it cannot be done, and despite his friend's
insistence, Hill declines.

Owen Glynne Jones, firmly rooted in his project, and reckoning
that a party of three will be indispensable, secures a second guide,
Clemenz Zurbriggen of Saas. Zurbriggen, being released from
an engagement and preparing to return to Zermatt, accepts the
windfall with joy. But Jean Vuignier is bitterly disappointed.

What a wrench he finds it to abandon the Ferpècle arête for the snowy levels of the Col d'Hérens, where a nurse could almost push her perambulator! Thinking that his recalcitrant employer declines for financial reasons, he offers to find a guide who will agree to conduct Mrs. Hill across the Col d'Hérens alone, and to pay this guide himself. Hill turns this touching proposition down; but yielding in the end to the insistence of Jones and his guides, he eventually agrees to join them, and instead of three there are now five men ready to leave for the Ferpècle arête.

The men left Arolla on Sunday, August the 27th.[11] It was their intention to bivouac at the foot of the arête. But the chalets at Bricolla detained them, and they spent in the hay a night which for comfort was beyond comparison with that which the Rocs Rouges might problematically have offered them. On Monday the 28th, at three in the morning, they set out.

Before them the Dent Blanche, like a motionless cloud, darkened the night. The stars trembled in the clear sky. A fragment of the moon, cut by a crest, gleamed palidly on the skyline. Close to a torrent they awakened a herd of cattle, and the bells jangled. After the last of the grass and the moraines, they trod the upper Ferpècle Glacier. There they uncoiled the rope.

Dawn broke. Formidable, dwarfing them by the upsweep of its pacified chaos, the Dent Blanche masked the east where the sun was rising. The snows which the climbers were ascending at a great pace were already reflecting the roseate gleams. Shafts of light filled the empty sky with their joyfulness. The Dent Blanche itself, a colossal and massive ruin in a frozen landscape, crowned itself with delicate hues. These fiery lights on the high crests accentuated the lividness of the abysses to which the determined gaze of the climbers was raised.

The glacier crossed, the two parties found themselves in the delta of the Grand Couloir, a strange isthmus connecting space and the earth, splitting the mountain from top to bottom. There the heavy silence was almost painful, as if it had to be lifted in order to move. And in the depths of these violet-walled chasms, cut sheer and picked out with ice, nocturnal shadows still lingered. The arête was revealed in profile, boldly outlined, marking the limit of a titanic tumult, pacified at last but still preserving a terrible shape in its final immobility.

Elias Furrer leads, followed by Clemenz Zurbriggen, and

260

behind these shock-troops, on the same rope, Owen Glynne Jones. Jean Vuignier and Mr. Hill form the second party and follow the others closely. Difficulties arise from the very beginning; the attack is going to be a serious affair. Great slabs follow one another, smooth and vertical; rock walls and great accumulations of shattered stone as well. At eight-thirty a party of two men is visible for a moment on the southern arête, but no shouts are exchanged between the two parties. The seconds are very solemn. Fissures run the length of the walls; the holds conceal traps; the climbers' efforts are often baffled by the treachery of the rocks. Henceforth the party is all on one rope, a party of five men with Vuignier tied behind Jones. The whizz of stones, and the noise they make rebounding in their fall, now enliven the empty immensity of the couloir. The glacier displays itself indistinctly very far below.

Half-way up the arête the way is blocked by bulging rocks, smeared with verglas. It is impossible to pass. Furrer unties himself. He perceives to the right a horizontal ledge whose gilded surface contrasts with the dark walls which it divides. He follows it, then leaves it for a chimney in order to regain the arête. Things look better above; but three hundred feet higher a precipitous spur juts out from the arête. There, clearly, he will not be able to pass alone. He calls his comrades. Zurbriggen's head appears in a breach, and the five men are soon regrouped, Furrer reassuming his place at the head of the rope. They all start forward once more.

At this moment, nine-thirty, the two climbers on the southern arête are visible again, quite near to the summit, slender silhouettes against the blue depths of the sky. But, as before, the silence between the two parties remains unbroken, as if by instinct those on the Ferpècle arête fear to distract their close attention even for a second. At ten o'clock the five climbers reach the base of the spur, known as the "Gendarme," a verticle pinnacle furrowed with sharp-edged fissures, wrinkled with slight depressions and speckled with snow, and resting against the ice slopes which decorate the lateral surface of the great couloir to the right. Just as the climbers approach the lower structure of the spur, in the axis of the arête they see the peak against the light, surmounted by a fiery crest.

"In less than an hour we shall be there," Elias Furrer declares.

Then they penetrate into the shadow and coldness of the wall, on the side of the couloir where a kind of ascending ledge turns them aside. An instant later the way is again blocked. A narrow chimney, communicating slantwise with a step, provides the only possibility of rejoining the arête. But this chimney is entirely coated with verglas, as thin as a skin but as hard as cement, on which the fingers can find no grip and where the point of an ice-axe proves useless and even dangerous. Furrer silently glares at the passage. Decidedly, nothing can be done there. His attention then travels to the left, attracted by a verticle wall only ten feet high, ending in an overhang. Above this it should be possible to refind the arête.

The party is motionless on the narrow band of rock, spaced at intervals of eight or ten yards, all on the same level except Hill, the last on the rope, a little lower down and still ascending. A few minutes later he hoists himself on to the ledge and so finds himself on the right wing. Nine yards in front of him is Vuignier; Furrer is on the left wing. To be exact, the latter is already at work. Outstretched against the wall, he has raised himself about five or six feet, but can make no further progress. He hesitates, gropes, feels the perpendicular rock, makes a false start and returns hastily to his old position. Checked on the right. Checked on the left. Yet five feet above him. . . . Five feet! The distance seems ridiculous! Laughable! But below him there are nearly 2,000 feet of precipice falling straight into the bay of the glacier.

Nobody speaks. Nobody moves. Tension grips their minds and weighs upon their breasts. Definitely, it is no good; Furrer will not succeed. Will he give it up and come down? Not yet. His hands tighten on the texture of the rock. Unable to turn round, he calls to Zurbriggen.

"Zurbriggen . . . quickly . . . an axe!"

Zurbriggen hurries forward carefully and reaches the foot of the wall. Jones has allowed the rope to run out and himself moves two or three yards in order to consolidate his position and to secure the rope. This brief dialogue follows between the two guides:

"Put it under my right foot."

"Like this?"

"Yes. Now lift it gently."

"All right?"

"Yes. Hold it tight for heaven's sake!"

"Higher?"

"Yes . . . go on . . . gently . . . farther . . . stop ! . . . steady !"

Furrer now has his right leg raised and bent at an acute angle, his foot on the axe head. This artificial support sinks an inch or two each time the man, with a supple but heavy effort, attempts to rise. Furrer turns to Jones; his face can be seen in profile, turned away from the wall.

"Herr Jones, can you come here?"

Jones frees the rope from the rock and draws near, taking in the slack line as he goes.

"Do you think it's any good, Elias?" he asks.

"Oh yes, it will be all right. Will you just help Zurbriggen to hold the axe?"

"Like this?"

"Yes . . . just a little lower."

"Like that?"

"A little higher . . . lean it against the rock."

"Like this?"

"Stop. That's right . . . don't move . . . now . . . hold tight . . . I'm starting . . . hold tight !"

Slowly, with infinite slowness, with an almost imperceptible movement, Furrer shifts to the right; his left foot abandons its support, hovers, scrapes the rock and reaches the small steel bar. His legs are now together, and he is standing entirely on the axe. Now can be seen a group from a bas-relief, a human pyramid fixed to the rock: to the right the guide, to the left the British climber, outstretched, shoulder to shoulder, faces lowered, riveted to the rock, but joined at the axe-handle which they force to the wall with strained muscles. Above them, erect on the axe-head, and harmoniously prolonging the symmetry of the two bodies, Furrer.

Furrer at this moment has succeeded in reaching the level of the overhang. His body as far as his chest, although thrust slightly backwards, even extends beyond the lip. His outstretched arms, fingers spread, cling to the slab, slide over it with slightly disordered motion, covering it with fevered touches, grappling haphazardly in indistinct asperities, then resting motionless. Furrer then attempts to re-establish himself. He has not yet left the axe-head, but already all the weight of his body is carried by his arms, which are suddenly stretched tautly like metal levers.

Nearly twelve stones depend upon these contracted joints. It is too much for them. They refuse to obey him. They yield . . . and yield again. Furrer forces them forward. They decline to hold him . . . they slip back a little . . . Furrer forces them in vain . . . they give way slowly . . . they slip. Furrer flattens them, crushes them against the rock, digs them in. But they yield always . . . slip back. Furrer beseeches them to hold. He presses upon them so hard that they should cut their way into the rock. But they do not hear the supplications of his agonised spirit. Destiny inexorably takes hold of them, lifts them gently, as studious fingers lift from the keys of a piano . . . lifts them . . . lifts them. . . . In a rush, Furrer falls backward. He tumbles upon Zurbriggen and Jones, demolishes the group, separates the welded backs, throws them down, and the three men, without a cry, without a word, without an exclamation, plunge into the abyss.

Hill, witness of the whole drama, then instinctively turns and desperately embraces a rock. He hears the silky rustling of the rope—like an octopus seeking its prey. There is a light, dry shock, and the octopus snatches Vuignier away. Hill hears him disappear. The light rustling draws nearer. The tentacle is about to seize the last man. The octopus hesitates, gropes. Hill knows himself condemned and waits. But the terrible rustling suddenly ends. He waits . . . he waits . . . silence falls. Without a blow, gently, the octopus has submerged. There is nothing now but a curious, far-off sound, like an alternating cascade.

Hill turns round; he is alone, the cornice is deserted. The little wall, stripped of the noble bas-relief of a few moments since, is bare. And then he perceives his former companions, already far below, sliding with terrifying speed. The bodies raise a soft sound as they crash against the precipice. Stones escort them in prodigious bounds. And Hill sees that tied to his middle is a nine-yard fragment of rope.

*   *   *

Pulling himself together and mastering his nerves,[12] the solitary man takes stock of his position. The situation is clear: to descend would be death; to wait for rescue on this hostile ledge in the middle of an almost limitless abyss would be death; and to attempt to ascend the wall which had repulsed Furrer's audacity would be death too. The solitary man turns round. From the depths of the abyss the last dull thuds arise, the smothered blows of the bodies which have completed their journey and of the last stones plunging into the snow. Then the silence closes in again as before, the great diaphanous silence of the heights.

Hill then examines the wall to the right, facing the still shaded couloir. There in bitter mockery, there where Furrer gave up, lies salvation, or at least the gleam of salvation. After all, better to make one supreme effort and fall than to die an hallucinating death here after a slow motionless agony.

Hill rolls his nine yards of rope into a bandolier and deliberately, axe in hand, begins his climb. He turns to face the unsurmountable spur on the right. The rocks confront him with their treacherous verglas. Nevertheless, he succeeds. He gains height, crosses a step whose grey shadow, streaked by sunlight, rises to meet a slope of ice. He passes over it, reaches the ice, and emerges into the sunlight. Its exquisite warmth effects a resurrection of all his strength; his body, his blood, his spirit, his senses are all recreated. Then he attacks the slope with a kind of furious intoxication. The ice splinters; the steps take shape. The dry blows of the steel are a diversion from his funereal thoughts, and a distraction from the terrible silence.

An hour after his departure from the ledge the solitary man rejoins the arête above the gendarme; the obstacle is passed. He can see again on the north side the great rampart which overlooks the Glacier de la Dent Blanche. His difficulties are ended, vanquished. He makes a short pause, then starts off again, an unusual figure in the sky of the Ferpècle arête.

In another hour he arrived at the summit. It was a little after mid-day. At that precise moment a joyful cry was raised a long way off; it came from the party seen that morning which, having rapidly descended, was just then reaching the foot of the southern arête and was saluting the human figure up above. The solitary climber saw nothing and did not answer. But, leaning against the ice-covered cairn with distracted eyes, he heard this happy shout leap from the immensity unfolded before him. After his fierce struggle and the death of all his comrades, life for him sang its own praises.

*   *   *

The solitary man begins his descent at once. The southern arête is the classic route. It is not particularly difficult, but it is nevertheless a serious undertaking, and Mr. Hill knows it well. Vuignier, in fact, had guided him there, and there is a vague irony in the way he finds himself there again, and his guide down below motionless on the snow.

The man advances along the crest, resolutely crossing the slabs from which the Lochmatters fell in 1882.[13] Obstacles of rock and ice follow one after the other. Clouds which had developed on the white plateau of the Col d'Hérens rise slowly, stretching out their supple platforms and welding themselves together. To guide himself the solitary man now and then follows the tracks of the unknown party in the snow, but when he arrives at last at the foot of the Grand Gendarme (13,054 feet), the thick mists envelop him abruptly. It is impossible to go on. Around him everything is obscured; he makes two or three attempts to start again, but the cloudy opaqueness hems him in. To force the descent would be reckless, and he would pay dearly. And a wind now rises, bringing squalls of snow.

So at the foot of a rock the man sits down on the stones. He moors himself to the rock behind him with the short length of rope, plants his axe in a fissure before him, encircles its shaft with his legs, and grips the head with his two hands. And he waits. It is now about four in the afternoon.

With twilight a bitter coldness freezes the clouds. Evening draws in. The winds blow without respite and the snow swirls thickly. The human form is soon no more than a vague figure thickly coated with ice and snow, a white block leaning against the frozen rock. Then it is night; immense night, almost without transition; a night overflowing with noise and the muted rustling of the snow. A night of eternity. But the solitary being is anchored to his rock, and also to his will. Fear might prowl about him, but if he sees it or senses it, he scorns or ignores it.

Thus the tempestuous night passes away to the regular and indifferent metronome of the hours. And the dawn, as if dredged from the lowest depths of the turbulent darkness, slowly brings back the day. But nothing changes in the day that is beginning (Tuesday the 29th), except the greyish tinge of the hours; the clouds and the cold, the snow and the wind, are without end. And this human form, over which the snow has cast its blanket, remains moored to its frozen rock; only a rare movement of the hands upon the axe-head, or of the feet against the handle, betrays that it lives.

Thus the morning passes. The mid-day angelus rings in the valleys. Then the thick mists lightly disperse and the white sheeted form rises to its feet. The man shakes himself, unties his nine yards of rope, loosens the line, rolls it methodically round his chest, uproots his ice-axe and tranquilly starts on his journey. Under the sun and the blue sky he tackles the thick snow and reaches the arête (12,830 feet). The snow slides on the ice beneath it, and in order to cut steps the solitary climber has to clear away the moving surface in which he is floundering. Soon he is stranded in the labyrinth of ravines on the Wandfluh, and there he loses three hours in futile efforts. When at last he reaches the Schönbuhl Glacier the sun is setting, and the vast shadow of the Dent Blanche lies across the glacier. The terrified man does not dare to set foot on the shadowy frontier which stretches across the snow; he comes and goes, climbs and descends again, seeking an escape from this opaque and recumbent wall, as if it contains evil and terrifying things. But the twilight abruptly submerges the shadow in its turn and frees the solitary man from his fears.[14] He moves on. The sharp peak of the Matterhorn and the frozen roof of the Dent d'Hérens, glowing incandescently, are drenched in a glory of gilded purple.

Nightfall finds the solitary man on the Zmutt Glacier. In the growing obscurity he trudges wearily along the track that runs the length of the moraine. For the third time since leaving the chalets of Bricolla it is night. A tranquil light shines down there in the darkness at the Staffelalp inn, and for a long time its beacon guides his stumbling steps. Suddenly the light is extinguished and the night becomes atrocious, sunk under the shadowy mass of the Matterhorn. Straying in the chaos of broken stone, the man loses his way, passes below the Staffelalp without seeing the inn, and collapses, exhausted and desperately hungry, on the grass beside the torrent. He falls asleep at once, with his fragment of rope still about him.[15]

*   *   *

When he awoke, the tenderness of an exquisite morning lay above him. He had slept like a little child, without interruption, until ten-thirty. Once again (Wednesday the 30th) he rose and set forth. Soon he rejoined the track, and at eleven-thirty he arrived at last at Zermatt, and the fragment of rope still encircled his body. Only then did he undo the knot.

For the scene of the tragedy on the Dent Blanche, see Plate 30.

[1] See Charles Gos: "Maupassant et la Montagne" (*Gazette de Lausanne*, 28th October, 1940).

[2] T. S. Kennedy, celebrated mountaineer of Whymper's generation, conqueror of the Dent Blanche amongst other victories. (See p. 79; note 6(*c*) to Chapter 17; and note 6 to this chapter.)

[3] See Charles Gos: "Alphonse Daudet et la Montagne" (*Journal de Genève*, 29th September, 1940).

[4] Cf. *Tartarin of the Alps*.

[5] Cf. *La Horla* and *Au Soleil*.

[6] Its first ascent had been accomplished on the 18th July, 1862, by T. S. Kennedy and W. Wigram, with the guides Jean-Baptiste Croz (Michel's brother) and Johann Kronig.

[7] Born in 1867. At his death he occupied the position of physics master at the City of London School. Concerning his climbs in the English hills, he left behind a charming book, full of interest: *Rockclimbing in the English Lake District*.

[8] On the 25th April, 1893, from Bricolla. The climb lasted $21\frac{1}{2}$ hours. With the guides Antoine Bovier and Pierre Gaspoz and Antoine Bovier *fils* as porter, all three from Evolène.

[9] Personal communication from Joseph Pollinger and Antoine Bovier.

[10] Celebrated St. Niklaus guide, conqueror of the two great arêtes of the Dent Blanche, that of the Quatres Anes (1882—see Chapter 13, Part III) and that of Ferpècle. Aloys Pollinger accomplished the "first" on the Ferpècle arête on the descent, with the famous English climber Mrs. E. P. Jackson and Prof. K. Schulz (the Zsigmondys' comrade on the southern face of the Meije—see Chapter 14) as travellers. The party spent a terrible night below the summit (25th to 26th August, 1884). The second guide was J.-J. Truffer of St. Niklaus. Four years later Aloys Pollinger reclimbed his arête alone, except for his traveller, Walter Gröbli (29th July, 1889).

[11] Cf. *Alpine Journal*, Vol. XIX, 1898–99.

[12] Mr. F. W. Hill writes: "It is difficult to analyse my sensations at that moment. My main feeling was one of astonishment that I was still there. I can only suppose that Vuignier had belayed my rope securely to protect himself and me during our long wait on the traverse."

[13] See Chapter 13, Part III.

[14] This hallucinating detail, strictly authentic, was given me by Mr. E. C. Oppenheim, a distinguished climber and member of the Alpine Club, who had it from Mr. Hill himself. It was at Toarmina in the middle of the Sicilian spring; below us the Gulf of Naxos spread its violet-coloured waves and Etna raised its light snows against the sky, crowned by a canopy of saffron-rose smoke. This recollection of the fearful tragedy on the Dent Blanche in so divine a scene was something extraordinary. Mr. Oppenheim concluded his reminiscence with these words: "I was seated in front of the Monte Rosa hotel at Zermatt when Hill arrived with the broken rope around his waist."

[15] The same evening a rescue party of thirty guides, led by Aloys Supersaxo (one of the future guides to King Albert I during his Swiss climbs), left Zermatt. Three climbers joined it: Dr. R. Lenk, Mr. K. Mayr and Mr. W. R. Rickmers. At 10.30 that evening the caravan passed the Staffelalp. The following morning (Thursday, 31st August) they reached the Col d'Hérens at six o'clock, where they were surprised by thick mists and squalls of snow. The rescuers descended the Ferpècle Glacier towards the base of the Ferpècle arête and, at the height of the Rocs Rouges, ascended the Upper Glacier which had been followed by the Jones–Hill parties on Monday the 28th. The long column reached the glacier bay enclosed by the arms of the giant couloir. Some 300 feet above the bergschrund the bodies of the unfortunate climbers lay at the edge of the last rocks, horribly mutilated and three-parts decapitated. A rescue party of Evolène guides, accompanied by Mr. Harold Spender, were already on the spot. High above them,

straight up, overlooking the bodies, the rock buttress stood out from the arête. One could see to the right of it the slope of ice by which Mr. Hill had escaped. The fall had been about 1,650 feet. Between the guides Elias Furrer and Clemenz Zurbriggin the rope was still intact.

During the evening of the 31st August the rescue party brought the remains to Haudères.

The medical expert acting on behalf of the examining magistrate for the Hérens district, reported as follows:

". . . I found in the school-room, four sacks enclosing the bodies of the unhappy victims. Having freed them from their wrappings I noted that all the bodies showed: (*a*) a complete removal of the posterior and upper part of the cranium, only the faces, horribly disfigured, remaining; (*b*) multiple fractures of the limbs and of various parts of the body; (*c*) death must have been instantaneous and a direct result of the injuries found on the bodies."

Aloys Pollinger *fils*, told me at St. Niklaus (1944) that, in climbing the Ferpècle arête a year after the accident, he had found Jones's torn knapsack in the rocks below the buttress; the knapsack contained, amongst other things, an aluminium flask filled with excellent brandy. The name "Jones" was still readable on one of the knapsack straps.

Furthermore, when the guide Maurice Crettex of Champex, with his son Nestor as porter and Sigward Mundi as traveller, climbed the Ferpècle arête on the 5th August, 1930, and unintentionally passed the spot where the bodies were recovered, they found vestiges of the accident still scattered around, such as torn footwear and fragments of rope and clothing.

Owen Glynne Jones and the guide Jean Vuignier were buried at Evolène on Saturday, 2nd September. The other two guides were buried in their native villages, Stalden and Saas-Grund. The epitaphs of Jones and Vuignier are as follows:

"In memory of Owen Glynne Jones who, with the guides Elias Furrer, Jean Vuignier and Clemens Zurbriggen, was killed on the Dent Blanche, 28th August, 1899, aged 31 years."

and (*trans.*)

"To the memory of our dear son and brother, the guide Jean Vuignier, born the 22nd September, 1866, and died on the Dent Blanche, a victim of his duty, the 28th August, 1899. You alone our help, oh Lord! Pray for him."

Mr. F. W. Hill died in 1935. "I met him at Riffelalp in 1928. He still did a little climbing. But we have never discussed the cruel subject of the Jones accident." (Personal communication from Col. E. L. Strutt.)

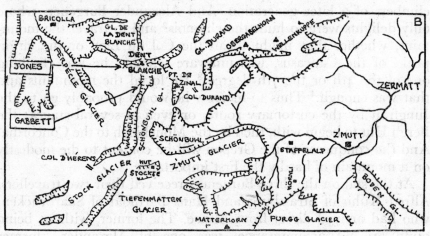

THE DENT BLANCHE AND ZERMATT

CHAPTER TWENTY-TWO

THE MADDENED WAVES OF SNOW

The death of A. Kühn, of H. Barthold and of the guides Alexander and Adolf
Burgener, Peter and Rudolf Inäbnit and Christian Bohren (Bergli Hut, July 1910)

I N the first week of July 1910, Alexander Burgener, the old
and glory-laden guide, at one time the guide and companion
of the famous English climber A. F. Mummery, arrived at
Grindelwald, supported by his two sons Adolf and Alexander.
On this occasion the conqueror of the Zmutt and Furggen arêtes
of the Matterhorn and of so many famous peaks[1] had no very
great plans. The psychosis of the famous north-east face of the
Eiger did not then exist. The alpinists of those pre-1914 days were
less ambitious; none then dreamed of the innumerable "last
great problems of the Alps" which were bitterly disputed by the
climbers of a later generation. And Alexander Burgener, whose
only delights were to hunt the chamois[2] and to travel the mountains, whether that might mean the Col du Lion or the virgin
peaks of the Caucasus, was unaware whether he was climbing
one of the 4th or the 7th degree.[3] He loved the mountains and
that was enough.[4] Thus to-morrow he would probably go to the
Jungfrau by the customary route, or even in several stages: the
Bergli Hut to begin with, then by the Mönchjoch to the Concordia.
And the conqueror of the Grépon will be content to die modestly
on a mountain of hardly the first importance.

  At the station the three Burgeners received their two travellers,
Alfred Kühn of Strassburg and Hans Barthold of Saarbrucken,
who had arrived direct from Alsace. The former, without being
quite an old acquaintance, was one of Alexander's former

270

"clients"; at exactly this time the year before they had climbed together two or three four-thousanders in the Valais. Such adventures draw two men very much together.

The same evening the guides and their employers were together in the café. The weather was gloomy. For close on two weeks the mountains had been floating in a sea of cloud. In the valley it had rained, but up above the snow was accumulating.

"Have you your *führerbuch*, Alexander?" asked Kühn.

The guide groped laboriously in his large pocket and extracted the precious *führerbuch* in its deer-skin case. Kühn opened it and his friend leaned over. They ran through it and stopped to read the last page. There Kühn himself had entered his testimony.

"Look here, Alexander, this fine weather is making fun of us! Do you remember those torrents of rain between Randa and the Festi Hut? They tumbled down just like they're doing to-night."

"That's right," Burgener replied, "but all we had to do was squeeze our way between the drops. Walking sideways like crabs, we got along very well."

There was a burst of laughter, and Kühn continued with his reminiscences:

"Just like the snow. . . . The snow! You might say that we love the snow too, you and me. . . . Listen, Barthold. Snow on the Dom, snow on the Nadelhorn, snow on Monte Rosa . . ."[5]

"Snow on the Matterhorn," Burgener interrupted facetiously. "I should have done better that day to have brought a shovel instead of an ice-axe!"

"A shovel?" questioned Barthold.

"Yes, a good shovel to dig a trench with. . . You could then have climbed up with your hands in your pockets."

There was more laughter. Gusts of rain swept against the windows. The wind raged.

"And if this weather continues," the guide went on, imperturbably, "we shall need an umbrella to climb with to the Bergli hut."

For three days the rain was intense. Sombre clouds veiled the mountains from the middle of their slopes, and when the wind repelled them belts of new snow were revealed. But the fourth day was very fine and the climbers, tired of the prolonged wait, took advantage of it to set out. A young local guide, Fritz Brawand of Grindelwald, accompanied them, replacing the guide Rudolf Baumann, prevented from leaving at the last moment.

In the train that took them to the Kleine Scheidegg, Burgener had his head out of the window. His tanned and heavily bearded face was raised to the heights of the Eiger, where the sharp Mitteleggi arête, foreshortened and terrifying, climbs towards the clouds. Its conquest had made a stirring story, of which Burgener knew a great deal. He himself was one of the heroes of the sensational victory.[6]

"It stirs you to see these parts again, doesn't it, Alexander?" one of the travellers asked.

"Me? No! I'm just watching if I can see the shine of that knife I lost up there. One of these young people might go up and look for it for me. . . ."

He laughed, and all the party with him, proud to travel under the orders of such a chief, as if sharing in his glory.

The Eiger's walls were streaming with light. The sun's iridescence trembled on the crests. When the climbers disembarked at the Eismeer station, the föhn was blowing; its warm gusts had swept the sky and burnished its sombre blue. Padded with deep snow the mountains were sparkling like solid blocks of mica. There, indeed, the glaciers shone in the way that made the poet Byron shout for joy. But contrary to the exultation of that impassioned romantic—who had not himself the outlook of a climber, laden with a heavy pack, ploughing through the snow, dragging his slow travellers along—Alexander Burgener was silent and gazed at the glaciers wryly. *Childe Harold* expressed his thoughts very well when he cried out in a burst of lyrical admiration, which the old Valaisian guide was, however, far from sharing:

. . . . Above me are the Alps,
The palaces of Nature, whose vast walls
Have pinnacled in clouds their snowy scalps,
And throned Eternity in icy halls
Of cold sublimity, where forms and falls
The avalanche—the thunderbolt of snow!

The avalanche! It was just that which troubled old Burgener. The way up to the Bergli hut was long. The glacier would be encumbered with soft snow. While below the hut there was a wide and extremely exposed reef of rock to cross.

"Well, are we ready, Alexander? . . . You're pleased aren't

you? What wonderful weather! Would you believe such luck! No shovel or umbrella to-day!"

"What about a sunshade," suggested Barthold.

"Yes, Herr Kühn," Burgener replied. "The weather's all right, but the snow . . . !"

It was very warm. The sky was too blue, the mountains were too clear, without perspective in the transparent air. The gutters were overflowing and the drainpipes gurgling. The snow was putting as much energy into melting as in the previous days it had put into falling. Large masses were sliding off the station roof and flattening themselves in the puddles with an irregular rhythm.

"Herr Kühn," Burgener then said. "I think we would do well to hire some porters as far as the hut. The snow is in an abominable condition. With less to carry we will move quicker, and the sooner we are at the hut the better. To-morrow . . . that's another thing. To-night, up there, the snow will freeze up, but to-day it's sticky, it melts and slides and sinks. We shall have to be careful."

A hoarse uproar rose into the motionless air like invisible clouds. The avalanches were roaring down the sides of the Mönch.

At the beginning of this too blue and too sunny afternoon the long caravan left the Eismeer for the Bergli hut;[7] two Grindelwald guides, Peter Inäbnit and his nephew, Rudolf Inäbnit, joined it at the station as porters. The eight men are now on the Kallfirn Glacier. They move in Indian file, covered to the knees in thick snow. The two Inäbnits lead, being the lightest of the party despite their loads, and they open up a path. A heavy warmth adds to the tedium of the monotonous tramp. The climbers' backs are wet under the packs; their eyes, behind yellow glasses, are turned down upon the surface which blazes with sunlight. From time to time a head is raised and searches for the hut on the promontory of rock, a dark islet in this ocean of snow. It can be seen for an instant, then it vanishes behind a white knoll. It reappears. A joyful and breathless shout salutes it: "The hut!" In fact, at the very point of the rocks, a kind of miniature Gibraltar raised above the head of the Grindelwald Fiescherfirn, a small square brown shape, too rectangular to be a rock, can be distinguished. From it a small plume of smoke is rising. Smoke rising from a roof!—a much-abused image, but one which, nevertheless, always speaks to the heart, above all when the roof is in the bitter solitudes of the high mountains. Slackened energies revive. A guide raises a prolonged shout.

It is five in the evening, but another hour must pass before the hut is reached. Burgener is anxious, and while he walks he examines the reef of rock more than three hundred feet high, at the summit of which the hut is perched. There is no other way to reach it. The slopes are literally cushioned with snow, and since the morning all this snow, now seen in diminishing perspective, has been exposed to the heat of the pitiless sun, burning it like the flame of a blowlamp.

The caravan reaches the base of the promontory and leaves the glaciers. Vertically, and strictly in line, the eight men slowly climb the reef of rock. From time to time some stony crests break the uniformity of this formidable cope. The stippled line of the climbers' track breaks the white expanse of the snow and trails like a blue ribbon upon the surface, just as if the guide who walks last unrolls it behind him. The eight men are now just below the culminating arête; the hut overlooks them from its perch on the left, smoke still curling from its roof. Its windows can be seen; its shutters are open. A man stands in front of the hut watching the laborious ascent; this is undoubtedly the hut-keeper who has been isolated on his rocks throughout the two weeks of storm, a stylite *malgré lui*, and he is happy to see his fellow creatures once more. To-night there will be company.

The eight men are now ascending a kind of combe which widens out between the spur on which the hut is built and a small rock tooth to the right. They will have to flounder in the wretched snow for another twenty minutes before reaching the arête. The man up above now moves. Clearly outlined, he descends the arête to meet the arrivals, to clear a way for them He hails them. They answer him blithely. They continue their ascent, and he his descent. He reaches the col on the arête to the left of the small rock tooth. He then leaves the arête and moves several metres down the slope towards the caravan:

"What! Is it really you, Alexander?"

"How are you, Christian?"[9]

"The hut," a breathless voice asks, "is it still very far?"

"Far? . . . Why! you're there . . . just a few minutes more."

It is six in the evening. The man from above, the old guide Christian Bohren stops. And the column, with the Inäbnits still

274

leading, stops also. They are at a height of about 10,800 feet. Six feet separate Bohren from the party.

Suddenly there is a sound like a thunderclap, splitting the infinite silence of the sky. But the sky itself remains motionless, an unchanging azure, while the mountain moves. From the small rock tooth to the right, as far as the eastern arête at the extreme left, slightly below the hut, the whole surface, split by a single stroke, gapes. The thick bed of snow tears itself from its icy foundation and slides irresistibly forward, folds itself up and breaks into pieces. In an instant the whole promontory capsizes, up-ending itself like a sinking ship. Engulfing the nine men, this formidable cataract then falls down upon the Grindelwald Fiescherfirn; it falls in immense soft waves, breaking into foam, crumbling in enormous masses with the rolling roar of explosions in a line of artillery fire. Then, spreading widely, it grows silent, like a mortally wounded beast which stretches itself out and gives up the struggle. Shudders run along its extremities, as if moved by nervous reflexes. A few great blocks still turn over once or twice, and in the divine silence, under the motionless blue of the sky, nothing has changed except this striated sheet of snow, pale grey, leaning upon the glacier.

Thus dies the great guide, Alexander Burgener. Those powerful arms which have mastered the virgin granite of the Grépon and Dru, open to the raging waves of snow. Everything collapses around him. He goes down in the midst of a tumultuous uproar. The snow fills his eyes with darkness; the snow closes his mouth. The terrifying tide carries him away. And he gives himself up.

* * *

On a squat block of rock in the little cemetery at Eisten, visible against a background of the distant Bietschhorn, a guide's badge is fixed. On the stone these simple words may be read:

ALEXANDRE BURGENER

1846   1910

DIPLM. FUHRER

SAC

Some days after the tragedy, the Ligurean section of the Italian Alpine Club, expressing and epitomising the emotion and sorrow of all the alpine associations and of alpinists everywhere, sent this telegram to the President of the Swiss Alpine Club:

275

"We learn with the deepest regret the news of the catastrophe at the Bergli hut. The members of the Ligurean section of the C.A.I. sincerely share the sorrow of their Swiss colleagues and weep with them for the victims of this terrible disaster which, at the beginning of the alpine campaign, plunges the whole great alpine family into mourning. Profoundly moved, we send you our sincere condolences and testimony of our fraternal sentiments in these days of distress."

For the scene of Alexander Burgener's death, see Plates 31 and 32. Burgener's portrait is reproduced in Plates 33 and 34.

[1] Alexander Burgener, born at Eisten in the Saas valley in 1846. He began his career as a chamois-hunter and he remained one all his life. In 1868 he worked as a guide for the first time; his employer was the well-known English mountaineer, Dr. Clinton Thomas Dent, President of the Alpine Club from 1887–90. Burgener and Dent travelled together every year from 1868 until 1878. In 1872 they made the first ascent of the Zinal Rothorn from the Trift side, and on the 12th September, 1878, after nineteen attempts they made the first ascent of the Aiguille du Dru (the Grand Dru) together with J. Walker Hartley and the guide Kaspar Maurer. But it was above all as guide to that famous climber, A. F. Mummery, that Burgener is renowned. These two climbers accomplished together the following first ascents: the Zmutt arête of the Matterhorn (1879); the Furggen arête of the Matterhorn and the traverse of the Col du Lion (1880); the Grands Charmoz, the Teufelsgrat of the Taeschhorn, the Aiguille Verte from the Charponez side, and the Grépon (1881); finally (1885), Alexander Burgener achieved the "first" on the famous Mitteleggi arête of the Eiger, on the descent. In 1884 he explored the Caucasus with his Hungarian employer, Maurice de Déchy (with a "first" on the Adai-Kokh); he returned there in 1886 with C. T. Dent and W. F. Donkin and they succeeded in climbing Tetnuld Tau for the first time. After that he left for South America with the celebrated German climber, Dr. Paul Güssfeldt, with the intention of exploring the Cordilleras; but he had hardly disembarked in the Argentine before he was laid low with sickness and had to return home.

[2] Eight months before his death, Alexander Burgener followed a herd of chamois alone and brought down four of them. The same evening he carried two of them down over his shoulders and only reached the valley after a four-hour march.

[3] Modern climbers have classed the mountains according to a scale of difficulty. The seventh degree is equal to "the extreme limit of human possibility," beyond which there is probably nothing but the resource suggested by Nietzsche, of "climbing on to one's own head in order to surmount the impossible."

[4] Like many great guides, Burgener concealed a sensitive nature beneath a rough exterior. Dr. C. T. Dent reported that, on arriving at the summit of the Aiguille du Dru, a victory which Burgener himself always considered as one of his greatest exploits, he saw tears of joy and pride in his guide's eyes; "all the same," he adds, "I could feel his emotion in his formidable handshake."

[5] I have before me a photographic reproduction of Burgener's *führerbuch*, his second, in which Alfred Kühn inscribed the following lines; his attestation precedes the penultimate testimonial by which the magnificent career of the great guide came to an end.

(*Trans.*) *"From the 5th till the 17th July, 1909, I travelled with Alexander Burgener in the mountains of the Saas-Zermatt region. The first ascents in 1909 were the Nadelhorn and Dom; of other climbs I mention particularly Monte Rosa. All the tours were successful under the most difficult snow conditions.*

(*Signed*) *Alfred Kühn.*

In addition the Matterhorn on the 21st July as the second climb for 1909 under very difficult snow conditions."

[6] This long and difficult arête, which had resisted numerous attempts, was finally conquered, on the descent, by the Austrian climber Moritz von Küffner, with the guides Alexander Burgener, Josef-Marie Biener and Anton Kalbermatten (3rd July, 1885).

[7] Cf. *Alpine Journal*, Vol. XXV, 1910–11.

[8] Quoted in *Alpina*, XVIIIth year, 1910.

[9] The guide Christian Bohren of Grindelwald, caretaker of the Concordia hut, was probably awaiting his sons in order to go with them to Concordia by way of the Mönchjoch and the Ewigschneefeld.

[10] The depth of the snow at its breaking-point was 2m. 40cm. (or approx. 7 ft. 10½ ins.). The avalanche divided into two branches: the left one (in the falling direction) swept away the Burgener party and carried off Christian Bohren; the right one overtook a party of Grindelwald porters on the Grindelwald Fiescherfirn—Christian Bohren *fils* and his brother Fritz, Peter Bleuler and Peter Kaufmann. The two first-named were on their way to the Concordia hut to reprovision their father; the other two were also carrying provisions, but for the caretaker of the Bergli hut, the guide Kaufmann. The four men were overthrown, dragged off and tumbled into some crevasses; they were half-buried, but they extricated themselves with slight injuries. Christian and Fritz Bohren clearly saw a man leave the hut, come down to meet the caravan of eight men and suddenly disappear, snatched away by the avalanche. It was their own father!

Just when Christian Bohren was descending towards the caravan, Kaufmann the hut-keeper, an old guide who had followed his profession as far away as the Caucasus, was bending over his stove, preparing a hot dish for the arrivals. A crack of the snow-slope made him jump into the air. He guessed what had happened, swallowed a large mouthful of cognac and rushed outside. But all he could see was the smoking avalanche rolling down. And where, only a moment ago, were eight men there was nobody. He called for Bohren, but Bohren did not answer; he too had been swept away. Then Kaufmann, carried away by his feelings, rushed down with all his strength to the help of the vanished men, his litre of cognac in his hand. He rushed down the length of the slope whose every inch he knew; he pursued the avalanche, growling, cursing, gesticulating. He pressed close behind it, but it fled before him like a maddened beast. He almost overtook it. Then his feet became entangled in the cascades of snow at its rear. He was forced to slow up to pass a wall of rock. There he lost headway, and when he reached the glacier all was over. Only a silent immobility remained.

After a moment he distinguished a long way off, at the head of the avalanche, three outstretched human forms, three dark shapes which appeared to move. So he resumed his disordered course, crossing the masses of snow, and came to the three figures: Rudolf Inäbnit, Fritz Brawand and one of Alexander Burgener's sons (Alexander). All three were cruelly injured. Kaufmann gave them generous libations of alcohol and strove to alleviate their pain. Inäbnit had one of his legs half torn away; it was attached by only a few fragments of skin, and the poor victim wanted only to draw his knife and cut it free. Of the other six men there was no trace. The massacre was complete.

From the Eismeer Station the ascent of the Burgener caravan had been followed through the telescope, so that the avalanche had been seen. A first rescue-party of three men left at once, followed at a short interval by a second column comprising some forty volunteers—railway employees, guides, porters and other mountain folk. It was night by the time the rescuers reached the scene of the tragedy. Acetylene lamps were lit, care having been taken to bring them, and by this wan light the six dead men were exhumed from their icy tomb. They were buried under only a thin layer of snow, as if an undercurrent had at the last moment brought them towards the surface. But their wounds were terrible. Their fall had been some two or three hundred metres (from 650 to 1,000 feet). Towards midnight the long column, still by the light of their acetylene lamps, descended the glacier, laboriously and terribly laden. The guide Rudolf Inäbnit died on the journey, having bled to death from the tearing away of his leg. The younger Alexander Burgener had, among other wounds, lost an eye.

The Oberland guides were interred at Grindelwald. The cemetery at Eisten, near Saas, received the remains of Alexander Burgener and of his son Adolf; the bodies of the travellers were taken to Strassburg and Saarbrucken respectively.

As for the younger Alexander and Fritz Brawand, they more or less recovered after long treatment in the infirmary at Interlaken.

[11] Two famous English mountaineers have written moving lines about Alexander Burgener. Capt. J. P. Farrar writes:

"Alexander Burgener is dead, but he will live for ever in Alpine history as one of the most dauntless mountaineers of his day. The leader of Mummery, of Güssfeldt, of Schulz, of von Küffner, to him belong the honour of some of the most terrible climbs in the Alps. If at last the mountains have beaten him he only shares the fate and joins the immortal ranks of such men as Michel Croz, as Christian Rangetiner, as Ferdinand Imseng, as Michel Innerköfler, Jean-Antoine Carrel, as J. J. Maquignaz, as Emile Rey, as Zsigmondy, as Purtscheller, as Mummery himself. One will remember him as one knew him in the heyday of his magnificent strength and dauntless courage, in his later days, when time seemed to have no power over him. The sound of his name to all those who know and appreciate such deeds as his which the Alps witnessed will not fail to cause that involuntary tightening of the heartstrings that is the truest tribute which man can pay to sustained and brilliant courage." (*Alpine Journal*, Vol. XXV, 1910–11.)

And Dr. C. T. Dent has said:

"If at the end he fell a victim to the mountains, we may feel sure that it was from no lack of prudence or foresight. The accident itself is but a proof that mountaineering can never be wholly devoid of risk. In Alexander Burgener's case the epithet 'treacherous' would be misapplied to the avalanche which swept him away. It was no underhand revenge that the great peaks took on one who had so often been their conqueror. He had identified himself so thoroughly and for so long with the mountains that at last they had just claimed him as their own." (*Alpine Journal*, Vol. XXV, 1910–11.)

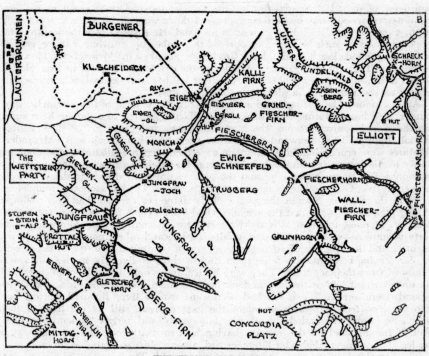

THE JUNGFRAU REGION

GLOSSARY

Aiguille (Fr.)	. . .	a sharp rock-needle.
Alp (Ger.)	. . .	a mountain pasturage.
Arête (Fr.)	. . .	a sharp ridge of rock, snow or ice.
Bergschrund (Ger.)	. .	a large crevasse separating the head of a glacier from the snow that remains attached to the rock (Fr.: *Rimaie*).
Chimney	. . .	a steep rock gully, smaller and narrower than a couloir (*q.v.*).
Col (Fr.)	. . .	a pass, or a depression on a ridge connecting two summits (Ger.: *Joch*).
Cornice	. .	an overhanging crest of snow.
Couloir (Fr.)	. .	a wide steep gully, often filled with snow or ice.
Crevasse (Fr.)	. .	a fissure in a glacier or snowfield.
Dent (Fr.)	. . .	a peak; literally, a tooth (Ger. *Horn*).
Firn (Ger.)	. . .	hardened snow on the upper part of a glacier (Fr.: *Névé*).
Föhn (Ger.)	. . .	a warm south wind, generally indicating bad weather.
Führerbuch (Ger.) .	.	official booklet held by every Swiss guide and surrendered by him for annual inspection by the cantonal authority; in it the employer may record his opinion of the guide's behaviour or abilities (Fr.: *Livret*).
Gendarme (Fr.)	. .	a rock pinnacle on a mountain ridge.
Ice-Fall .	. . .	an extensive fracture of a glacier caused by a sudden change in the level of its bed; the ice breaks up into great crevasses and throws up fantastic formations of ice, known as *séracs* (*q.v.*).
Joch (Ger.)	. .	see *Col*.
Kamm (Ger.).	. .	a ridge or crest.
Kessel (Ger.)	. .	a mountain basin; literally, a kettle or cauldron.
Mayen (Valais)	. .	a spring pasture.
Moraine (Fr.)	. .	debris of rocks and stones left by a moving glacier; *lateral* moraines lie along the sides, and the *terminal* moraine lies at its extremity.
Névé (Fr.)	. . .	hardened snow on the upper part of a glacier (Ger.: *Firn*).
Piton	. . . .	a stout iron pin with a ring at the end, used in rock climbing to secure the rope.
Rochers Moutonnés (Fr.)		boulders worn smooth by glacier action.
Sattel (Ger.)	. .	a saddle or depression.
Séracs (Fr.)	. . .	fantastic ice-formations in the shape of towers and needles, often of great size, formed at an ice-fall (*q.v.*).
Tal or *Thal* (Ger.)	.	a valley.
Traverse	. . .	a horizontal passage of a mountainside; often used in respect of the ascent of a mountain from one side, followed by its descent by the other.
Verglas (Fr.) .	. .	a thin coating of ice on rock surface; very tough and very treacherous.
Wand (Ger.)	. .	a wall, face or cliff.

DRAMATIS PERSONAE

The Numbers given refer to the chapters concerned

Almer, Ulrich, 9
Arkwright, Capt. Henry and Miss, 5
Aufdenblatten, Peter, 15

Balfour, Prof. F. M., 13 (I)
Balmat, Alphonse, 8
Balmat, Jean, 8
Balmat, Mathieu, 1
Balmat, Pierre, 1
Bär, Wilhelm, 16
Barthold, H., 22
Baumann, Peter, 6
Bean, Dr. J. G., 8
Bennen, Johann-Josef, 3
Beytrisson, Pierre, 11 (II)
Bider, Gustav, 16
Biener, Franz, 6
Bohren, Christian, 22
Boissonet, Mr., 3
Borckhardt, F. C., 15
Brantschen, Josef, 11 (II)
Breton, Joseph, 8
Burgener, Adolf, 22
Burgener, Alexander, 22
Burgener, Franz, 7

Cachat, Auguste, 8
Carrel, Jean-Antoine, 18
Carrier, Pierre, 1
Castagneri, Antonio, 17
Couttet, Auguste, 8
Couttet, Joseph-Marie, 1
Couttet, Sylvain, 5
Craven, W. E., 11 (I)
Croz, Michel, 4

Davies, John, 15
Devouassoud, Julien, 1
Douglas, Lord Francis, 4
Durnford, Joseph, 1

Elliott, Rev. J. M., 6

Fischer, Johann, 9
Fuller, B., 2
Furrer, Elias, 21

Gabbett, W. E., 13 (III)
Gay, Olivier, 7
Gorret, Charles, 18
Gosset, Mr., 3
Graf, Johann, 8

Hadow, R. D., 4
Hamel, Dr., 1
Henderson, Gilbert, 1
Hill, F. W., 21
Hopkinson, John, and family, 20
Hudson, Rev. Charles, 4

Imseng, Ferdinand, 12
Inäbnit, Christian, 11 (I)
Inäbnit, Peter, 22
Inäbnit, Rudolf, 22

Jones, Owen Glynne, 21

Knubel, Johann, 10
Knubel, Niklaus, 10
Knubel, Peter-Josef, 10
Krönig, Fridolin, 15
Kühn, A., 22
Kühn, Gottfried, 16

Lauber, Joseph, 6
Lewis, W. A., 10
Lochmatter, Alexander, 13 (III)
Lochmatter, Josef-Marie, 11 (II), 13 (III)
Lüscher, Mr., 11 (II)

McCorkindale, Rev. G., 8
Maquignaz, Jean-Joseph, 17
Marinelli, D., 12
Marke, Mr. and Mrs. G. B., 7
Marshall, J. A. Garth, 9
Maurer, Andreas, 13 (II)
Moseley, Dr. William, 11 (I)

Paterson, N. H., 10
Pedranzini, Battista, 12
Penhall, William, 13 (II)
Petrus, Johann, 13 (I)
Phipps, Rev. P. W., 6

Randall, J., 8
Rey, Emile, 9, 13 (I), 19
Roberts, A. Carson, 19
Rochester, J. M., 2
Rubi, Peter, 11 (I)

Schiess, Dr., 11 (II)
Schulz, Prof., 14
Simond, Edouard, 8
Simond, Michel, 5
Sinigaglia, Leone, 18

281

INDEX

Tairraz, Auguste, 1
Tairraz, Fernand, 8
Tairraz, Frederic, 2
Taugwalder, Peter (*père et fils*), 4
Tournier, Francois, 5
Tournier, Joseph, 5

Vavaseur, F., 2
Villanova, Count Humbert of, 17
Vuignier, Jean, 21

Wettstein, Dr. Alexander, 16
Wettstein, Heinrich, 16
Whymper, Edward, 4
Wilkinson, Miss, 7
Winhart, Nicolas, 5

Ziegler, Karl, 16
Zsigmondy, Dr. Emil, 14
Zsigmondy, Otto, 14
Zurbriggen, Clemenz, 21
Zurbriggen, Peter, 7

1. (*opposite*) THE TOMB OF MICHEL CROZ IN THE OLD CEMETERY AT ZERMATT

3. *(above)* THE COL DU GÉANT FROM THE ITALIAN SIDE, WITH PART OF THE MONT BLANC CHAIN (SOUTH-EASTERN FACE)

1. Col du Géant (11,053 feet). 2. Aiguille du Géant (13,166 feet). 3. Grandes Jorasses (13,806 feet). 4. Courmayeur.

×. Approximate site of the accident described in chapter 2. ××. Approximate point where the victims were recovered.

2. *(opposite)* MONT BLANC (CHAMONIX ASPECT) SEEN FROM LA FLÉGÈRE

A. The Summit of Mont Blanc (15,771 feet). B. Mont Maudit (14,649 feet). C. Aiguille du Midi (12,608 feet). D. Vallot Refuge and Observatory (14,311 feet). E. Dôme du Goûter (14,118 feet). F. Aiguille du Goûter (12,582 feet). G. Aiguille de Bionassay (13,287 feet). H. Grands Mulets (10,010 feet). I. Pierre Pointue (7,328 feet). K–K–K. Glacier des Bossons. L. The Tongue of the Glacier des Bossons (partly masked by the woods) where were discovered the remains of some victims of the Hamel, Arkwright and Randall accidents (see chapters 1, 5 and 8). M. Chamonix.

1. Approximate site of the Hamel accident (see chapter 1). 2. Approximate site of the Arkwright accident (see chapter 5). 3. Approximate site of the Marke accident (see chapter 7). 4. Approximate site of the Randall accident (see chapter 8). 5. The presumed and approximate point (about 13,380 feet) where the Villanova party disappeared in 1890 (see chapter 17). This point is in fact behind the arête marked, on the rise from the Col de Bionassay to the summit of the Dôme du Goûter.

4. THE NORTH (ZERMATT) FACE OF THE MATTERHORN (14,780 feet) SEEN FROM THE EAST ARÊTE OF THE ZINAL ROTHORN (see also Plate 12 for the characteristic features of the Matterhorn).

A–A–A. The route followed on the ascent and descent by the Whymper party (Hörnli Arête). B. Furggen Arête. C–C–C. Zmutt Arête. D. Italian Arête. E. Col du Lion (11,736 feet). F. Tête du Lion (12,211 feet).

×. Site of the Whymper accident (see chapter 4). × ×. Point where the victims were recovered on the Matterhorn Glacier. The depth of the fall is about 3,500 feet. Whymper estimated it at 4,000 feet, which appears to be a little exaggerated.

(*a*) IN 1865 (at 25 years of age)

(*b*) IN 1908

6. EAST FACE OF THE SCHRECKHORN

A. The Summit of the Schreckhorn (13,386 feet). B. Indicates the direction of the Lauteraarsattel. C. Lauteraar Glacier.

×. Site of the Elliott accident (see chapter 6).   × ×. The approximate point where the victim was recovered.

7. THE UPPER SLOPES OF MONT BLANC, SEEN FROM THE AIR (CHAMONIX SIDE)

A. The Summit of Mont Blanc (15,771 feet). B. Mur de la Côte (base 14,268 feet, summit 14,579 feet). C–C. Rochers Rouges (highest point 14,779 feet). D. Vallot Refuge and Observatory (14,311 feet). E. Bosses du Dromadaire (14,885 feet). F. Grand Plateau (minimum altitude 13,000 feet).
1. The Hamel accident. 2. The Arkwright accident. 3. The Marke accident. 4. The Randall accident (see chapters 1, 5, 7 and 8 respectively, and also plates 2, 8 and 9).

8. THE ITALIAN SIDE OF MONT BLANC (EAST FACE), SEEN FROM THE NORTH-WEST BUTTRESS OF THE AIGUILLE DU GÉANT

1. The Summit of Mont Blanc (15,771 feet).
2. Mont Blanc de Courmayeur (15,642 feet).
3. Aiguille Blanche de Péteret (13,507 feet).
4. The Summit of the Rochers Rouges (14,779 feet).

5–5. The upper slopes of the Brenva Glacier.
6. The upper levels of the Glacier du Géant.
7. Dames Anglaises (11,815 feet).
8. The Buttress of the Aiguille Noire de Péteret.

×. Approximate site of the Randall bivouac (see chapter 8 and also plates 2, 7 and 9).

9. THE EAST AND SOUTH-EAST FACES OF MONT BLANC (THE ITALIAN SIDE) SEEN FROM L'HER-BETET, IN THE GRAIAN ALPS

A. The Summit of Mont Blanc (15,771 feet).
B. Mont Maudit (14,649 feet).
C. Mont Blanc de Tacul (13,937 feet).
D. Aiguille de Bionassay (13,287 feet).
E-E. Glacier du Brouillard.
F. Aiguille de l'Innominata (12,192 feet).
G-G. Glacier de Fresnay.
H. Aiguilles de Péteret.
I. Glacier de la Brenva.
K. Brouillard face.
L. Col de Fresnay (approximately 11,800 feet).
M. Arête du Brouillard.
N. Pic Luigi Amedeo (14,668 feet).

1. Approximate site of the Marshall–Fischer accident (see chapter 9).
2. Approximate site of the Balfour–Petrus accident (see chapter 13 (1)).
3. Approximate site of the Randall tragedy (see chapter 8).

X. Approximate point reached by the Marshall party in 1874.

10. THE EASTERN SUMMIT OF THE LYSKAMM, SOUTH-EAST (ITALIAN) FACE

×. Approximate site of the accident in 1877 (see chapter 10). ××. The place where the victims were recovered on the Lys glacier.

11. THE NORTH (SWISS) FACE OF THE LYSKAMM, SEEN FROM THE GORNERGRAT

A. Eastern Summit (14,888 feet). B. Western Summit (14,695 feet). C. Grenz Glacier.

×. Approximate site of the accident in 1877.

12. THE MATTERHORN (ZERMATT ASPECT), SHOWING THE EAST (LEFT)
AND NORTH (RIGHT) FACES

A. Swiss Summit. B. Italian Summit. C–C. Furggen Arête. D. Furggen (East) face.
E–E–E. Hörnli (North-East) Arête. The usual route from Zermatt and more or less that used by
Whymper's party in 1865. F. North Face. G–G. Zmutt Arête. H. The Shoulder (about
13,450 feet). I. The old hut. K–K. Furggen Glacier. L. Hörnli hut (10,820 feet).
M. Matterhorn Glacier. N. Site of Whymper's bivouac in 1865.

×. Approximate site of the Moseley accident (see chapter 11 (1)). × ×. Approximately the
place where the victim was recovered.

13. THE
ITALIAN
(SOUTH)
FACE OF
THE MAT'
HORN, S
FROM
BREUIL

A. Italian
mit.

B. Swiss Su

C. Pic Ty
(13,921 feet

D. Furg
Arête.

✕. In the c
of this s
ledge, knov
the Cra
(13,498 feet
the refuge v
Joseph P
schen died
chapter 11

14. (*opposite*) THE MACUGNAGA (NORTH-EAST) FACE OF MONTE ROSA, SEEN FROM THE APPROACH TO THE MONTE MORO PASS ON THE ITALIAN SIDE

A. Dufourspitz (15,204 feet), the highest point of the massif. B. Nordendspitze (15,127 feet). C. Grenzgipfel (15,075 feet). D. Grenzsattel (14,602 feet). E. Zumsteinspitze (14,966 feet). F. Signalkuppe (14,964 feet). G. Monte Rosa Glacier. H. Belvedere Glacier.

1. The bivouac on the first (1872) ascent and the present site of the Marinelli hut. 1–2. The crossing point of the Marinelli couloir.

✕. Approximate site of the Marinelli accident (see chapter 12). ✕ ✕. The place where the victims were recovered.

15. THE AIGUILLE BLANCHE DE PÉTERET (SOUTH-EAST FACE)

A. Summit (13,507 feet). B. Col de Péteret (12,949 feet). C. Arête of the Mont Blanc de Courmayeur. D–D–D. Glacier de Fresnay.

+. Presumed and approximate site of the Balfour accident (see chapter 13 (1)). ++. Approximate place where the victims were found (see also plates 8 and 9—the Aiguille Blanche as Balfour and his guide would have seen it from the Col du Géant—and note 8 on page 134).

16. THE WETTERHORN

A. Grosse Scheidegg. B. Wetterhorn (12,149 feet). C. Mittelhorn (12,165 feet). D. Rosenhorn (12,106 feet). E–E. Hühnergutz Glacier. F–F. Grindelwaldfirn. G. Krinnefirn. H–H. North-west aspect of the Wetterhorn, overlooking Grindelwald.

×. Approximate site of the Penhall accident (see chapter 13 (11)). × ×. Approximate place where the bodies were found.

17. THE WEST FACE OF THE DENT BLANCHE (14,318 feet), SEEN FROM THE AIR

A. South arête (the usual route). B. West (Ferpécle) arête. C. Grand Cornier (13,020 feet).

O. Point from which the Jones party fell (see plate 30 and chapter 21).

×. Approximate site of the Gabbett accident (see chapter 13 (III)). × ×. Place where the victims were found.

18. THE MATTERHORN (ZERMATT ASPECT), SEEN FROM THE AIR

A. Grandes Murailles.   B. Grand Combin (14,164 feet).   C. The Shoulder.

X. Approximately the place where Burckhardt died (see chapter 15). See also plates 4 and 12.

19. THE MEIJE (SOUTH FACE), SEEN FROM THE PYRAMIDE DUHAMEL
A. Pic Central (or Doigt de Dieu, 13,022 feet).   B. Pic Oriental (12,828 feet).
×. The chimney in which Zsigmondy fell (see chapter 14).

20. THE MEIJE (SOUTH FACE), SEEN FROM THE NEIGHBOURHOOD OF THE REFUGE CHATELLERET

A. Grand Pic (13,077 feet). B. Brèche Zsigmondy. C. Pointe Zsigmondy. D. East arête and the direction of the Pic Central. E. Carrè Glacier. F. Brèche de la Meije (10,824 feet). G. Refuge du Promontoire (10,145 feet). H. Glacier des Etançons. I. Le Promontoire. K. Pic du Glacier Carré (12,667 feet).

×. Approximate site of the Zsigmondy accident (see chapter 14). × ×. Approximately the place where the victim was found.

21. THE SUMMIT OF THE JUNG-
FRAU (13,670 feet), SEEN FROM
THE ROTTALHORN (in the fore-
ground the Rottalsattel)

×. Site of the bivouac. The route of
the descent is shown and ×× marks the
point from which the victims fell in the
accident described in chapter 16.

22. THE JUNGFRAU FROM THE
SOUTH-EAST

A. Gross Doldenhorn (11,962 feet).
B. Rottalhorn (12,615 feet). C. Rottal-
sattel (12,713 feet). D. Summit of the
Jungfrau. E. Jungfraujoch (11,385 feet).
F. Point 3470 m. (11,382 feet). G–G–G.
Upper part of the Aletsch Glacier.

1. Site of the bivouac described in
chapter 16.

×. The point from which the fall
began. ××. Place where the bodies
were found.

This illustration is taken from the
brochure *Bericht über das Unglück an der
Jungfrau*, by A. Fleiner.

Heinr. Wettstein
geb. 1859

Karl Ziegler
geb. 1853.

Alex. Wettstein
geb. 1861

Gottfried Kuhn
geb. 1863

Wilhelm Bär
geb. 1863

Gustav Bider
geb. 1863.

23. THE VICTIMS OF THE JUNGFRAU TRAGEDY

Reproduced from A. Fleiner's brochure.

24. THE SOUTH-WEST SECTOR OF THE ITALIAN FACE OF MONT BLANC, SEEN FROM THE AIGUILLE DE L'AIGLE

A. Col de Miage (10,985 feet). B. Aiguille de Bionassay (13,287 feet). C. Col de Bionassay (12,766 feet). D. Dôme du Goûter (14,118 feet). E. Arête leading towards the Vallot refuge, les Bosses and the summit of Mont Blanc. F. Italian Glacier de Bionassay. G–G. Glacier du Dôme. H–H. Chain of the Aiguilles Grises. I. Italian Glacier de Miage. K–K–K. Rochers du Mont Blanc. L. Aiguilles Grises hut (10,073 feet). M. Quintino Sella hut (11,057 feet).

1. Point 4003m. (13,130 feet). 2. Point 4153 m. (13,622 feet). 3. Point 4080 m. (13,382 feet) and the presumed place where the Villanova party disappeared (see chapter 17).

25. ITALIAN (SOUTH) FACE OF THE MATTERHORN SEEN FROM THE CHATEAU DES DAMES

A–A. Zmutt Arête. B. Furggen Arête. C. Mischabels (14,942 feet). D. Täschhorn (14,758 feet).
E. Breuiljoch (10,722 feet). F. Tête du Lion (12,211 feet). G. Col Tournanche (11,380 feet). H. Col du
Lion (11,736 feet). I. Luigi-Amadeo hut (12,566 feet). M. Glacier du Lion. N. Matterhorn Glacier.
O. Pic Tyndall (13,925 feet). P. Rope ladder. R. The summits (Italian to the left, Swiss to the right).
S. Rionde. T. Tiefenmatten (west) face.

The line H–I–O–P–R marks approximately the normal route from Breuil—the Arête du Lion (or south-west arête).

×. The place where Carrel died (see chapter 18).

26. GUIDO REY BESIDE CARREL'S CROSS AT RIONDE

27. (*opposite*) LANDSCAPE AT BREUIL

29. THE PETITE DENT DE VEISIVI, SEEN FROM AROLLA

A. Summit of the Petite Dent (10,460 feet). B–B. South-east arête. C. Col de Zarmine (10,045 feet). D. West-north-west arête.

×. Approximately the site of the Hopkinson accident (see chapter 20). × ×. Approximately the point at which the victims were found.

28. (*opposite*) AIGUILLE DU GÉANT (13,166 feet), SOUTH-WEST ASPECT, SEEN FROM THE AIGUILLE MARBRÉE

×. Approximately the place from which Emile Rey fell (see chapter 19).

30. (*opposite*) THE NORTH AND EAST FACES OF THE DENT BLANCHE, SEEN FROM THE AIGUILLE DE LA TSA

A. Summit (14,318 feet). B–B. South arête (the usual route). C–C–C. West (Ferpécle) arête. E. Glacier de la Dent Blanche. F. Upper Ferpécle Glacier. G. Grand Gendarme (13,054 feet). H. North-west face. I. Taeschhorn (14,758 feet). K. Ferpécle Glacier.

O. Approximate site of the Gabbett accident and direction of the fall (see chapter 13 (111)).

×. Approximate site of the Jones accident (see chapter 21). × ×. The place where the victims of the Jones accident were found.

31. BERGLI

*. The Bergli hut (10,823 feet). **. The point where the avalanche began and the Burgener accident took place (see chapter 22). ***. The place where the victims were recovered.

32. THE EIGER AND THE MÖNCH, SEEN FROM THE METTENBERG

A. North arête of the Trugberg (12,905 feet). B. Ober-Mönchjoch (11,870 feet). C. Mönch (13,468 feet). D. Eiger (13,028 feet). E. Grindelwald-Fiescherhorner Glacier. F-F. Kallifirn Glacier. G. Kleine Scheidegg. H. Mitteleggi arête. I. North face. K. North arête of the Eiger, bounding the famous north-west face.

1. Bergli hut (10,823 feet).

×. Approximate site of the Burgener accident (see chapter 22). ×× . The place where the victims were recovered.

34. ALEXANDER BURGENER

33. A PHOTOGRAPH OF BURGENER AND HIS TWO EMPLOYERS, TAKEN A FEW MINUTES BEFORE HIS DEATH

35. CHARLES GOS

THE AUTHOR